Managers and Mantras: One Company's Struggle for Simplicity

Managers and Mantras: One Company's Struggle for Simplicity

Charlotte Butler
and
John Keary

John Wiley & Sons (Asia) Pte Ltd

Singapore • New York • Chichester • Brisbane • Toronto • Weinheim

This publication is designed to provide accurate and authoritative information in
regard to the subject matter covered. It is sold with the understanding that the publisher
is not engaged in rendering professional services. If professional advice or other expert
assistance is required, the services of a competent professional person should be sought.

Other Wiley Editorial Offices

John Wiley & Sons, Inc., 605 Third Avenue, New York, NY 10158-0012, USA
John Wiley & Sons Ltd, Baffins Lane, Chichester, West Sussex PO19 1UD, England
John Wiley & Sons (Canada) Ltd, 22 Worcester Road, Rexdale, Ontario M9W 1L1, Canada
John Wiley & Sons Australia Ltd, 33 Park Road (PO Box 1226), Milton, Queensland 4046,
Australia
Wiley-VCH, Pappelallee 3, 69469 Weinheim, Germany

Library of Congress Cataloging-in-Publication Data:

Butler, Charlotte
    Managers and mantras : one company's struggle for simplicity / Charlotte Butler and
John Keary.
        p. cm.
    Includes bibliographical references and index.
    ISBN 0-471-83558-7 (cloth : alk. pbk.)
    1. Management.   2. Inchcape & Co.   I. Title.   II. Keary, John.

HD31 .B862 1999
658 21—dc21

                                                                    99-043202

Typeset in 11/13 point, Goudy by Linographic Services Pte Ltd
Printed in Singapore by Craft Print Pte Ltd
10 9 8 7 6 5 4 3 2 1

Contents

Acknowledgments

T his book would almost certainly never have been written if Sir George Turnbull had not seen fit to make Inchcape a founder member of the Euro-Asia Centre at INSEAD. As a result of the senior management programs held at Fontainebleau and the case studies sponsored by the company, the authors formed a working relationship and began to share a fascination for this unusual group. The announcement of a demerger in March 1998 was both a punctuation mark in the evolution of the business, and a trigger to start writing about the organization and the twists and turns of management thinking over the past four decades.

We owe a considerable debt to the company for granting us permission to produce the book, giving us access to internal sources of data and for allowing us to quote from *Two Centuries of Overseas Trading* by Dr Stephanie Jones. Beyond the data and the dry facts are the opinions, experiences, and feelings of employees at all levels, past and present. Their contributions have transformed the nature of this account and enriched our understanding of complex events. We especially thank all those who first gave us lengthy interviews, and later took the time to respond to our follow-up queries in order to ensure that we developed as good an insight as possible. In this context, it should be noted that Inchcape plc wishes to make it clear that the views expressed in the book by Inchcape managers represent their personal views, and not those of the company. Also, the company does not in any way accept responsibility for the contents of the book.

We should also like to express our gratitude to the Inchcape family and to Inchcape Family Investments Limited. From them, too, we received generous help, both in the form of interviews and permission to quote from the biography of the first Lord Inchcape, again written by Dr Stephanie Jones.

Beyond the current and previous members of the organization is another circle of contributors, consisting of academics, consultants, and analysts, who gave up their time to be interviewed and to offer their wisdom and counsel. In the first category, we particularly wish to put on record our thanks to the Euro-Asia Centre, which encouraged the writing of this book and made available many of its own sources, including the set of case studies specially written for the Inchcape Programs.

For their patience in the face of our constant bombardment with questions and requests for clarification, we should like to thank all our contributors. We have also been struck by the huge enthusiasm shown by 'insiders' and 'outsiders' alike for the subject, and their strength of feeling about a range of issues. This was never a bland or boring company.

Throughout the past year, we have been acutely aware that we have seen only the tip of the iceberg. There are many, many people with whom we had neither the time nor opportunity to talk. Hundreds of thousands of people across the world have helped shape this story, and we acknowledge their unconscious contribution.

Finally and inevitably, we must thank our families and close colleagues who helped in a myriad of ways but, above all, endured our moods and smoothed the path for us to write and think.

Charlotte Butler
John Keary

Introduction

◆

In 1957 the Inchcape group, an overseas trading company, was launched on the London stock market. During the next twenty years, under the leadership of the third Lord Inchcape, the group expanded profitably and at a rapid rate. To the plaudits of the City (London's financial community) and the investment analysts who followed its progress, Lord Inchcape acquired company after company in a series of friendly takeovers that made the group a global concern before ever the word became fashionable, and at a time when most other U.K. companies remained firmly anchored in their home bases.

Under his autocratic but paternal leadership the group's managers, like their chairman, remained untroubled by any of the new management concepts winging their way across the Atlantic and infiltrating the ranks of other British companies. And as long as the profits continued to roll in, nobody questioned the way in which the group was managed. On the contrary, Lord Inchcape was hailed as "the man with the Midas touch," a shining example to all.

But by 1979, as the group's results began to plunge due to changing economic circumstances and the revelation of mismanagement, the plaudits turned to criticism. The stock market turned its back on the golden boy, who now became leader of "a colonial dinosaur." The group was labeled an anachronistic mess, in need of a firm dose of modern management to rescue it from certain disaster.

During the next twenty years the group received precisely this. By 1982, amid rumors of a takeover or the imminent break-up of the group, Lord Inchcape had been "persuaded" to retire from active management of his group. During the next few years the group's senior ranks were culled and in came a team of professional managers, dedicated to restoring Inchcape to financial health. In carrying out this task, help and advice was readily available from the serried rows of management consultants and business school theorists, whose influence over the strategies and operating practices of companies in the United States and Europe would grow enormously during the 1980s. Over the next fifteen years, Inchcape plc, a lesser-known English patient, was subjected — at no small expense — to examination and treatment by all these expert practitioners of management medicine.

Following the theories then being expounded by top consultants in the management field, the new chief executive and his team of executive surgeons went to work on the ailing Inchcape body. The famous diagnostic tool, the BCG matrix, was used to analyze, dissect, and then prune its businesses. Restructuring and control were prescribed for the organization, in order to wipe out the deadly virus of free-wheeling entrepreneurialism that had flourished under the old decentralized organization.

After a successful transplant operation, Inchcape plc emerged with a centralized structure under the control of a head office containing new departments, for planning and strategy, and an enlarged, powerful finance department. It also received a life-giving transfusion of new managers, professional in outlook and with a strong grasp of key financial ratios — return on investment was their mantra. Whether Inchcape was now a conglomerate, a holding company, or a strange hybrid, no-one was sure, but what it was being given, according to the health bulletins issued to the financial press, was focus, simplicity, and, possibly, in the fullness of time, synergy. These were all words the stock market wanted to hear and, once again, Inchcape began to receive praise. The new chief executive announced, with some ceremony, that Inchcape plc was no longer an old-fashioned middleman doomed to extinction, but an international marketing services and distribution group. The analysts were excited by the news, and the rising share price reflected their approval.

Meanwhile, at therapy centers in the U.K. and France, the group's managers were undergoing treatment by the business school doctors to ensure that the group would stay on the path of financial rectitude. They were instructed in the use of new management techniques for financial control, and learned the importance of delivering shareholder value and developing core competencies. Later on, they found themselves empowered. Discussions on the nature of Inchcape's corporate culture revealed that it was firmly focused on strict budgets and the bottom line. Some puzzled over how this could be squared with being a caring company whose people were its greatest asset, but there was never time to follow up this dichotomy. Visitors from the center beamed their approval as the troops all sang from the same hymn sheet and genuflected toward the City temple.

In the next few years the patient seemed to respond extremely well to treatment. The results improved, profits went up, and the City reclaimed the group as one of its favorite sons. The crowning achievement came on June 19, 1991, when Inchcape was admitted to the exclusive ranks of the FTSE-100. At a triumphal rally in Luxembourg in 1992, the group's then leader proclaimed it was time for growth. Inchcape was prescribed a new wonder drug called "acquisition" which, if taken in judicious quantities, would make the group grow to become even healthier, and immune from the pernicious contagion of recession that was then striking down other companies.

Alas, it was not to be. As the group's management overdosed on acquisition, Inchcape reinflated in a way reminiscent of its earlier incarnation. However, this time the image-conscious leadership presented it as a complex set of businesses. By 1993, profits, badly affected by the failure of the yen, were on the slide and the patient found itself back in the emergency room. Despite ruthless treatment from the business medicine men, and cosmetic surgery to give it yet another new profile as a "marketing and distribution company," Inchcape's financial decline continued. Feverishly, the leadership worked to assure the City that all was well, or that all would be well, given time. The underlying pulse was strong, and would once more beat soundly in the very near future.

Unfortunately, its protestations fell on deaf ears. "Very near future" was too long for the stock market to wait and, once again, the City turned its back on the group. As the share price plunged, the patient was subjected to the currently popular downsizing and restructuring treatment involving the amputation and sale of its body parts, but failed to respond. The final blow came with the collapse of the Asian markets in the summer of 1997, after which it was only a matter of time before all support systems were turned off. Amid rumors of a takeover, the specter of break-up reappeared.

In March 1998 the demerger of the group was announced. The patient's limbs — some healthy, some diseased — would be lopped off and offered to whoever wished to buy them. Given the continuing poor prospects for Inchcape's Asian businesses and its falling share price, any buyer was likely to get a bargain. However, declared the group's top management, from this operation would emerge another, healthier Inchcape, focused and ready to take its place among the City élite once more. The round would begin again.

Thus, the forty-odd years between 1957 and 1998 saw Inchcape plc perform an expensive and complicated minuet with the stock market and its satellite partners, the investment analysts. What did this performance actually achieve, and who gained from it? Certainly not the shareholders, including, it should be remembered, many of the group's own managers, who bought shares at £6 in May 1992 only to see them floundering at £1.14 by March 1998. And if not the shareholders, for whose benefit was this performance played out?

Put at its baldest, the Inchcape story — or perhaps saga — is a detailed account of a complex organization's quest for value, and its attempts to transform itself in turbulent markets. But beyond this familiar territory, the Inchcape experience raises important questions about the nature of the relationship between companies, the City, and fashionable institutions such as management consultancies and business schools whose power has so markedly increased over the last two decades, and who have so abundantly provided the mantras of our title.

During the last fifteen years, consultancy has grown from a puny infant into a seriously overweight adult, a huge industry that has successfully propagated the notion that companies need the expertise of its practitioners. In 1996 the top thirty management consultancies earned almost US$30 billion from businesses and governments worldwide. Inchcape was a prime user of consultants throughout the period covered by the book, enlisting their aid on crucial issues such as restructuring and the ongoing search to find a new, profitable business on which the group's future could be secured. But did the senior managers who commissioned the numerous reports feel it got value from them, or would they agree with Lord Weinstock that management consultancies are "invariably a waste of money"? Did they digest and implement the advice so expensively commissioned, to the benefit of the whole organization? Or did they just accumulate a stack of reports that gathered dust in various cupboards at head office?

Consultants themselves are, of course, a prey to fashion. To be impressive and credible, they need to know and quote the current theory, the latest idea from the business schools authenticated through the pages of the august *Harvard Business Review* and an ever-growing stable of specialist management journals, for business schools have been another high-growth industry during the last two decades. Consultants and business school theorists have a symbiotic relationship. Often, they are one and the same: business school gurus act as consultants, and the consultancies recruit from the business schools, which churn out ever-increasing numbers of young "wannabe" executives who have been force-fed the latest line on management thinking.

Inchcape turned to both the consultancies and business schools for help. This help took several forms: weighty reports about future strategy and the viability of certain businesses and industries; new recruits in the shape of MBA graduates; and business school training for its managers via company-specific programs, tailored to the group's needs.

One of the obvious results of these contacts was that Inchcape executives were exposed to the latest management ideas or mantras, undoubtedly the most important way in which consultancies and business schools influence companies throughout the Western world. Research output from the business schools has expanded enormously over the past fifteen years for, in order to gain promotion, business faculty are required to publish more; hence the corresponding rise in the number of journals to provide an outlet for an increasingly specialized profession. Consequently, a succession of management theories, based on research into what is judged to be the currently successful company, has come and gone. Browse through the back numbers of any management journal and recall exhortations to be "large" in order to benefit from economies of scale, while remaining nimble and flexible; then to re-engineer, downsize, and unbundle, or even perhaps to find the "optimum relationship" between slack and innovation, to leverage "knowledge management" in order to embrace "value proposition" and "enabling conditions."

Unfortunately, as experience has shown, today's big idea may well be tomorrow's myth, to be replaced by the next fad. Often they leave confusion in their wake, being written more by academics for academics in opaque jargon rather than for harassed managers. For despite the successive introduction of case studies, computer simulations, and multimedia cases, the problem of relevance still lingers over much of the output from the business schools. Originally, the word "focus" meant a funeral pyre in classical Latin. Many managers might be excused for feeling that a funeral pyre would be a fitting end for many of the management theories with which they are regularly bombarded through the business press.

The Inchcape top management embraced many contemporary management theories, and in the early 1990s, business school faculty were invited to run board-level workshops and lead discussions about vital topics such as the succession, and the future strategic direction for the group. But how deeply did the mantras and workshop conclusions touch the rest of the organization and, ultimately, were they a benign or damaging influence on the group's strategy and operating methods? Did Inchcape fall prey to fashionable ideas about focus and simplicity to its own detriment? Or were the theories the right ones, but their implementation faulty; did the mantras float impotently among the top ranks, leaving the rest of the management untouched — or were they misinterpreted?

Another set of questions concerns the much vaunted product of the business schools; the modern, professionally trained manager. At Inchcape, many of the group's managers, who had lived through previous business downturns in the volatile sectors in which they operated, were swept away in the name of professionalism. But did the new team of professional managers, respecting all the modern precepts of business theory and financial strictness, finally achieve any better results than the *laissez-faire* style of the third Lord Inchcape and his band of discredited entrepreneurs? What are the strengths and weaknesses of the modern professional, as demonstrated by the Inchcape experience?

The most popular subject in business literature is leadership, and Inchcape's story necessarily provokes discussion of the question. Over the forty years covered by this book, Inchcape plc was headed by five men. All of them had to lead the group through periods of major transition. All of them, to a greater or lesser extent, re-engineered the group of businesses they inherited. All were men of acknowledged ability, yet they had quite different management philosophies. One of them was the high-flying product of our twin influencing bodies, a graduate of a leading business school who went on to spend several successful years with a top consultancy. What conclusions about the effectiveness of different leadership styles can we draw from the group's performances under them? How far was leadership important in influencing the success or failure of Inchcape? Or did other factors have a greater impact?

Taking another perspective, what can Inchcape's experience tell us about the role of leaders in a modern multinational? Are they the long-term, strategic thinkers that business literature likes to evoke, or are they in reality prisoners of their own ambition and of external pressures such as the stock market? Are too many business leaders, under the multiple stresses of today's business environment, virtually outsourcing their strategic thinking to external forces?

And while the corporate mandarins at the top of Inchcape were immersed in the search for focus and simplicity, what were the operating managers doing? Often dismissed as unable to "see the big picture," these people nevertheless operate at the sharp end, where theorists and senior managers rarely spend a great deal of time. What effect, if any, did the different visions, mantras, and strategic directions announced at successive group conferences or in *Inchcape World*, the in-house magazine, have on them and their performance? Their opinion was rarely canvassed by corporate head office; what ideas might they have contributed had anyone asked them?

If leadership was not the determining factor, then what about the role of history? It could be argued that Inchcape's final transition to a single-activity company was inevitable from the beginning, as the nemesis of history caught up with a diversified trading group that no longer had a role to play in an increasingly specialized world. If so, did the strenuous efforts of the professional managers who headed the Motors, Coca-Cola Bottling, Insurance, Testing, Marketing, and Shipping businesses, in conscious or unconscious collusion with the stock market, merely stave off Inchcape's final break-up? Few companies are as old as Inchcape, or have been so buffeted by world events, economic downturns, stock-market crashes, and wars. Throughout all this, Inchcape adapted and changed, but always survived in some recognizable form, and was never taken over. What kept it going for so long as a complex, diversified conglomerate when every comparable firm had either disappeared or made the transition to simplicity years ago?

It was consideration of these and other issues that provoked this book about the evolution of the Inchcape group over the past forty years. In the course of writing it, we drew on in-depth interviews with over sixty people, including all the key players still living. At the end of the interview, we invited each of them to pick out the main contributory factors in Inchcape's final break-up. Many identified the usual suspects, such as the result of history catching up with it, poor management, following wrong advice from outside experts, throwing out the old strengths or competencies without replacing them with new ones, and so on.

However, top of the list for many, especially in the latter years, was the role of the City and its highly influential acolytes, the analysts. It was an unexpected response that, after further probing, left us with another set of questions. Did the City analysts, by alternately praising and criticizing the group's performance, sometimes on superficial evidence, fail Inchcape? Was Inchcape's top management so mesmerized by the share price performance that they sacrificed long-term considerations in a bid to win short-term praise? Could the end result, given another strategy less dictated by concerns about City opinion, have been different? Which, in turn, raises the question of whether or not the City is a good mechanism for judging company performance.

Latterly, the beginnings of a backlash against an overreliance on consultants and theorists has been discernible in business literature. This book is a contribution to this debate. It does not claim to have any hard and fast, universally applicable answers; to do so would be to fall into the same trap as the consultants and theorists are accused of doing. However, it does attempt to discuss what the proper relationship between companies and these two powerful groups should be, in order to provide a healthy balance. And based on our findings, to this dynamic duo we add a third key influence: that of the stock exchange.

In the case of Inchcape plc, clearly the eyes of its leaders were firmly riveted on the London share price, but the principle could equally apply to a company registered on the New York or Hong Kong stock exchanges. In today's business world, consultants, business schools, and the stock market form a potent mixture, each offering its own yardsticks for success — a Bermuda Triangle into which a company's sense of its own capability and best interests could easily disappear. Did Inchcape fall into this void and, if so, was it of its own accord, or because it was pushed?

The theory of a void, or hole, into which a company can fall, was one that continually haunted us during our researches. We were also intrigued by the frequent use of the word "gaps" by many of our interviewees. Respondents spoke of gaps between theory and implementation, in communications, between field managers and their corporate colleagues, culture gaps, and so on, so that the Inchcape saga became riddled with the notion of unbridged gaps in the group's management and business structures. Undoubtedly, their existence affected the outcome, though to what extent only became clear when we reached the end of our study.

These, then, are the main themes that have emerged during the course of our research into the long march of the Inchcape group. In writing the book, we have tried to avoid too much hindsight and concentrated on reconstructing what actually happened, and why. For the early history of the group we had two main sources; first, the history of the Inchcape group written by Dr Stephanie Jones, and her biography of the first Lord Inchcape. Second, we have been able to draw on the case studies prepared by the INSEAD Euro-Asia Centre during 1989–92, which included the views and insights of two crucial figures who are sadly no longer with us, the third Lord Inchcape and Sir George Turnbull. Many Inchcape senior and middle managers were also interviewed at that time, and their taped thoughts, impressions, and visions for the future have provided a rich resource, untarnished by hindsight and subsequent memory lapses.

Another valuable source has been the two business schools, the INSEAD Euro-Asia Centre and Ashridge Management Centre, where Inchcape management courses have taken place. Faculty members from these schools were involved with the company over a number of years, acting variously as teachers, consultants, and conference speakers. In doing so, they gained an overview of Inchcape, its leaders, and the process of transformation it underwent, which they have generously shared with us. The same applies to several of the consultancy firms who worked with the group at different stages in its development, and in some cases organized workshops around key themes. They, too, have helped us enormously by discussing their impressions and recollections of Inchcape.

As these acknowledgments demonstrate, this book is by no means an attempt to denigrate either consultants or business schools, of which we are both fully paid-up members. The two have important roles to play in helping organizations steer a path through an increasingly complex and competitive environment. We do, however, question whether their capabilities have been overestimated, so that companies now have an almost Pavlovian response in times of trouble or when deciding on a change of strategy, and look first to outsiders for inspiration rather than to their internal resources. Neither business schools nor consultants are infallible, but there has been a tendency, self-assumed or not, for them to take on that mantle. In the process, have they perhaps undermined the belief of companies in their own competence?

Add to that the manifestly growing power of our third influencer, the City, and a depressing scenario emerges of chief executives and their boards almost buckling under pressure — pressure from a steady drip of articles in the business press urging them not to be caught out by ignoring the latest management idea and failing to restructure this or leverage that; and pressure from shareholders, who avidly follow a company's daily share price and devour the latest assessments from the analysts about its potential to be a winner or a loser. In today's business world, it seems, the middle way of concentrating on a steady performance is no longer a viable option. Is this picture merely a caricature, or does it contain a kernel of truth and, if so, what can be done about it?

In writing this book, we hoped to find some of the answers to this list of questions, but, realistically, perhaps the most we can hope for, given that management is not an easy game to play, is to have at least provided a few insights for managers at all levels in companies who might find themselves in a similar position.

At a recent conference held at the Euro-Asia Centre in Fontainebleau, one speaker observed: "We are all the victims of fads and fashions. This is fine when we are talking about fashion as applied to clothes, but it is a little worrying when we are dealing with billions of dollars." The remark is a very appropriate lead into the rest of this book.

The End of
An Era

From Merchant Prince to Colonial Dinosaur

◆

"There are few more impressive sights in the world than a Scotsman on the make."

J. M. Barrie's famous remark could be aptly applied to the two most famous entrepreneurs associated with the overseas trading group that became Inchcape plc. The first was the founder, who began life in 1852 as plain Mr. Mackay and was subsequently ennobled for his services to a grateful nation. The second was his grandson, the Third Earl of Inchcape, nicknamed "the man with the Midas touch" by an admiring business establishment for his acquisitive triumphs of the 1970s.

During the century spanning the two men's activities, the Inchcape empire underwent periods of rapid growth and prosperity, followed by more difficult times as changes in the world economic and political situation affected its various businesses. In response, the group's portfolio was several times restructured and reoriented, subsequently emerging ready to go on to further growth and runaway success until the next enforced change. For this sometimes volatile performance, Inchcape was alternately praised and criticized by contemporary business observers, who watched the group with interest, if not always comprehension. In the light of its later development, the rollercoaster progression of the Inchcape operations under family leadership could be taken as a template for the whole of its history.

OUT OF INDIA

The roots of the Inchcape group lay in nineteenth-century India and the trading expansion associated with the growth of the British Empire. As the tentacles of the Empire spread across the Indian subcontinent, trading agencies were formed to take advantage of the shipping and mail contracts granted by the British government. One such group of merchant partnerships, Mackinnon, Mackenzie and Company (MM&C), was founded in 1847 in Calcutta, Ghazipur, and Cossipore. Through its key role as owner and manager of the British India and Steam Navigation Company (BI), MM&C grew by spawning shipping agencies on all major trade routes in the region and beyond. By the outbreak of the First World War, it had established related partnerships in Singapore, Borneo, China and the Far East, the Persian Gulf, Australia, and, later, East Africa.

As described by Dr Stephanie Jones in her study of the group's founder, much of this growth was due to the workaholic James Lyle Mackay, the first Earl of Inchcape. Landing in Calcutta as an apprentice in 1874, within twenty years he had taken over MM&C and transformed it into one of the greatest commercial empires to come out of India.

Luck — and a very strong constitution — played an important part in this meteoric rise. The family had longstanding maritime connections — his great-uncle, Captain William Mackay, survived the 1795 wreck of the *Juno* (commemorated in Lord Byron's epic poem, *Don Juan*) by existing on a diet of distilled seawater and four old coconuts for twenty-three days until rescued. Mackay himself twice fell overboard on his first return voyage to Archangel in Russia at the age of seven, which may have influenced his later decision to settle for a more land-based career. In 1872 he became a trainee shipping clerk with Gellatly, Hankey Sewell & Company, the leading cargo-loading brokers in London for many major shipping lines. Two years later he won a coveted posting in India with MM&C, India's premier managing agency house and shipping line.

Legend has it that he was not the first candidate chosen, but leapfrogged two others who hesitated to accept, one wanting to take his long-awaited summer holidays, the other seeking parental permission. The orphaned Mackay said he could sail that night if necessary, and got the job. After successfully expanding MM&C's business in Calcutta and impressing the senior partners by his energy and commitment to the firm, in 1878 he moved on to Bombay. There, he vastly increased the company's revenues derived from handling the thriving opium trade. Two things stood out in these early years: the speed with which Mackay learned Hindustani and took care to respect the local customs, and his "careful financial management." The first, an ability to operate as a local, was to become one of the Inchcape group's greatest strengths, while financial management, under less "careful" control, was to become one of its greatest weaknesses.

While Mackay's grasp of the local language gave him an advantage over his more ethnocentric colleagues, another talent that marked him out was his ability to act quickly and seize any commercial opportunity. Years later, his acceptance of a contract to carry a lucrative consignment of camels, despite a lack of steamers, was still remembered in Bombay. His ideals were "efficiency, economy, and making the most of wealth-generating opportunities," and his fast-rising salary reflected the high regard in which he stood with the management back home. This money he largely invested in Indian-based businesses. Mackay's work also led to his involvement in public affairs; he served on the Bengal Chamber of Commerce committee, eventually becoming its president, and in 1891 he was elected to the Viceroy's Legislative Council.

In 1893 he returned to England at the request of the failing Sir William Mackinnon. On Sir William's death that same year, although the chairmanship passed through the family to Duncan Mackinnon, Mackay was perceived as the real power. Duncan's retirement in 1913 left Mackay as head of the group; when the last Mackinnon was killed in Flanders in 1917, Mackay, by then Lord Inchcape, took over all the MM&C companies.

In the intervening years, both his entrepreneurial and troubleshooting skills were prominently displayed. In 1898, Mackay negotiated the end of a potentially serious strike at BI by convincing the strikers that the company could not afford pay rises — "quite an achievement in view of BI's record earnings that year." By 1900 he was in Australia where, demonstrating "a shrewd eye for dubious accounting practices," he turned round the Australasian United Steam Navigation Company (AUSN), in which he had built up a substantial interest. Back in India, in 1906 he seized an opportunity to take over the struggling Binny & Co., then the largest merchant firm in Madras. Bought at a bargain price, this proved to be another successful long-term acquisition. Branching out from river steamers, he invested in the valuable tea estates, including the Upper Assam Tea Company, controlled by the Mackinnon cousins, the Macneills. In 1910 these estates were "bringing in gross proceeds of almost half a million pounds"; five years later, Mackay took them over at the request of the Indian government, adding them to his other interests in Australia and East Africa.

During these years he also found the time to serve on seventeen committees and, in 1901–2, following the failed Boxer rebellion, spent twelve months negotiating a new commercial treaty with China. In his diary, he described the "complex, time-consuming, and exasperating nature of the negotiations." Later managers trying to do business in China would have recognized his feelings of frustration, though they may not have had to suffer the near death of a wife and daughter from typhoid, as Mackay did. His work was rewarded by a peerage in 1911, which came shortly after his second knighthood, the Order of the Star of India.

However, his greatest achievement during these years was the merger of BI and P&O in May 1914, "one of the most shrewd deals of Inchcape's life." In what was described as "the first reverse takeover," Mackay merged his own BI with its more powerful rival, P&O, and then became successively managing director and chairman of this enlarged shipping power. Later Inchcape leaders, one of whom allowed a similar reverse takeover (only this time to Inchcape's definite disadvantage) might have profited from observing the brilliant way the operation was negotiated and implemented.

So, having landed in England as a little-known expatriate in the twilight years of Queen Victoria, by the time the First World War broke out, Lord Inchcape had become the greatest shipowner in the land. Of the 12.5 million gross tons of shipping under the British flag — representing about two-thirds of the entire world's seagoing tonnage — the combined fleet of the P&O and BI shipping lines then under his control accounted for one-eighth. It could truly be said that, "If Britannia ruled the mercantile waves in 1914, then Inchcape was her merchant prince."

The first Lord Inchcape successfully steered his empire through the disaster of the First World War, despite the disruption of trade, losses of ships and men, and government requisitions that trailed in its wake. His ships contributed decisively to the war effort by carrying both passengers and military stores. However, as today's City analysts would have appreciated, despite his heavy involvement he managed to keep the share price "at a high level." Lord Inchcape even found the time to expand his banking interests and make further acquisitions, including several shipping lines in Australia and New Zealand. His public work during these years was so important that he was one of the few individuals allowed a petrol allowance for his motor car. According to *The Times*, "probably no civilian outside the Cabinet discharged during the war a greater range of administrative activities."

However, in 1918, Inchcape the businessman had to face a changed world. British shipping had paid a substantial price for victory in terms of lost tonnage, markets, and privileges, and would never regain its former pre-eminence. As the inevitable postwar boom was followed by a slump and then continued depression, the P&O line was found to have enormous liabilities. The returns paid by Inchcape to shareholders, it emerged, had been based on a policy described as "skilled accumulation followed by skilled juggling."

Although the volatile shipping industry continued to be dogged by problems of government interference, lower profits, high rates of tax, and increased competition, Lord Inchcape continued to grow in this field, acquiring the old established General Steam Navigation Company. He funded this expansion through the foundation, in 1920, of the P&O Banking Corporation, which had branches in India and China.

Despite Lord Inchcape's high profile as chairman of P&O, the Mackinnon interests and his own personal merchant stakes in shipping, oil, insurance, tea, communications, railways and harbors, coal, banks, textile mills, refrigerated meat, and general merchanting remained equally important to him. Expanded during the postwar years, these family investments would eventually form the basis of the Inchcape group.

He also found the time to continue his heavy involvement in public affairs in both Britain and India, though his justifiable hopes of becoming Viceroy were ultimately dashed by the Prime Minister, Asquith. The wide variety of assignments Lord Inchcape covered are a testament to his appetite for hard work, and the general respect in which his wide expertise was held. The British government's gratitude for the negotiation skills and salesmanship he displayed on its behalf in India and the Middle East found expression in the earldom, granted in 1929.

Also influential in financial and monetary affairs, Lord Inchcape was one of those wielding the 1922 Geddes Axe. This committee, an attempt to apply tough business standards to the public accounts and cut government expenditure, was not a success. Inchcape himself failed to enhance his popularity by supporting heavy cuts in teachers' salaries on the grounds that "he was personally none the worse for having received but little formal education." A letter to *The Times* in 1925 demonstrated his disillusionment; he wrote that "perhaps the best person to introduce real Government economy was Mussolini."

By 1931, with both Inchcape's health and the P&O results

deteriorating, Alexander Shaw (later Lord Craigmyle), acting chairman of P&O and Inchcape's son-in-law, took over the reins of power and initiated a complete restructuring. He did so in the face of opposition from Inchcape, whose views now seemed increasingly out of step with the modern world.

On his death, the first Lord Inchcape was variously described as "a Napoleon of Commerce" and "the last survivor of Britain's feudal shipowners." According to *The Daily Mirror*, he was so overbearing that "no shareholder would dare ask a question at AGMs." Other obituarists were kinder, however, saying that "few men have sat on so many Royal Commissions, mostly as Chairman, and still fewer have saved the State so much money" and referring to him as "the world's best ship salesman."

His management style could aptly be described as hands-on, in that he never delegated any major decision. Despite his prolonged absences in India, he knew exactly what was going on, keeping "in touch by telegram on all matters of importance." His fellow directors "sent me regularly my weekly bag and I turned up in Leadenhall Street after six months' absence with as full a knowledge of the affairs of P&O and our Allied companies as if I had never been away." His total commitment to his companies was illustrated by the way he put his own money into P&O, in order to maintain public confidence.

The first Lord Inchcape's biographer summed him up as "a businessman who was very lucky, but who capitalized on every stroke of luck to the full." In current jargon, this was due to the way he leveraged his extensive knowledge of shipping and trade affairs — the success of his acquisitions was attributed to the fact that "Inchcape always did his homework." Methodical, precise, and a man for detail, yet in his early days "innovatory and radical," Inchcape never shouted or lost his temper, and prided himself on the fact that "I never fail to keep my work, and I always clear up my desk at night." Today's business writers might also describe him as someone who knew his own core competencies and stuck to them; in 1921, he declined the throne of Albania on the grounds that "it is not in my line."

For Lord Inchcape, retirement was never an option. Up to his death, all official mail was redirected to the yacht, moored in Monte Carlo, on which he lived. None of the directors dared contradict his orders. He died in May 1932, and the news of his death was withheld until the stock exchange closed. When it reopened, "the whole market fell noticeably." How times were to change.

TRANSITION

Not until 1948 did the family find someone to rival the first Earl's entrepreneurship and business skills — or talent for making money. His son, Kenneth, although always involved in the Inchcape activities, lacked his father's ambition. His early death in 1939 was followed, five years later, by that of Lord Craigmyle. However, in 1948 the Third Earl of Inchcape, also called Kenneth, took over the family inheritance. The next thirty years were to see another remarkable transformation stage in the Inchcape saga.

In the intervening years, the businesses had gone through yet another cycle of depression and war. During the Second World War, some of the Indian activities repeated P&O's performance during 1914–18 by both contributing to the war effort and achieving record profits. So, while BI lost over half its tonnage in the service of the Admiralty, the Binny textile mills churned out khaki uniforms and prospered. Similarly, while the Middle East businesses suffered manpower shortages as expatriate managers were called up, the African and Australian interests experienced growth. In fact, the effects of the war on Inchcape's interests demonstrated the value of a long-held Inchcape business mantra, the value of spreading the risks.

As the third Lord Inchcape took over, the political complexion of the region in which the first Earl had built up the family fortunes was changing rapidly. On world maps, the pink tide that had indicated the all-conquering spread of the British Empire was pushed into reverse by the counter charge of decolonization. Independence for India, Pakistan, and Ceylon came in 1947–48 and as the winds of change began to blow over Africa, there was political unrest in the Gulf. With the new governments came the threat of higher taxes, a clamor for localization and, inevitably, nationalization. It was clear that a radical rethink about the focus of the family holdings was needed; in a changing world, they could no longer survive in their present form or geographical orientation. Fortunately, Kenneth Inchcape was the man to supply this radicalism.

GETTING OUT OF INDIA

Born in 1917 and despite having what his grandfather might have seen as the disadvantage of an education — albeit at Eton rather than Arbroath Academy — Kenneth Inchcape was to demonstrate that he had inherited all his grandfather's toughness and determination. Before the outbreak of war he studied law at Cambridge, and then saw active service at Dunkirk and in Italy with the XII Royal Lancers, the same (though now mechanized) cavalry regiment in which his father had served during the First World War. Demobbed in 1946 he went to India where, shades of his grandfather, he spent two years in the MM&C shipping agency in Calcutta "learning the ropes."

He returned to England in 1948 and took stock of his inheritance; director of eighteen companies and a partner in nine others, mainly India-based but also in East Africa, the Persian Gulf, and Australia, their activities covering tea, cotton, engineering, shipping, and insurance. The majority of these businesses had made large profits during the war, and their recent earnings were substantially higher than in the 1930s. However, the threat of the crippling death duties — a very real one, given the advanced age of many of the partners — to which privately owned companies were subject meant that this inheritance could soon be whittled away.

Kenneth Inchcape quickly realized that such a myriad collection of investments, respected old businesses though they might be, was in no shape to survive the pressures and threats of a changing world. Still generally organized and run as partnerships rather than limited companies, the firms operated quite independently of each other. Divided in this way, they would never stand up to change, but together, their joint resources and skills harnessed under a centralized management, they might represent a profitable core round which Inchcape could grasp new opportunities and rebuild.

In a move that was to be repeated by Sir David Orr and George Turnbull forty years later, and by Philip Cushing ten years after that, Kenneth Inchcape decided on a program of rationalization and reorganization. The shortening intervals indicate the quickening speed of change, but in every case the motivation was the same; rationalization in order to release capital to feed the growth of those activities chosen to take the whole forward.

In a first phase, capital would be raised by selling off shares and then invested to strengthen the remaining companies. In a second phase, these would then be grouped as subsidiaries of a main holding company. At some point, the decision was taken to launch this holding company in, as Dr Stephanie Jones described, a "package attractive to would-be investors" on the London Stock Exchange, along with its satellite subsidiaries. Two crucial figures in seeing through this highly complex operation were Hugh Waters, Kenneth Inchcape's right-hand man, and an old friend, A. W. Giles of Barings. The two men were closely involved right from the beginning, and the close relationship with Barings was to last until the present day.

Since the whole exercise was designed to satisfy the stock exchange and the investing public, sentiment was not allowed to cloud judgment. So in the first phase, the 48% interest in the tea, jute mills, and river steamers of Macneill & Barry Ltd. in India was sold to the local Tata group, leaving Inchcape with a 52% controlling interest plus £500,000 in cash. In 1956–57 the jewels in the crown, the MM&C shipping agency companies, were sold to P&O for £2 million. These moves left the family portfolio less narrowly concentrated on shipping, and gave Inchcape a cash mountain for future investment.

During stage two, almost every business was reconstituted, a task involving the resolution of many legal and taxation problems, complicated by the involvement in the laws of countries outside the U.K. Family interests were rearranged, and partnership firms were — often with difficulty — converted into limited liability companies. The object was to gain tax advantages, satisfy national policies in the host countries, and make the retirement of managing partners, and local and European staff easier.

In phase three, a program of evaluation and disposal, again to be echoed forty years later by Sir George Turnbull, took place. Each holding was examined to decide its fate. The basis on which companies were chosen for sale or retention was that they had "a good geographical spread of business" and "a favorable profits or assets ratio," words that could have been written at any time during the 1980s.

The final act was to form a U.K. holding company to act as the financial base of the new group. This now comprised seventeen companies with interests in six areas, arranged into three principal subsidiaries. A prospectus was then drawn up, and at the end of October 1958 the Inchcape Group plc, an international trading company, was floated on the London Stock Exchange. The value of the company's market capitalization was £2.25 million and the first year's pre-tax profit was £737,000. The issue was favorably received by the City and business press of the time, and by May the next year the middle price of an ordinary share had risen from 25s per share to 31s3d. Two years later, Inchcape acquired and moved into its new headquarters in the City of London at 40 St. Mary Axe.

By his actions, without the benefit of any business training or outside advice, Kenneth Inchcape "not only preserved the value of his grandfather's assets but increased their worth several times over." As a result, the refocused group, under the umbrella of the respected Inchcape name, could grow in new directions. For these and later actions, his half-brother, Lord Tanlaw, described Kenneth Inchcape as "a business genius. He saved the business by converting them into private companies and then into the public company of Inchcape" so that it could then "become a sort of multinational conglomerate." Lord Tanlaw, then managing director of the Gray Dawes Bank, had in fact argued for keeping family control through the privatized bank, "as did the Swire family. But my brother disagreed, so there it was."

Certainly, it was seen by contemporaries as a major tour de force, and as Hugh Waters later recalled, the third Lord Inchcape was widely praised for his "vision and enterprise." The public launching of an international general trading company was unprecedented, but, as the rise in the share price indicated, he had produced "an acceptable amount and spread of assets and risks and income of the right kind, and in the right countries." Later leaders could not claim as much.

THE ACQUISITIVE YEARS

During the first few years after its formation, recalled the later director of group accounting and treasury, Colin Campbell, the group "did very little." At this time, Inchcape still had a massive investment in India. As Lord Tanlaw, who spent six years in Calcutta recalled, "In the 1960s, Inchcape was employing 30,000 to 40,000 people in India itself. Binny's composite textile mill was the biggest in the world, employing 15,000 people. Then there were thirty tea estates, the jute mills and engineering."

However, the businesses were being hit in various ways; tea prices fell after a series of droughts, the textile industry suffered from government restrictions, and some steamer business was lost. In addition, "the tax structure was making it impossible for overseas or absentee landlords to make profits and the need to Indianize overseas investment was a political pressure," although this last point affected Inchcape least. As Lord Tanlaw observed, "We didn't mind at all as we employed Indian officers throughout the group. In fact the first Englishmen we employed was in 1939 — until then, they were always Scotsmen or Indians." But these developments confirmed the poor future outlook in the subcontinent, at a time when political instability in East Africa and Iran was reining in activity there.

However, in the decade from 1965 to 1975, a combination of boom conditions generally, fast rates of growth, and the falling pound sterling signaled a different economic climate. During this period, the Middle

East businesses began to take off, as did Nigeria where the oil revenues began to flow through. Everything seemed to go well at the same time, and during these years, Inchcape plc made its great leap forward.

Growth came in two ways: internally, through the expansion of existing businesses; and externally, through a widely acclaimed program of acquisition. From 1966 onward, the Third Earl orchestrated a series of mergers that transformed the group and earned him a reputation for shrewd judgment and astute dealing.

Colin Armstrong, who joined the group in 1981, credited Kenneth Inchcape with a farsighted philosophy in his approach to growth by acquisition. "I've heard it said, and I think it is true, that once the Inchcape group was floated, he had paper. A lot of the other big, family overseas businesses remained in private hands and so faced a lot of problems with inheritance tax, and couldn't liquidate their assets. So when Lord Inchcape bought them up, he gave them shares in Inchcape. He said, 'We will take your company over, but leave your name on the door, and you can continue the same management. All we need is "x%" return per annum in London.' So they were all friendly takeovers. The family owners encouraged them, and the managers were reassured they wouldn't have to change their ties or their logos. There was a lot of wisdom in that strategy." Certainly, the willingness of many companies to accept shares in Inchcape showed its strength in the City, besides making the group's expansion easier.

The Third Earl's strategy succeeded brilliantly. As strong growth gave the company a high market rating, the company took advantage of this to issue more shares to fund further expansion; it was a winning syndrome, which for some time showed no sign of ending. During this time, the Inchcape price/earnings (P/E) ratio climbed ever higher, demonstrating strong market approval of this "expanding and dynamic international holding company with a reputation for honesty and fair dealing."

The merger with the Borneo Company in 1967, described as "the single most important vital transaction in the post-flotation history of the group," radically transformed both the geographical distribution of assets and the income of the group. Lord Tanlaw recalled that the merger was "due to family connections, or if you like sentiment, to link up with my mother's part of the world. It was a joint family decision. The Borneo Company fitted in because our families are married to Brooke and Mackay. These are the two basic roots. When Lord Inchcape's mother died his father (and mine) married Leonora Brooke, who was the eldest daughter of the third Rajah of Sarawak — my grandfather."

Family connections apart, there were many synergies in the merger; both firms were active in shipping and insurance-agency work, and operated jointly in the U.K. and Australia. However, the acquisition of the Borneo Company and its interests in Canada, the Caribbean, Hong Kong, Singapore, Brunei, and Thailand also doubled Inchcape's sphere of operations, and added two important activities for its future development: motor vehicle distribution, and the timber and construction industries. By tripling the group's pre-tax profit, the Borneo acquisition also enabled it to go on to further diversification in new markets. "The Borneo Company," observed Lord Tanlaw, "gave Inchcape a new lease of life, as it then spread out across the world."

To emphasize the friendly nature of the merger, the Borneo board joined that of Inchcape. Two particular ex-Borneo directors, Robert Henderson, a major shareholder in the company, and Peter Heath, were to play important roles in later events. The entrepreneurial Heath was generally considered one of the architects of Inchcape's growth, as his knowledge of the countries and companies involved was instrumental in making the later Far Eastern acquisitions that became the mainstay of the group. Another important figure was Donald Caswell, company secretary, whose encyclopedic knowledge of the group was invaluable. During this acquisition, Inchcape again called on A. W. Giles of Barings to act as advisor. These men formed a solid team on whom Kenneth Inchcape relied during this heady period of growth.

Heath was also a crucial figure in developing the Toyota motors business. An episode in the early 1970s, recalled by Colin Armstrong, provides an insight both into Lord Inchcape's business style, and how contemporaries viewed the nascent Japanese automotive industry. Heath informed Inchcape that he had the opportunity to acquire a Japanese motors distribution franchise, Toyota, in Singapore. However, when Kenneth Inchcape, who was at that time on the British Export Council and a senior figure in business and political circles, talked to colleagues — ministers and other businessmen — about this, there was a horrified reaction. "It was considered absolute sacrilege for a British trading company to think of doing business with a Japanese company. He took tremendous flak but had the courage of his convictions and told Heath to go ahead, telling him 'Say you couldn't contact me because it was the weekend, and we'll sort it out next week.' The rest, as they say, is history."

The Borneo merger was taken as a template of Inchcape's management style; firm but entirely fair. It was not a bad image for the more gentlemanly times in which business was conducted. Like his grandfather, Kenneth Inchcape was seen to have done his homework in preparing the acquisition, and the way in which it was carried out won approval both from the City and international observers. It also soothed the fears of future targets, whose managers could see the benefits of having Inchcape's growing financial clout while retaining the family name, together with the autonomy — and pensions — of its management. No-one could ever accuse Kenneth Inchcape of being an asset-stripping predator, and this favorable reputation also soothed those served by the acquired companies; few agencies were lost as a result of an Inchcape takeover.

An important spin-off from the merger was the 1970 investment in the BEWAC Motor Corporation in Nigeria. This motor distribution business was also a Birmingham-based distributor, the main principal in both cases being British Leyland. This growing interest in the motor industry, and new involvement in motors distribution in the U.K., was then solidified by the 1973 acquisition of Mann Egerton, one of the leading U.K. distributors of British Leyland cars and commercial vehicles, and a distributor of Ford agricultural tractors and machinery.

With this move, Kenneth Inchcape achieved his aim of strengthening and enlarging his U.K. base in order to meet new tax legislation and reduce dependence on foreign remittances. Money could then be left in the overseas businesses to fund future investment. However, at the time, Inchcape's involvement in the motor trade was frowned on as "not quite the thing." Lord Tanlaw recalled, "We were very rude about the business and Motors people at first, but then it started to make money and we had to pay attention to it."

Subsequent acquisitions confirmed the group's new geographical focus on the Far East. To its new 100% holding in Gibb Livingston & Co., in 1969 Inchcape added another long-established Hong Kong business, Gilman (Holdings) Ltd. This, too, was a family sell-out and, as Lord Tanlaw emphasized, a valuable one since Gilman's interests in specialist marketing, exporting, and engineering gave Inchcape an important arm for the future. The next great coup, the acquisition of Dodwell & Co. in 1972, introduced Inchcape to Japan. Yet another family business, Dodwell had long-established shipping agencies and trading interests in Hong Kong, Japan, and elsewhere. As its chairman pointed out to his shareholders, "... it would be hard to find a better partner with whom to merge." Inchcape's softly softly approach had again paid off.

In 1972, Kenneth Inchcape even made a bid for P&O, of which he was a director. Inchcape and P&O had gone their separate ways since the death of the first Earl, the only common denominator being that Kenneth Inchcape was a shareholder in each company. Now, this move brought him a great deal of notoriety in the press, as it unveiled a lengthy disagreement between himself and the P&O board over its bid for Bovis, the construction firm. Eventually, after much drama, both bids were dropped and in 1973, Lord Inchcape followed in his grandfather's shoes by becoming chairman. The next year, he took over Bovis at a fifth of the cost of the original bid.

In 1974, *Management Today* profiled the Inchcape group. In the light of later developments, two comments stand out. The article noted that as a result of the Mann Egerton acquisition, the Motors business worldwide accounted for 40% of the group's profits. However, Sir Hugh Mackay Tallack, chief executive of the time and Kenneth Inchcape's cousin, was reported as saying that Inchcape had "no desire to become just a motor company." In the same article, Lord Inchcape himself was quoted as saying that he foresaw "a great danger in getting too diverse." But by then, it was already too late.

The 1975 Anglo-Thai acquisition, Kenneth Inchcape's last major move, was an exception in the hitherto smooth progression of the group. As Commander Michael Wall, Inchcape's Public Relations Controller, later recalled, the vituperative nature of this contested bid "shook Lord Inchcape rigid. No-one had ever refused to join the group before," and he vowed never to do such a thing again.

However, by gaining Anglo-Thai's substantial trading operations, and wines and spirits distribution in Southeast Asia, Hong Kong, Japan, and Australia, Inchcape's new orientation toward Asia was entrenched. It also eventually got another new board member in Roy Davies, who was later to be seen as a possible successor to Lord Inchcape.

The deal brought greatly increased profits. In 1977, Inchcape posted a record £73 million in pre-tax profits (from £37 million in 1976), representing an 80% growth in EPS over the previous year. The City once more applauded strongly; the group's prestige was at its height.

The program of acquisition had been rounded off a year earlier in 1976, when Inchcape increased its stake in Bain Dawes, one of the largest unlisted Lloyds insurance brokers, to 100%. Insurance broking was yet another new business that was to have an important influence on the group's future.

In the next years, the emphasis was more on developing the

profitability of Inchcape's U.K. assets and internal growth, as exemplified by Gray Mackenzie, Inchcape's Persian Gulf agency, which was making huge profits there. The smaller, later acquisitions included Poons, an industrial and project caterer in the Middle East and Australia, and, more notoriously, an associated French company, Peschaud & Cie (heavy equipment transporters). In Hong Kong, Neil Pryde Ltd. (sailmaking) and the Mazda motor franchise were added, while in the U.K. the acquisition of Pride and Clarke Ltd. brought the exclusive Toyota distributorship that was to play such a key role in the group's evolution.

As it turned out, 1977 marked the high point of Inchcape's performance. It was then the twenty-eighth largest British company by market value. Three years later, the group's market capitalization stood at £400 million, over 175 times the value of the original launch in 1958. It had over 700 principal subsidiaries and associated companies operating in over fifty countries, the main areas of activity being the Far East, Southeast Asia, the Middle East, Africa, and the U.K.

However, by then the economic climate was changing and, as a series of shocks hit the group, later events were again foreshadowed by the drop in the median share price from 460p to 270p by the end of 1981, with the market capitalization at under £225. The glory days were over, leaving Inchcape in danger of sliding down the greasy pole of City opinion into near oblivion.

For the expansion of the Inchcape group during the 1970s, Stacey Ellis, director of strategy and planning under George Turnbull and responsible for a later restructuring, put the third Lord Inchcape in an élite league of genuine entrepreneurs and creators. "He took over at twenty-eight and had the vision to sell India. He saw there was no future there and went into Southeast Asia. He sold his heritage and started afresh. Everyone said he was mad, but he was right." Ellis recalled Kenneth Inchcape coming into his office to discuss a critical article that had appeared in the *Far Eastern Economic Review*. "I said to him, 'Remember, you are one of fewer than ten people since the war who have built up an empire. We are the civil servants; we will never have the flair that you have.'"

Unfortunately, Kenneth Inchcape's time of triumph was over. His freewheeling entrepreneurial style was now out of date. It was almost time for the civil servants to come in and introduce a new note of sobriety and control.

Entrepreneurs, Fiefdoms, and Shocks

◆

In 1977 the Inchcape group had reached its zenith after a decade of achieving an annual compound growth rate of 43%, an impressive performance by any standards, as the City appreciated. There had been widespread praise for the way Kenneth Inchcape had used the favorable economic climate to play the 1960s' acquisitions game to put together his group, or conglomerate as it was more usually described. Unfortunately, the economic shifts that occurred in the late 1970s were to prove less favorable to this strategy, and all the factors that had made the group so strong in earlier times had begun to work against it. Deconglomeration was now the order of the day, along with an emphasis on return on capital, ideas that completely passed the group and its management by. Within a few years, Kenneth Inchcape's recipe for success would be relabeled a recipe for disaster. Such are the vagaries of management fashion.

In fact, there had been a very sound method in the apparent madness of Inchcape's strategy of growth by acquisition. The common denominator of all the group's activities was a trading orientation, and the Third Earl was clear that its main strength was an ability to do business in the most remote parts of the world. Whenever goods needed to be shipped from A to B, Inchcape plc could arrange it, relying on its long-established name and experience in trading. It followed that any opportunity to extend this strength should be taken, as such a move could only enhance the group's overall performance.

Kenneth Inchcape's mantra, which became the yardstick applied to potential acquisitions, was: "We are prepared to engage in a new activity in a familiar area or a familiar activity in a new area, but we would not

— unless there were especially good reasons — attempt a new activity in a new area." It was considered, and by and large events bore out the truth of this belief, that the territorial spread of the group and the diversity of its interests spread the risk. By having many eggs in many different baskets, the group was able to survive setbacks; a loss in one part of the world could be offset by success in another. On the other hand, as the 1977 Harborn episode was to demonstrate, when a group member veered from this rule, the consequences could be disastrous.

CRISIS IN COCOA

The revelation of the Harborn losses was the first shock to hit the group and signal to the outside world that Inchcape's fortunes were not as firmly grounded as it believed. Inchcape had gained control of Harborn Holding B.V., a small venture employing no more than a dozen people, as part of the Borneo acquisition. A Dutch commodity trading and broking company, Harborn traded in cocoa futures, well known as a high-risk business and an activity in which, as it was recognized too late, the group should never have been involved.

Since cocoa was largely an Africa-produced commodity, Harborn was placed under the jurisdiction of the Main Board director responsible for Nigeria and Kenya. Inchcape's activities in these countries then included motor distribution, windows and airconditioning equipment, tea, dairy farming, shipping agencies, and ordinary agency work — activities not, at first sight, compatible with the cocoa business. The Inchcape director himself had no knowledge of the cocoa industry and little of this small company, and the hands-off approach of the Inchcape center had allowed Harborn to run its affairs without interference. In fact, as the then deputy chairman and chief executive, Sir Michael Parsons, wrote later, no-one at Inchcape's London head office knew anything at all about commodity trading "other than in connection with the company's substantial interest in tea, which was a commodity operating under its own very different set of rules."

In the mid-1970s the world's supply of cocoa was unexpectedly and sharply diminished as a result of unfavorable weather conditions. Consequently, the price of cocoa rocketed, with catastrophic results for those trading in cocoa futures. Many cocoa traders suffered losses, and some lost very heavily indeed. Among the latter was Harborn Holding B.V. As Sir Michael Parsons described, "Having sold short, Harborn found itself having to make physical delivery of high-priced cocoa against contracts made at previous low prices, or make settlements at or near market differences. In short, they had guessed market trends wrongly, had not hedged, and suffered substantial losses as a result." The problem first appeared in 1977 but, because of the futures trading, its effect was spread over the next two years.

Inchcape's finance division had first scented trouble at an earlier stage, alerted by a rise in the company's borrowings. The director responsible was dispatched to Harborn to investigate, but was reassured by its manager that the problem was only temporary, that it was due to a Romanian debtor who was unable to repay in the short term because of political problems, and that matters would soon be resolved. The explanation was accepted, but, in fact, the Romanian debtor did not exist and the debts were actually losses. Prompt action by the center would have limited the damage, but because the true state of affairs had been successfully concealed, the company was allowed to slide deeper into debt as it tried to trade out its losses. When a halt was finally called, these losses amounted to over £25 million, spread over two years. As the *Far Eastern Economic Review* reported, one Inchcape director later admitted, "We didn't have the expertise to monitor that," while Lord Inchcape himself attributed the disaster to the fact that "We broke our usual rule of not going into a new country with a new business."

Although the actual amount of cash lost was not in itself a crippling sum, it compounded an already difficult situation. The Harborn crisis came at a time when the group was still growing rapidly, and therefore absorbing a great deal of working capital. To meet these demands, the group had extended its borrowings and now, the urgent necessity to pay off the Harborn losses in addition to this burden of debt put the group close to its borrowing limits.

More seriously, the Harborn losses shook the City's previously favorable view of the group. The episode implied a disturbing lack of financial controls and cast doubt on the quality of Inchcape profits. These, as analysts began to realize, could not be maintained at such high levels for much longer, given the changing economic situation. Inchcape was about to run out of growth.

In fact, the finance division had already recognized that several of its most fertile cash cows, such as Nigeria and the Gulf ports, were beginning to dry up and that unless alternative sources of income were found, the group would soon find itself in trouble. In preparation for this, two convertible bonds in the Euromarkets had been issued, the money to be used for further acquisitions to compensate for anticipated losses. However, the cash was largely used to pay off the Harborn losses, and a valuable opportunity was lost.

Equally important, Harborn brought Inchcape's management style to the attention of the outside world. And as the structure and organization of the group came under scrutiny, the analysts didn't like what they saw.

STRUCTURE, WHAT STRUCTURE?

Business theory in the United States during the 1960s was dominated by Alfred Chandler's seminal work on the relationship between strategy and structure, published in 1962. It is highly doubtful that Kenneth Inchcape ever read this work, for, as Colin Armstrong observed, "He was of the generation when business theory was not fashionable." However, the group he created faithfully reflected the truth of Chandler's conclusions about the influence of a company's strategy on its organizational design.

A business historian, Chandler's work was based on a review of over a hundred American firms between 1850 and 1920, a period he described as "the formative years of modern capitalism" during which business enterprises, under pressure from a changing environment due to shifts in markets and technologies, moved from being small, owner-controlled enterprises toward the modern, multi-unit firm. Chandler examined in depth the evolving structure of four companies — DuPont, General Motors, Standard Oil of New Jersey, and Sears Roebuck — to see what factors affected structure, and in what sequence. From his studies he identified a distinct pattern: that the structure of an organization was related to its strategy, and that structural adaptation always appeared to follow the pursuit of a chosen strategy — ergo structure followed strategy.

For Chandler, there was a crucial distinction between the two; strategy was "the determination of long-term goals and objectives together with the adoption of courses of action and the allocation of resources for carrying out those goals." Structure was "the organization which is devised to administer the activities which arise from the strategies adopted." As such, it involved the existence of a hierarchy, the distribution of work, and lines of authority and communication.

Chandler concluded that new environments created new strategic choices that, in turn, called for the development of new structures. The structure developed by his sample firms was a divisionalized one which, he observed, required new administrative offices and structures. These were run by a class of professional and technical managers "committed to the long-term stability of the firm" and responsible for "coordinating and planning work, and allocating resources." The role of management in developing structure was central to Chandler's analysis. As he wrote in another work, "the visible hand of management has replaced Adam Smith's invisible hand of market forces."

Chandler concluded that "growth without structural adjustment can lead only to economic inefficiency" — that is, firms that expanded but failed to progress toward a new type of divisionalized structure and management hierarchy would risk losing profitability, and being left behind. The group's history during the final years of Kenneth Inchcape's leadership was to demonstrate the truth of this. Then, his strategy of acquiring distant and unrelated businesses, unaccompanied by the appropriate structures, began to have a disastrous effect on the ability of the group's central management to control, resulting in serious financial weakness.

THE CONTINGENCY THEORISTS

Meanwhile, a set of British theorists were also focusing on the interaction between organizations and the environments in which they operated. Like Chandler, they analyzed how the need to function successfully in different environments led organizations to adopt different strategies and structures. Their research led them to conclude that there was no one best way of structuring an organization — it all depended, or was contingent upon, circumstances.

For these contingency theorists, two key factors in an organization's structure were the degree of differentiation and integration, both of which could be viewed from horizontal and vertical perspectives. Vertical meant looking at how much variation occurred at different levels hierarchically in the organization; horizontal referred to variation across the organization at the same level. So, for example, allowing decisions to be made away from the central authority at lower levels in the hierarchy created vertical differentiation.

Three contingencies were identified as affecting the degree of integration and differentiation appropriate to an organization: its size, the kind of technology it employed, and the nature of the environment in which it operated. Of the three, research into the external environment and its structural implications had most relevance to Inchcape's problems at this time. Burns and Stalker (1961) developed two new classifications for management methods and procedures: the mechanistic and the organic. Their conclusions were based on a comparison of twenty English and Scottish industrial firms, to see how their organizational structure and practice varied according to the different environments in which they operated. They found that in a stable environment, what they called a mechanistic structure (characterized by formalization and centralization) would be effective, whereas a more changeable, fast-moving environment required a more organic (flexible and adaptive) structure. Emery and Trist (1960) expanded this work by identifying four kinds of environment in which an organization might operate: placid randomized, placid-clustered, disturbed reactive, and turbulent-field. While mechanistic structures were effective in the first two, the other two required more flexible approaches.

Perhaps most relevant of all, however, was the work of two Harvard Business School theorists, Lawrence and Lorsch (1967), who carried this research further. Their investigation into ten firms in three industries showed that the more turbulent, complex, and diverse the external environment in which an organization operated, the greater the degree of differentiation necessary among its internal subsets — that is, the need for a greater number of different units in order to deal with all the different parts of the environment. However, they also warned that, given a very diverse external environment, coupled with a highly differentiated internal environment, the imposition of an elaborate integration mechanism was necessary to avoid the sub-units going off in completely different directions.

Under Kenneth Inchcape, the group took part of this theory — the degree of differentiation — to heart. Plotted on any scale that set turbulence and complexity in the environment against its implications for appropriate differentiation in the organization, Inchcape would probably have fallen off the edge. Unfortunately, it had omitted to ensure that the all-important integration mechanism was in place to compensate. For in effect, the Inchcape organization consisted of a collection of fiefdoms, in which the barons who ran them followed the mantras of autonomy and entrepreneurship, without thought to the possible consequences or reference to the central authority. Entrenched in their kingdoms and independent habits, they were to prove an almost insuperable barrier to every effort to change the group over the next decade.

AUTONOMY AND FIEFDOMS

Given the geographical spread of the business and difficulties of communications, and Kenneth Inchcape's own view on the value of freedom, the emergence of fiefdoms as the predominant organizational feature of the Inchcape empire was inevitable. Their degree of autonomy was exemplified, at its most extreme, by the Anglo-Thai group. Such was the bitter legacy of the takeover that Anglo-Thai's chief executive refused to let any Inchcape member into its building (which in Singapore was next door to the Inchcape Berhad office), insisting, "Your style of management is bloody hopeless." However, to the Inchcape managers, the spirit of independence that characterized the organization and their managerial style was the outward and visible sign of the group's inward strength.

THE HOLE AT THE CENTER

At the hub of this empire was Kenneth Inchcape himself. The way in which he led and organized his group reflected a philosophy and personal style that was in turn heavily influenced by his army training: autocratic but paternalistic, firm but *laissez-faire*. In recent years, many business theorists have appropriated the vocabulary and theories of the military world and offered them as suitable models for strategic planning and leadership in business. As practiced by Kenneth Inchcape, this model did seem to point up some distinct limitations.

Colin Armstrong, recruited in 1981 to run Inchcape's South American operations, found him "quite an enigma. He had great compassion for people and earned great loyalty from the old stagers, though Inchcape did not pay well. He commanded tremendous loyalty and respect, but could be very tough when he wanted to be. He had vision … He chose people he got on with." Public Relations Controller, Commander Michael Wall likewise found that Lord Inchcape preferred to work with those he knew and trusted, and was not good at personal relations or at choosing new people. Lord Tanlaw described his half-brother as "a business genius of the old sort. He was the proprietor of the company and ultimately, the buck stopped with him. It also started with him. He inspired people to do things and he saw that they were done. And if Lord Inchcape didn't approve of it — and I had lots of rows with him — then it didn't get done. If he didn't like it, you couldn't do it … he was quite frightening across the desk, and he was the boss. He made decisions and followed them through. He had no time for people who were incompetent."

Although this attitude was acceptable as long as Lord Inchcape remained intimately involved in running the group, its downside emerged later when he became distracted by other responsibilities. At that time, believed Lord Tanlaw, Kenneth Inchcape was surrounded by "too many people who agreed with him too easily. He needed more people to stand up to him. He had this strong, forceful presence which needed some courage and ability to stand up to, and those executives who did often found that it did not do their careers too much good. This is the weakness of a proprietorial system."

Famous for his formidable memory, Kenneth Inchcape had accurate recall of everything that was reported to him in the course of his yearly inspection visits. Richard Owens, who joined Gray Mackenzie in 1964, remembered that "If you bumped into him on the stairs, he would know exactly what was going on." His style of management, observed Lord Tanlaw, meant that decisions were made and implemented with speed, "as opposed to an endless round of committees, reports and accountant systems so by the time it has gone through, you have missed an opportunity." Like his grandfather, every day Lord Inchcape pored over a folder of consolidated material in a bid to keep track of events. However, the gaps in the material were to become more telling.

Although many who worked for the group found Lord Inchcape awe-inspiring and irascible, his autocratic manner hid a shyness that made it difficult for him to address large groups, or to be comfortable with people until he had known them for twenty years. Philip Leavers, later information technology manager at corporate headquarters, recalled the annual Christmas party, when all the head office staff would be introduced individually in a receiving line to shake hands with Lord Inchcape. This was the only time most people working there actually saw their chief, and Leavers recalled that for himself, then a young man in his first job, it was something of an ordeal. However, he wondered whether Lord Inchcape might not have been equally nervous. John Duncan, director of corporate affairs under George Turnbull, found him "sensitive to criticism and very sensitive to the press."

Reflecting both his background and time, the two qualities Kenneth Inchcape prized above all were loyalty and integrity. Anyone who served the group well could depend on his support and appreciation. It was said of him that he never sacked a man or sold a company. Like all builders, he could not destroy and, until later events forced his hand, "disposal wasn't a word in his business vocabulary," commented Michael Wall. However, as Lord Tanlaw recalled, "People thought they could be fired, though he never did. They were in fear and trembling of him, so people got things done."

Below Lord Inchcape in the organizational structure was the Main Board, several of whom were family members. Each Main Board director, with the exception of the finance director, was said to "have a responsibility" for a range of businesses. The directors were recruited from the ranks of those who had been successful at running one of the companies in some part of the Inchcape empire. After at least twenty years with the group, usually at the age of about fifty, such a man would be brought to London and would be said to "have a view" over, for example, Hong Kong or Thailand. He would then oversee three or four managing directors in that area, and act as their link man. "Overseeing" usually meant that the director would go out and visit that area, the frequency of their visits increasing as transport by ship gave way to air travel. Lord Tanlaw recalled that, in his day, "All the executives from the Inchcape Board lived permanently on airplanes, which was very wear and tear. They went overseas to see that the policy was implemented." However, Main Board directors did not belong to the boards of the companies they oversaw (which were staffed by local people) or have any direct involvement in them.

Alastair Macaskill joined the board in 1984 following a successful period of leadership in the Gulf. "It was an experience to join the board. There was a whole history of convention, of what you did and how you presented yourself ... It was the format of how you presented that mattered; you didn't go into great detail. You were supposed to give a broad-brush picture with concise details. The business was done sensibly and effectively. They knew the business, and hence you didn't have to reiterate all the building blocks ... It was very gentlemanly but, equally, with great point to it. Something could be phrased extremely subtly but you realized it could be either criticism or praise — but never fulsome. That was something you had to learn."

After Main Board directors came another level, the controllers. They too would have spent many years working in some part of the Inchcape empire, and would be assigned to look after that area. These controllers would make periodic visits to the territories under their jurisdiction.

This "loose" control meant that the center played a reactive role to events, guided in its judgments by the men actually living and working in the territories and exercising little or no control. A management committee, composed of executive directors and controllers, met once a week, but was not considered a decision-taking body. It merely existed to receive reports on current activities and to inform those present of developments taking place. Although there were guidelines for the managers in the field to work to, there was "nothing so formal as a written policy."

This, of course, reflected Kenneth Inchcape's belief, borne out by the group's success, that in an entrepreneurial company the man on the spot was in the best position to assess opportunities and make decisions. He had quickly recognized that the nature of the Inchcape businesses meant that local initiative and freedom to act was critical, and since the group's inception had encouraged a "see it and seize it" approach. Thus, the group had no research staff, relying instead on "our lines of communication." Director James Millington-Drake, a cousin of the Third Earl, was quoted as saying, "We're never wanting for projects; people come to us with ideas."

THE BARONS

In the territories, then, although each company had a nominal link with someone on the board, the entrepreneurial spirit was equated with a minimum of control. As Lord Tanlaw recalled, "There was no fax, you had your weekly letter and that was all. You were left pretty much on your own. The whole policy of Inchcape was that the overseas companies had autonomy."

Alastair Macaskill, who went out to the Gulf in 1954, confirmed this. "You had cables in those days and mail wasn't bad, but it was probably ten days or so. Telephone — you had to book calls via Cable & Wireless, and go to their booth to take it. There was much more autonomy, and the managing director in London had usually succeeded from the operation ... The pattern was, you had someone in London who had lived and breathed the organization and knew exactly what he was talking about." Later, senior people would return to London on leave every two years (then annually) for discussions, but once back in their fiefdoms each managing director acted and lived like a king.

So, a written plan for expansion might be a two-page memo from the local chief executive to the Main Board member responsible for his area, while some bought businesses almost at whim, as exemplified by the purchase of Neil Pryde Ltd., bought by a Hong Kong manager who was a keen sailor. On the whole, this loose organization had paid off; in the 1960s and early 1970s, Inchcape men had been in the right place at the right time, and the group had profited.

Richard Owens, then a young manager in the Gulf, recalled how, during the glory days of the 1970s, the scramble for acquisition meant that "any possible idea was considered. We were trying to get away from the 'booze and boats' image, so we looked at anything. Money was no object. And because of the oil boom, there was great congestion at the ports and so we moved in and hoovered up every port contract. It was all go, and we were the shining stars. Until the boom died in 1978." Such abrupt endings to an apparently lucrative window of opportunity were another type of risk run by the group, while loose control left ample room for disaster if management was not on top of its task or was performing badly. A strong character, as many of the barons were, could keep the center in ignorance of the true state of affairs in his company. When Colin Armstrong joined the group in 1981, he found that "People who, when I joined, had been involved in problem areas all said the same thing, they didn't know what was going on till they got a nasty surprise."

The company heads also had great status in the local community. Gray Mackenzie "had a pretty high profile in the community and was well respected ... You had standing with the banks and the Residency in Bahrain and the oil companies. Those were the circles we moved in," said Macaskill. Privileged access to those who ran the country was long one of the group's great strengths, as Lord Tanlaw emphasized: "In India and in Asia, Lord Inchcape and the family and the executives knew all the families who ran the country. India is run by 250 families. It still works like that today. All the Chinese empires in Malaysia and Hong Kong are run by families, and if you want to get on, you have to know the family ... that's how you win or lose business."

Macaskill illustrated the value of these personal contacts in negotiating contracts: "When I was in Dubai, Abu Dhabi was beginning to show signs of coming to life and I spent two years making friends with Shakhbut the Ruler. I spent a lot of time driving up and down to Abu Dhabi, and it was a three-hour drive on the sand — no roads ... I negotiated an agreement with Shakhbut in late '59 ... it took eighteen months of constant visits a couple of times a month, going to the *Majlis* (the ruler's court), getting your face known, and eventually the effort resulted in an agreement. For Macaskill, this illustrated the great Inchcape strength of "knowledge of the community in which you worked. You ignore that at your peril."

INCHCAPE WHO?

The other aspect of this freedom was the way in which the companies acquired by Inchcape had been allowed to preserve their own identity, rather than being forced to integrate into the group. As a long-serving member of the board described, "It was always company policy to allow each business to retain its own name and traditions. Even the firms in

London weren't housed together, and there were many instances of the right hand not knowing what the left was doing."

This policy was initially seen as another of Inchcape's great strengths, the magnet that had attracted companies to join the group, knowing that as long as they produced satisfactory results, there would be little contact with the center. As far as the staff and locals were concerned, being bought by Inchcape made little difference; managers thought of themselves as Dodwell, Gilman, or Mann Egerton men, wearing their own company tie. Thus, a survey of Dodwell's Hong Kong employees found that most of them thought that the company was self-owned. When told that this was not so, over 50% of them responded that in that case it must be owned by Jardine Matheson (one of Inchcape's Hong Kong competitors). The idea of a corporate identity was never even discussed until 1977, when Michael Wall remembered designing a logo, tie, flag, and corporate letterhead.

Commercially, keeping the old names made good sense as it enabled the companies to keep the goodwill and loyalty associated with them, but the negative side of this was that there was no attempt to exploit potential synergies in the customer base. The management focus was extremely narrow, being limited to their particular company and their particular region, so there was no tradition of one Inchcape company recommending a service offered by a fellow subsidiary. Rather, managers in each subsidiary kept their customers and their experience of particular markets firmly to themselves, despite the fact that this could lead to Inchcape companies competing against each other. However, this too was considered to be a strength, as it enabled the group to cover the widest possible range of brands through different companies.

A GENTLEMAN'S CLUB

Inchcape's management recruitment and training policy was a further reflection of the paternalistic and *ad hoc* attitude that permeated the group. Recruitment was narrowly based, resting mainly on kith and kin, which meant, according to Richard Owens, "You came from Arbroath, you'd served in the Black Watch, and you'd been to Fettes [the Scottish public school]." Another route was via personal recommendation by an old boy network of company personnel. In this way, you felt comfortable and "fitted in."

In the early days, Kenneth Inchcape relied on a core of men he had known during his army days, and with whom he had strong bonds. This culture was continued, and thus Inchcape executives were "chaps" rather than "managers," and were measured in terms of their soundness or not. When Michael Wall joined in 1974, everyone he met at head office seemed to have been in the company, man and boy, for the last twenty years. He was struck by the lack of office politics compared with other companies he had known, and by the emphasis on protocol. So, office allocation at head office was rigidly controlled. "The controllers sat on the first floor, the Main Board directors on the second, and personnel, finance and other services were on the third and fourth." No-one removed a jacket — let alone married — without permission.

Since a career with Inchcape was a job for life, there was little emphasis on remuneration. Neither was there an idea of professional training, except in languages. Gray Mackenzie chaps were sent to school in Beirut to learn Arabic; Dodwells' people learned Japanese. Michael Wall, who shared a secretary with the India controller, remembered being amazed by the way all the old India hands at head office chatted in Hindi. Thus, there was no need for any large personnel function at the center. Its primary task was to oversee the payment of pensions to retired Inchcape employees.

All this resulted in a culture characterized by long and loyal service, security of tenure, and steady progress up the company ladder — as long as no major mistake was made. The career path was straightforward. Managers were recruited straight from school or university and sent out as temporary assistants to an area to learn the language for a year. Once they had done that, they would become full assistants. Because the continuity of management in an area was considered to be a source of great strength, they would spend their entire career in that region, acquiring the experience and expertise that made them so valuable to the center. If successful, they would rise to be number one in that area, and their ultimate object after that would be to return to England and join the board.

Alastair Macaskill's career was a classic example of this route. He joined Inchcape in 1954, having been referred to the London managing director of Gray Mackenzie by his uncle. After three weeks in London he asked to go out to the Gulf where he found "a friendly reception, a very cohesive feel, everybody seemed very cooperative." Having learned "the basics" of Arabic, he spent his first years as a shipping assistant. He was promoted to manager in Bahrain in 1970, "which was really to understudy the General Manager who was the head man in the Gulf. It was generally accepted that if you attained that post, you were to succeed to the top position, which I did."

The retirement age, strictly adhered to, was fifty-five in the overseas territories. In fact, a postwar bulge of young managers joined the group between 1945 and 1950, which meant a corresponding exodus thirty years later. In 1982 the retirement age for the rest of the group was sixty.

Thus, there was little or no cross-fertilization; the geographical focus of company managers would remain tied to one area, where they would have an intimate knowledge of the local situation and understand the nuances of political and economic life. The management system, explained Lord Tanlaw, was based on the Indian "box-wallah system, by which people didn't get home leave for three years, and then you had six months' leave. This meant you identified with the host country."

But although specialists in the sense of knowing their own local area, they were generalists in terms of their management skills. "I learned to be Jack of all trades," said Macaskill, "and hopefully master of some." Lord Tanlaw recalled that, in India, "When someone went on leave, you took over their job. You knew nothing about, say, insurance or river steamers, but you knew that all businesses were the same. Under the managing agency system, you had experts to make the ships or the jute mills run, and you did the business side, working out the margins or whatever, until the chap came back. That way, you had a very wide range of knowledge about how the businesses ran." Or as another old hand described it, Inchcape managers were prepared to have a go at most things, with varying degrees of expertise. They would sell almost anything they could for a profit, and do their best with the opportunities as and when they came across them.

In many of the smaller businesses, the quality of management was poor, being entrepreneurial without any of the commensurate qualities of anticipation and flexibility, or the ability to calculate risks. This, believed Armstrong, was a characteristic of many small or family-owned business at that time. "Of all the qualities looked for by the top people when choosing managers, business sense was not a high priority. It was almost considered *infra-dig* by the owners. It was considered more important to be a character, and an upstanding gentleman, a British subject looking after the interests of the company and participating in the local community. It was old Empire very much personified. Wonderful characters and it was great fun, but the extreme of too much fun and not enough work compared with today. I saw the end of it when I joined the group." Tony Simpson, an old Africa hand from the 1960s, confirmed this picture, recalling that the cost of living in East Africa was said to be based on the cost of lunch at the Mombasa Club.

The same type of management prevailed in the U.K. Clive Hall, then a young general manager for Mann Egerton, recalled how every six months his chairman would invite him to "come over for lunch, dear boy." Hall would go over to headquarters in Norwich and after "very large G&Ts" would talk about what was happening. Or a phone call might ask him, "Are you free for lunch?" and then the Rolls-Royce would arrive and the chairman would begin with, "How are things?" As Hall recalled, "It was a friendly system of management, but you knew the plot and by the end, he would know exactly what was what." John Bartley, on the other hand, who was working in Hong Kong in the 1970s and 1980s for another company, was not impressed by the Inchcape managers he observed. "The outside perception of the people who were running it was of fat cats, I think, who had been around a long time living a very high life on the hog ... They were not exactly a laughing stock, but respect had gone."

FINANCIAL CONTROLS — AN OXYMORON

The Inchcape policy of minimal interference extended to financial controls, which contemporaries described as "casual." A chartered secretary, who eventually became the first finance director, headed an accounting department. This did secretarial accounting and tax work for a few Inchcape subsidiaries and the family trust, besides the financial analysis of possible investment opportunities. The relationship between field and center concerning financial responsibility was not at all clear cut, and the center's effectiveness depended very much on the personalities involved. Until 1982, for example, group finance directors were not expected to visit one of the group's subsidiary companies without first receiving clearance from the chief executive of that company.

At the beginning of every financial year, the different businesses would send in budgets and plans that would all be added up and presented to the board. However, there was no automatic expectation that the budgets would be adhered to, and no real sanctions if companies failed to reach their targets. Although the financial department was concerned by cash levels and profitability, such issues were not uppermost in the minds of the general managers of Inchcape companies, and there was little emphasis on the measurement of financial performance. Failure to reach a target did not necessarily carry negative associations, and could usually be excused on the grounds of changing economic circumstance, hard times, or unforeseen problems. In fact, if having a presence in an area was considered the most important criterion, then a company might be allowed to run at a loss for several years. At most, recalled Commander Wall, a non-performer might be "given a good boot up the backside."

Alastair Macaskill had little recollection of any financial control. "I suppose there was a budget, presumably ... If you required funding you constructed the case and it was agreed with the managing director, who checked it out with his colleagues and the bank and you got your funding and off you went ... You learned most of the procedures in the first two-and-a-half years. You had no other formal management training or accounting; it was common sense ... Of course, it was your responsibility to make sure there was no monkey business going on. In my briefing from Charles Noble he said, 'I don't mind if you make a mistake, provided it is (1) a very small mistake, and (2) you don't repeat it."

What each company earned, it expected to keep. At one extreme, this practice led to the classic example of the Anglo-Thai group, bought by Inchcape mainly because of its cash mountain, which the management hoped to use to offset Inchcape debts. However, although Anglo-Thai was happy to give Inchcape its monthly results and budgets for the year, what it had it would hold! There would be no grouping of Anglo-Thai cash with that of the Inchcape group.

The reporting of results was not at all consistent; there was no standardization of the type of information sent back to the center. Each company reported separately, using different ratios. The figure companies reported back to the center was their profit before tax (PBT). Until 1981, this was the sole parameter on which a company's performance was judged. Those businesses that had accumulated cash had the benefit of that cash, and it counted in their PBT. There was no central control over a company's borrowings, and so an operating unit could build up massive borrowings over the years, without the center taking any direct action. Indeed, it could even be regarded as a successful company as long as its PBT result for the year appeared reasonable, while a steadily increasing PBT was regarded as the sign of a healthy business. There was no regular procedure laid down to enable the center to take a more penetrating view of the financial state of the individual Inchcape companies. Some companies, as Harborn showed, could run up huge borrowings without the center being aware, and even make their own banking arrangements. There was not, as Brian Ashworth who later joined as group planning director, remarked, "a profound understanding of the significance of gearing" among the Inchcape management of that time.

A final feature of the Inchcape group's financial organization was the unpredictable reporting date of its group profits. Although the overseas companies reported at the end of each calendar year, in 1980 it took until August for the 1979 results to arrive, be consolidated, and published. Inchcape, according to an observer who had followed it for many years, was "one of the slowest reporting groups in the U.K., if not the world."

The Inchcape group reflected the theory and practices of the time when it had been formed, a pattern many other British companies had followed. However, while other British companies were now adapting and going forward, Inchcape had stagnated. And as Bob Carpenter, another analyst who followed the group, observed, "Once an entrepreneurial company starts to fall behind, not only do you fail to see things changing, you are also hurt by matters outside your control." This was about to happen to Inchcape, as it lurched from one crisis to another.

MORE BAD NEWS

Within a short time, the group was hit by further blows. The rapidly deteriorating economic situation in Nigeria, it became clear, was killing off the Motor business, BEWAC. In Malaysia, poor management at Inchcape Berhad resulted in the loss of the foundation of its trading activity and profit, the Toyota franchise. Even more of a drain on the group, ultimately, believed Colin Campbell, was the Peschaud affair.

This French, heavy equipment transportation company was involved in servicing the oil industry. Headquartered in Paris, it was a mini-Inchcape with subsidiaries in French West Africa and the Middle East. The company, in which Inchcape held a 70% stake, entered into a contract to build an electricity generating plant in the Yemen. Typically, it had done this without reference to the Inchcape center. The project was a disaster, overrunning in time and money, and although Inchcape sold Peschaud in 1983, it could not sell the plant. With court cases ongoing in Paris and Lyon, Inchcape was to write off £20 million over the years.

Such a series of disasters, which an alert central management might have been expected to foresee and forestall, rocked those inside the group and further disquieted outside analysts. Robert Morton began following the group in 1980–81, as a young analyst with Simon & Coates. His first impression of Inchcape was that it was "a shambles," a company where "the senior management didn't know what was going on." He was not surprised when "everything hit the buffers." Other people were coming to the same conclusion; there was no visible hand on the Inchcape tiller.

So the Harborn crisis proved to be not a "one-off" crisis, but a symptom of a far deeper and potentially fatal disease that afflicted the group: complexity and lack of control. Its real importance was the weakness of the state of Inchcape it revealed, and the blow it dealt to the confidence of both those involved in running the group and those outside observers, analysts, and investors who had suspected but until now been unable to confirm the real extent and nature of its problems. The City, as Lord Inchcape knew, liked steady results and no surprises. In the past three years, Inchcape had produced declining results and several nasty surprises.

Kenneth Inchcape's philosophy, which had worked well during the last twenty years, had been the right one for its time. While communications were slow and uncertain, an overseas trader like Inchcape necessarily had to give the men on the ground the freedom to follow up and seize any opportunity. However, the corollary of this was that the different Inchcape managers in their separate far-flung fiefdoms would not necessarily come up with businesses that had anything in common, as a glance at the list of Inchcape's portfolio of activities at this time, ranging from business machines to car, truck, and tractor distribution, tea and timber to tramp and liner services, wines and spirits distribution to sawmilling, watch distribution to insurance, helicopter to oil support servicing, testing to contract catering, plus many others, made clear. And the other side of autonomy and freedom, as events showed and as Lord Tanlaw observed for himself, was that over time, "Too much power went overseas, and you lost control."

So, Lord Inchcape and his group were revealed as out of line with contemporary business philosophy and practice. In his day, acquisitions had appeared and been absorbed almost by magic; Inchcape had thrived simply by being a large international group. But by the 1980s, business heads were expected to take action and control growth. He had built up a federation that, to him, was held together by values such as trust and loyalty. Now, outsiders were describing it as "a rag bag," and demanding he produce professionalism, focus, and control.

But as Kenneth Inchcape was well aware, he and his board — many of whom were coasting toward retirement — were too old to face the challenge of adapting to this new environment. To compound the problem, he had failed to train or find a successor who could implement the necessary change. Neither was there a younger tier of managers coming through with new ideas and energies, since localization had reduced the number of expatriate managers. Tony Simpson recalled that in East Africa, their number had been reduced from 147 to 7 by the end of the 1970s.

In addition, at this critical time the Third Earl was becoming increasingly involved with P&O, which had been seriously damaged by the oil shocks. From 1978 on, efforts to restructure P&O took up more and more of Kenneth Inchcape's time and energy, and he "took his eye off the Inchcape ball." He even transferred the finance director, Oliver Brooks, who had made a great contribution to Inchcape's growth in the previous decade, to P&O to help sort out the mess there. A good team, they were both missed by those left to cope with the group's problems. Several outside directorships also took up Lord Inchcape's time, along with his duties as Prime Warden of the Fishmongers' Guild in the City. As Lord Tanlaw recalled, "I think that the real problem came when he was offered the chairmanship of P&O. You cannot be chairman of two companies … however great a genius, you can't ride two horses of that size at once. That's when the lack of control came in …" This situation was compounded when Kenneth Inchcape cut down his traveling time. "If you are the proprietor, you have to travel if you are to be as hands-on as he was. And when you don't see him around, when the cat's away, the mice will begin to play …"

Put at its bleakest, by the beginning of the 1980s the Inchcape group was outdated, out of control, and almost running out of time. Outside analysts now thought of it as a "colonial dinosaur," an anachronism that had lost its way and its vitality. No longer the stunning acquisitor of the previous decade, its image was that of a Leviathan swollen by undigested acquisitions, out of joint with the times, lacking the strategic concepts and structure that would enable it to survive, and vulnerable to takeover and the breaker's yard. Although it had not been apparent at the time, the Harborn loss was a key turning point. Change was on its way.

Bob Cowell, then an analyst with Hoare Govett, saw the group as at sea in the modern world. "The world began to leave Inchcape behind. It was set up to take advantage of how long it took to do things. Then the businesses got together to get more muscle at the bank or whatever, but then it became unmanageable. It needed modern business controls to measure the risk, group cash, and impose budget discipline, but because of the fiefdoms these could not be applied." In 1981, under the impetus of outside events, the first steps toward change were about to be taken.

Enter the Consultants

D uring the 1970s, management consultancy was the growth industry. It began, as all good things are said to do, in the United States and the best-known names were McKinsey & Company, Booz Allen and Hamilton, A.T. Kearney, and the Boston Consulting Group. Management consultancies had been in existence for some time, but during the heady period of economic growth of the late 1960s, companies had not felt in need of their services, and so the consultancies had lain dormant. With economic hard times, their renaissance was greeted with relief by managers beset by the problems of deregulation, the oil shocks, and increased competition from Japan and Germany. By 1979, *Business Week* estimated that the industry was growing by 20% a year and becoming a highly competitive field, attracting business school faculty members who were virtually abandoning their teaching to go into consultancy. Aggressive marketing of their services turned consultants into "one of the hottest new specialties." They never again went away.

As the consultancy craze demonstrated, Inchcape was not the only international jigsaw that was falling apart. In the U.S., as Chandler had noted, "By the late 1960s, growth through the acquisition of enterprises in distant or unrelated businesses had become almost a mania." This strategy, he observed, had led to a breakdown of communications between center and field, and a weakness in the ability of top management "to maintain a unified enterprise whose whole is more than the sum of its parts." Famous companies like Sears Roebuck and DuPont were in trouble, and there was even talk of the giant AT&T being broken up. Soon, acquisition mania was being followed by "as unprecedented a number of divestitures."

So, just as most companies had gone through the same acquisitive phase, they now all obediently took the restructuring path to undo what they had just spent the past decade doing. They read that it was time to divest and, instead, concentrate on a smaller number of activities where they had the strongest capability. The new mantras for the 1980s were focus and simplicity, and the consultants were ready and waiting to help them achieve this. It was the start of a lucrative pattern; articles would appear in the business pages about a need for companies to re-engineer, find their competence, assess and manage risk, add value, and so on, and the consultants would devise the techniques and tools to help them do so. They were the business plumbers and, similarly, always cost more than the original estimate.

WELCOME TO THE MATRIX

Many of the consultancies had developed their own diagnostic tools with which to entice their clients. Most popular were models for strategic planning, used by the fashionable marketeers. Once simply part of "selling," they were dedicated to the elevation of marketing into a reputable science. They were the first of the business theorists to raid longstanding academic fields, such as military history, appropriating their concepts and vocabulary to cloak their theories in respectability. So, Napoleon's victorious battle dispositions, for example, could be reduced to an example of "effective resource allocation."

The PIMS project, developed by the Marketing Science Institute in the 1970s, was the first effort to develop an empirical base for strategic planning, whereas the Boston Consulting Group model (BCG matrix), developed in 1960 by Bruce Henderson, and the GE-McKinsey matrix, were portfolio classification models. Although various pitfalls and limitations were later associated with the use of these models, their spread was rapid and their influence far-reaching, evidence of their potent appeal. Of course, what companies did not then realize was that each tool had a sell-by date, after which it was time to adopt a new one.

The portfolio approach to marketing attempted to manage the product mix (the range of products making up a firm's businesses) in order to balance short-term gains with longer-term profitability. BCG's two-dimensional growth-share matrix became a very popular model for achieving this, spawning a vocabulary to describe different types of business that passed into everyday use. It involved plotting the firm's portfolio of strategic business units (SBUs) on a four-celled matrix in terms of the growth rate of the market in which it competed (vertical axis), and its market share relative to its largest competitor in that market (horizontal axis). On the basis of its position on the matrix, company strategists could both analyze a unit's potential to decide on the appropriate strategy and funding for it, and at the same time consider the overall health of the firm's portfolio.

The four cells of the matrix each represented a different portfolio category, characterized by a catchy label, to which certain strategies were considered appropriate. So, the lucky "stars" were businesses or products with a high relative market share in a high-growth market. Although cash users in maintaining their position, they might also be the key to future success, so the strategy would be to build them until, when market growth slowed, they became cash cows and it was harvest time. "Cash cows" were market leaders in a slow- or zero-growth market. Throwing off more cash than they needed, this excess could be used to fund other growing businesses, such as those in the star quadrant. The recommended strategy would be to hold or, if its position in the market weakened, to harvest.

The "question marks" operated in high-growth segments, but had only a low market share. As the name indicates, these could either prove to be a drain on resources or, if they had a distinct competitive advantage, might in time become stars. A company with a lot of question marks in its portfolio would have to decide which to build and which to divest. Finally, the poor "dogs" were to be found cowering in the low-growth, low relative market share sector. Harvest and divestment were the two recommended strategies here.

The GE matrix was a more complex, multi-factor portfolio model, developed jointly by the consulting firm McKinsey and General Electric (GE) in the early 1970s. Designed to overcome some of the limitations of the simpler BCG model, it used return on investment (ROI) as the criterion for assessing an investment opportunity. It became very popular with managers wishing to measure which products were in attractive markets and had a competitive advantage over their rivals. In using this model, the companies themselves chose the criteria most relevant to their businesses, assigned ratings, and then ranked them on a scale of 1 to 5 (1 being the least favorable and 5 the most favorable). These scores were then translated into values for the two dimensions, market attractiveness and competitive position, of the 3 × 3 matrix. The values were then plotted on the matrix to give planners an idea of their strategic options, which, like the BCG categories, ranged from invest/grow to build/rebuild and harvest/divest.

As ever, the U.K. lagged behind the U.S. in adopting these new ideas and tools, and the Inchcape group was a long way back in the domestic field. But, in fact, a highly diversified group such as Inchcape was made for such models and, as will emerge, once it was endowed with a team of strategic planners, they attacked the task of plotting and assessing the health of their portfolio with relish. As they anticipated, the sight of a heavily crowded quadrant or zone labelled "dogs," into which too many of its businesses fell, proved a timely spur to change when presented to the group's top management. The Inchcape planners used such matrices to plot not only the performance of their businesses but also to analyze the spread of territorial risk, commissioning a series of reports from consultants on potential risks and changes in the world environment. Like many other companies, Inchcape found the consultancy habit very easy to acquire.

A 1979 *Fortune* article on the value of consultancies concluded that the results of using these outside agencies were mixed. However, it believed that the use of consultants should enable business people the better to use their imagination and inventiveness, "qualities that no set of tools can replace." Unfortunately, this message seemed to get lost along the way. In the 1980s, corporate restructuring in the U.S. reached record proportions, providing an even greater market for the consultants and that elite core, the business gurus.

By then, consultants had begun to publish their work in order to reach a wider audience. When Peters and Waterman brought out their bestselling *In Search of Excellence — Lessons from America's Best-Run Companies* in 1982, it started off a craze for business books that has never since slowed. Famously, five years later only a third of the companies featured in the book were still in excellent shape, but by then the world had moved on to the next fashionable concept. During the 1970s, managers also learned that to be credible, even the most everyday term — from "management" to "planning" to "investment" — must be prefaced by the word "strategic." A *plan* was no longer acceptable; it had to be a *strategy*. It was a disheartening time for many older managers, dealing with the consequences of economic change on their operations, and seeing the first wave of confident young graduates from the business schools, fluent in the new business vocabulary, recruited and rising rapidly up the corporate ladder.

Inchcape might have been interested by one of those bright young MBAs, a certain Charles Mackay (no relation to the founding Inchcape family). He had graduated from INSEAD in 1969 and then spent the next six years with McKinsey, where he rose rapidly through the organization before returning to line management. This route would eventually lead him to Inchcape, and the chief executive's chair.

But this was in the future. In 1980 the immediate problem for the management was how to tackle the problems that diversification had brought to the group. Some attempt had already been made to analyze the sprawling portfolio. Donald Caswell had produced a memo that examined the group's acquisitions, from the Borneo company onward, in an attempt to identify and define a pattern of success, but it had little impact. As Michael Wall recalled, in those days, "corporate strategy was not seen as a necessity."

More important, Inchcape's field managers, scattered in developing countries where ideas of professional management had not yet penetrated, had no inkling that the group was in trouble and that they needed to change their ways. This was to have serious implications for the various remedies tried by the third Lord Inchcape and his team.

Kenneth Inchcape himself had by now realized that there were grave problems in the higher management of his group. Recently, in his preoccupation with P&O, he had let the reins of control slip at St. Mary Axe. Now, he was determined to act quickly and restore Inchcape to health, so that it should be in good shape for his successor. He had also grasped that there was no-one within the group capable of pinpointing what kind of change the group needed and so, although it was hard to accept that outsiders should be brought in, he decided to make such a move. During his work with P&O, he had come across the Corporate Consulting Group (CCG). At the end of 1979, he returned full-time to Inchcape to take control, and invited CCG to carry out a strategic analysis of the company. Its mission was to examine its problems and "initiate a process of strategic change, which will position the company for its next period of development."

THE CONSULTANTS' REPORT

At the start of its investigation, in February 1980, CCG sent a letter to Lord Inchcape in which it identified the group's basic problem as "the need to establish a system of direction and management that is capable of sustaining momentum through a change of leadership. The main issues concern the role, structure and accountabilities of the center of the Group in its relationship to the operating parts."

In the next few months, the CCG team examined in detail the group's background, its strengths, and the ingredients of its leadership and culture, and reported back their findings. Delicately, they sketched in the fact that the success of the group so far had been achieved within a particular leadership and management culture characterized, among other things, by trust, personalized leadership, and decision-taking that "did not require complex systems and structures for effectiveness." They also noted the strong "entrepreneurial flair and print of the Chairman," which had given rise to the fatal lack of financial responsibility among the group's operating management. Because of the family heritage and powerful personality of their chairman, those in the field felt no personal accountability for any losses or setbacks they might cause; the buck would always stop with Kenneth Inchcape.

The consultants then went on to list the problems facing the group. It was a long list: the explosive rate of growth of the group and the resultant size; the diversity of Inchcape's worldwide businesses; the increasing complexity and sophistication of the trading environments in traditional markets; the bunched retirement of a key leadership group between 1980 and 1983; the absence of a generation of central management "skilled in leadership of large complex international businesses"; and the continuation of systems and structure of management relevant to an earlier, more personalized leadership requirement. It ended with "the need to change the 'Investor and Fire Brigade' role of the center."

The consultants' final conclusions were that, "the rate of business growth has been so fast in the last decade as to preclude the development of management resources and organizational systems at the center appropriate to current and future needs." Put more baldly, there was a big hole in the center of the group, a hole that needed to be filled by professional management, expertise, and systems.

Their recommendations were presented to Lord Inchcape in a report. In essence, this said that there should be "a new role for the center which was different from the past and which as a result had to be populated with different types of people ... and a new organization for the Group." The new organization should be one "which clearly outlines and identifies the accountabilities of individuals."

However, CCG emphasized, these should be complementary to the "essential qualities and strengths of the current system." These included entrepreneurial skills, local knowledge, and speed of response, and the need for decision-making to remain as close to the marketplace as possible. The consultants, then, were aware that, by exercising too strict control, the center risked destroying one of the company's key strengths — the ability to respond quickly to an opportunity — so throwing out both baby and bathwater simultaneously. In fact, this dilemma lay at the crux of Inchcape's problem, and was an issue with which every subsequent leader struggled; how to balance central control and operational freedom.

The final recommendations, the introduction of a "strategic business unit, sector-type organization," introduced the vocabulary of modern business to the group. This structure, the consultants concluded, would best correspond to the organizational needs and the portfolio nature of the group, enabling its businesses to remain close to the marketplace, but with very clear accountability and a well-defined relationship with the center.

STRUCTURE AT LAST

The building blocks of the new structure were product units, strategic business units (SBUs), and sectors. The product units would be decentralized and specialized, in order to retain local trading skills. The SBUs, which represented the core of the structure, would be composed of groups of product units, positioned for control and development at an intermediate level between the marketplace and the center. To enable them to function efficiently, with high-quality management resources, it was recommended that the SBUs should have a minimal size of £5 million per annum PBT and a maximum size of £20 million per annum PBT. The sectors were composed of grouped SBUs, to enable strategic management at the center.

At the center, the consultants recommended the establishment of three key functions: personnel, finance, and planning. As a result, three new men were recruited: Peter Lumsden for Finance, Brian Ashworth for Planning, and Tom Bradbury for Personnel. This first influx of professionals, who were "managers" rather than "chaps," represented another radical move for the group. In fact, an earlier attempt had been made to introduce graduate entry, but the experiment had been shortlived, since the existing managers had made it clear they did not want "university people" coming in. The task of this new heart was to pump blood more effectively round the group, "to provide the control and support necessary for effective central and SBU accountabilities." The final appointment was of a group chief executive, accountable to the board and to whom the sector executives would report.

Kenneth Inchcape accepted the recommendations of the consultants, and decided that they should form a major part of a conference planned for 1981, and optimistically entitled "Inchcape into the Eighties."

LOGIC AND ORDER

The new organization and structure inaugurated as a result of the CCG report marked the first attempt to put the mish-mash of companies into more logical order. The guiding principle in grouping the businesses would still be geographic, but the nature of the businesses would also be taken into account. Thus, no longer would Nigeria be bracketed with U.K. commodities for no logical reason, nor the U.K. Motor businesses kept separate from those in Hong Kong. On the other hand, Thailand still had two managers, reflecting its origins rooted in the two companies, Anglo-Thai and the Borneo Company, and their mutual antipathy. No-one expected Rome to be built in a day.

Similarly, although the whole chain of command was altered to a more clearly defined system, some idiosyncrasies remained, built in to accommodate the chairman's wishes. For example, the role of the deputy chairman, who had no operational responsibilities, was unclear without the knowledge that he was an old and trusted member of the family. Most of the longserving senior men who had been actively involved with the businesses were designated sector directors. A new deputy chairman was appointed, and James Millington-Drake, Kenneth Inchcape's cousin who was expected by many to be his successor, became responsible for group planning.

In carrying out their mission, the consultants had focused on getting into place the processes and organization considered necessary for a modern organization, with the underlying assumption that these would then trigger the necessary change. Their strategy had been to seed key players in the organization, who would then act as time bombs and initiate new practices.

So, what was the verdict on this first intervention by outsiders in the group's affairs? Undoubtedly, it was a success in that it identified Inchcape's weaknesses and initiated a change process, something no internal body had been capable of doing. However, in retrospect, the consultants themselves considered they had failed because they had "misjudged the pace and ability of the organization to take on the rate of change necessary." They had thought that by getting the right processes and organization in place, "getting the lines on the chart," and seeding the organization with key players who would work around Lord Inchcape, change would eventually occur. They knew that, in reality, a key issue was "a new corporate vision," but equally, they were aware that was not something Lord Inchcape was ready or able to address since "even the organization issues seemed pretty indigestible to him."

So, although the consultants had pinpointed the faults and suggested changes, they could not ensure they were fully implemented.

Emotionally committed to the empire he had built up, at heart Kenneth Inchcape wanted to do the right thing, and so he accepted the consultants' conclusions. However, through no fault of his own, he lacked the understanding of the processes and culture the CCG report implied. At the age of sixty-four, he was too much a prisoner of the past to do so. He accepted the words, but at a different level of understanding; the concept of line and staff, of SBUs, was alien to all his previous experience, and he did not fully appreciate the different role the center would be forced to play. Observed Brian Ashworth, who watched the struggle, "He wanted the company to succeed, but he could not break out of his past chains. The change from transaction management to process management and, most important, the change in culture, was just too much to expect from him."

The truth of this is demonstrated by the fact that before the full report was distributed throughout the group, it was rewritten by Lord Inchcape. Horrified by the "business" jargon used in the report, he rewrote the document "in English" to make it comprehensible to his managers.

TRAUMA IN THE RANKS

Kenneth Inchcape's problem was shared by most of the Inchcape management. One senior executive refused to accept the new system, saying "I only report to the chairman and that's that." Out in the operating units the reaction was even more extreme. To them, the center was a remote entity that had never impinged on their daily habits and activities; they had no idea of the seriousness of the situation, and the urgent need for change was never explained. Therefore, it was an even bigger shock to them when the report ushered in a new philosophy and business vocabulary. As one contemporary observed, its impact was "traumatic."

Apart from the organizational changes, the operating management were most affected by the new emphasis placed on accountability, and the concrete reality of the monthly and quarterly reporting forms (MRs and QRs). These were standardized throughout the group, and were not greeted with enthusiasm. Wrestling with the new forms, and providing the required information, enormously increased the workload at operating level, and imposed a great strain on the Inchcape management. Tony Simpson estimated that the finance staff spent a third of their time filling in the new forms. Staff resentment was further reinforced by the knowledge that not everyone was obliged to bear the new burden of paperwork. The stronger fiefdoms, such as Dodwells and Anglo-Thai, resisted change and negotiated their way out of filing reports, so conformity was still not achieved.

At the same time, little training was given in the new working methods, and no-one explained what exactly was expected of them. The operating managers felt hard done by, that the monthly and quarterly reports were too much of a one-way traffic. Many thought that they could have benefited from talking to those analyzing the reports and clarifying the issues involved. It was difficult for them to accept the new regime which judged them by their actions, but gave zero feedback. "Inchcape seemed to go from one extreme to another," recalled Simpson. In protest, the older managers closed ranks and became even more insular: they would only look after themselves. As Michael Wall recalled, under the new system all the "boxes" became boundaries, and none of the managers were prepared to talk across them. "It wasn't a happy time." The next months marked an era during which the lack of business success mirrored the decline in company morale.

Between 1981 and 1982, then, change was introduced to the Inchcape group. However, given the strong resistance in the field, and the gap in terms of people available and the systems needing to be operated, it remained much more of a paper exercise than the radical overhaul required. The consultants' report had led to the necessary mechanisms being installed, but they were not yet operational. On the whole, Inchcape continued to run much as it always had; the time bombs would take some time to explode.

THE PLANNERS TAKE A TURN

Following up behind the work of the consultants, the new team of corporate planners moved center stage to tackle the job of reshaping the group. This team was composed of Brian Ashworth, John Style (a member of the Inchcape family), and group economist Peter Stubbs, under the overall leadership of James Millington-Drake. The complementary partnership of planning and finance showed an appreciation that, in future, the two functions had to work together, and leave no room for parts of the group to play one off against the other.

Until this time, analysis had taken the form of "people writing essays, with no real insights." Now for the very first time, Inchcape was subjected to a severe catechism; what activities should the group be involved in and where should the profits come from? In attempting to answer these questions, the team hoped to gain a better understanding of the actions that needed to be taken regarding the businesses. They would then try to find the levers to change the shape and destiny of the group. Twenty years on, a different team of planners would be asking virtually the same set of questions, and seemed no nearer to discovering the answers.

Obviously, the key man in implementing any real change was Kenneth Inchcape. Therefore, the planners set out to convince him that the setbacks were not just temporary or due to a problem in the world economy, but to the fact that the group lacked the strategic structure to plan for, and overcome, its difficulties. It was decided that the most effective way to do this was to highlight the remarkably high rate at which money was being lost in a number of parts of the group. They therefore wheeled in the portfolio matrix tool, on which they began to plot the group's numerous businesses. If it had been an instrument of torture, the pain felt by the group as a result of this exercise could not have been worse.

For the efforts of the planners succeeded magnificently. Through this portfolio analysis, they were able to demonstrate that "a significant number of parts of the group were not only *not* generating cash, but were absorbing it at an alarming rate." The figures had always been available, but had never before been fully understood, or set out in such stark relief. Of the group's assets, two-fifths had a zero cash flow at operating level. Brian Ashworth recalled looking at one business that was generally regarded as successful, on the basis that its PBT was growing. PBT, it will be remembered, was until then the only parameter used to judge a business's performance. A closer look, however, revealed that its profitability was declining and that it was "absorbing cash at a horrendous rate and fast approaching crisis." "We tried," said Ashworth, "to get across the notion that the group was hemorrhaging money, and that a lot of businesses were in fact cash disasters."

His attention firmly riveted by these startling revelations, Lord Inchcape was forced to accept the necessity for a critical review and, an example of thinking the previously unthinkable, the disposal of those assets that had become a drain on the group.

THE FIRST REVIEW ...

The central planners did not know enough about the component parts of the Inchcape portfolio to be able to make any immediate judgments about their future. Therefore, as part of an effort to grasp the complex nature of the group's businesses and to integrate them into an overall strategic framework, further attempts were made in 1981 and 1982 to analyze the portfolio of activities and, on the basis of these findings, prepare a corporate strategic plan.

Over the next eighteen months, Brian Ashworth initiated various studies to examine, on a business-by-business basis, the market prospects, risks, and competitiveness of the Inchcape portfolio, as well as the rates of return. Whether anyone outside his small planning group knew what he was talking about was another matter.

In March 1982, an "Inchcape Group Corporate Strategic Review," covering the period 1982–87, was produced. The main focus of this was to introduce the methodology for reviewing the group's portfolio of businesses, "The Business Policy Matrix." The planning team's reservations about the board's lack of familiarity with strategic analysis was demonstrated by the fact that the Review began with a section entitled "What is Corporate Strategic Planning?" In the next few years, the Inchcape directors were to receive a crash course in the subject.

From a survey of the world political and economic outlook for 1982/83 and some longer-term business trends, with particular emphasis on the threat posed to Inchcape's traditional agency business by the emergence of strong manufacturing and service industries, the Review extracted some key messages for the group. The first was that it needed to capitalize on opportunities to exploit its main asset, its international presence, and to expand in specialist services. Second, it therefore, needed to identify the strong businesses that provided opportunities for profitable growth, and which should be developed. Finally, it needed to release cash for more profitable use from weak, unprofitable businesses facing unattractive markets.

Using the matrix logic, the planners then reviewed the Inchcape portfolio. Each Inchcape business was assessed in terms of the attractiveness of the market in which the activities operated, and the relative competitive strength or weakness of each activity.

Based on its position in the matrix, each business was then prescribed either a strategy of "Development" or submission to a "Critical Review." The former was for businesses with a strong or moderate competitive position in an attractive market, the latter for those with weak or moderate competitive strength in a market of low attractiveness. For those businesses with an average or a weak competitive position in an unattractive or moderately attractive market, the proposed strategy was one of "Selective Reinvestment." It was all good textbook stuff.

The picture that emerged from the use of the matrix revealed that businesses in the first category (Develop) represented 20% of the group's business assets (although even they showed "little real growth over the period 1980–83"). Those in the second category (Critical Review) represented 22%, and those in the third (Selective Reinvestment) 58%. Although this analysis was based on a very crude database, it did give a clearer indication of the need for the group to refocus and concentrate its efforts.

Having established the group's financial profile, the Review next considered the scale of improvement required to secure the group's financial viability, and then the route to doing so. In the process, it argued that the group needed a return of 22% (trading profit/business assets).

From all this, the planners concluded that the route to financial viability lay in raising cash from the sale of non-viable businesses and the group's holdings in property. Interestingly, among the options here, the Review put forward the possibility of divesting from the Toyota business in Malaysia, and the U.K. motor business, Mann Egerton. Through these and other actions, the group aimed to raise £100 million for reinvestment in selected activities on which future growth would be based.

Finally, the Review considered the future geographical shape of the group, concluding that rather than seek to increase its activities in the U.K., it should instead look to Japan, Hong Kong, and Australia, then deemed to have attractive economic prospects. Southeast Asia and the Middle East were seen as growth economies but with risks. South America, North America, and Europe, too, were described as potential growth areas, but "how and in what?" The planners did not know.

At the outset, the Review had highlighted the need for Inchcape to develop in activities where, given the threats to its traditional agency activities, it could control the skills and know-how for success against increasingly international competition. In fact, this would be another refrain that would haunt the group for the next two decades. For now, it gave the planners their next step: to identify and exploit opportunities in businesses in which the group already operated and which possessed the potential for growth, a strong service content, an international scope, and in which Inchcape had an international edge. Growth in these businesses would be pursued internally, and through acquisition. The sectors thus identified were: insurance, motors business, testing and inspection, retailing in the Far East, aviation services, oil industry services, wines and spirits, and resource industries and services.

FOLLOWED BY ANOTHER

The bit now firmly between their teeth, in March 1983 the planners produced a second "Corporate Strategy Review" for 1983–88. This followed a similar format to its predecessor, presenting the board with an updated set of business policy matrices demonstrating the potential, or in many cases the lack of it, of activities according to their place on the market attractiveness/competitive position matrix in the light of the latest results. It was followed by a second set of matrices showing the distribution of assets in the various regions of the world, categorized according to their growth potential and territorial risks.

The data revealed some fundamental cash traps. Only 19% of the group's businesses were performing well, providing reasonable returns and substantial positive cash flow. Of the remainder, 32% of the group's assets fell into the critical review segment, being non-viable cash consumers, and 49% had turned in "an uneven financial performance with returns below the level required for financial viability in a number of businesses." From this it concluded that there was "potential for significant rationalization and performance improvement in component parts of this sector of the matrix, including reduction in working capital." An analysis of the group's profile by country, plotted on a growth-risk matrix, showed that 48% of its fixed assets were located in high-risk, low-growth territories. This came as something of a surprise to both the planners and the board.

In conclusion, the Review endorsed the earlier program of divestment from a certain number of low-contributor businesses. However, it also noted that "SBU initiative and flair remained the cornerstone of the Group's development," with the qualification that SBU management should be selectively strengthened, and that the planners should monitor progress on the above initiatives. It reiterated Inchcape's blueprint for acquisitions related to its existing businesses, and then went on to look at the criteria for "A.N. Other Activity." This new activity should be in specialized services or distribution that could be self-financing, had significant entry barriers and a world scope, and a significant presence in developing countries. Among the sectors identified were: electronics distribution, industrial products distribution, industrial commercial services, healthcare, leisure, and security services. An initial investment of around £30–50 million was anticipated for 1983/84.

These findings confirmed the view of Philippe Haspeslagh, Strategy Professor at INSEAD, who later became involved in helping the group plan its future, that the real value of portfolio techniques was the learning that top managers got from its preparation, and not the methodology itself. The planning team had learned some unexpected facts about the business, findings that provided concrete evidence of the strategic challenge facing the group. Unfortunately, because it was carried out by a cabal in the ivory tower of St. Mary Axe, the implications of these conclusions were not disseminated to the rest of the group. Communications, as the next years would show, were never the group's strongest point.

These strategy reviews were to be the first in a series of initiatives, each one of which raised two other critical issues. Could their conclusions be fully implemented, and were the measures advised enough to guarantee the control and stability that the group needed to restore its internal prosperity and external credibility?

THE ROBA MANTRA

The other revolutionary step taken by the planners as a result of their financial diagnosis was to introduce a financial ratio for the group; return on business assets, or ROBA. Their 1983 Report identified that "the return needed to achieve the objective of financial viability for the Group is a 16% Return on Business Assets (Fixed Assets + Working Capital) at the prevailing inflation rate of 8% per annum"; achieving this return was to present a real challenge to the operating management.

ROBA was not a concept the group had ever heard before and, as might be expected, it did not take readily to the notion. One difficulty was that no attempt was made to train managers in how to calculate it or what was expected of them. Instead, there was further confusion as young, professional accountants, apparently speaking a foreign language, replaced the old financial secretaries and tried to impose restraint.

Little did the field managers know, ROBA was a financial ratio that was here to stay. Used, overused and much abused, later managers became adept at manipulating their asset base to achieve the "right" results, and so keep the center unaware of the real financial state of their businesses. It was ironic that this practice reached its apotheosis under the new, professional managers; the older, financially inept ones, lacked the skill to do this.

... AND A NEW CULTURE

The planning process undertaken during 1981–83 marked the introduction of a business culture that ran directly counter to the old one. As a result of portfolio planning, managers gained the first intimations that certain businesses, and certain areas, were in future to be more favored than others. Tony Simpson, ex-managing director of Inchcape International Trading who later held the Africa desk role in London, recalled his own horror when he heard that as a result of the findings, Inchcape was to get out of Africa. As he observed, "There had been no discussion or explanation with those involved at an operational level, which would have eased the path of disengagement and probably improved the group's returns on the sale of assets." Things would never be the same.

It was the start of a more aggressive management style that was difficult for the longer serving managers to accept. Low morale led to further decline in the businesses and meanwhile, at this critical point, Kenneth Inchcape had re-immersed himself in P&O's affairs.

WAR AND COCA-COLA

The outbreak of the Falklands War in 1982 had meant that the P&O's ships were once again pressed into service to ferry troops and ammunition, and provide hospital care for the wounded. Within hours of its outbreak, Lord Inchcape was in touch with the office of the Prime Minister, Margaret Thatcher, and remained closely involved with the company's efforts throughout the war. Once this was over, he became involved in a takeover battle with Trafalgar House and in fact, stayed on as chairman of P&O until 1986. He tried to do both jobs, coming to St. Mary Axe at 5 p.m. after a full day at P&O, but it was too much for one man and worked to the detriment of Inchcape.

Despite this, Kenneth Inchcape made one final, very important decision that was to affect the group's future almost as much as his support for entering the Toyota business. In 1982, Colin Armstrong brought before the board a proposal to purchase three Coca-Cola bottling plants in Chile. Their owner had gone bankrupt through diversifying into too many other businesses, and Armstrong saw them as a sound strategic investment since his experience told him that "there are two big businesses that survive, whatever happens in a country. One is the brewery, the other is the soft drinks bottler. I knew that these were both big cash generators, and that is what you need in a volatile economy." He had just recruited Sergio Mardones from Ford Brazil, where he had been their number 2. Together they aimed to put South America on the Inchcape map. Armstrong had told Mardones to look for a bottling business and he had come up with the Coca-Cola opportunity. With a major name like that, he and Mardones believed, they could not go wrong. Unfortunately, their ideas did not find a receptive audience.

As Armstrong recalled, "I put the project to the board and we discussed it. And then suddenly someone from the Middle East said, "We can't invest in Coca-Cola because they are on the Arab boycott list, and Gray Mackenzie will be drummed out of the Middle East.'" Gray Mackenzie was, of course, an important contributor to the group's profits in those days, but, fortunately for Armstrong, "Roy Davies then perked up and said that this didn't make sense, as we sold Ford all over the world and they, too, were on the boycott list. So then Kenneth Inchcape was left to decide, and he gave the go-ahead. He was instrumental, and gave me a lot of help." The Coca-Cola business was to be one of the big successes in Inchcape's later glory days. It was a pity few people realized what a good business it was until it was almost too late.

By the end of 1982, the Inchcape group stood at a crossroads. Some steps towards change had been taken, but, as INSEAD-EAC professor, Philippe Lasserre, pointed out, they were mostly of a cosmetic nature. Most of the strategic thinking had been carried out by a small group of managers, cut off from the mainstream of the group. Although, on paper, Kenneth Inchcape had accepted the conclusions of the consultants, nothing had occurred that seriously moved the group forward. The main center of gravity still lay in the territories, and the third Earl himself was not prepared, mentally or physically, to undertake the huge cultural overhaul that was needed.

As the planners and senior managers were aware, nothing further could be done until Kenneth Inchcape, and many of his board, retired. Unfortunately, like his grandfather, he showed little sign of wanting to step down. But with Kenneth Inchcape occupied elsewhere, and almost daily public arguments taking place between himself and his number 2, Peter Foxon, the non-executive directors finally decided things could not go on as they were.

Three of them, Sir Robert Henderson, a merchant banker, Sir Eric Norris, and Peter Baring, approached the retiring chairman of Unilever, Sir David Orr, and asked if he could "come on board" as chairman to help Inchcape through the next period of change. Lord Inchcape, he was assured, would accept him, although, as Sir David understood it, "clearly he had reservations about leaving his group." The phrase reflected the diplomatic, understated culture in which Sir David had spent his working life, one that would not be out of place in St. Mary Axe. On

December 31, 1982, the third Lord Inchcape retired, remaining on the Board as a non-executive director and becoming life president as from January 1, 1983.

The group's 1982 Corporate Review had opened with a quotation by President Sadat of Egypt: "A man who cannot change his way of thinking will never be able to change reality and will never therefore make any progress." Lord Inchcape should, perhaps, have taken a warning from this; it was said shortly before Sadat was assassinated.

The Great Caretaker Takes Great Care

*"I was interested in keeping busy and knew quite a lot about
Inchcape because of my interest in overseas business.
It seemed to me a nice sort of company, doing the sort of things
I was interested in, in the sort of places I was interested in.
So I thought the fit would be quite a good one, and I thought
it would take up only about one day a week and that seemed
about right. When I got there, I saw that there was
a lot more to be done."*

Looking back on his decision to take over as chairman of
Inchcape, Sir David Orr smiled at his own *naiveté*. His vision of a
cozy, one-day-a-week retirement job was shattered within a few
days of his arrival at St. Mary Axe by the realization that he had a major
turnaround on his hands rather than the gentle reorganization he had
envisaged. Was the revelation of the extent of Inchcape's problems a
shock? "No, but let's say a surprise." Sir David's capacity to take surprise
in his stride was to be tested to the full during the next two years.

Described as a "tough, no-nonsense businessman with a first-class
management record" but with a reputation for caution, Sir David Orr
had risen through the ranks of Unilever to become its chairman in 1974.
Retiring at the age of sixty in line with company policy, but "feeling that
he still had a few good working years in him," he had accepted the
invitation to join the Inchcape board in September 1982 and take over
as chairman from January 1, 1983.

There were few men Kenneth Inchcape would have accepted as a successor, but Sir David was one of those few. Like Lord Inchcape, he had enjoyed an excellent war record, followed by a wide business experience with a company whose activities were international. A tall, impressive figure and an entertaining speaker, whose speech still showed a trace of the Irish brogue from his home town of Dublin, he was to win wide respect and affection from those who worked with him at Inchcape.

Sir David already knew Kenneth Inchcape "in the way that business people at our level knew each other" and respected him as "an instinctive entrepreneur and a very, very good businessman." As Sir David acknowledged, "He was not keen on my coming, though he was very nice and we got on well together. But he didn't think that he should have had to go."

Sir David's diplomatic approach, honed in the understated environment of Unilever, was to stand him in good stead in handling the group, given that he was the first from outside the family to exert control at the top and that Lord Inchcape, by then life president, continued to take a keen interest in the running of "his group." Sir David "never discussed what we were doing with him, because I knew he would be against it. Kenneth by then thought we were doing the wrong thing, but he said, 'I will be loyal, and that's that.'"

From the first, Sir David saw his term of office as a bridging period in which his role was clearly defined; to guide the group through the next difficult years of change and, most important, to find a suitable successor to carry on the work of recovery.

MAPPING THE FUTURE

His initial perception of the group was that it was overdiversified, that the company had "a large number of divisions that were not performing well and was in a number of different business areas that were inappropriate." In fact, despite a few recent disposals, Inchcape had interests in more than 500 companies operating in some forty-four countries, and marketed the products of some 2500 manufacturers. He concluded that the group had "run to the end of the road as far as growth was concerned, and had not yet identified where it wanted to go in the future." It was Sir David's task to map out that future.

The planning process was one that Sir David greatly enjoyed, and so it was with enthusiasm that he took over the leadership of the Planning Action Committee (PAC) that had been responsible for initiating the first changes under Lord Inchcape. Led by Brian Ashworth, they had been busy analyzing the group's businesses in an attempt to find focus and future growth; now they received a new lease of life under Sir David. The PAC was made up of Sir David himself, Peter Foxon who was then managing director, Brian Ashworth the head of planning, and Peter Lumsden the finance director. The various planning reviews and documents they produced between 1983 and 1985 testify to their dedicated attempts to plot the long-term future of the group, and to ensure that it grew in a profitable direction.

PLANNING 1: A DIRECTION FOR THE FUTURE

In response to the situation unveiled by the two reviews of 1982 and 1983, the first efforts of the PAC under Sir David were directed to a further rationalization of the Inchcape portfolio. Their strategy was to dispose of businesses that were performing badly, or were peripheral to what was seen as mainstream Inchcape activities. In this context, an important move was Inchcape's agreement with a French insurance group, Worms & Cie, eventually signed in 1984. By this, Worms transferred their minority holding in Bain Dawes to Inchcape, in exchange for additional shares in Bishopsgate Insurance. The deal enabled Inchcape to get out of the insurance underwriting business in exchange for a 100% interest in the insurance broking business it wished to develop. Inchcape's involvement in this activity was to provoke a lot of debate over the years, and provide a great deal of work for various consultancy firms that produced a stream of reports about whether the group should be in or out of the business.

As the Worms deal illustrated, the PAC had been slowly working toward a clearer definition of what exactly the group should be involved in. The program of critical review and disposal had helped them to distinguish which directions offered the best prospects for future growth, and to sift out the "nuggets" from the dross in the group's portfolio. The results of this exercise were set against an analysis of the key economic and business trends for the future in order to establish where the greatest potential for Inchcape lay. The PAC concluded, "The Group needs to exploit its capabilities in service and distribution activities ... [and] ... to capitalize on its geographic coverage."

These conclusions formed the basis of Sir David's first statement as chairman in 1983. This identified two main functions for Inchcape: first, as a professional distributor, marketer, and seller of the products and technologies of principals; and second, as a skilled provider of specialist services. In the first of a series of renaming ceremonies, the Inchcape group was pronounced "an international specialist service and marketing

Group." Sir David also defined the group's traditional strengths, or core competencies as a later generation would know them. These were "an international trading network that is outstanding, if not unique, a culture that can cope with the needs of a service industry, and a name that stands for integrity."

Inchcape's new look reflected the way that threats to Inchcape's traditional agency work, identified in the 1982 Review, were becoming reality. One of the most important was the localization policy of the governments in several countries where the group had longstanding ties. In Iran, for example, 120 years of agency work by Inchcape's subsidiary Gray Mackenzie had ended in 1982 when the Iranian government decreed that henceforward, the shipping operations in all Iranian ports were to be confined to wholly-owned Iranian companies. In Malaysia, where there was a move toward *Bumiputra* ownership of companies, Inchcape took the initiative by floating its interest in its subsidiary, the Timuran Company, and retaining only a minority 49% stake. By being one of the first companies to take *Bumiputra* partners, Inchcape won considerable goodwill from the Malaysian government.

To compensate for these and other losses, Sir David proposed to concentrate on the development of specialist services. The priority areas here were Inchcape's existing activities of insurance broking, port management, aviation, liquor distribution, and office automation and information technology. These were identified as meeting the criteria for development and investment in the near future.

The conclusions of the 1983 "Corporate Strategic Review" provided the main themes which were to run through Sir David's chairmanship: to secure financial viability by improving profitability and by the further rationalization of the Inchcape businesses; to give investment priority to existing businesses with the potential for growth; and to consider adding, through acquisition, a new activity to the Inchcape portfolio.

A NEW BUSINESS?

In the identification of an attractive new growth business, the criteria for selection were that it should be a specialist or distribution activity, that it should have an international dimension with an orientation toward those rapidly developing countries where the group was based, and that it should be cash-generating.

The PAC looked at three particular sectors: security, industrial catering, and inspection and testing. To help them evaluate the possibilities for each, studies were commissioned from McKinsey and Booz Allen. In 1984 the exercise culminated in the acquisition of Esperanza, International Services Limited, and Transcontinental Services N.V., later renamed Specialist Services International (SSI). A major international group in the inspection and testing industry, SSI was to be the type of single-activity SBU that the PAC expected would form the basis of the group's organization in the future. It also fulfilled Sir David's objective of giving Inchcape a new leg on which it could stand more securely.

Over the years, as with insurance broking, there would be a long debate about whether or not Inchcape should be in the inspection and testing business. At the time, it was seen as a logical extension of its other marine and insurance activities, or as it would later be labeled, part of the "search for synergy" that later swept the group. But its critics always claimed that Inchcape's lack of expertise in this sector made it open to exploitation, and that the added risk from exposure to South American business methods made it "not our sort of business." Criticism was especially fierce during its early years, when it turned in a series of poor performances. In fact, Inspection and Testing became a new type of fiefdom, run by Richard Nelson in his own style with little reference to the rest of the group. But it also proved, eventually, to be a profitable investment. Meanwhile, Inchcape's progress was to be rudely interrupted by an unwelcome intruder from the past.

ANOTHER NASTY SURPRISE

Even while Sir David and the PAC were happily immersed in formulating their plans for Inchcape's future, a crisis was brewing which would underline the superficial nature of the changes that had taken place previously. Before the end of his first year as chairman, Sir David was faced by a disaster in Thailand. It plunged the group into heavy losses and demonstrated that although the group *looked* different in 1983, in reality it continued to operate exactly as it had in the worst days of the late 1970s.

Lord Inchcape's only hostile acquisition had been the Anglo-Thai Corporation, bought in 1975. Because of this hostility, and because the Anglo-Thai management contained some strong characters, the company had been left even more severely alone than was usual. The company regarded itself as a separate entity, and relations between the center and Anglo-Thai rarely rose above freezing point.

Part of Anglo-Thai's business was the sale of Ford tractors and cars, and in 1981 it had requested extra resources from the center to finance expansion into the hire purchase business. At that time the group was highly geared and did not have the borrowing powers to finance the project and so it was turned down. Anglo-Thai then turned to the Greyhound Corporation, formed a 50–50 joint venture to finance their scheme, and re-presented it to the board. This time they were allowed to go ahead, and Thai Greyfin opened for business. The subsequent disaster arose from the agreement that, although Anglo-Thai only owned 50% of Thai Greyfin, it was responsible for 100% of its debts.

Early results looked good, and business expanded rapidly. However, as it later emerged, Thai Greyfin was fast outrunning the market. The salesforce, secure in the knowledge that Anglo-Thai was guaranteeing all bad debts, were selling tractors to people who had no possibility of paying for them. The waters were further muddied by their practice of rewriting the hire purchase contracts for defaulters. Anyone who had not paid for several months merely got their contract rewritten, including arrears of interest, and this made it impossible for investigators to tell for how long a contract had been running.

In 1983 the Anglo-Thai debacle caused Inchcape an £8 million operating loss out of pre-tax profits, and a further £22 million in extraordinary losses (from an annual turnover of £45 million). Worse, it caused the City to lose total confidence in the group's ability to manage its affairs, remembering that this was not the first time in recent years that the group had been rocked by "a nasty surprise."

FURTHER LOSSES — AGAIN

For Sir David, the Anglo-Thai losses underlined the failure of all the central controls so recently put in to avoid such a development. The dismal financial situation was further compounded by bad results from Malaysia, where the downturn in the construction market had resulted in losses for the B-Trak earth-moving equipment business run by Inchcape Berhad. An outside analyst commented that this was yet another example of the failure of the Inchcape management to anticipate and deal with a foreseeable risk. As far as the center was concerned, these losses further confirmed the weakness of the Inchcape Berhad management, which in 1981 had lost the Toyota franchise for Malaysia. Another running sore was the Peschaud Company, whose losses continued to drain the group, besides the costs associated with outstanding judgments in the French courts.

WHAT TO DO ABOUT "THE MANAGEMENT"?

The events of 1983 brought it forcibly home to Sir David that "the management team which had performed so well during the years of growth were ill-suited to working within the constraints exercised by a planned management at the center." At first he had hoped to find suitable people for promotion internally, but by the end of 1983 it was apparent to him that this was not going to be possible. Looking round, he realized that several of the senior managers, such as Peter Foxon and James Ritchie, were of retirement age, while Lord Inchcape's son, Peter Glenapp, had ruled himself out, preferring life as a gentleman farmer. As Sir David recalled, "He knew he lacked the qualities of decisiveness and toughness his father had *in excelsis*. Peter was very sensible and able, but not tough; it was not his style at all."

The early death of the only other candidate, Sir James Millington-Drake, in January 1983 left Sir David with no option but to look outside. To find a successor to himself, a chief executive who, working with a professional executive team, would be strong enough to change the management culture once and for all, became his priority.

WHO NEXT?

Sir David's first idea was to find someone in the fifty- to fifty-five-year age group. "Unfortunately, I couldn't find anyone with this type of overseas interest and the business ability the company needed. It needed a tough, hands-on executive." With the help of headhunters, Sir David interviewed and looked around for a long time, but couldn't find anyone to fit the specification except, finally, for George Turnbull who "had exactly the right experience but wasn't in the right age group." Interestingly, Turnbull reminded him of someone else. "George was an instinctive businessman, to some extent like Kenneth Inchcape. They had the same entrepreneurial feeling."

Sir David took a long time deciding, and discussed his doubts about his age with George himself. "But in the end, he was obviously the best-qualified person to take on this task. I knew he was a good operator; in particular, I knew of his interest and experience in the motor industry, which was very important to us at that time. So, finally, he came on board." The news caused a rally in Inchcape's share price, and was a huge relief to Sir David. The recruitment of George Turnbull was perhaps his greatest gift to the group, and in the year they worked together before the final handover, their relationship was "terrific." Sir David felt that they made a good team. "I had experience in the international field and of professional management, and George had the tough drive and decisiveness that we needed very much indeed." After Turnbull assumed power in June 1986, Sir David stayed on as a very active deputy chairman.

NEW FACES AT THE TOP

Between 1983 and 1986, Sir David's concern about the quality of the Inchcape management led to the recruitment of other new people, including several from Unilever. The change was made easier by the retirement of some longserving board members, which made room for the appointment of younger men trained in the corporate management style. Two key appointments announced in March 1984 were Alastair Macaskill, who moved from the Gulf to become executive director responsible for Toyota (GB), Inchcape Europe and Aviation, and, shortly after, Stacey Ellis, who became an executive director responsible for the troubled Malaysia, Thailand, and Singapore region. As Sir David recalled, Ellis was "very good at strategic thinking" and "played a big part in the new strategy." In September, another key figure appeared in the shape of Derek Whittaker, a long-time colleague of George Turnbull who later took over responsibility for the motors business throughout the group. With the influx of these men, the influence of Brian Ashworth and his team diminished. Once seen as the "new breed," they were now themselves considered old-fashioned.

FINANCIAL NON-PERFORMANCE

The depth of the management problem was illustrated most strongly by the failure of all attempts to impose financial controls on the SBUs. One of the main preoccupations of the PAC was how to improve the group's lamentable financial performance, and a recurring theme in group reviews was a plea to the SBUs for faster progress in meeting performance criteria, for greater professionalism in the appraisal of capital expenditure, and so on. The attitude of Inchcape's operational managers toward the ROBA concept illustrated the perennial nature of the problem.

First introduced in 1982/83, this attempt to impose an across-the-board control mechanism on the group had featured in every strategic plan since that time. Every year, a group-wide profitability objective, a minimum ROBA, had been set, beginning with a target of 16% in 1983. In 1984 the minimum was raised to 18%, and this remained the long-term target toward which the group was asked to work. The SBUs were asked to provide plans to achieve this minimum return, and the resultant objectives were first built into budget guidelines from the center, and then into their own budgets by the SBUs.

Despite the fact that throughout this period the 18% target was never achieved, it was effective in raising the level of results from the SBUs. In 1983 the group ROBA was 9.1%, in 1984 it was 11.4%, and the estimate for 1985 was 15%. Progress of a sort, but still leaving a long way for the group to go.

The other constant refrain of the Inchcape center was for performance improvement plans to reduce working capital and overheads, and though the group began to move in the right direction, here too progress was painfully slow. However, the center had some success in getting the group's gearing down, from over 100% in 1982 to 69% by 1985.

A TAKEOVER?

The year 1983 marked a very low ebb in Inchcape's fortunes. Unable to offset the Thai losses against tax, the group paid a crippling £37 million out of pre-tax profits of £53 million. As a result of the collapse of the property market, it also took, a year earlier than necessary, a write-down of £43 million on its Hong Kong properties. One broker estimated that in that year, the group's return on capital employed of nearly £700 million was 1.6%.

At this point there were rumors of a takeover threat, which remained rife over the next few years. The seriousness of the threat is difficult to determine; some alleged that no-one would have been "willing to take on such a mish-mash, whatever the discount to assets." On the other hand, given the break-up value of the Inchcape interests and the low share price, others believed that a real possibility of takeover existed. Whatever the truth of this, the group's position appeared vulnerable to many City watchers; one internal calculation put its market value at £300 million against a computed break-up value of £700 million.

PLANNING 2: DISPOSALS ...

Against the depressing backcloth of events out in the field, the PAC continued to immerse itself in the planning process. In part motivated by the desire to forestall any takeover bid, they returned to the task of stripping down the group. Guided by the same business policy matrix as in 1982/83, the PAC initiated a second major phase of critical review and disposal. Once again, the relative value of the Inchcape businesses was plotted on a matrix, using the two axes of competitive position and market attractiveness.

Again, businesses falling into the critical review quadrants were given the chance of a reprieve if they produced a viable long-term plan to improve their position, after which the final decision was taken as to whether to dispose of them or not. The outcome was the sale of many businesses that appeared to have poor prospects, and had no part to play in the core strategy formulated by the PAC. The group got out of peanut farming in Malaysia, its wine business (the later highly successful Hunter Valley) in Australia, besides the ill-starred Peschaud, the watch division of Gilmans, and a miscellany of others spread throughout the world in Canada, Singapore, Jamaica, Angola, Panama, and Ecuador.

Another important decision was to continue the phased sale of all property owned by the group, which in 1984 realized a profit of £44.5 million. The net effect of this disposal program was to reduce the number of Inchcape businesses and to release £105 million in cash by 1985.

THE X FILE

The cash was to be used to make major investments for the future, and a two-pronged search was initiated, in sectors where the group already operated and in new growth opportunities. The criteria for any new activity remained constant, with emphasis on the need for "a high degree of technical sophistication ... where we can develop some elements of specialization."

Throughout 1984, "Project X," the search for a new activity, was carried on. The SBUs were invited to identify existing and new activities as investment candidates and present them to the board, a task they entered into with enthusiasm. This was more like the old days. The PAC then acted as a filtering unit to knock on the head any that did not fit in with their strategic objectives for the group. Studies of other likely candidates were commissioned from consultancies such as Booz Allen and Hamilton. The group had got the consultancy habit with a vengeance.

Among the businesses considered were a duty free shoppers operation, a pest control business, a U.S. broker operating in the energy sector, and a specialist construction and consumer goods testing business. These were all sectors in which the group already operated. Among the possible new ventures were an international software packages company, an airport and hospital management business, and a computer maintenance business. But at the end of the day, it appeared that no new activity offered a better opportunity than those identified as strong in Inchcape's existing portfolio. It was decided to call off the search, and instead concentrate on "developing the group's existing operations into world-class businesses, run by a world-class management." It is not recorded whether or not anyone smiled at the incongruity of this.

TERRITORIAL STRATEGY

The PAC also continued to review the group's territorial strategy, and a number of initiatives were taken to try and gain a truer perspective on the future prospects for the group in the regions where it operated. The group economist, Peter Stubbs, led a series of territorial studies, and again the results were plotted on a matrix. As a result, the Far East and Southeast Asia were starred for priority treatment, with selective investment in Europe, North America, the Middle East, and Australia. The decision taken earlier to withdraw from Africa was confirmed, so cutting one of Inchcape's historic ties.

Investment in South America was to be restricted, despite the best efforts of Colin Armstrong, responsible for the South American and Caribbean businesses. He had hoped for more sympathetic treatment from Sir David Orr due to his experience of the successful Unilever operations there; Armstrong was to be disappointed. Although Sir David was not "anti," he was "careful." Regarding them as volatile economies, he was wary of investing Inchcape's hard-won cash there, despite the fact that in the 1982 Review, South America had been identified as a strong prospect. It is ironic, in view of later developments, that at a time when Sir David was casting round for a new business, the later phenomenally successful Coca-Cola bottling operations were under his nose.

In retrospect, Sir David also felt that he could have given more support to the nascent bottling business in Chile, but "to go for that, and to do the job properly, would have needed an enormous amount of money. I didn't like to gamble so much of Inchcape's money on it."

The Middle East and Hong Kong were the subject of particular scrutiny during these years because of potential problems. Anxieties about the former were due to the downturn in the oil industry and the Gulf War, while the future prosperity of Hong Kong was overshadowed by the negotiations taking place between the British and Chinese governments on the colony's future after 1997. The PAC decided to stay in both areas, but in the former to reduce their costs, and in the latter to concentrate on expanding Inchcape's business with China.

Inchcape had capitalized on its historic links there, having continued to do business throughout the years since the Communist takeover in 1949. Fortunately, the earlier speculation about the sale of Mann Egerton had not materialized. By 1983 the U.K. was Inchcape's strongest growth area.

REORGANIZATION

In the new organization set up under Lord Inchcape, the SBUs had been mainly based on existing companies that encompassed a range of activities, grouped regionally. Now, the first tentative steps were taken toward setting up functional SBUs and, one of the most controversial moves, the introduction of business streaming.

The origins of the business stream concept are unclear. Some believe it was part of the Unilever vocabulary brought in by Sir David Orr; others give the credit to Stacey Ellis. INSEAD's Philippe Haspeslagh believed it was the logical continuation of the switch from a country-based to a product-based organization. Streaming, he noted, made sense to Inchcape as a word "since it means to take a bunch of disparate things and make them flow together."

What is clear is that once adopted, it became Inchcape's strongest weapon for achieving the ultimate nirvana, focus. First introduced under Sir David, widened under the leadership of George Turnbull, business streaming reached its apotheosis under Charles Mackay, who eventually implemented global business streams. Although undoubtedly a force for good in some activities, whether they were a suitable mechanism for all Inchcape's businesses was a subject for hot debate later on.

The new SBU concept implied the consolidation of a specific type of business — for example, insurance broking — into a single business stream covering that activity throughout the group. This meant that responsibility for that activity would no longer be divided among various sector directors according to the regions in which it was carried on, but could be placed under one centralizing authority. It was envisaged that this functional organization should be an adjunct to geographical management, but such a move cut right across Inchcape's former emphasis on territorial responsibility.

For the first time, the word "global" entered the everyday vocabulary of the Inchcape managers at the center. To them, the great advantage of this type of "global" organization was that it would enable them to exploit possible linkages between operations in the different regions, and to gain a sounder idea of the long-term potential of a particular activity. Initially, two fledgling business streams were set up, Inchcape Aviation and Caldbeck International (which covered the wines and spirits business). Inchcape's new activity, Inspection and Testing, later became a third business stream. Although the Shipping stream was left under the direct operational responsibility of its several geographical managers, a shipping services coordinator was recruited to introduce a "light functional dimension" — a compromise by any other name.

THE PERSPECTIVE FROM THE FIELD

Despite the best efforts of Sir David and his team to re-engineer the group, the management problem in the operating units continued to represent an apparently immovable obstacle in their path. Relations between the center and the operating units had become increasingly strained as those "out in the sticks" watched the changes from afar and noted the changing emphasis without understanding the reasons for it.

On the one hand they felt themselves harried and beset by the new financial controls, required to send in returns by stricter and stricter deadlines and, worst of all, to stick to budgets and achieve targets. On the other hand, they understood quite well the consequences of selective investment; if some businesses were being marked for stardom, others were clearly for the axe. The overall effect was to make them entrench themselves behind barriers that effectively cut them off from a center they regarded as interfering and unsympathetic. With no personnel function operating in the regions, this problem was impossible to resolve and a stalemate existed in which the field management fought a rearguard action to defeat the efforts of the center to enforce a change of attitude.

SHOUTING INTO THE VOID

The problem of communications between those at the center and those in the field was one that, for the moment, remained unresolved. Despite a vast amount of traveling by the chairman, it was impossible to develop any sense of common responsibility in such a widespread, diverse group, and this void effectively defeated all the efforts of the central planners to implement new strategies.

The PAC attempted to communicate the fruits of their labors through two conferences held in 1984. The first, a group conference, was held in March; the second, for SBU chief executives, was in December.

THE WAY AHEAD

The December 1984 conference introduced George Turnbull as group managing director. His involvement gave a renewed impetus for change, building on the work of slimming down the group already begun by Sir David and his team. In the next year, yet further studies were undertaken of the businesses in order to look at their future potential for growth, and distinguish the likely stars from the dogs. To many, it was a process that seemed to have been going on forever. Were there any stars to be found? Or was Inchcape just a huge kennel for unwanted strays? The latter view seemed to be confirmed when, as a result, a third list of disposals was drawn up. Turnbull, meanwhile, departed on a lengthy tour of the group so that when he finally took over, he would be in a position to understand and assess its disparate businesses more fully.

During the conferences, Sir David reiterated that the two main building blocks for the future were to be specialist services, and marketing and distribution. He also emphasized that the *sine qua non* for the group's future strength was efficiency of operations and the achievement of strict financial objectives. Renewed emphasis was laid on the achievement of the ROBA target and it was decided to hold quarterly review meetings which would focus on the progress made by the SBU directors in achieving budget plans.

The theme of the conference was "The Way Ahead," and it ended with a picture showing the Inchcape man, confidently striding down the road sign-posted "efficiency and enterprise" toward a "profitable future." Such optimism seemed justified by the 1984 results, which showed increased profits from the group's tea interests (12% gross profits on only 1% of turnover), and success in the new Chinese market for its Toyota sales.

An upbeat article in the *Far Eastern Economic Review* of August 1984 demonstrated the success of Sir David's efforts. According to this, "the group has been the subject of a spate of reports by stockbrokers, most of whom are recommending Inchcape on a recovery view." However, there was a sting in the rider that "in part, this is just a matter of analysts concluding that the performance simply can't get any worse, especially after sweeping provisions made in 1983." Some analysts, it noted, were talking of pre-tax profits of up to £70 million in 1984, and one even went so far as to forecast earnings of £90 million for 1985. Inchcape, they clearly believed, had finally turned the corner. Given its "greater focus, stronger management and a continued upturn in world trade, with especial demand in East Asia," things could only get better.

As if to mock every effort, 1985 was another bad year for Inchcape with another set of disappointing results. However, by then Sir George Turnbull was firmly in the driving seat. Although the recalcitrant field managers did not yet know it, major change was finally on its way.

Turnbull Turns it Round, 1986-92

"You *Will* Achieve"

"In the areas of marketing and distribution our aim will be to achieve a standard of such excellence that we will become the natural choice of any principal wishing to sell his goods or services in our territory."

Now, let's get on with it." With these words, George Turnbull signaled not just the end of his speech as chairman to the chief executives of the Inchcape group, but the end of an era in its history. Although few of those assembled to listen to their new leader realized it, Turnbull's assumption of power in June 1986 marked the final demise of the old Inchcape, whose results, as described by Turnbull, told "a sorry story of underestimates, underperformance, management failures ..." More ominously for some, his words also signaled the beginning of a much more ruthless, hands-on style of leadership, and the implementation of a professional management culture that emphasized achievement through teamwork and, above all, obedience to strict financial controls. In effect, the speech signaled the beginning of a long-awaited turnaround for the ailing group, but in the process, a lot of blood would be spilt.

A NEW LEADER

At first sight, George Turnbull seemed a surprising choice to take over the group. When he had originally been mooted as a possible successor, Sir David Orr had considered him "too rich and too successful" to want to take over the chairmanship of Inchcape. However, within ten days of first meeting Sir David to discuss the appointment, George Turnbull had made up his mind to accept a job he thought offered "something interesting." One observer described the appointment of the "millionaire apprentice lad" as "shrewd and imaginative," for the whole of George Turnbull's career so far had been spent in the motor industry, where he enjoyed "a star reputation." The Inchcape executives might have profited from a close study of his previous career, which would have given them plenty of clues about his likely business focus and management style.

A "Motors" man to his fingertips, Turnbull had started out as an indentured apprentice at the old Standard Motors, later to merge with Triumph and become part of the British Leyland (BL) group. Having picked up an engineering degree at Birmingham University, he made his name in the stormy, highly political environment of BL where, by 1969, he was deputy managing director. Following a policy row with the BL chairman, Lord Stokes, and his failure to become managing director, in 1973 Turnbull moved on to South Korea and Hyundai Motors, where the challenge was to set up a car industry from scratch. That he succeeded rapidly and only too well is history, and a source of some grief to his erstwhile colleagues, who had to face this aggressive new competitor.

Turnbull then migrated to Iran as deputy managing director of the National Motor Co., which "assembled cars from kits of parts supplied by Chrysler in Britain." When Iran erupted into revolution he returned to the U.K., and another challenge as chairman of the troubled Talbot U.K. There, he gained a reputation as a "hatchet man," but five years later the "slimmed-down" company that he left was able to announce a net profit for the first time in ten years. It was from there that he joined Inchcape, taking up the post of group managing director in 1984. The understanding was that if all went well, he would become chief executive in January 1986 and take over as chairman from Sir David in June 1986; a timetable that was maintained.

These standard biographical details apart, perhaps the Inchcape management would have found even more enlightening the information that George Turnbull had been a star rugby player, captain of his county, Warwickshire, and, in his own words, "a fairly robust player." After meeting him, one interviewer noted the similarity between George Turnbull's rugby playing and management style, concluding that, "He still gives the impression that it might be wise to keep out of his way if he's running with the ball."

To Turnbull, Inchcape represented yet another in a long line of challenges. His whole career demonstrated how much he relished such a situation, and also his preference for freedom of action and willingness to take tough decisions. A forceful character, who "got on well with others and got things done, rather than a strategist or intellectual," he became familiar figure to the staff at Inchcape. Square-jawed and square-cut, with heavy-rimmed spectacles, he looked confident and purposeful. A blunt speaker with little time for frills or graces, he appeared tough and even bullying but was inwardly shy, and needed to prepare carefully for public events. Speaking "off the cuff" was a source of real discomfort for him. However, timekeeping came naturally, and this meant that his team had ready access to him at short notice.

Both Derek Whittaker and Sir David Orr described Turnbull as one of the most sensible people they had known. Noted Whittaker, "George's great strength was that he had an abundance of experience; his feet were always firmly on the floor. He recognized everyone's strengths and weaknesses. He was not an over-sophisticated person; his great *forte* was common sense and communication — up, down, sideways with all his employees ... George manipulated us all."

Turnbull brought a completely new tone to the group. He left no doubt about what he expected and so, where once exhortations to achieve budget targets had been firmly but politely phrased, "You *will* achieve" became the order of the day. The two planks of the new culture he introduced were "Do not ever have red numbers" and "No surprises." In the spirit of another firm leader of the time, there was no alternative. He believed in professional management and teamwork, and anyone who did not work in that way was not encouraged to stay around. In the early period he bullied and pushed the group into change, providing the iron hand in the iron glove it had long needed. Decisions were taken quickly, with a minimum of agonizing and a constant striving to "keep it simple." Work was compressed into relatively short but highly effective days. Energy was conserved for the extra pressures of a heavy travel schedule.

Turnbull's "Twelve Management Maxims" soon became the mantras of his senior team. Six of these set out his management style: "I will not tolerate barons or prima donnas; I reward loyalty but don't mistake it for ability; I don't believe in the comfort zone for anybody; I always remind headquarters staff that they are overheads; I delegate the capacity to make mistakes; and I give everyone an opportunity to acquire extra management skills." The other six concerned his approach toward the businesses: "We must ask ourselves, do we understand the customer base? We are in business to handle the possible; we must be internationally competitive in every business stream; we should always regard cost reduction and productivity as an endless street; we must recognize and respect our competitors; and, finally, earnings per share, return on business assets, and use of funds are the yardsticks which we use at Inchcape." The message was loud and clear.

THE CHALLENGE

George Turnbull's task was to complete the work of reconstructing the group begun by Lord Inchcape and Sir David Orr. This involved first restructuring the Inchcape businesses to give the group a coherence it had hitherto lacked, and then extracting greater performance from those businesses destined to be the key to the future. He also had to find linkages between the different activities pursued by the group and so "make the whole greater than the sum of the parts." This, the vogue phrase among business theorists at that time, proved highly attractive to Turnbull, as to many other chief executives struggling with an unwieldy conglomerate, and was a frequent refrain over the next few years. The search for this ideal state, translated into the search for synergies, became a long-running and influential theme throughout Turnbull's time at Inchcape.

As Turnbull saw it, an urgent task was to replace the old cult of the individual by a professional management style capable of running a modern, multinational company. Another was to rebuild morale and confidence, both internally and externally. Internally, he had to establish an efficient management structure, which required a significant change in the relationship between the center and those in the field; he had to create an environment of greater openness and trust between the two, and a greater sense of mutual interdependence. Externally, he had to convince the City that the group's reputation for unforeseen disasters was a thing of the past, and that the new Inchcape was ready not just to survive, but to be a winning competitor in the second half of the 1980s. His ability to achieve all of this would, in great part, depend on his success in building financial stability into the group through the introduction of strict financial controls.

To reach his decision about the group's future, George Turnbull served another period of apprenticeship. During the sixteen months between his appointment as group managing director and actually becoming chairman, he traveled twice round the group. His major objective was to gain an understanding of the company and its activities to enable him to assess its disparate component parts, but his tour caused panic in the ranks. Dale Butcher, who had been persuaded by David John to join the group to "revamp the group controllers' department," recalled his first impressions of the group at this time: "It was a shambles — in terms of no-one was quite sure who was meant to be doing what, and there was a crisis brewing ... There was the thud of George's feet around the world, and every department thought George had given them the brief to sort things out and was busily recruiting their teams. I am sure that George knew what he was doing at the time, but it was a bit like organized chaos. The old guard was sitting there and the new guard was getting its troops in — a palace revolution."

Old hand Alastair Macaskill spent quite some time traveling with Turnbull during this period. He recalled him saying, "I have great difficulty with Inchcape. The one thing I find most difficult is that everyone is so damned polite to each other." In fact, said Macaskill, "He was astute enough to understand this and made it work for him."

Turnbull concluded that the group was clearly divided into three main types of activity. The first involved the marketing and distribution of other companies' products; the second was giving a direct service to customers where Inchcape marketed its own service; the third comprised the resource-based businesses where the group actually owned the resource (tea and timber) and marketed them from source.

From this conclusion, he set to work with the central planning team to look critically at the Inchcape businesses against his management maxims. Prime place was given to Inchcape being internationally competitive in everything it did and to a knowledge of the customer base "in order to understand the business, that should be in an expanding market, profitable, and preferably above average in terms of margins." Moreover, as part of understanding the customer base, Turnbull demanded the necessary expertise to run the business. Where this was lacking, he foresaw a major task in recruiting the right kind of people to develop the company for the future. By January 1986 he had "a pretty good idea of the parts of the company I thought were sound and should be strategic in the sense that we would develop them for the future, and those parts which had very little relevance."

A NEW STRATEGY

On this premise a strategy for the future was drawn up and presented at the chief executives' conference held in February 1986. At that conference, Turnbull outlined how the group should be run in the future and explained his objectives for it. He then presented the new strategy, at the same time making it quite clear that, under him, the group would be run according to that strategy. The implications of this for the Inchcape management were clearly spelt out.

The plan represented the center's perception of what was going to happen during the next year; it would dictate what future actions were taken and would be reflected in budgets and targets for the businesses, and in discussions with the banks, the institutions, and all interested outside parties. From now on, the Inchcape management would be required to work within planned commitments. As George Turnbull went on to explain in terms that left no room for doubt, this meant a new style in which the watchword was teamwork not individuality, and reduced local authority coupled with strict financial control as opposed to entrepreneurial flair and uninhibited spending. Pointing to the history of unauthorized financial commitments and huge exposures that had so undermined the group in the past, George Turnbull drove home the message that the system whereby the group was run as a loose confederation of companies allowed to go their own way was finished. From now on, they would do it his way.

The 1986 strategic plan was to be the basis for the future of the group. It embodied George Turnbull's view that Inchcape should aim to be an internationally competitive services and marketing company, a global player. However, first there was a lot of work to be done in transforming Inchcape to give it the structure and management necessary to achieve these objectives.

A NEW TEAM

"… there is obviously a major task to be performed in recruiting the right kind of people: aggressive people who can out-think the competition."

Turnbull knew he would need a team of "totally professional" managers at the center, people suited to the new Inchcape he wished to build. These would be men (and all the new managers were men) of high caliber, proven experience in their individual fields, and imbued with the modern management culture. To him it was evident that such men would have to be brought in from outside, a potentially delicate problem as he wanted no "night of the long knives" which would be bad both for the group's image and morale. Accordingly, Turnbull tried to make his personnel changes gradually, and in this was aided by a rash of retirement that fortuitously broke out, both at board level and in the regions. Between 1984 and 1986, five directors left, replaced by younger men who brought the average age down ten years to forty-seven or forty-eight. In dealing with the board, George Turnbull was able to rely on the unstinting support of Sir David Orr who had moved over to become deputy chairman; his diplomatic approach was the perfect complement to George Turnbull's more robust style.

In the end, Peter Lumsden, the finance director fell an early victim to the clash of cultures and was replaced by Rod O'Donoghue. Bob Goodall was recruited as personnel director, John Duncan became director of group corporate affairs, and Stacey Ellis was brought in from Southeast Asia to lead the planning team. George Turnbull also recruited professionals to lead the work of reconstruction in the regions. Unlike their predecessors, they were to be based in their territories; Charles Mackay was to go to Hong Kong and take over the Far East. David John, who joined the group in 1981, moved from Bahrain to Singapore to head up Southeast Asia. His erstwhile boss, Alastair Macaskill, returned to the Middle East. Derek Whittaker, an old and trusted colleague from the British Leyland days who had been acting in a consultant capacity, took over responsibility for the motors businesses throughout the group. All except Bob Goodall and John Duncan were made executive board members, those based outside London flying in once a month for briefings and board meetings.

George Turnbull wanted them to be the best people he could get, and it was his presence that convinced many of them to join Inchcape, a company some of them knew by reputation and would not have found attractive, given the old management style. The new recruits shared a common culture; they were professionals, tough and aggressive, and above all, under Turnbull's forceful leadership, team players; he wanted no more of "the baron's syndrome." They were also, perhaps even more crucially in view of Inchcape's past record, finance-trained and well versed in the avoidance of financial risks.

Yet, being team players did not preclude individual ambition, and several of the new recruits obviously saw their current task as a stepping stone en route to the top job when Turnbull retired. Three candidates were to emerge: Charles Mackay, Stacey Ellis, and David John, each with their own styles that they proceeded to stamp on their particular territory within the group. So, although the old "baron's syndrome" was eradicated, it was replaced by a more modern version that was played out through the adoption of another business theory gaining much credibility at the time: the building of a corporate culture. In the long run, their actions served only to confound attempts to find a cohesive entity for the group, and to build further barriers between managers who were being encouraged to bring down such walls.

Mackay was perhaps the most openly ambitious. Joining BP after leaving school, he had read Law at Cambridge thanks to a university apprenticeship scheme, and then spent six years climbing the corporate ladder as he directed operations in Algeria, the Eastern Congo, Burundi, and Rwanda. He then persuaded BP to send him to the international business school, INSEAD, where he graduated top of his year. From there, he moved into the consultancy world and a different experience, spending six-and-a-half years with McKinsey. After McKinsey he returned to senior line management, first with Royal Pakhoed, a Dutch oil storage, property, and transport conglomerate, and then with the British firm, Chloride. The highly successful, multilingual, and internationally minded Mackay was then recruited by Turnbull in the course of a long plane journey. With his background and track record, Mackay was just about as ideal a representative of modern, professional management as you could get; it was little wonder that Turnbull saw him as a brilliant addition to the Inchcape team he was building, and his eventual successor.

Short and stocky, Mackay's hyperactive style was betrayed by the constant juggling with keys and pens in his pocket. Rarely seen with his jacket unbuttoned, and even more rarely in shirtsleeves, he was notorious for his lightning command of figures and would relish every opportunity to prove his mastery. Even the most numerate managers were seen to emerge ashen-faced from a meeting to discuss capital expenditure or more trivial accounts. "When he left Hong Kong," consultant Nick Allen recalled, "at his leaving party, they gave him a six-foot model calculator." To many, it seemed that only the computer chess games Mackay played daily seemed to offer him any real challenge.

Mackay's management style was demonstrated by his high-profile leadership of Inchcape Pacific Ltd (IPL). This Far Eastern empire, centered on Hong Kong and a miniature version of the Inchcape group, became known for a ruthless, fast-moving culture. Like the progress of Napoleon's armies across Europe 200 years earlier, it left a changed landscape in its wake. Indeed, Mackay's video appearances exhorting his troops to further effort did, some felt, betray an unnerving identification with the first French Emperor.

Stacey Ellis had joined Inchcape in 1984 and successfully carried out the task of cleaning up the Southeast Asia sector. There he had seen Inchcape at its worst, "a Byzantine organization with no control, no clear lines of communication, and no idea where it was going." In 1987 he returned to the center to take over the planning function, progressively handing over responsibility for Singapore to David John.

In contrast to his two younger rivals, Ellis gave a somewhat old-fashioned impression, both in language and appearance. Urbane, and with a fondness for striped "City" suits, he looked like the successful accountant that he in fact was. He was at his happiest unraveling a set of complex figures, but experience with Haw Par in Singapore and Inchcape's Southeast Asian companies had given him an acute commercial "nose" and a cultural sensitivity lacking in some of his colleagues. Together with George Turnbull, Sir David Orr, and Rod O'Donoghue, Ellis formed the chief executive office which was represented on all the committees set up to oversee the running of Inchcape.

David John was both the youngest of the three and the most approachable. A rugby-loving Welshman with a fund of stories and a vast collection of contacts stretching across the world, he revelled in getting on with people and was well-liked by employees at all levels. Based in Singapore in charge of Southeast Asian operations, John had immediate success without, apparently, causing any of the resentment associated with the rise of IPL.

In fact, none of these was as close to George Turnbull as Derek Whittaker. An old pal from Turnbull's British Leyland days, he shared Turnbull's love and encyclopedic knowledge of the car business. In contrast to the smooth professionalism of Mackay, Ellis, and John, and despite his accountancy training, Whittaker's accent and style were more Arthur Daley than Arthur Andersen. Behind the used car dealer exterior hid a keen, experienced brain that, within a few years, turned the motors business into the backbone of the group. When he and George were both in the U.K., the two met up before 8 a.m. to discuss any new projects. As Whittaker recalled, "George would say, 'You show me the figures in a month's time, and if they look right — go and do it.' We did the paperwork afterwards." Whittaker had access to George Turnbull at any time, and knew, or appeared to know, everything that was going on. He was to be instrumental in Inchcape's turnaround.

A NEW STRATEGIC DIRECTION

Stacey Ellis led the planning team at the center. His perception of Inchcape's problem was the same as everyone else; it was too disparate, and because the center lacked an understanding of what was going on in the field, "it could monitor but not control." Moreover, as past events had so often proved, it had not always monitored the right things.

The aim of the planning team was to guide the future development of the selected core businesses; to do that, they needed to gain access to the right sort of information and to understand it thoroughly. Another dimension of this was the need to ensure the optimum allocation of the group's resources. The disposals program had brought in a considerable sum, but having shorn Inchcape of all its fat, the center did not want to risk an investment that might go wrong. For the first years there was a strict rationing system with regard to acquisitions; they had to be in the budget, and be in line with the overall strategy. This aimed to build on the group's traditional strengths: its international spread; its reputation for integrity and honest dealing; and the experience and expertise of its people in operating throughout the globe.

A New Set of Managers

Bob Goodall arrived in Inchcape from a senior human resources position in Merck. A keen sportsman with a spare physique and a laconic style, his first task was to try and understand the new environment in which he found himself. After working in a highly structured organization with long time horizons, generous margins, and ample resources, Inchcape was a profound culture shock.

His initial perception was that the group's personnel function existed primarily for the administration of the head office and a select number of British expatriate managers. This was brought home all the more forcibly when he started exploring the personnel records. File after file was on British expatriates, and each consisted largely of minute details on their leave arrangements and furniture allowances. Records of achievement or personal development were almost always lacking. Even more striking was the total lack of Chinese, Japanese, Indian, or other foreign names who were the men and women earning the money that paid for the lifestyle enjoyed by the expatriates.

Although previous efforts to install an appraisal system, and to set up a central committee to encourage cross-postings, had achieved some success in the face of stubborn opposition from local operating units, there was little else in the way of data on the Inchcape workforce. Consequently, Bob Goodall was to spend his first nine months collecting information and setting up the machinery for his department before he could even begin functioning on an international basis.

His mandate from George Turnbull was top management development; responsibility for "upgrading our standards of professionalism in our training, recruitment, and quality of management generally." A great part of this task would involve trying to forge a new and positive relationship between the center and the regions. Not surprisingly, the many changes they had seen had left the men in the field negative and poorly motivated. They had withdrawn behind invisible barriers, set on protecting their particular territory. Echoing the spirit of the planners, Bob Goodall and his team set out to break down these barriers and build new lines of communication based on feelings of interdependence and mutual respect rather than suspicion and hostility.

Inevitably, part of bringing about this change was a clear-out of the old senior-level management throughout the group. In fact, a whole generation of Inchcape managers was approaching retirement (the age of fifty-five for those in the field), and so once again it was possible to put down the old guard fairly humanely, and replace them with new people. The picture was not uniformly bad; some of the managers at the local level were "very good," and had the potential to metamorphose into the kind of managers the group required, given the right encouragement.

Bob Goodall then turned his attention to providing this encouragement. He discovered the existence of sound plans for the training and development of a new generation of Inchcape managers produced by his predecessor. The reason for their failure was quite obvious to him; like so many other Inchcape plans, they had been made in a vacuum at the center. Because there was no personnel function in the field, there was no-one responsible for executing them, and hence the training programs, too, had disappeared into the black hole. "I literally didn't know where to focus my energy: there was so much that needed to be done."

NEW FINANCIAL CONTROLS

"We are going to make sure that we achieve the budgeted trading profit of 87 million for 1986 without any slip-ups, vulnerabilities, old sores, etc., emerging unexpectedly at the last minute ... we will be lean and mean ..."

In a rare understatement, George Turnbull described how "it became very apparent to me as soon as I became chairman that I had to make some significant changes in financial control." To him, it was clear that the imposition of strict financial controls on the group's management would be critical to its future success. Until this had been achieved, he knew that he could not "sit in London and feel that we were not running great risks and big exposures round the world."

The group's history of volatile results, and its penchant for huge, unforeseen losses due to a crisis in a faraway territory, were well known to Turnbull. He also knew the reasons for them. They had occurred because "subsidiary companies had entered into major financial commitments and created huge exposures for the group either without authority from the board, or without the board's fully understanding the nature of that commitment" — he was determined that nothing like that would ever happen under him.

Accordingly, improvement of the group's financial performance figured largely in the 1986 plan. He was at his most formidable as he spelt out his demands to help fulfill group objectives — "I must insist that a 5% overhead reduction is achieved" — and his expectation that the core businesses achieve a minimum 18% ROBA by 1988. He also made it abundantly clear that, in future, local management would have greatly reduced authority to commit the group on capital and bank loans, and have to endure tight financial controls. This meant planning, setting out a budget, and, most important of all, gaining approval for that budget. Once that budget had been approved, the necessary funds would be released. However, if later on anyone did have a bright idea — a once-in-a-lifetime opportunity they could not bear to refuse but that was not in the budget — then "the process of getting approval for it would be long and tortuous." Such a tight rein would keep the group moving in the direction envisaged by the center, stop unwelcome diversions into unrelated businesses, and ensure that there would be no nasty surprises to upset the annual results.

Part of the solution to this problem lay in having authority levels that would impose automatic discipline, and these were quickly put in place. At that time, anything over £2 million had to go to the board; anything under that was dealt with by the capital executive committee. For sector directors, the authority level was £250,000, and £50,000 at SBU level.

The rest of the solution lay in tight controls and shortened lines of communications between the center and the regions. Communications had always been Inchcape's biggest problem. Under the old system, those in the different geographical sectors reported to directors resident in London, and it had always been difficult for the center to find out exactly what was going on because of the number of parties the information had to go through before it reached the board. George

Turnbull wanted a homogeneous finance function running through the company, one where everyone had a clear understanding of their responsibilities and the limits of their authority. The most important building block in realizing this was the appointment of a new finance director, Rod O'Donoghue.

O'Donoghue was charged with the task of setting up the kind of finance function suited to a modern, multinational company; it was an awesome task. He found a fragmented organization, in which managers operated within their own little boxes. His predecessors had not tried to run the group as an integrated body, but had "acted as the finance directors of a holding company." They had stayed out of operations as much as possible, and lacking any leadership from the center, there had been no progress toward the setting of standards, or showing those in the field how to operate their finances. Communication between center and field was at best confused; no-one knew who they should talk to in the field, and those in the field had no understanding of the center's role. Previously, for example, the central finance function had not been allowed to talk to those in the regions, other than via the financial people working for the individual sector director.

Out in the operating units, each of the geographical sectors had a sector assistant whose job specification was broader than finance, and whose effectiveness depended on the attitude of the individual director. Below sector level came the SBUs and below them the operating units, each of which usually had a financial team headed by a financial executive. The reporting structure, as O'Donoghue found it, was "quite good, though very slow." There was a common format for the monthly reports that were sent in for budgeting purposes, and a quarterly process that reviewed the budgets in greater depth.

O'Donoghue arrived from Pritchard Services where he had been group finance director, but his formative years were with Xerox. This experience and his personality were critical to the way he would tackle his task. A tall, almost ascetic-looking person, he had a deep belief in order and structure and a typical attention to detail. Less typically, for a senior finance person, he coupled this with a relaxed, informal style and a mildness of manner, which would enable him to penetrate parts of the organization that had previously resisted all attempts at scrutiny or rigor.

A NEW CORPORATE IMAGE

A major preoccupation of the new Inchcape management was to project a clear corporate image for the group as one of today's successes rather than yesterday's has-beens. The urgent need to efface the memory of the old Inchcape and all its works was pursued in a coordinated program, managed from the center. Accordingly, in an attempt to distance it from the previous "overseas trading group" tag with its old-fashioned connotations, mention of Inchcape in press reports was always prefaced by the description "the international services and marketing group."

John Duncan, director of group corporate affairs, was given the task of communicating the message about the new Inchcape. His objective was to make external perceptions of the group match the new reality, and to do so he targeted three key audiences whose image of the group and what it stood for needed to be changed: the City and business media; the investment community; and the Inchcape employees.

The challenge, as he saw it, was to convince the first two groups that the backward-looking, Victorian Leviathan with a propensity for "shooting itself in the foot every so often" had been replaced. Today's Inchcape would be a modern, international company with a new strategy, a new management style, and hence a new culture. To address this challenge, a program of communications was put in place, focusing at first on the broking community, and then opening out to include City analysts and the investment institutions. The third group, the Inchcape employees, had to be encouraged to feel part of the Inchcape group, and proud to work for it.

In dealing with the City, the major objective was to raise confidence in the group's future prospects and belief in its sustained revival, and thus improve the rating of the group's shares. The effect would be twofold; as a defensive measure it would help to discourage any likely predator, while the improved rating would also enable the group to use its shares to finance an investment if the need arose.

In communicating with Inchcape's own people, he had to overcome the legacy of acquisitions and all their subcultures which had been allowed to flourish under the previous holding company mentality. These cultures were overlaid with loyalty to supplier companies, such as Toyota or Coca-Cola, which inevitably had far more direct relevance for most employees and made Inchcape seem, at best, a very remote entity.

A keen cricketer, and a member of the MCC, Duncan came from American Express, bringing to Inchcape public relations professionalism, and wide contacts in the City and the financial press. A wordsmith and an amateur cartoonist, his acid wit and acute sense of the absurd or pompous could humble the unwary. In an important sense, he occupied the role of court jester at the center, preventing the new team members from taking themselves too seriously or becoming downcast when their efforts ran into the inevitable wall of cynicism posed by the operating executives.

ALL TO PLAY FOR

With the exception of Charles Mackay, George Turnbull's new team was made up of keen sportsmen who could wax lyrical about cricket, rugby, soccer, and golf. Often a serious discussion would be started, or punctuated, by some comment or banter of a sporting nature. The unwritten code of the team was "work hard, play hard," and this energy and commitment soon became translated into the style of the organization.

In retrospect, they all looked back on the years they spent working under Turnbull's leadership as the happiest of times. They were unanimous in their admiration for the way he welded them into an effective force for change. As John Duncan recalled, "We were a good team because George said to us, 'I want you all to be friends — good friends — and that's an order!' He could be brutal with some people. He couldn't stand the barons, or anyone who didn't deliver, or who tried to play games. Under George, we had a good sense of comradeship. We were all different personalities, but we had shared interests, especially in sport."

Stacey Ellis recalled that "It worked very well. Although George, Rod, and myself were basically at the center, George was terribly careful to make sure we were never seen as senior to the barons in the field. It was always that we were different. And he always talked about humility at head office." Another of Turnbull's senior managers once remarked, "George will take a decision, and then he will go." Once he had reached a decision about what the group needed, obtained approval for his strategic plan, and got his top management team into place, George Turnbull proceeded to go at a cracking pace.

CHAPTER

6

The Glory Days

"Over the next 2 years the Group needs to effect a major rationalization of its activities. As part of this process, 3 sets of objectives have been set — namely to improve our financial performance, to reallocate our resources so that we can be 'bigger, better in fewer businesses' and to improve the caliber of management thereby bringing about a change in management style and philosophy to one committed to management by objectives." (Extract from the 1986–88 Group Strategic Plan)

"The trick is to have the controls but make the strings from the center almost invisible," George Turnbull was quoted as saying. Few in the field would have agreed with his choice of words. For them, the strings put in place between 1986 and 1988 were only too visible, and sometimes pulled tight enough to choke them. Those years saw radical change finally implemented throughout Inchcape by Turnbull's team of whiz-kids, using the 1986–88 Group Strategic Plan as their blueprint.

It was not rocket science, merely the classic turnaround route beginning with reducing expenses and eliminating losses, then on to profit improvement and growth — first organically and then by acquisition. Under Turnbull, the first stages were accomplished with dizzying speed.

"A MAJOR RATIONALIZATION ..."

"It soon became very obvious to me that the group had activities all over the world that had very little relevance to one another that were the product of the 'entrepreneurial flair' of the old-style management."

"There is only one thing you must do and do urgently — fix it, sell it, or close it."

George Turnbull's words conveyed his attitude both toward the old Inchcape and the task in hand. For the former, he could see little of value that should be kept and so, for the latter, the goal would be to carry out a root and branch pruning operation. Turnbull had been preparing this during his period of apprenticeship, as Dale Butcher, then with the controllers' department, recalled: "We used to get loads of requests from George — for instance, 'Tell me how many companies are actually making money, and how many losing.' We did this huge exercise to get people in the field to tell us. First they had to tell us what companies they had got — cattle ranches and hotels here and there. We had about 180 companies out of which thirty or forty were making £100 million profit, and the rest losing £130 million. We had lots and lots of loss makers all over the place, so George could see if we got rid of them, there was a lot of earnings growth. That was the focal point of Inchcape's strategy, and the way forward then." For Butcher, a young man newly joined but who had glimpsed the old Inchcape, the contrast was "hugely exciting." Some of the older members were understandably less enthralled.

The same month that he finally took over in June 1986, Turnbull presented his plan for the future shape of Inchcape to the board. It was, he later recalled, "virtually a list of companies that should be kept and a list of companies that should be disposed of, and the reasons why. The board then had about six weeks to chew it over." His method of presentation was direct and virtually an ultimatum: "I want it approved."

The overall strategy behind this fourth list of disposals since 1979 was that Inchcape would get out of businesses where it had no hope of being a major player in world terms, and stay in those where it could. Over the next two years, the group got out of a number of activities that had once been at its core. One of these was port management, which it had successfully carried on in the Gulf States through its subsidiary, Gray Mackenzie. With rising oil prices, no home base, and the privatization of British ports, it was clear to George Turnbull that this no longer represented a profitable future. Over time, the group sold its fleet of ships in Bahrain and got out of the business altogether.

The strategy similarly dictated the sale of Inchcape's catering business, which had long serviced the Australian mining industry, and its aviation business. Even more controversial was the decision to speed up the sale of all Inchcape's property throughout the world, including the group's headquarters in the City, which was sold for £22 million. The shock of all this to most of the old Inchcape managers was tremendous.

Not all of them were negative, however. Macaskill recalled rationalizing the operations in North America. "We had a peanut factory in Holland — it was a principal supplier to Mars — but who knew about peanuts, for heaven's sake? We had a cold rolling mill in Montreal ... a rail ferry from Thunder Bay across Lake Superior ... a tool distribution company in Canada; we had this aviation unit, which did not really fit. I think I sold something like twenty-three companies and this sort of thing was a new experience for me, because I had been a builder ... but I saw the ultimate advantage of it, because the group developed a degree of focus."

"... Bigger and Better in Fewer Businesses"

As Sir David Orr recalled, from the start, both he and Turnbull "saw the need to identify big businesses and places where we wanted to concentrate, and not get bogged down in smaller things. There was no tradition of getting rid of poor performers; it was part of Kenneth's loyalty. We felt we should be more focused rather than wandering off over different things. We felt we were in some very good and some very poor businesses, but we didn't treat them differently. We thought we had better find out which were the good ones ... we all took part in this but George directed it, and Stacey put the polish and the numbers on it. We all joined in."

Stacey Ellis was also concerned to prepare the group to meet a perennial threat, the loss of principals. Always one of the hazards of a middleman such as Inchcape, the process was now being speeded up by the trend toward globalization. "Brand owners were starting to say, why should I allow another company to affect my brand in a territory, because if I am developing a brand on a world basis, I must control that brand. Therefore, the people we served were beginning to question if they needed us, and were we damaging them, since the guy in the territory runs it territorially, and the brand owner wants to build a global brand. Also, the territories were becoming more transparent with improvements in communications, and the second generation in these developing countries had been to business schools, got MBAs, and talked the same language as the brand owner.

"So Inchcape faced a problem, in my and George's mind, that we couldn't go on as we were with a myriad of businesses. First, because the

City doesn't understand it, and in that case you are at a discount; and second, we didn't have the arguments to persuade them. Life was changing and we had to become global. Therefore, we had to face a big sea change. What the hell were we to do?"

What Stacey and his planners had been doing was once more subjecting the Inchcape businesses to the good old BCG matrix, in order to assess their viability. "At one point we had about seventy businesses, and then we got them down to forty, and then we tackled them a bit harder, picking out the worst businesses and selling them off. Simultaneously, we continued the program of disposing of the property. We probably disposed of several hundred million pounds of businesses making very negligible returns, and put it into other businesses to build them up. So inevitably, the profits were going up because we had this money moving from non-performing to performing businesses."

As a result of this process, by 1986 the group had been reduced to ten core businesses that fitted Turnbull's criteria of having the capacity to influence results, and a predictable customer base. Then accounting for three-quarters of group profit, they were the shape of Inchcape's future.

Five of them — automotive distribution, business machines distribution, buying offices, insurance broking, and inspection and testing — were designated growth businesses, on which the energies of the management would be focused. Strategic investments were planned to encourage rapid growth in these activities. The other five, which inevitably became referred to as "the second division," were: general marketing and distribution, wines and spirits, tea and timber, and shipping agencies. These were to be allowed to grow organically in line with their own markets. The ten were highly publicized, appearing on the cover of the Annual Report as an equation of 5 + 5 = Greater Global Performance. This received much attention in the press, translated into the image of ten balls being juggled in the air.

One of the analysts who had been watching this process, observed that, "If you go back in history you will see that one of the great corporate PR ideas was to refer to ten balls in the air. They had an 'A' team and a 'B' team within the ten balls, and the 'B' team grew faster than the 'A' team. It was just classic."

BUSINESS STREAMS WIDEN

After this energetic bout of spring cleaning, Turnbull and his planners then turned their attention to the way the businesses were organized and run. Since 1984, Inchcape had been slowly moving toward a business stream organization that grouped businesses by activity. Stacey Ellis had introduced business streaming in Singapore; Charles Mackay would do the same in his Hong Kong-based territories. In fact, of the ten core businesses, all except marketing and distribution were streamed by definition, so it seemed a natural evolution to make following business streams the *modus operandi* throughout the group. However, since it was not viable to scrap the old system completely, the new organization was a mixed matrix comprising both business streams and the old geographical concept.

Not surprisingly, the overall effect could be confusing, and in some instances success depended on the responsible people enjoying a good working relationship — or more realistically from the manager's point of view, whichever one was nearer. For example, the responsibilities of the Hong Kong- and Singapore-based sector directors of Inchcape Pacific and Inchcape Berhad, with their geographical focus, cut across Derek Whittaker's group-wide functional responsibility for Motors. So a Motors manager in Hong Kong would report both to Charles Mackay as head of Inchcape Pacific Ltd. (IPL) and to Derek Whittaker as the London-based head of Motors. However, outsiders judged that the new organization gave the group a much sharper profile, seen as evolving in response to market needs. And they were the audience Inchcape had to please.

"Who are we? What do we do? What is the strategy?"
(Group planning document, 1987)

The — to Inchcape — revolutionary concept of planning, introduced following the advice of the CCG consultants in 1984, had not been a total success. This was because it had largely taken place in a vacuum. Members of the old planning action committee had gathered information during their travels to the outlying parts of the group, but once a decision about future strategy had been reached, the planners had simply announced their verdict to the operating managers. They then left them to understand the plan and be motivated (or not) as the case might be. This had left the managers with the distinct — and by no means unique — view that the corporate planners were arbitrary and negative, their only function being to knock on the head all the "brilliant ideas" suggested by those out in the field.

Under Stacey Ellis, the central planning function operated quite differently. In addition to the yearly exercise that covered the whole group, they decided to work through the core businesses one after another, putting each under a microscope to discover how it worked and achieve a real understanding of it. What was more, they would accomplish this by working closely with those in the field! Together, the optimistic scenario ran, they would collect and analyze the data, argue issues through, produce a draft document, and argue again until agreement was reached. On this basis, they hoped to reach informed judgments and develop a plan in partnership with the operating units. Harmony would reign over the group.

The value attached to participation from those in the field was emphasized by having the person in charge of the business stream present the plan to the board. This, it was anticipated, would result in greater motivation and enhanced authority for the plan from those who were to implement it. Once all the business streams had been investigated, the planners expected to have a sound idea of "the group raft" in all its dimensions. From this they would know which were the growth areas, and what were the limiting factors to growth in terms of money, people, markets, and so on. For the first time, they would be able to look at the group as a portfolio.

"DESPERATELY SEEKING SYNERGY"

As they worked through each of the core businesses the executive committee put in some "objective pegs" — growth potential, geographical risk, etc. The profile of the group obtained from these agreed criteria was to enable direct comparisons to be made between the businesses. The exercise would also enable the planners to spot any potential linkages or — another mantra that had crept into group vocabulary — "synergies" between the businesses. These could then be developed to make the whole greater than the sum of its parts; such linkages could be "the pot of gold at the end of the rainbow."

One of the earliest writers to use this concept was H. Igor Ansoff. Despite his erudition, he will probably be associated most with the familiar expression, "Two plus two equals five." As a later writer, John Kay noted, throughout the 1960s and 1970s, the main thrust of corporate strategy was to create a diversified business portfolio: either by seeking synergy between old and new businesses, or by using portfolio planning to justify unrelated diversification. By the early 1980s, evidence was piling up to suggest that unrelated diversification was not adding value and sometimes two plus two equals less than four. Conglomerates like Litton Industries went broke, and TRW and ITT slid out of fashion. The fashion changed abruptly, with terms like "stick to the knitting" and "core business" becoming common coinage. Then raiders like KKR and T. Boone Pickens shook up the U.S. corporate world and forced attention onto shareholder value. This gave an even stronger push toward the break-up of conglomerates. By the 1990s, the fashion in strategy had moved onto mission statements, which commonly encompassed corporate and business strategy — the "what" and the "how" rolled into one. And, simplicity and focus ruled.

Synergy might have appeared to be lost out in the noise, but as two recent business writers, Andrew Campbell and Michael Goold, observed: "Managers and academics are fascinated by synergy. It has become one of management's top priorities. It is a way of getting extra performance, creating new businesses, and making more profit from the existing situation. It is a logic that drives acquisitions and empire building. It is a glue that creates community out of disparate entities." Perhaps not surprisingly given such a build-up, they found that "synergy initiatives often fall short of management's expectations." Interestingly, they noted that although "when a synergy program founders, it is usually the business units that take the blame ... the true cause more often lies in the thinking of the corporate executives themselves."

Their overall message was that synergy is worth pursuing and the gains can sometimes be spectacularly worthwhile. However, they also cautioned against what they term "mental biases" and the flabby thinking that might follow. Too often, the sources of synergy and the potential downsides of any action are not thought through in a systemic way. Too often, the "mirage" of synergy becomes an excuse for rigor. They also make the important observation that because many organizations are complex and chaotic, synergies often work well without the presence of a "parent" — they emerge at a lower level.

At Inchcape, George Turnbull certainly seemed to be fascinated by the theory, so this particular mantra had a long run before finally being abandoned in favor of "empowerment" and "competencies." In a speech to delegates from the four service activities at a September 1989 conference, he focused on the advantages of exploiting synergy between their businesses: "In a stream of activities where we buy, ship, insure and test a range of products and know literally thousands of customers and suppliers, we could serve principals and clients more completely by co-ordinating some of our activities in different ways."

The search for synergy between the group's activities continued throughout Turnbull's time as leader. According to Stacey Ellis, the idea was seen as a useful vehicle to keep both Inchcape employees and outside observers happy. "George wanted to make progress in an orderly fashion and maintain the high level of morale he had achieved throughout the group. Therefore, an exercise was started to see what, if any, synergy existed between the ten business streams, not just the service activities. If such a linkage could be demonstrated, then this would keep the City at bay whilst we progressed with our strategy. George and I were doubtful if such synergy existed, and the last thing we wanted was to 'force' buying decisions in any part of the group ... George's idea was that if there is something there, let's do it. If not, the very exercise of doing it will bring the group closer together."

An article in *Inchcape World* in May 1991 reproduced Turnbull's speech and added: "The synergy idea has been gathering strength as the Group completes its transition into global business streams ... Although in its early days as a Group activity, synergy is spreading through Inchcape's businesses world wide and is beginning to generate additional revenue."

Future editions of *Inchcape World* reported on the progress managers were making in their search for opportunities to exploit synergies with other group companies, by highlighting stories in a box marked "Synergy." The box was highly appropriate since, ultimately, the implementation of the theory was to founder partly on the barriers standing between Inchcape managers from different businesses — who neither knew nor trusted each other. The secretive insurance world did not lend itself to trust within the stream itself, never mind with outsiders, so each business remained within its own box. The principals, too, did not always prove amenable to suggestions that, for example, they change shippers and use Inchcape boats to transport their goods. As Ellis observed, "The theory was good, but the practice was always more difficult."

But this lay in the future. In 1987, hopes of finding synergy were still strong, and outside consultants were used to carry out market studies of core growth businesses in the hope of identifying them. Booz Allen carried out a study of the European Business Machines market, with the active involvement of the Inchcape Pacific business machine managers. A corporate memo on the subject cited the aim of "getting value for money by gaining synergies, if the interests of the Group are taken into account in framing the terms of reference for the study."

A change in geographical emphasis was also in the pipeline. Just as Kenneth Inchcape had seen that India was no longer the focus,

Turnbull believed that Inchcape would have to start expanding more in Europe and the U.S., to lessen its dependence on its earnings from the East.

All this took place in the context of Ellis's wider aim of setting a rhythm for the group, a rhythm that was "How fast can we sensibly grow? If we grew too slowly, no-one would be very happy — the City wouldn't be happy. But if we set the pace too high, and it was out of kilter with the potential rhythm of the group, then that will only upset everyone. Therefore, we chose a rate — about 15–16% per annum, and into it was built a 3–4% inflation figure — so the underlying growth was about 12%. It doesn't sound very strenuous, but when you look at the City over twenty years, only about thirty companies have ever achieved it. So it was really quite challenging."

Extrapolating from this 12% growth target, Inchcape center used the May 1988 Management Conference, held in Bahrain, to announce the goal of reaching £200 million by 1991. The return on capital was set at 20%, which was required to produce the cash flow to fund the group's expansion. These targets were, as Stacey recalled, "very similar to a number of other companies we talked to." He and his team then began to examine the relative contribution each of the ten businesses could make toward reaching this target. Their conclusions would lead them into some tense tussles with the business heads about which activities should remain in the group portfolio.

"... CHANGES IN MANAGEMENT STYLE AND PHILOSOPHY"

"... no-one is running an independent, stand-alone activity ... If you want to live in an ivory castle, go and live on your own ..."

As the above demonstrates, in describing the management culture he wished to implement, George Turnbull did not mince his words. "We must adopt professional management to replace entrepreneurial management ... The group must operate as a team ... From now on, length of service or availability will simply not appear on the selection criteria for a senior post; skills in marketing and distribution and knowledge of financial controls certainly will."

To support the directors sent out into the regions to sort out the businesses, four new sector assistants were appointed. New people were also brought in to head the insurance and automotive operations, and other specialist appointments were made. The senior management in the

Middle East was strengthened, as was the planning function in all the major SBUs. People came and went at a rapid rate.

At the center, Bob Goodall and his personnel team were equally busy recruiting new personnel managers to set up departments in all the group's main subsidiaries. Goodall then set out a complete statement of what he saw as the human resource needs of Inchcape, and what should be the prime objectives of the group personnel function. This was endorsed by the board and then sent out to all the chief executives. The main thrust of the document was that Inchcape needed "a change in the culture and strength of its management."

John Duncan described one of the key differences between the old and new cultures. "When I joined Inchcape in 1986, all the office doors down the corridor were kept firmly closed. There was a nameplate on each door with full title, and everyone was formal both in manners and dress. I remember Bob, Rod, and me meeting in an office in the early days and we said, 'How are we going to play this? What sort of culture do we want?' And we decided it would be shirt sleeves and first names — friendly, informal, but immensely professional. We all traveled a lot to spread the new culture, the new type of Inchcape person. Professional but relaxed. That was the '80s' Inchcape."

As Goodall quickly realized, the horizons of the Inchcape personnel were extremely limited, reflecting the way the group had evolved. They thought of themselves as Dodwell men who were loyal to the Dodwell name and traditions, or as Mann Egerton men, part of the clannish automobile world. They never thought of themselves as Inchcape employees. But with the group moving toward a business stream organization, this local focus clearly had to be replaced by one that was both international and mobile. Besides an expertise in the products in which they dealt, the new business stream managers would need to have an understanding of different markets and cultures and be able to work both with each other and, most difficult of all, with the center.

The personnel team first introduced a performance-based reward system, to ensure that every manager had a set of key objectives, consistent and contributory to the objectives of the SBU in which they worked. In this they tried to ensure that those objectives were broader than short-term profit. Managers were then to be appraised annually and rewarded against these objectives, both in terms of bonus and their career progression. Each manager's performance was to be measured against two things: specific financial measures directly related to the budget, and up to five broader and more qualitative objectives. Part of Inchcape's problem in attracting high-caliber staff had been its reputation as a poor paymaster — the honor of working for the group had been thought to make up for any shortfall in cash terms. This was corrected.

A more adventurous move was the setting up of management training programs at group level. By allowing its managers to meet in a neutral place away from their own companies, it was hoped to break down some of the barriers and give them a real sense of belonging to a multinational group. In a bid to encourage a more international outlook, the INSEAD Euro-Asia Centre in Fontainebleau was chosen as the venue. To help new Inchcape managers understand where the group was coming from, and reinforce the message of why the current emphasis on financial control and professionalism was necessary, Professor Philippe Lasserre orchestratd the writing of a set of cases that laid out Inchcape's past history.

As Bob Goodall recalled, "This was the first time we had embarked as a group on a management training program of that nature. The group had sent people, the high-potential ones, singly to Harvard and the like, but there had been no attempt at middle management, and we decided to correct this. We decided at the outset that we wanted to focus on Asians; we wanted to give a message to pay attention to managers other than expatriates. We looked at Asia but could not find a provider that met our needs. INSEAD had the Euro-Asia Centre; we happened to be a founder member, though we never used it. Because they were looking for business, they were very flexible and cost-effective ... It was paramount that we did not want the business school provider to be in the U.K." Later, the Inchcape *caravanserai* moved on to the Ashridge Management College in the U.K.

Another device was to move people around the group to demonstrate that opportunities for international development did exist, and to reinforce the point that mobility and experience of different countries and cultures would be expected of those wishing to advance in the future. Again, this was a Turnbull hobbyhorse. He was eager to broaden the group's management base through the promotion of local people to senior positions in the regions, so he wanted to attract local talent to work for Inchcape, give them international experience, and get them into top positions in their own territories.

These changes in remuneration, training, and career development were generally well received, and had a considerable impact on the caliber and average age of the group's senior management. Young, local managers were particularly enthusiastic about the change to a performance-oriented, more demanding culture. The older expatriate managers who could not adapt largely voted with their feet, though pockets of resistance to the new regime remained for some time to come.

POACHERS OR GAMEKEEPERS?

Meanwhile, Rod O'Donoghue was working on the all-important finance function. Having created central functions for treasury, tax and information systems, he, too, decided to concentrate on demolishing the walls between field and center. Unlike his predecessor, Rod O'Donoghue tried to give a clear lead to his managers, travelling the group and enjoying a high profile as an approachable figure. However, the Inchcape managers were not to be fooled; they realized early on that whatever happened would cause them pain.

His first move, to replace the old sector assistants by sector controllers, was viewed with a great deal of nervousness, and for a long while their role was mistrusted and misunderstood by the Inchcape management. However, though based in London, they spent a lot of time traveling and working in the field so that, over time, they did become familiar figures. After six months or so, the controllers came to be seen as both challengers and supporters, working with and on behalf of those in the field. They were instrumental in drawing the center and the field closer together in understanding; they could give a true picture of what was happening and at the same time, the theory went, ensure that the center was aware of the issues those in the field wished to discuss. In this way, it was hoped to avoid any more unwelcome surprises.

Another safeguard was the imposition of a new treasury function. Previously there had been no coordinated approach to cash management — to his horror, O'Donoghue had found that money was being borrowed from 150 different banks across the group. A centralized cash management process was set up in all the group's major monetary centers, beginning with the U.K. and going on to cover Singapore, Hong Kong, the U.S., and Australia. At the same time, he decided to regionalize the group's currency exposure. The units had previously managed this, sometimes with hazardous results. As a result, the group's exposure in currencies was managed out of two regional centers (London and Hong Kong).

Another innovation was the treasury management committee, which met monthly and brought together the treasury and tax people at the center to look at the group's worldwide position. It received a structured set of information concerning currency exposure and banking positions, and it ensured that no-one in the field could create a relationship with a bank without approval from the center.

At a Finance Workshop held during the 1988 Bahrain conference, O'Donoghue distributed a paper outlining his ideas about the future financial structure of the group. The paper was discussed in an open forum, and by the end of the meeting, O'Donoghue felt that "we knew what we were trying to do." The distribution of such a paper became an annual event, comparing what the group said it would do with what it actually achieved. In theory, at least, those in the field could measure the performance of the center as readily as the chairman could. There is no record of how many people took advantage of this.

ROBA REVISITED

Under the new leadership, a minimum 18% ROBA target was finally achieved, though O'Donoghue believed that to have a flat rate across the group was not ideal given the very different characteristics of the businesses. The process of setting the rate was refined for each territory to take into account inflation rate, tax, etc., but it remained difficult to make allowances for the relative risk, political or economic, associated with a given region. And the innovative Inchcape managers, who objected strongly to the new concept of teamwork and sharing when it came to cash, still found ways of keeping their profits out of the clutches of the mercenaries at the center. Blocked at one end, entrepreneurialism found another outlet.

AN INFORMATION STRUCTURE TO HELP US

The information structure and the data on which those at the center focus turned out to be another Achilles heel for Inchcape. To gain a balance between data creation and data use, and not to focus on collection at the expense of analysis and use of the information, was always difficult for the group to achieve. A further difficulty was how to ensure that the right sort of information was collected.

In fact, as many other companies discovered, getting the information technology function right could prove to be a bottomless pit into which the promise was always that "the next system, the next update, will be what we want." The first information systems strategy, developed in 1987, with the objective of giving the group common systems solutions for common business needs, was based on assumptions about the existence of synergies. Unfortunately, the first attempts ended in technical and logistical disaster, culminating with the replacement of the initial information systems director after eighteen months. For Inchcape, this was to be a home-grown failure for several years to come. Despite promises at every conference, central resources and central control proved inadequate to achieve even a group-wide e-mail system until the mid-1990s. There was a distinct element of *Schadenfreude* in the field's view of this failure.

The information collected was the raw material for a series of committee meetings at the center, aimed to keep close tabs on what was happening, and avoid any old Inchcape-style nasty surprises. The most important was the monthly executive committee, which looked at the group's results and at those decisions (in particular, capital) that had to go through that committee before going before the board.

Sector briefings were held weekly to communicate matters of importance and "anything that has happened in the world that week" that might affect the Inchcape businesses. Afterwards, the sector controllers reported back to their directors based in the regions.

Quarterly reviews were conducted by the chairman, Rod O'Donoghue, Stacey Ellis, the relevant sector controller, and the group controller. They were an attempt to drive performance and keep a finger on the key issues facing the group across the world. During them, each of the chief executives, supported by their chief finance officer and perhaps one other executive, reported on their operations. This meeting was meant to be a forum for debate about key issues, risks, and opportunities to ensure that field and center were talking about the important things, rather than a court presiding over the trial where the chief executive was the defendant. However, few chief executives felt that this was actually the case.

Yet, in support of the theory that companies have their own genetic code, despite all these precautions Inchcape experienced a mini-crisis in Australia during this period. The problem, involving Inchcape's Business Machine activity, was one of wrong pricing in the marketplace and a newly established management. Although the center was receiving post-acquisition updates and monitoring the situation via the responsible sector controller, its reactions were far slower than they should have been, and in retrospect it was recognized that serious mistakes were made in handling the situation. The episode sounded a strong warning that the controls were still not 100% foolproof.

Burnishing the Image

Under John Duncan, the corporate affairs department played a major role in selling the new, risk-free, focused Inchcape to the City analysts and the stock-buying public.

In dealing with the City, the major objective was to raise confidence in the group's future prospects and belief in its sustained revival, and thus improve the rating of the group's shares. Among the analysts and business press at this time there was, Duncan recalled, "A fair degree of ignorance and not a lot of understanding of Inchcape. The general view was that the group didn't make sense and that it had been badly managed. That it had gone from one disaster to another and was a potential takeover target." One quote, he recalled, spoke of "100 businesses in 100 countries." To remedy the lack of market makers was one of his first tasks. "We had to get enough brokers in to make a market for our shares, and for this we got a lot of help from Capels. George, Rod, and I met them. At the time we were a Beta stock; we wanted to become Alpha."

With the active support of George Turnbull and Rod O'Donoghue, the department implemented "an exercise, aimed at marketing the Inchcape capital base." The eventual aim, written into the group's strategic plan, was "to see the Group's shares rated at a par or at a premium with the *Financial Times* Industrial Index." Turnbull's ultimate ambition was to propel Inchcape into the FTSE-100.

A big effort was implemented to improve the group's relations with the media and improve the group's image. "What we had to do was explain the reality," John Duncan recalled. "The perception was out of kilter. The objective was to get a level playing field and stress the quality of the management and the quality of the businesses. The first was clear, but it was always difficult to achieve the second. We tried like hell to convince them that the businesses had quality, but they always insisted that we were in the hands of our principals who could take them away, and they always focused on Toyota, though, funnily enough, we were safest with Toyota. But the fact that we didn't control our own destiny was always seen as a problem. Yet we were in high-growth markets, like the Far East and Southeast Asia. It was very difficult, but George Turnbull set out his strategy of first- and second-division businesses. Then we had to get the message across to the marketplace." The star here was George Turnbull, who carried out an exhaustive program of interviews, briefings, and lunches to obtain the widest possible coverage for the group in the press.

Using an old contact at *The Sunday Times*, Duncan sold the idea of a story on Inchcape. He promised an exclusive interview with George Turnbull, since no profile had been previously done. On the Friday night before the profile was published, Duncan sat down with the journalist in her office at Wapping and watched the screen as the story was put together. "It was vitally important to get it right." The story, headed "New tricks give bite to an old dog," came out on February 8, 1987, headed by a picture of Turnbull and O'Donoghue in front of the Lloyd's building. The result, Duncan noted, was immediate. "Bob Goodall was recruiting then, and the headhunters said it had made their job easier. There were compli-mentary letters from the banks, and a very good response from the staff."

Unfortunately, the same newspaper dealt a blow to the group two years later when the timber business fell foul of the paper's "Insight" team, hot on the trail of environmental enemies. An emotive article entitled "Log'em and leave'em" could have been damaging, but, a sign of the new Inchcape, Duncan's department was well prepared to meet and refute the accusations fully. On the other hand, the comment by one manager that the article did not do too much damage (compared, say, with Nestlé's powdered milk experience) because no-one had really heard of Inchcape, seemed rather back-handed, given the intense efforts to raise recognition of the name.

Despite this hiccup, by 1987 Inchcape had become a growth stock, basking in the good opinion of the City and the business media. "Turnbull turns it round" was the headline of the July edition of *The Financial Weekly*. The largely admiring profile described how "the generalship of George Turnbull has slimmed down this sprawling conglomerate ... and produced spectacular profits growth ... Inchcape was back from the dead, having completed one of the most dramatic and rapid corporate rehabilitations the City has seen for years." Even the crash of October 1987, though it brought the group problems in Hong Kong and in its Motors operations, caused only a ripple in the relationship. This, believed Duncan, was because "we told our audiences, 'Look at the quality of the management, the strategy makes sense, our finances are strong, turnover is increasing.' We were going well, and could repeat that performance as we were in growth markets."

The 1986 results were the first of a series of triumphant announcements and, as time went on, Duncan and his team got better at communications with the business world. "We were very open. We knew the people we were talking to, the journalists and analysts, and even the fund managers." Previously, relations with fund managers had been handled by brokers, but the confident Inchcape now brought in a specialist investor relations manager to deal with them directly. All the main Inchcape performers received media training and were equipped with a "bible" of questions and answers covering every issue likely to be raised in interviews. These managers would, literally, be singing from the same hymn sheet.

Trend data produced by MORI for Inchcape on the six factors that investors and analysts considered most important in evaluating companies demonstrated how far Inchcape had come. By the fall of 1987, Inchcape had a 49% increase in the perception of quality of management among analysts, and 26% among investors. On average, both City groups showed substantial improvements in their image of Inchcape, with institutional investors improving their ratings by six points and analysts by seventeen points. When Turnbull began his work at Inchcape, only a handful of analysts followed the group. By the time he stepped down, there were between fifteen and twenty of them. However, as Duncan observed, "They still got the name wrong, spelling it 'Inchape'."

Duncan's team also spent a lot of time improving communications with Inchcape employees across the group. Duncan revamped the old Inchcape journal, which had featured old photographs of nineteenth-century Inchcape pioneers, bringing out *Inchcape World*, a three-times-a-year magazine carrying articles on present-day employees throughout the world. Video reports were produced for internal and external consumption. Distributed to the regions three times a year, they brought everyone up to date on what was happening, and increased awareness of the group's activities. At first, the self-consciousness and awkward body movements of the executives in front of the cameras made them rather an amateur affair, but as time went on, some of them began to look more comfortable, and even to enjoy their taste of stardom.

In retrospect, John Duncan felt that "during the five or six years after 1986, there was trust between us and the analysts. These were the good times." This was because, "During George Turnbull's time, we told it like it was. We never over-egged it, and we worked hard on explaining what was happening." However, he conceded that, "We persuaded them that we were much more focused than we really were. We sold them the three parts — motors, marketing, and services — but really we were still a ragbag. However hard we tried, it was true that there was not a lot of sense to it. We had tea and timber; both very cyclical businesses, so getting steady growth was always going to be difficult. In Southeast Asia we were Dyno Rod, cleaning drains. In Thailand we had an army of Mrs Mops — teachers who would clean offices at night. We had cattle in Papua New Guinea, where we virtually ran the town." Duncan and his team had successfully covered over the gap between the perception and reality in the short term, but as he and some of the others knew, it was still there, threatening to re-emerge during less favorable economic times.

THE RESULTS

"The market loves you if you bring in year-on-year steady growth. It doesn't like surprises." (John Duncan *et al.*)

Under Turnbull's leadership, between 1986 and 1989 Inchcape delivered dream results. Nineteen eighty-six saw a dramatic increase in profits before taxation to £86.1 million (up from £46.2 million in 1985) and the first dividend increase in ten years. Despite some sober voices who pointed out that, in real terms, this result was still some way short of the 1977 figure, the City as a whole reacted with enthusiasm and lavished praise on the magician who had worked a miracle.

John Duncan remembered the dramatic delivery of the first set of results. "We were crammed into the boardroom at St. Mary Axe. It was full of analysts and journalists, and we had a screen at one end of the table for slides — so old-fashioned compared with today. And we made up a board that said '£86 million — up 86% in '86.' It was a great feeling." One very bullish analyst, Mike Smith, then with Chase Manhattan Securities, was quoted as saying, "There might be better places to put your money taking the short-term view, but most people [in the City] would be pretty positive about Inchcape in the longer term."

That was just the start. From then on, profits grew to £116.2 million in 1987, its share price outperforming the market by 36%, and the year after, a 27% rise in profits before tax to £147.7 million. Inchcape was suddenly fashionable. Gearing at the end of 1988 was down to 10%. One analyst called Turnbull "the shareholders' champion."

By February 1987 the share price had risen in twelve months from 303p to 560p. *Investor's Chronicle*, in June 1989, made Inchcape an "Eastern Promise" and one of its "tips of the week," noting that, "On a prospective PE ratio of under 10, the shares are inexpensive and well worth tucking away." In September 1988, Bob Carpenter at Kitcat & Aitken, a long-time follower of the group, recommended Inchcape shares as a "buy for re-rating and growth potential," since "the shares had consistently outperformed the market over the past two years." He noted that the price had moved ahead without a break, until the October 1987 crash. "In the aftermath, strong support came in at 130p ... the price moved up to around 180p and just when it looked to be flagging, the board announced a share split (each £1 share was split into four of 25p)." The next year he again recommended them as "a growth investment — buy for medium term potential."

Other analysts were equally enthusiastic. Hoare Govett's November 1988 summary observed that, "Recent price action has been disappointing, which is at odds with the group's strong growth potential. We regard the trading outlook as very positive, while the rating still fails to reflect fully the substantial changes at Inchcape. Buy and Long Term Positive." With perhaps greater insight, it noted that, "Valuing a company like Inchcape is difficult because it is unique." Bob Havard at James Capel rated Inchcape shares as A/1, along with another later fallen angel BTR, and Bowthorpe Holdings, Racal, and Guinness. He, too, commented that "Rating undervalues continuing strong growth. Buy." In September–October 1988, Morgan Stanley felt that the shares represented "good value," while Cazenove's research department concluded that, "There is enormous potential from the Group's Pacific Basin position, which offers the most attractive long term growth prospects." In fact, the enthusiasm among the analysts was such that, as one senior manager rather ruefully recalled, "it was impossible to control." The question was what did they mean by long term? Was it the same as that of the Inchcape center?

The business journalists also wrote flattering reviews: "Inchcape in the fast lane," "Inching ahead with Toyota," "Inchcape soaring," "Confident Inchcape," and, inevitably, "Inchcape keeps on motoring," were the headlines in April 1989. It was all too good to be true.

THE PERSPECTIVE FROM THE FIELD

From the results and external reactions, it might be inferred that George Turnbull's changes were greeted with enthusiasm by his troops in the field. But just as an improved GNP alone does not give a real indication of how a country's subjects view a new regime, so it was with the Inchcape management. According to Charles Mackay, sector director of Inchcape Pacific, the initial reactions were shock and suspicion, followed by the realization that, on the whole, the changes were "a good thing."

Overall, the promotion of local people in the regions had a tonic effect. Derek Whittaker frequently cited the success story of Alan Tan in Singapore. Promoted to the Inchcape Berhad board by David John, Tan "performed an outstanding success story" in turning round the Motors business there. In 1988, profits were up 32%, and under his management Borneo Motors achieved the Triple Crown, being number one in three separate market sectors for Toyota: passenger cars, commercial vehicles, and taxis.

However, the negative side of the changes tended to emerge forcefully during training programs at the Euro-Asia Centre, when the field managers were given the opportunity to discuss the changes and assess how they were working out in practice. As a result of the Turnbull treatment, managers out in the regions felt under tremendous pressure to perform, and so suffered greater stress. Subject to judgment, and given much harder targets to meet, they naturally missed the good old days when they were left more-or-less alone. The gradual acceleration in the timing for reports, from the fifteenth of the month to the tenth, with the eventual aim of getting it down to the seventh, was a constant lament. On the other hand, as Bob Goodall noticed, although the regular financial deadlines were kept, the far less arduous personnel requests for completed reports and information were not! The weight of the finance function had clearly made itself felt.

Information collection was another endemic cause for complaint; those in the field not always perceiving the necessity for the different types of information required, and regarding many of the central demands as a wasteful duplication of effort. The view of one senior executive in South America — "I am the best-paid clerk in the business. Quarterly reports ... monthly reports ... I write and I write and I manage nothing" — was shared by many of his colleagues.

Again, it was felt that the information flow was all one-way. While the central planners constantly made demands on the operating units, they paid little attention to the warnings or advice from the field when taking crucial decisions that would have important consequences for them. The logic of the center, they believed, did not always fit the local situation, and could get in the way of good business practice.

Furthermore, the emphasis on central control was leading to unnecessary duplication of effort, and too much emphasis on meeting targets that forced short-term tradeoffs. The controls gave rise to "blanket policies," which did not sufficiently differentiate between local conditions and the needs of the different activities.

Although most accepted that the old Inchcape — so decentralized as to be almost out of control — could not have continued, there was a feeling that the pendulum had swung too far the other way. While appreciating the achievements of George Turnbull and his team, there was a sense among some of the old hands that "*C'est magnifique, mais ce n'est pas l'Inchcape.*" In getting rid of some of the old evils so efficiently, had they thrown the baby out with the bathwater? The clearance of the old businesses had not been followed by the introduction of new, profitable activities, and a frequent question asked of the central planners who visited the seminars was: "Where will the growth of the future come from?"

This point was often linked to the dreaded "E-word" that George Turnbull had banished from the vocabulary of his managers. The entrepreneurial spirit that had characterized the old Inchcape, they argued, had had value. Granted that there was an urgent need to restrain the entrepreneurial excesses of the old days, and cut out the "seat of the pants" stuff, but was the result an environment that discouraged risk-taking completely? And wasn't risk-taking an intrinsic part of an overseas trading group, which was what Inchcape basically remained?

The central representatives were quick to refute such accusations. One of the senior men said, "George is very willing to step into the unknown as long as he thinks the story is worth reading and the book is worth getting to the end of ..." They maintained that they did indeed "try to get their minds round risk and opportunity" — but then, muttered the cynics, they *would* say that, wouldn't they?

Moreover, despite the efforts of the center to travel and talk to the troops, tensions and resentments remained. Among the older generation it was felt that by clearing out the old central management wholesale, the group had torn up roots which could still have made a valid contribution in terms of expertise and continuity. "Today's senior managers," observed one old hand, "spend a great deal of time trying to forge relationships and open doors which would have been instantly accessible ten years ago." They also resented the tendency of the relative newcomers to see themselves as white knights charging to rescue the apparently total incompetents of the old Inchcape.

After all, the new Inchcape's debt to its past was considerable, and the group's prosperity under Turnbull was largely built on the strength of acquisitions made by the old leadership. In a conservative business like shipping, it was the old-established reputation of Gray Mackenzie that still brought in the business in the Middle East. Longstanding loyalties like this remained important to the new Inchcape, plus the group's other traditional strengths; its global coverage, and its reputation for integrity and honest dealing. All the new management had done was manage better the strengths that the group already had.

While there was general agreement that the videos and other central efforts to communicate had been excellent, the experiment of having field-based sector directors was not voted an unqualified success. The overstretched sector directors seemed to spend most of their time flying between London and their areas of responsibility. Rather than an aid to better communication, some operating managers felt that the regional headquarters had become an effective screen between themselves and London head office, able to filter out the rays broadcast from the central sun and manipulate the information flow.

But overall, their verdict was that the new, streamlined Inchcape had a much-needed sense of direction, and there was general approval of the clearer objectives that were given, the emphasis on teamwork, and the professional approach. Managers knew what was expected of them, were better motivated, and felt confident about the future. Perhaps most important for many, though not all, was the fact that they received much better incentives and remuneration.

Turnbull's stick-and-carrot approach, then, seemed to have worked. Now a performance-driven company, the rewards were there to be taken, and the systems were in place to drive them to that reward.

GLORY DAYS

By 1989, George Turnbull could justly pride himself on a job well done. Inchcape was once more experiencing a period of glory. The "A" team businesses had been expanded through acquisition to the tune of approximately £100 million, though this sum was broadly in balance with the sum raised by disposals. Of these core businesses, Motors, the backbone of the group and of course George's particular specialty, had enjoyed spectacular success, though this performance had to be put in the context of an unprecedented expansion of the car market which created conditions from which all motor manufacturers benefited.

Inchcape's relationship with Toyota was now in excellent repair, due to the successful performance of the businesses. The new Greek Toyota franchise, for example, acquired in 1986 when it had only 3.5% market share, had grown to a 16.5% share by 1989. Under Derek Whittaker, the group also developed well-publicized plans for exploiting Europe's single market, due to open for business in 1992. In preparation, Whittaker went on a spending spree, buying up several U.K. and continental dealerships covering BMW, Ford, Renault, and Mercedes-Benz.

Not to be left behind, Inspection and Testing acquired ETL, a U.S. business, and Bondar Clegg. However, the most important buy was an insurance broking business, Clarkson Puckle. Merged with Bain Dawes, the new company, Bain Clarkson, became number three in the U.K. and the twelfth-largest insurance broker in the world. From Bain Clarkson, the group hoped for substantial growth, but as time would show, the move actually entrenched Inchcape in a business that it did not know well and that was about to change rapidly, and not to Inchcape's advantage. As Insurance experienced "a difficult period" due to a downturn in the market, Inspection and Testing, too, suffered a setback in Venezuela. Buying Services was in the midst of a prolonged recession from which it would never recover, and Business Machines had endured the Australian losses and subsequent reconstruction.

Ironically, the five "natural growth" businesses had grown at a faster rate than had their more favored brothers. Some of them had also been enlarged, Inchcape Pacific Ltd. (IPL) acquiring Hutchison Whampoa's marketing and distribution and shipping businesses in November 1989 for £56.5 million. This situation implied a re-think by the center planners, once they had completed their review of each individual business stream. A slight warning note was struck by *The Daily Telegraph*, which noted in April 1988 that, "Turnbull has yet to show he can move from recovery to growth ... Excellent though they are, the overall figures for the year to December owe a great deal to loss elimination and tightening up on cash management. These are the easy parts."

However, such carping was forgotten in the celebrations that greeted the news that in the Queen's "New Year Honours List" of December 30, 1989, George Turnbull received a knighthood. Sir George Turnbull resumed business in the New Year with sleeves rolled up, confident that he was ready to tackle the next phase of Inchcape's turnaround.

"Like Speaking a Swiss Language"

Sir George Turnbull had a firm
Which had not reached its peak.
He sent us all to Fontainebleau
To sharpen our technique ...

T he annual invasion of the Inchcape boys (very few girls ever made the trip) for the management training programs that took place at the INSEAD Euro-Asia Centre (EAC) every summer between 1987 and 1994 was always a highlight for the Center's administrative staff and its faculty. Enthusiastic, friendly, always ready to crack a joke, and hard-working in a laidback sort of way, the Inchcape crew guaranteed that the next two or four weeks, the length depending on whether the program was for general or advanced managers, would be action-packed.

Among the good burghers of Fontainebleau, the arrival of the Inchcape crew was the signal for careful citizens to lock up their daughters to remove them from the dangerous sphere of the Motors men. The restaurant and cafe owners put out extra tables and chairs on the pavement, and prepared to stay open until the small hours.

Sessions ran from 8.30 a.m. to 5.30 p.m. every day — though they often overran. On several evenings, VIPs from the center flew in to give a presentation and answer questions put by participants. Often they would stay for dinner and be drawn into the amusements on offer. The daily sessions involved a great deal of reading preparation — *too much*, was the frequent complaint — but the Inchcape managers, even those whose first language was not English, seemed to thrive on the challenge.

The program was coordinated by Professor Philippe Lasserre, whose facial resemblance to the well-loved British actor Alistair Sim and generous hospitality made him a firm favorite. In temperament stereotypically French, his excited gestures as he dissected the Inchcape strategy always guaranteed a lively session.

The program offered relief from the stresses of the real world, and a chance to meet colleagues from other businesses and countries, and to learn new techniques and jargon they could take back with them. All of them returned to the office with bulging files of notes and presentations, though how much of what they learned was of active use later was difficult to track.

That the programs were considered valuable by the Inchcape center was demonstrated by the special board workshop that took place in 1990. It was attended — reluctantly by some members, who were not impressed by this new-fangled business school mumbo-jumbo — by all the Inchcape board. But with George Turnbull a keen supporter of executive education, no-one was allowed to escape. Moreover, although these respected members stayed at the decidedly up-market Aigle Noir Hotel, they demonstrated a similar ability to enjoy themselves. Staying up in the bar drinking whisky until very late was one of George Turnbull's favorite relaxations, as John Duncan recalled. The search for the Inchcape culture should perhaps have begun and ended there.

Of all the modules taught, the most popular, and the one that consistently achieved high ratings in the post-seminar evaluation, was the two days conducted by Andre Laurent, Professor of Organizational Behavior at INSEAD. Laurent had spent many years researching into cross-cultural issues and had encountered managers from multinational companies throughout Europe and the U.S. However, long after any detailed memory of the faces passing through had vanished, his abiding impression of the Inchcape managers was that "They were never dull."

In the early years this was a gross understatement, as the sessions became virtually a battleground in which representatives of the old and new Inchcape, of businesses that were clearly rising stars and those that feared they were shortly for the chop, fought a fierce and often highly emotional verbal duel over the changes taking place. Later, as the old guard died out and the participants grew more homogeneous in training and outlook, the sessions focused on what sort of group Inchcape had become. Visitors from the centre were often shocked at the vehemence of the feelings expressed, and went away with much to chew over, given a rare chance to see how others saw them.

The question that invariably ignited the groups concerned corporate culture. Did the group have one? If so, what was it? Participants often arrived at the Euro-Asia Centre having given little thought to this subject. By the time they left, as their final presentations showed, it had become a central focus for all their thoughts and concerns about the group's future.

WHY A CORPORATE CULTURE?

In the 1980s it was almost *de rigueur* for companies to claim possession of their own corporate culture. By this was meant an organizational self-image that reflected a company's prevailing attitudes with regard to what it could and could not become, which values were important to it and which were not, and which behaviors were acceptable to it and which were not. Much research into the subject of organizational culture focused on measuring how employees saw their own organization — for example, did they believe that it promoted teamwork and trust, rewarded entrepreneurialism, or stifled initiative. Inchape, being such a diverse company both in terms of businesses and people working in it, was a paradise for such researchers.

According to theory, the culture sets the tone of a company both internally and externally, affecting both the spirits of its personnel and its relationship with the outside world of analysts and investors. Organizations were thus seen to have personalities and so, like their human members, could be flexible, conservative, innovative, or anachronistic.

Cultures could also be described as thick or thin; the former characterized by the existence of many shared assumptions and the latter fewer, implying that it would have a weaker influence on organizational life. A strong organizational culture gave employees a clear understanding of "how we do things" and was seen as desirable. However, as one of the best-known writers on organizational culture, Edgar Schein of the Massachusetts Institute of Technology, pointed out, "The dilemma is that we don't know what we are hunting for." This comment could have been the mantra of the Inchcape managers.

Schein concluded that the content of an organizational culture was primarily derived from two sources: the prior assumptions that founders, leaders, and employees brought with them when they joined the organization (which in turn depended on the culture of the national, religious, ethnic, etc., communities they came from); and their learning experiences within the organization. The notion of ongoing learning implied that culture was subject to development and change, but since values are not quickly changed, such changes would be "incremental and evolutionary rather than radical and revolutionary." Schein also believed that leaders played a key role in maintaining and transmitting culture, their signals being transmitted via mechanisms such as how they reacted to crises, who they recruited, promoted, and demoted, and so on.

The advent of globalization led to an offshoot based on research into cross-cultural organizational behavior; the study of multicultural issues arising when managers from different cultures work together. Prominent here has been the work of Geert Hofstede and Fons Trompenaars, both of whom compiled rich databases in order to examine the topic. Hofstede concentrated on identifying the factors on which nations appeared to differ consistently, while Trompenaars investigated the impact of cultural differences on doing business and managing. Of practical interest for companies involved in globalizing their operations, and so employing people whose fundamental cultural assumptions might clash with those underlying the parent company's values, was to discover how an organization could coordinate a multicultural workforce through creating a "strong" organizational culture.

For Inchcape, the issue of cross-cultural competence — or incompetence — was an important one, especially given the strong British culture associated with its founder and subsequent generations of managers. Cross-cultural issues and organizational change were areas in which Andre Laurent specialized, and he found an abundance of rich material arising from his sessions with Inchcape.

As ever, the theory of organizational culture first took practical shape in the U.S., where it became the mode for successful chief executives to give interviews in which they earnestly, and sometimes reverentially, ascribed their commercial achievements to their strong corporate culture. Inevitably, a corporate culture became marketed as yet another "got to have." It could take different forms; be proclaimed through a lengthy mission statement in the Annual Report or be a short, catchy slogan employees could recite like a mantra, while even claiming *not* to have one could be taken as a statement of intent. Whatever type, the corporate culture was seen as something that, properly managed, could give the company that vital competitive edge.

The cultivation of a corporate culture was associated with that other mantra, strategic focus, considered equally necessary for success in the marketplace. The importance attached to this even led some U.S. companies to hire anthropologists to help develop the right type of culture, which, generally speaking, was a marketing culture. This meant a company becoming more marketing-driven; studying the needs of its customers and then positioning its goods or services to meet those needs in a way that positively differentiated company "X" from the rest of the field.

With focus already at the heart of its strategy, a corporate culture had a clear appeal to Inchcape. In its climb from the slough of despond into which it had fallen by the early 1980s, one of Turnbull's key objectives had been to effect a change of culture. It was also an issue with important implications for the future, both for the motivation of Inchcape's personnel and for relationships with its customers and principals. It also related to the group's acquisition strategy, since research had shown that when a carefully planned merger failed to produce the expected synergies, one of the most common reasons for that failure was a clash of cultures. The more the Inchcape managers delved into the subject, the more controversial it became. Since cultures are firmly rooted in the past, the argument inevitably began there.

THE GREEN AND THE BLUE

If the culture of an organization reflects behavior patterns developed on the basis of what worked well in the past, then clearly the old Inchcape mindset was entrepreneurial and incurably independent. It was what Laurent had christened a green or "being" organization, in which the tasks were the excuse for developing relationships, and people were defined by who they were and by their affiliation. In the case of Inchcape, this meant by being Scottish and products of the same school and regiment.

This culture reflected the beliefs and values of the group's founder, the Third Earl of Inchcape. He prized integrity and company loyalty, and was proud of Inchcape's reputation as an honest trader. He was the dominant force through the successful growth years of the 1960s and early 1970s.

By the end of the 1970s, however, this mindset of "the venerable Inchcape" was no longer appropriate to the changed business environment, and a different culture was needed. This was to be provided by George Turnbull, in order to turn the group into a modern, international company. To do this, he had to initiate a complete change in the outlook of the group's management.

Consequently, the objective of the new leadership was to replace the green culture of the old Inchcape by what Laurent described as a blue or "doing" culture, associated with some of the most successful competitors of the decade. A blue culture was more aggressive in character, the emphasis being on achievement. In this type of culture, relationships — which were instrumental to the task — were marked by a degree of competition between individuals, with performances evaluated and measured against strict standards. Under Turnbull, the new Inchcape culture was characterized by task-oriented teamwork instead of individualism, and control instead of autonomy.

The field perception of this new, blue Inchcape was of a finance-driven, bureaucratic, and risk-averse organization, and the changes associated with its advent — rationalization, strict financial controls, and new management systems — caused considerable anguish. The changed role of the center was much resented, as they made clear during the sessions. The center they characterized as a traffic light permanently on red, restricting their freedom of maneuver and presiding over an internal competition for scarce financial resources that left them frustrated. The legacy of independent action, and the negative impressions associated with the new culture, were the most difficult obstacles for the post-1986 management to overcome.

The early changes at Inchcape followed the classic pattern (a contemporary example was Chrysler under Iacocca) being precipitated at a time of crisis and associated with the advent of a strong leader, "the right man at the right time," leading from the top. According to the authorized version, the cultural change should then have gone on to gain critical mass and, finally, the momentum to involve the whole company in a sustained effort lasting for a considerable period. The final result should have been a culture that cemented the organization together and enabled its component parts to work in a gloriously harmonious and integrated effort.

However, this classic pattern is usually associated with monolithic organizations, where the imposition of a common culture from the center is relatively easy. Even then, the change is neither quickly nor easily achieved. Apart from a natural resistance to change, other barriers can make it a lengthy process, and it may require a considerable investment of time and resources to accomplish.

Inchcape plc did not fit into this simple mould. The federalist character of the old Inchcape meant that, until the late 1980s, the name "Inchcape plc" had been just a convenient umbrella. Because of its history, Inchcape plc was an organization made up of distinct local groups lacking any sense of an overall corporate identity. Their loyalty and cultural roots lay in the entities that made up Inchcape plc, rather than in the parent body. In Chile, for example, Inchcape personnel focused on Williamson Balfour; a name which, as Sergio Mardones later wrote, "has extraordinary value in Chile, and gave us the image of a solid, prestigious company with a long presence in the country." Historically, both personnel and customers identified with these old company names, and even after 1986, many remained unaware of belonging to a larger group on a worldwide basis; indeed, some, like those who joined as a result of the TKM acquisition in 1992, remained positively hostile to any such notion. Alan Reed, manager of Mann Egerton Jaguar, recalled how even at a conference held six years later, one speaker clearly thought of himself in terms of the TKM company, Wadham Kenning, while "another person at the dinner table said, 'I've been with this company for nineteen years,' and again, he was thinking of Wadham Kenning." How to bring them together or establish any common corporate identity would be, therefore, a major challenge even under normal circum-stances. To change a long-established identity was a still greater one.

This was immediately apparent whenever those at the center tried to examine reception of the changes they had implemented, and to judge how far they had succeeded in changing minds and hearts. Despite consistent efforts to get the message across that there was now a new Inchcape, they found it almost impossible to know how far down the organization change had reached. The map of where they were going was clear to them, but were they taking the rest of the organization with them? Was any remaining resistance substantial, or was the new culture winning acceptance? The messages from the EAC programs were one important way of finding out.

A WARM RECEPTION

A cultural change that requires a challenge to long-held behavior patterns, or the disruption of former assumptions or positions, will almost inevitably cause confusion and loss of morale. If there is a company-wide perception that change is necessary and that there is no alternative, then this motivation can make the transition smoother. In the case of Inchcape, the disparate spread of its interests and the poor channels of communication meant that the perception of an urgent need for drastic change that existed at headquarters was by no means apparent to those out in the field. This lack of understanding clearly made the acceptance of the new management and culture harder for some than for others. As one old hand described the impact of the new management, "It was like being taken over without being actually acquired."

Accordingly, instead of acting as the glue that binds everything together, the effect of the new culture was rather to cause a rift in the organization. This was an early reaction among the field managers, and the gulf between themselves and the center was made sharper by the new breed of senior managers at headquarters; all finance trained, with a common vocabulary and attitude toward business practice. What was this new Inchcape? What had they, the old managers, been doing wrong?

Thus, the immediate result was not one new Inchcape, but an organization with two cultures. To some extent the situation was eased by the retirement of many old hands, who were duly replaced by managers more receptive to the new ideas. However, the center did not want a mass exodus of all its field management, whose expertise and experience was still needed. Not unnaturally, those remaining formed the nucleus of the awkward squad, those most critical of the new culture.

Fortunately, not everyone had the same negative reaction to the changes. The center was encouraged by getting a very positive response — especially among local personnel who had long felt their careers blocked by the Anglo-Saxon phalanx that headed the businesses. And as the group's results improved, the perceived effect was to increase motivation for working in the new environment.

By the end of the decade, the blue culture seemed to have prevailed, and the center did appear to have brought about a considerable revolution. However, if "culture is an iceberg and behavior is just the visible tip," then while the center was able to influence that visible tip — make managers keep to budgets and deadlines — by reward systems, there was no guarantee that they had managed to shift the underlying assumptions. Like the metaphorical liner turning in the ocean, the maneuver would take a long time to complete. Moreover, year after year the Inchcape managers put forward some persuasive arguments that the imposition of a central culture was unnecessary and counter-productive. Some of the reasons for this, reasons that had vital strategic implications, were brought out during the Laurent sessions.

SYNERGY STOPPERS

The diversity of the ten core businesses, each with its own specific skills and loyalties, was one clear differentiating factor. To be a successful insurance broker demanded different skills from running an inspection and testing business, which inevitably resulted in different value systems.

Moreover, with the exception of insurance and shipping, all Inchcape's businesses could be said to be local ones dealing with local customers, some of whom were also global. This meant that winning or losing a contract would still depend on the performance of the people on the spot, and on other local factors. Such considerations, it was argued, would always work against the emergence of a tight culture. Instead, the emphasis should be on management flexibility and freedom to respond to local situations and the particular demands of each business. In this, the views of the Inchcape management seem to bear out Andre Laurent's research conclusions that, "International companies of the future are going to have to look less and less like corporate headquarters and subsidiaries, and more and more like centers of competence in different parts of the world."

A further barrier was represented by the "black holes" of ignorance that the businesses had about each other. Rarely, if ever, in the past had there been an opportunity for the Shipping lion to lie down with the Motors lamb and appreciate the problems, opportunities, and demands peculiar to each business. There was general agreement on the need for greater enlightenment across the group, both to allow opportunities for synergies to emerge, and to foster a common *esprit*, a view heartily endorsed by the center.

WHAT IS INCHCAPE PLC?

By raising the profile of the name "Inchcape plc" and making it more than a mere cipher, the center hoped to foster a common sense of identity and lay the old federal concept to rest. However, this policy met staunch resistance from the old hands who asked "What does Inchcape bring to the party?" and even dared to question whether or not the businesses would be even stronger if they were freestanding. One Bain Clarkson representative even went so far as to claim, "Business would be significantly damaged if the name were changed to Inchcape."

In fact, where it would have been counter-productive to destroy the corporate identities of the old Inchcape, and the goodwill and customer loyalty along with them, the center had been content to leave the old company names extant. Thus, the name "Inchcape plc" appeared in very small letters at the bottom of the notepaper used by companies such as Gilman's Office Machines, and this dual identity continued in many of the business units. But such instances only reinforced the confusion — among both personnel and outside customers — about their relationship with Inchcape plc.

Fortunately for the future of Inchcape plc, ultimately most agreed that there was a competitive advantage to be gained from belonging to a larger group. Increasingly, the "Inchcape muscle" gave them leverage with their principals, and enabled them to differentiate themselves from competitors by being part of the more powerful whole. The role of Inchcape plc in the future, it was hoped, would be to pull the diverse units together, and more was expected from the center in terms of systems, of seeing and implementing synergies and providing financial clout.

CULTURAL DIVERSITY

The multicultural character of Inchcape's personnel, customers, and principals was believed to be yet another barrier to the imposition of a tight corporate entity.

The culture of the old Inchcape management was exclusively British and expatriate-driven. The new Inchcape group was concerned to promote local managers to the highest levels; a change that those working in the field agreed was long overdue. The companies all employed local personnel, and the influence of their cultures was reflected in the companies in which they worked. Only in the Gulf, where recruitment difficulties had left U.K. expatriate managers dominant, did the company still "feel British" and colonial in culture. As Kalpana Prathap recalled, when she joined the Inchcape Middle East human resources department at the end of 1991, "We were still issuing crockery and cutlery for our expatriate managers." To change this culture would take a lot of hard work, backed by strong support from the top management, as "there were many blockers in the way."

In fact, here the center did not seem to be moving fast enough for the field, who pointed out that Inchcape remained a U.K. company operating in different countries, rather than a true multinational. Even by 1991 the group had no European or Asian directors at group level, and there was no senior expatriate manager working outside his or her own area of origin, other than British. Why not, participants asked? We are working on it, the center invariably replied. However, in retrospect IPL's Paul Cheng felt that, "Deep down, I think there is not total trust in local management in the field. We in the East feel that the total trust is not there with our Western colleagues."

Another great debate centered on the need for a strong relationship between the Inchcape subsidiaries and the principals they served. The multicultural character of those principals, from the Japanese culture of

Ricoh or Toyota to the entirely British culture of British Home Stores, was a very large gulf to bridge. Moreover, where those principals themselves had a strong culture, the subsidiaries were obliged to absorb and "keep in step" with it if they were to succeed. Toyota GB managers, for example, claimed that their company had "a 100% Toyota culture."

These factors seemed to strengthen the argument that people from a single culture cannot effectively manage a global company, as Inchcape was, but must reflect global thinking by having different cultures represented at the highest levels. Only this would allow the group to optimize the quality and effectiveness of its very diverse human resources. Moreover, if the top management was unable to recognize and appreciate the implications of cultural bias when it occurred, it would not handle certain situations sensitively or effectively. David John believed that those in the field had a point here, since "I don't think that anybody at the center realized the subtlety of managing partners in the Middle East ... They had international experience, but that had been mostly in Europe." He further thought that, "The other problem we had — and I was as guilty as anyone — was underestimating to what extent somebody who had managed successfully in one culture could manage equally well in another. In fact, that was not always the case." This seemed to bear out the theory that, "While the global nature of the business may call for increased consistency, the variety of the cultural environments may be calling for differentiation." This was the paradox: on the one hand there was the desire to establish a common corporate culture; on the other hand, there was the need to be sensitive to national cultures and not to stifle the initiative of local business units. It was bound to be a difficult balancing act, compounded by the existence of an ethnocentric head office.

The situation most criticized by those in the field was where the needs and actions of the blue center were seen to work against those of the green periphery. For example, necessity had forced the Inchcape center to keep a strict control on financial budgets; the emphasis had been on short-term targeting, with profit as the main objective. This perspective was, however, at odds with the long-term view adopted by other cultures, notably the Japanese principals of Inchcape, who preferred to invest and build up market share over time. Such a conflict of interest could place the subsidiaries in the difficult position of trying to serve two conflicting masters.

Other examples were quoted of the repercussions that could occur if the logic of the center did not fit the logic of the local situation. A strategic move applauded in Europe, for instance, might be viewed quite differently in the Far East, as apparently occurred over "the liquidation of the group's property [which] was misunderstood and negatively interpreted in Hong Kong, though it made good financial sense to London." In this case, the sale was perceived as signaling a lack of commitment to the region and discouraged local people from joining the company. Entrenched in the British culture of its personnel, the center was thought too prone to fall into the trap of thinking "what motivates me also motivates others."

As far as the subsidiaries were concerned, headquarters did not make enough allowance for the effects of cross-cultural bias. They saw no evidence of consideration at the center being given to the distinct success factors specific to a particular region; the speed and flexibility needed to succeed in Asia, for example, as opposed to other factors that may be specific to South America. If there had been, they argued, the Inchcape subsidiaries would have been even more successful. As it was, "we develop our own plans and strategies, but we can only do things that fit in with London's plans," whereas the locals from rival companies, free from such constraints, "see an opportunity and grab it." What they wanted was "an explicit recognition by HQ that its foreign subsidiaries may have preferred ways of managing people (and situations) which could be more effective locally."

Planners and finance executives visiting the seminars as emissaries from the center claimed that they did listen and respond to such complaints "when they thought the time was right" — for example, in raising the cap-ex levels once it felt financial discipline had been sufficiently tightened. They also felt that as time went on and the changes bit deeper, such issues would become increasingly irrelevant. But, as Laurent's own surveys of successive Inchcape groups of managers confirmed, in fact these questions remained a bone of contention.

Always present at the seminars were representatives from two of Inchcape's Asian subsidiaries, both of which had carried out important cultural change programs. Their descriptions of how the programs worked sometimes gave a different gloss than the one given by their senior management.

"Yes, We Care"

Inchcape Pacific Limited (IPL), the group's Far East subsidiary headquartered in Hong Kong, was formed on January 1, 1987, by "collapsing" five old-established trading hongs whose diverse activities had overlapped and, in some cases, competed with each other. Under its new chief executive, Charles Mackay, the businesses were reorganized into business streams under specialist directors, some brought in from other parts of the group. They were then run with strict control.

Between 1987 and 1991, IPL's financial results improved dramatically year by year. While these were a source of great pride to everyone connected with IPL, the organizational changes, together with the disappearance of many old hands, caused confusion, insecurity, and a loss of morale among its personnel, as a 1989 company-wide Staff Attitude Survey revealed. It found that though over 70% of respondents believed that their company had a good future in the territory and 80% said they enjoyed their work, more than 50% felt that they were "kept in the dark" about IPL's goals and aims. Only 45% felt they understood clearly what was expected of them, 60–70% (depending on the company) felt that they did not understand how their performance was measured and that they were unfairly evaluated, and 40–60% said they were dissatisfied with their working environment. These figures were not out of line with similar surveys in other companies, but were nonetheless disappointing.

In effect, the survey showed that although IPL had efficiently cut off the old roots that had hampered its growth in the past, it had not yet put down any new ones that were visible and meaningful to those who worked for it. Thus, one general manager described it as a company "run by hired mercenaries," meaning the new expatriate managers who had no stake in the community, while another referred to its culture as "a culture of change." For many, IPL had failed to provide a motivating vision; the profit objectives and financial incentives offered were not by themselves enough to convince people that they had a place and a future with the company.

The new management style also brought problems in its wake. Traditionally, the Chinese had been used to bosses who directed them and did not ask their opinion. They therefore found it difficult to adapt to the new European managers who asked their opinion during meetings or, even worse, asked them to prescribe a course of action. Those that enthusiastically embraced the new responsibilities were then brought up against the problem of career development for locals within IPL.

In 1987, when IPL was formed, the aim was to localize the company within a short time. However, the fears associated with the Chinese takeover in 1997, accelerated by the events of June 1989 in Tiananmen Square, made this almost impossible to achieve. With every crisis, the queues outside the Canadian and Australian consulates grew longer and the exodus of skilled locals accelerated. A confidential survey carried out within IPL showed that a high proportion of their senior locals planned to leave within the next two years. The shortage of managers of the right caliber led to more expatriates being brought in to fill the gaps, and this increased resentment among those remaining. Local managers, even those with previous experience in international companies, believed that their promotion path was blocked. As Paul Cheng, then head of the Consumer and Industrial business stream put it, "If there is a senior post to be filled, and an experienced local is suggested, the reaction is: 'He needs a few more years' experience.' A relatively inexperienced expatriate is then preferred, the justification being that, 'We should give him a chance to prove himself.'"

Recognizing some of these problems, the IPL leadership put considerable resources into an improvement of motivation and communication, expanding the central personnel department and opening a human resources center to conduct in-house training programs. A mission statement was followed by the launch, in April 1990, of a "Yes, We Care" (YWC) program. Publicized through an in-house newspaper, this was designed to demonstrate to customers, principals, and staff that it cared equally for them all. The concept was personified by a model of a three-legged stool distributed to about 150 managers. The legs represented respectively customer, principal, and people care, the interdependent trinity vital to the continued success of IPL.

These moves created an expectation among its local personnel that IPL was really going to address their cultural needs, though there was also a fair amount of cynicism, expressed by expatriates and locals alike, that any real changes would follow. As one said, "What you saw in Hong Kong made you cynical. You have to train people and take your time to get the climate right. When you have middle managers who still shout at their subordinates and a program like YWC, it makes the program a laughing stock. You cannot impose a culture from the top ..." Charles Mackay's anointment as Turnbull's chosen successor made it likely that "Yes, We Care" would be rolled out across the group. Whether this would be a good or a bad thing was a hot topic during seminars at the EAC.

"PEOPLE, MARKET, PERFORMANCE"

It was generally acknowledged that of all the Inchcape subsidiaries, Inchcape Berhad, based in Singapore, had one of the best records on communication and motivation. Inchcape Berhad, too, was transformed from "an old-fashioned, colonial company with low morale" into a performance-driven one with record profits. Its PMP program, launched in March 1989, was similar to that of IPL's "Yes, We Care," also being based on three building blocks: People — Market — Performance. However, PMP rested on foundations laid during the previous two years.

When Stephen Looi joined Inchcape Berhad in 1984, it was still a colonial company run by expatriate managers. Then, in April 1987, Inchcape Berhad got a new chief executive, David John, and Stephen Looi became the group's personnel manager. He came with excellent credentials: a good degree, an MBA from IMD, and experience with Ford and Beechams. Despite this, before David John arrived he was not allowed access to the expatriate salaries. These were maintained "confidentially" by the chief executive's secretary.

David John gave the personnel function a much higher profile, moving Looi to head office, and placing him two doors away from his own office to make communication and consultation easy. The new direction was also underlined by giving Looi exactly the same external status symbols as his expatriate predecessor, which sent a strong signal throughout the group. To further emphasize the demise of Inchcape Berhad's colonial past, the executive dining room and toilets were done away with, though not without strong protest from some who resented this "American fad for egalitarianism."

One of the first things Looi initiated was an opinion survey. This identified communication as one of the main problem areas. There was a strong division between the unionized staff and management, which was thought to be aloof. The findings of the survey were used as input for a five-year plan. In the short term, action was taken to improve communications and break down divisions.

A successful innovation was the introduction of "skip level" dinners, held once a month, when David John met managers on a level below his main board directors for dinner in a hotel. This enabled him to get to know the divisional managers, and vice versa. The first round of dinners were business-specific, but having worked through those, managers from different businesses were mixed up, so Timber, Motors and Services managers not only met David John again, but also met each other. The third round of dinners switched to David John's house, and spouses were invited. Some managers had worked for the group for twenty years, and never before been invited to the chief executive's home. The dinners led to cocktails and beer bashes, with the eventual aim of getting the directors to start their own round of "skip level" dinners.

David John was very involved with the programs that took place at Inchcape Berhad's new training center, attending every opening of a new course. He was, recalled Looi, "an HR director's dream because he kept out of the way. He said, 'You tell me when you need me, what to say, when to be there.' He was very supportive ... When the Muslims had a New Year party, he would be there."

Two audits measured the extent of Inchcape Berhad's efficacy. The first, carried out by the training manager, showed some gaps and reported complaints that there was not enough local news about what companies were doing. The second, carried out by the Industrial Society, found that the system was working well and that people felt they were learning a lot from it.

PMP grew out of a concern that Inchcape Berhad should formally announce its core values to the staff. After two years of "playing around with ideas and talking about values," Looi came up with five values he thought were important. These were subsequently cut to three: people-centered, marketing-oriented, and performance-driven. Looi saw people and performance as two balancing factors: "People without performance is irresponsible; performance without people is impossible."

The two-year gestation period was, Looi believed, important. It allowed the values to evolve slowly and make an initial impact. "Change must come from the top, but it must also have ownership at the bottom. The way to do this is to demonstrate through actions that the company means what it says and that these values do matter to it, so that it may be perceived as a PMP company even before the concept is announced. Otherwise, the response will inevitably be one of cynicism." PMP aimed to discourage negative behavior, and to engender a sense of belonging and commitment, so that people felt they were important and could trust the leadership of the company. With the ground prepared, said Looi, the culture was easier to propagate. By 1990, Inchcape Berhad had only three expatriate managers, though they were all in top positions.

THE INCHCAPE IDEAL

At the end of every session at INSEAD EAC, participants worked in groups to come up with their own ideal Inchcape culture. From every program, for whatever level of management, the belief emerged that the most appropriate culture for Inchcape would be one containing elements of both green and blue. It would combine the green elements intrinsic to the company's *modus operandi* (not least being the green nature of its most important principals, Japanese companies such as Toyota and

Ricoh) with the blue elements. These would prevent rampant entrepreneurship from ever leading the group to the edge of financial disaster again.

In this way, the presentations of Inchcape managers generally concluded, the group would turn the richness of its cultural diversity into its greatest competitive strength for the future; its people really would "become its greatest asset." Its differentiation would be that of a multifaceted group, with centers of excellence throughout the world. By breaking down the regional insularity, Inchcape plc would finally become a truly international company. Such conclusions commonly brought applause and nods of approval from everyone present. That such a consummation was "devoutly to be wished" by all sides provided reassurance for those at the top, demonstrating that, despite all the criticisms, both the center and the field shared the same vision of what should constitute an ideal Inchcape culture.

However, in the oft-repeated words of the group's personnel director, Bob Goodall, "Saying it ain't doing it," and throughout the Turnbull era, such a culture was not readily apparent group-wide. The experience of one young Chinese manager demonstrated that actions did not always measure up to words. After a four-hour meeting with a senior British manager from the center, the two had got into the lift together. As they descended, the senior manager spoke not a single word to him. "That hurt a lot. You realize that for them, you are not an individual. Did he think we all looked alike?"

So although everyone could see that the context had changed, doubt remained about the nine-tenths underneath. New top management appointments in the *Inchcape Bulletin* throughout 1990 featured British graduates of Glasgow University, Christ's College Cambridge, and Leeds University. This gave little comfort to those looking for hard evidence that the all-British group was undergoing a real transformation. Such a set of appointments signaled an altogether different message and, in this context, the designation "International" only provoked a cynical laugh.

The five years of George Turnbull's leadership passed in an atmosphere of excitement and achievement as the financial results spread confidence and optimism. Noticeably, by 1990–91 the Inchcape seminars had become far less combative and divisive when discussing the group's culture. Later, when Inchape held programs at Ashridge, program director Richard Phillips noticed that, "There was very little whingeing about corporate, which struck me as unusual." This unanimity was interpreted as indicating widespread acceptance of a new Inchcape culture by a new generation of managers who shared a common professional approach and knew nothing of the old Inchcape. Finally, it seemed that the gap between field and center had been bridged.

However, it was equally clear that the group was still far too blue for the comfort of most of its managers. When, as he did with every group, Laurent asked them to name "Two Do Be" and "Two Don't Be" characteristics that it took to succeed at Inchcape, the first list always began with "achieve performance and budget," and the latter with "don't fail financials." As the initial glow of the Turnbull years began to fade, the group's personnel began to clamor for more than a target of "£x" million profit to motivate and sustain them for the future; no culture could be built on such a short-term focus. When ominous rumors of retrenchment began to be heard throughout the group, its employees needed to know that they were not just being led by "a body of turn-around artists," or being groomed to become a branch of Toyota Motor Co. Was there a real vision at the center of where the group was going, and an agreed set of core values they could all unite behind?

The final presentations at EAC programs frequently included a call for a group mission statement in order to provide a binding element. But was such a statement a credible alternative, or would it of necessity be so all-encompassing as to be meaningless? What effect would coming organizational and personnel changes rumored to be in the pipeline , have on ongoing programs such as PMP and "Yes, We Care"? Would they, as some feared, "kill them off" by resulting in an emphasis on "Performance" and "Market" at the expense of "People," and so leave a legacy of cynicism about any future efforts to build a culture? Who would provide the vision in future — the center, the London-based business stream heads, or the country managers? Did anyone know? And how soon would they tell the rest of the group?

From 1986 on, the word "change" was the most popular word in the vocabulary of Inchcape's top managers. How many more changes, its other ranks wondered, must Inchcape go through before it achieved some form of stability and a recognizable culture? Was the nature of the group such that it was destined to have a culture of eternal change? Or was any centrally imposed culture a chimera?

The argument went round in a circle. Most memorably on one occasion, a group of managers concluded that the Inchcape culture resembled "a jigsaw for which there is no lid to show the overall picture," and in a phrase which Laurent quoted in every subsequent seminar: "Talking about the Inchcape culture is like speaking a Swiss language." It was a conclusion that remained true for many years to come. Indeed, by the mid-1990s, even the center seemed to have thrown in the towel and admitted that an Inchcape culture was a logical impossibility.

For many Inchcape managers, the EAC seminars on culture were a cathartic experience, enabling them both to air their complaints and to examine vital questions thoroughly. Their arguments reflected the fact that the fantastic span of the group's interests, both geographically and operationally, threw up important barriers to cultural coherence. They further argued that because these differentiating factors were intrinsic to Inchcape's success, they could not be destroyed and would always be there to work against the establishment of a centrally directed corporate culture. Both Inchcape and its managers were to pass through many changes in the years between 1989 and 1998, when the demerger of the group was announced. But perhaps that announcement represented an acknowledgment of the truth of this contention. All along, those in the field had got it right. But of course, no-one would ever admit it. Perhaps the last word should most appropriately go to the ever-fertile managers, who composed and sang this anthem for one of Inchcape's many closing dinners in Fontainebleau:

> *Now Sir George Turnbull had a firm*
> *With wise new chaps galore.*
> *Strategy and synergy*
> *Will make them cry for more.*
> *With a blue firm here*
> *And a green firm there*
> *Here a blue, there a green*
> *Everywhere a business dream ...*
> *Sir George Turnbull had a firm*
> *With brand new managers*
> *OH! ... INSEAD!!*

What's My Line?

◆

By 1990, Inchcape had emerged strongly from the "turbulent eighties" and seemed well positioned to meet the challenge of a new decade. Yet although many people within and without Inchcape applauded the group for having so successfully undergone profound and rapid change, Turnbull's view was that there was still a long way to go. An April 1990 article in the press about the group confirmed how right he was: "The whole thing looks like a mess. There are lots of small activities with barely a hint of what the modern world describes as 'critical mass', and precious little control over most of the products that pass through the group's hands." However, it went on, "On the other hand, such a rambling structure is rather reminiscent of those great Japanese trading houses such as Mitsubishi, Mitsui and C. Itoh. And lack of focus does not seem to have done them any harm, although it must be said that they are rather larger than Inchcape."

So far, Turnbull had moved piece by piece in order to manage the possible, but "the management structure of a company is a living thing: it must be massaged." Therefore, he believed, it was important for him to keep on traveling, to get out and about to meet people and encourage them to work together.

Turnbull was well aware that now came the difficult part; to find the growth that would make the group secure. In one aspect, continuity was maintained. Just as change had been one of the key themes of the eighties, so it continued to be the outstanding feature of Inchcape in the early 1990s.

SLOWDOWN

In April 1989, Bob Carpenter at Kitcat & Aitken, while recommending the shares as a "buy for medium potential," noted that "there have been recent signs that this phase of outperformance ... has run its course for the time being." His words were prophetic as, in 1990, results were flat at £174 million, reflecting the economic slowdown affecting many parts of the world. Profits were also reduced by currency fluctuations.

George Turnbull and Stacey Ellis were well aware that they now had to produce a new direction for Inchcape if it was to remain flavor of the month with the City. So, in the next eighteen months, they tried to deal with the many unresolved issues that had left question marks hanging over the group's future.

ORGANIZATIONAL INCOHERENCE

Inchcape had always been a mass of competitive environments; that was one of its strengths but also one of its weaknesses. Such a mass made it difficult to understand the whole, as the stock market frequently complained. In declining the offer of the throne of Albania in 1921, the first Earl of Inchcape had said, "It is a great compliment, but it is not in my line." Almost seventy years later, successive chief executives grappled with the same issue; what exactly *was* Inchcape's line?

Many analysts remained concerned that the group had not yet determined its strategic priorities and goals, a key point being the number of core businesses. Ten was considered far too many for even the most experienced juggler to operate successfully and, in the light of their uneven performances, it was clear they needed to be sorted out further. Marketing and Distribution, for example — by then expanded to include Consumer and Industrial, which itself incorporated the wines and spirits business — was the "biggest box of tricks." Arguably, it could be split into several business streams. By contrast, many questioned the validity of Business Machines as a freestanding business stream, especially in view of its Australasian failure.

The major challenge would be to find rational linkages between the group's businesses and ways of using its international spread more effectively. As a 1988 article in *Management Today* had asked, "What connection, if any, exists between selling Mercs in the Midlands and Jags on the Peak [in Hong Kong]? Is it realistic to talk of 'global business' and being internationally competitive when you lack control of the product and source of supply?"

Optimists within the group still hoped that this would be possible with the four services businesses; others were highly skeptical. Some analysts took the view that only through finding and exploiting such synergies could the group make the whole greater than the sum of its parts. Without this, as McKinsey's Roger Morrison commented,

Inchcape would remain "a collection of different businesses which frankly bear little relation to each other."

Connected with this issue was a new piece of management theory that had surfaced as a result of the group's training sessions at the Euro-Asia Centre. This concerned the question of what exactly were Inchcape's core competencies? As the managers had learned, identifying a company's core competencies had become an inescapable duty. They had to be cherished and spread via best practice, and any company that failed to do so courted disaster. A great deal of time was to be devoted to this new mantra.

QUALITY MANAGEMENT

Another constraint which Turnbull saw would hamper the group's future growth was a continued lack of the right caliber of management. Some of the businesses still needed better people, especially at senior marketing levels. The drive to recruit local managers continued strongly, but having trained and promoted local talent, would Inchcape be able to keep them working for the group? Was it capable of integrating different cultural biases into its "very British and very male" management outlook, and exploit them to the group's further advantage?

One appointment with important consequences for the future was that of Philip Cushing, who joined the group in April 1990 to run its Southeast Asian subsidiary. His arrival in Singapore, as a local paper noted, marked three firsts in his career. He was "Inchcape Berhad's first managing director, it was his first appointment at Inchcape and his first outside the UK." It further commented that despite all this, "Mr Cushing is not most people. He seems to have everything under control," though he admitted to "a little cultural and corporate shock." The shocks would get much bigger later on in his career with Inchcape.

Cushing recalled two lasting memories of his very first week, "... which may have been more important in my overall philosophy than I even realized. The first was that David John did not let me unpack, and sent me on a plane from Singapore to Papua New Guinea ... The second one was when I got back after this first week. My new secretary arranged for me to be met at the airport with a 'blue bag,' probably about overnight bag size — it was full of paper; this was my induction ... Three days later, when I surfaced for the first time, I really grasped what diversity meant."

BUSINESS STREAMS — THE LOGICAL SOLUTION?

Where is the organizational coherence?" had been a question long haunting the group planners. So far, Turnbull had opted for the gradual change to a business stream organization, based on a pragmatic working arrangement. But despite being presented as a streamed organization for the sake of clarity, the group was still run geographically, and although there was now a business strategy for each of the streams, there was no explicit territorial strategy, which some felt an important omission. Even this issue was not clear cut, since the service businesses, which were in principal global, did not need a geographical strategy, whereas the local marketing businesses definitely did. Function versus geography — it was a debate that would run and run.

In October 1990 the group held a management conference in Torquay. Its brief was to examine the critical issue of how Inchcape should organize its businesses for the future in order to achieve its stated corporate objective "to establish Inchcape firmly as the world's leading international services and marketing group." Planning director Stacey Ellis gave an overview of the group's history and its current position in which he focused on some of these concerns voiced by outside brokers. In particular, he emphasized the need to improve the rate of growth and the quality of the group's earnings in order to raise its share rating.

The conference went on to discuss the businesses and their prospects, ending with unanimous agreement about what the group's future direction should be. A few months later, in March 1991, the results of that unanimity were revealed. From January 1, 1992, the entire group would be structured and managed on a global business stream basis in four main areas: Motors, Marketing and Distribution, Services, and Resources. However, in all subsequent references, the consistent emphasis on "our strategic development in three areas" rendered Resources something of a lame duck from the start. These new global streams would be the "engines and focus" for future growth. Each would be run centrally by a director, in most cases based at London head office.

According to Sir George, this reorganization would make Inchcape more coherent in global terms and increase its international competitiveness in those areas that had already seen important investments and acquisitions since 1986. Another benefit would be to allow the group to respond more rapidly to its principals. Having the business stream directors at the center would provide a mechanism for talking to them and possibly offering them new horizons, as their knowledge of group performances in all areas would allow the directors to suggest additional services. This would both broaden the group's business base with its principals, and strengthen its relationship with them. Between the four services there was also the ever-tantalizing possibility that synergies between them might finally emerge on a worthwhile scale.

Both these assumptions were to prove contentious, especially when it came to running the Marketing businesses in the Middle and Far East. Dale Butcher recalled that some consultants had been invited by Turnbull to do some work on the subject. "It was probably a consulting firm that came along and said, 'In a global world, you cannot afford to have eight different people looking after this product; it needs to be managed globally.' I think George was quite influenced by consultant-speak at the time."

COUNTRY MANAGERS

The global approach was to be balanced locally by the appointment of senior executives as country managers. They would be directly responsible for the activities of one of the major business streams in their area as part of that stream's global management structure, there to provide a focus for local coordination.

The business streams would have an allegiance to the country managers and a responsibility to support them. In many cases, as Charles Mackay observed in a 1992 interview, it was anticipated that the country manager would be the executive in charge of the Marketing stream in the territory, "since he is likely to have the best knowledge of the local trading environment." George Turnbull saw only synergy between the country and business stream managers; there would be no conflict. This was good in theory, but time would tell if this was a naïve assumption.

WHAT NEXT?

Like many others, Stacey Ellis recognized that the group's turnaround had been achieved during very favorable economic circumstances. In the last three years, Inchcape had been "riding a number of growth forces in the world" through its involvement in the expanding motors trade and revived shipping business, and geographically via its strong position in the booming Pacific Rim. A hard landing would put the new management and structure to its first real test. How would it fare then?

For despite the heavy emphasis on strategic planning and strict rationing in order to ensure the optimum allocation of resources, the Australian mini crisis could be described as a pale echo of the old Inchcape. In the light of this, outside observers questioned whether the group really was now shock-proof. Even more important, would it turn out to be recession-proof?

A warning note had already been struck by an otherwise laudatory article, looking at prospects for the strengthened management team of Mann Egerton. "Growth does not come easily in motor vehicle retailing and some analysts, perhaps carried away by the excitement of Turnbull's restructuring, may have been over-estimating likely profit performance." *The Financial Times*, too, had noted in 1987 that "Inchcape is hardly slim-line, despite the somewhat cosmetic labeling of its areas of activities … For all its realignment, Inchcape has not lost its colonial charm, nor shrugged off the risks associated with a far flung empire. Although trading conditions have conspired to give a good performance across the board, Inchcape will ever be vulnerable to the vagaries of currencies, commodity prices and the economies of developing nations."

HELP ARRIVES

To help gain a clearer picture, the group again turned to the business schools for help. Philippe Haspelagh's introduction to the group had occurred two years earlier, when he gave a presentation to the executive board seminar at the Euro-Asia Centre. Later, in 1991, Haspeslagh was asked to prepare the first of two board-level workshops. He decided to focus on a discussion of "what type of diversified firm they wanted to be, and to review what the objectives and mission were, whether the business portfolio was right, and help them identify core competencies in terms of giving some basis for coherence to the portfolio." He would also discuss the organizational approach, which would mainly concern the relationship between the center and the units.

Haspeslagh's role was that of facilitator, to create a discussion. To promote debate, he presented various profiles of diversified companies "in terms of to what extent they fully owned the business, how they created value, how financially driven they were, how strategic they were, and so on," and administered a questionnaire. The questions focused on four main areas: "the ambition they wanted to own, the style they wanted to develop, the competencies Inchcape should deepen and the opportunities they should go after." As Sir George's health deteriorated, it was Charles Mackay who became the key figure in these workshops, though the corporate staff and business heads were also involved. The fruits of this exercise, refined into the new strategy, were to be influential in the way Mackay ran the group.

ONE GREEN BOTTLE ...

It was within this context that Stacey Ellis and the planning team continued their careful examination of the business streams, often working in conjunction with the stream management to try and avoid friction between field and center. As Ellis recalled, "We recognized that once the target of £200 million had been achieved, it would only take some five or six years to double this to £400 million if the growth rate of 15% was to be maintained. This inevitably gave rise to two questions. The first was, did the ten streams have the growth potential to achieve this target? The second was, did each of the ten have the mass to make a useful contribution to these targets? There was considerable debate about the minimum size a business stream could be ... Mathematically, with ten business streams, each one should have the immediate potential to reach a profit of £20 million and grow to £40 million over the medium term. As an initial guide, we set a target of £15 million for the next two years, increasing to £25 million over the next five years. These were deliberately set low so as not to raise too much debate and demoralize those directors whose streams might not be able to reach these targets."

Despite these measures, it soon became clear that some businesses would never get anywhere near the financial criteria. Tea, for example, produced fluctuating profits which, Ellis estimated, "could never get beyond £5 million or so. Its profits were cyclical due to fluctuations in the tea price, and the business was not international. Tea had one merit in that Inchcape was a major presence in India due to the high profile of tea, and this benefit would be lost if the tea company was sold." After spending some time examining how the group might be able to leverage this advantage, the planners were unable either to find another business in India that fitted the strategy, or a new business it might enter in the next few years. Therefore, Ellis concluded, "in my mind and in George's mind it had to go. The question was timing, as it had to be sold when the international price of tea was high."

Colin Armstrong, the sector director responsible for Tea, tried to save the business, protesting in vain that, despite the then high taxes in India that had so reduced the stream's profit, "We had one of the outstanding plantation businesses in the world." He saw it as "a classic case where we were so inbred with short-termism — you had to be increasing the profits every year. George was never comfortable with the business anyway; to be cynical, it didn't have four wheels." However, as Ellis observed, "None of his arguments answered the fundamental question of profitability which had averaged some £2–3 million over the last several years."

In June 1991, Inchcape sold all its tea interests (except for a tiny business in Ecuador) for £30.4 million, so severing further the links with its colonial trading past. The year following the sale, the Indian government loosened controls and the taxes came down.

Ellis acknowledged the emotions engendered by the decision. When he arrived to give a speech on behalf of the group at a pensioners' lunch, having just announced the sale of Tea, he remembered that "I was nearly lynched … I changed my speech and concentrated on Tea, but although there were one or two understanding nods in the audience, I was under no illusion that the message I had was not popular … In their eyes, we had sold their birthright." On the other hand, a cartoon produced for one of the final presentations on Inchcape's strategy at an EAC training session showed a smiling Sir George, armed with a bow and arrow, turning away from a darts board in which the section marked Tea had received a bull's eye. The caption read, "Jolly good shot, Sir."

The deal left Timber as a lonely outpost of the Resources business stream. After careful examination it was decided that, for many of the same reasons as Tea, this stream too should eventually be sold. Ellis believed, "It could never grow; nor could it make the returns we required … And you had Greenpeace and Friends of the Earth — although we did it better than anyone else, we were a Western target for them."

SERVICE ON FOUR FRONTS

Of the four services streams, Inspection and Testing finally began to show signs of improvement after several early false starts. The stream consisted of three fundamentally different businesses: inspection, product testing, and foreign trade supervision. This last activity worried Stacey, first because of the political risks and, second, because Inchcape might find itself in conflict by inspecting a lot of its own products coming in for distribution. He believed the future lay more in high-tech labs and the environmental side of Testing, as "this was highly skilled with very attractive returns and enormous growth potential." He was also interested in exploring the medical field, since "In Europe, government laboratories were being privatized and as the technology advanced, it opened up more and more opportunities." After research indicated a likely increase in pressure on state environmental bodies to reach higher standards, the group targeted environmental testing in the U.S. as offering significant future potential. Accordingly, it acquired four companies to form the core of a network of testing companies being established in the U.S. and Canada.

As the Inchcape center appreciated, the enormous attraction of Shipping Services was that much of it worked on negative working capital, which gave the group a very attractive cash flow and helped raise its return on capital. However, it was also another cyclical activity. The stream prepared for the inevitable downturn by carrying out a restructuring program of its operations, especially in the Far East. Heavy investment in new communications and data management systems was made to increase efficiency and put the stream in a good position to face harder times.

To the planners, it was clear that if Inchcape was going to succeed in this business, then it needed to be global. However, the major part of the stream's profits still came from Japan. In 1992, the growing importance of Singapore as a regional hub for future operations was underlined by the combination of several Singapore shipping agencies to form a regional office, Inchcape Shipping Services, Singapore, which would serve Southeast Asia. But the most striking development at this time was the continued growth in shipping and shipping-related businesses in North America, where there was a gaping hole in the stream's network. This gap was plugged by acquisition, notably of the Southern Steamship Agency whose chief executive, Win Thurber III, initially became a keen Inchcape supporter. These purchases enabled Inchcape to offer its principals an even wider range of services and make good its claim to be the world's most comprehensive shipping agency network.

According to Ellis, "Even after this acquisition the Shipping stream did not make a large contribution to the group's profit." However, despite being hit by exchange effects and the weakness of the US dollar, profits were maintained in 1990 and improved in 1991.

For Insurance Services, 1990 and 1991 were designated as years of consolidation for Bain Clarkson, the offspring of a merger between Bain Dawes and Clarkson Puckle. Although it met Inchcape's criterion of being an international business, unfortunately insurance broking, too, suffered from cyclical profits. Already a highly competitive market, 1990 saw a sharp fall in the U.K. brokerage business, which continued depressed in 1991.

Bain Clarkson's level of profit, Ellis recalled, "was not as high as the better companies ... We brought in some consultants who had expertise in this field and the 'education' of the senior management started. After about a year, we developed a plan which Simon Arnold and I put to the board to grow the company into one of the top three brokers in the U.K." In fact, Bain Clarkson's profits were to grow significantly over the period so that at one point, Insurance contributed almost two-thirds of the services stream's profit.

To Stacey Ellis, "Buying Services initially appeared to have all the characteristics we were looking for. The sourcing was predominantly in Southeast Asia and the Far East, but could be on a global basis. Although many of the customers were European, there was every reason why North America could be added, and the customer base could also be on a global basis." He spent a considerable amount of time examining the business, visiting most of the offices and talking with senior staff.

Unfortunately for initial hopes, several fatal flaws appeared in the structure of this business, not least being the low level of commission retailers were prepared to pay, and the fact that buyers would always be looking for any opportunity to set up their own operation and cut out the middleman once it had grown to a critical mass. Buying Services was also suffering from an unprecedented downturn in world retail markets at a time when it had invested heavily in information technology, plus the establishment and relocation of offices. The net result was to put it into loss for 1990.

So, after having supported its growth, Stacey Ellis later began to question whether the stream could realize "the potential we all thought it had," which led him to argue for limits on the amount of time and capital that should be expended to breathe life into the operation. The business fell within Mackay's Hong Kong empire and, as one onlooker recalled "Charles wanted to make it global so he would have a global business run out of Hong Kong, the same as Singapore had. We tried to ramp it beyond its capabilities. I am not sure there was a global Buying Services business to create, but we spent a lot of money trying ... There were frequent debates between Hong Kong and London ... Stacey would ask probing questions about where things fitted in strategically and the rationale of doing it, which used to frustrate Charles." For the moment, Buying Services was reprieved.

So, by 1992, hopes of leveraging the "natural synergy" thought to exist between Inchcape's service activities had been severely reduced. The efforts of the country managers, originally charged with producing incontrovertible evidence of its existence, did not seem to have been rewarded by any major success.

MARKETING — THE STRUGGLE FOR COCA-COLA

In 1991, the renamed and enlarged Marketing and Distribution business showed "a very good increase in profits." The operations continued strong in the Far East, with a record level of trading with China. Expansion into Vietnam received an impetus when Inchcape became exclusive agent for Unilever. So, despite lower profits in Singapore, Malaysia, and Thailand, great hopes were voiced for building up the Marketing stream to become the second leg on which Inchcape could stand more securely. The results during 1990–92 seemed to bear this out, and throughout the period, acquisitions to boost the group's aim of becoming the leading independent marketing company in the regions where it operated continued.

Ellis, however, believed that the consumer and industrial side could be built up into a sustainable business, "where we actually dealt with the end customer and could service behind it ... That I quite liked but in those days, branded products were probably 70–80% of turnover so again, we were trying to tell people steeped in this that the future lay in that. We did make a bit of progress." The fast moving consumer goods (FMCG) side, he realized would always be threatened by principals deciding to do the business themselves, once volumes had reached a high enough level.

The Marketing stream's success story of these years was, in fact, the South American business where in Chile, despite a deep recession, Williamson Balfour retained market leadership for Coca-Cola. Dale Butcher believed that in assessing the businesses, though George Turnbull mostly "got it right," he badly misjudged the potential of Coca-Cola bottling. "He was quite keen to get rid of Coca-Cola bottling in Chile because that was deemed by planning, in those days, to be manufacturing. If they said it was manufacturing and non-core, then it would take heaven and earth to sift their view on that, which was wrong. Also, they had a 'down' on South America; no-one understood the inflation rate in South America ... but it was all based on U.S. dollars anyway. So everyone had a view on South America, but no-one actually went out there and looked at the actual business. We could have lost bottling in South America ..."

Sergio Mardones, later chairman of the board and CEO of Balfour Williamson, had been recruited by Colin Armstrong back in 1981 to develop the Williamson business as Chile's country manager. He was a considerable coup, as he had twenty-one years' service with Ford in Chile, Brazil, and the U.S., and in joining such a small company was taking a considerable risk. Since then, he had steered the company through the country's deep recession and fought alongside Armstrong to get Inchcape into the bottling business. He had also won a valuable Ford tractor franchise.

He had always believed firmly in the potential of the two businesses, but as he wrote in his history of the company, "I had a very difficult position during these years, trying to combine the Coca-Cola investment covenants with Inchape-imposed investment limitations." In 1989, Pepsi returned to Chile and a price war ensued. While he was engaged in this battle, he heard that George Turnbull was planning the sale of all the South American companies, including Coca-Cola bottling, since "our Coca-Cola operation at that time, in spite of our strong opposition, was classified as an industrial operation that did not fit into Inchape's core businesses." Such was his belief in the future of the business, he and his managers decided "to form a company to be ready for the possibility of a management buyout."

The director responsible for South America, Colin Armstrong, was no less alarmed. Having lost tea, he found himself once again on the defensive — to paraphrase Oscar Wilde, to lose one business might be regarded as a misfortune; to lose two would look remarkably like carelessness. As Armstrong recalled, "George was never comfortable with Latin America because he didn't know anything about it." Armstrong thought that, strategically, the bottling business was a good antidote to the group's perennial worries about losing principals. "I was always conscious of Inchcape's weakness in being an intermediary everywhere, and you can lose an agency or franchise just like that, as has happened. The big thing about the Coca-Cola business, or the bottling plant, is that you are the owner of the factory, not the principal, and they cannot just come along and say you have lost it. What they do is negotiate you out of the business and find someone else, so you will never find yourself with three months' termination.

"So that was always a strength to me, but I remember having a big argument with George Turnbull because when he developed his ten core businesses, one of the many things Inchcape was going to get out of was anything to do with industry, and this was classified as an industry. I remember a big battle with George and Stacey about this being an industry and I said, 'It's really just putting liquid into a bottle — really, it's the distribution business, which is where you make money, but here, there is security for that distribution. And yes, it does demand investment, but much less than you are generating if it is a success.' So anyway, it was reclassified as a distribution business and not put up for sale."

Finance director Rod O'Donoghue recalled the battle: "In the early years, I was very demanding on the economics that were necessary to invest in South America because the risk profile was high at that time. Therefore, I probably contributed to the limitation of the group's exposure to bottling. I think it was 1990, George and I went down to South America to decide ultimately what to do with the businesses. We came back much more positive than we expected to ... George was against manufacturing because to him it was an extremely serious skill ... Remember his background." O'Donoghue also believed that part of the problem was Turnbull's distrust of Americans. "I don't think George would ever have formed an easy relationship with Coca-Cola ... As a generalization, he did not like doing business with Americans."

Stacey Ellis, on the other hand, believed that "George had an open mind on this, but wished to be convinced of the argument before investing further funds. He wanted to see the operation himself, and be convinced that the local management believed in the future of Coca-Cola there. He often did this by simply putting some obstacles up for the management to shoot down, so he could judge their belief and commitment." As he recalled, the board approved a major investment in the business in November 1991.

Mardones and Armstrong were to have further battles to get approval for money spent to defend market share against a determined attack by Pepsi. "Coca-Cola didn't like that sort of thing, so you just throw money. They throw some, but the bottler is expected to do so too, and it doesn't matter if you lose money in this case. Again, this is a medium-term view, but I was in a short-term view company," said Armstrong. However, Mardones recalled that "Inchape's commitment to our Coca-Cola operation changed completely when Charles Mackay became Inchcape's CEO ... a five-year investment program of US$30 million with local resources was approved." By 1997, the bottling business had a net turnover of US$251.9 million, giving an operating profit of US$13.1 million — not a bad return given that Mardones calculated Inchcape's investment in the business at US$5.3 million.

THE HEARTLAND

Motors, however, was the dominant element in the group. The real expertise of Inchcape lay there, and between 1986 and 1989 Derek Whittaker had guided his teams to record-breaking profits. Of its three very different parts — two distribution and one retail — the largest and most important was the import Toyota franchises in the U.K., Belgium, Ethiopia, Singapore, and Hong Kong, followed by the country franchises for the non-Toyota makes and, finally, the Mann Egerton retailing business.

The close relationship with Toyota fostered by George Turnbull and Derek Whittaker was confirmed in January 1990 when Inchcape reached a "pioneering" agreement with Toyota. This gave it an exclusive contract to distribute Toyota vehicles in the U.K. for eighteen years. In return, Toyota would purchase, in three stages at a cost of £60 million, a 51% interest in Inchcape's distributing subsidiary, TGB. Toyota would also take a 4.9% stake in Inchcape. The start of production of Toyota cars at the Derby plant by the end of 1992 was expected to herald good sales in Europe. This would enable Inchcape to concentrate on importing the "more lucrative models" whilst Toyota's cheaper models were produced locally. The end of 1991 saw Inchcape negotiating with Japanese automakers to market their vehicles in Vietnam and, until 1993, growth in the Far East, Southeast Asia, and Continental Europe balanced the retailing squeeze that hit Mann Egerton in the U.K.

Stacey and his team looked at this market in some detail, and came up with some surprising findings. "We looked at some 200 different outlets. The study showed wide variance in performance, but despite all our research we could not find any constant link between performance and any other factor ...The best performer was simply due to the quality and drive of the manager of that operation. This came as a complete surprise, and upset all the previous thinking". The study also highlighted that the trade's profit was under pressure from several factors, and that profits looked as if they might be undermined for the next few years. Such findings, added to forecasts about Toyota's possible future moves in Europe, led Stacey to have second thoughts about the long-term future of even this business, "the jewel in Inchcape's crown," as Turnbull had christened it in an interview with *The Financial Times*.

For although the Motors business had so far contained the greatest opportunities, this cyclical activity could quickly go into decline and threaten the group's profits. If, as many observers forecast, the trade suffered a downturn or even a recession in the near future, where would Inchcape compensate for the loss? The disparity in the contribution to the group's operating profit between Motors, at just under 50%, and all the other businesses put together, remained as wide as ever. Of the new activities, Business Machines had not so far been a success, and Inspection and Testing Services (ITS) represented a big investment that had not yet paid off. Such reflections were to be interrupted by the need to consider a project for a major acquisition in Motors, brought up by Charles Mackay.

ACQUISITIONS?

Clearly, if growth was not going to continue for some of the business streams, then the group must make acquisitions in adjacent growth businesses. Its ability to do so had recently been strengthened by Toyota's £60 million payment for its stake in TGB, which would leave Inchcape virtually "debt-free." The question that exercised the mind of the planners was — what to buy, and where? Europe and the opening of the integrated market in 1992 were seen as the next window of opportunity, given the group's expertise in car distribution and insurance broking. However, in Europe, where the group was unknown, it would not be able to rely on its traditional competitive advantages of knowing the countries and markets well.

Moreover, the group's recent acquisition record had not been notably successful, as *The Financial Times* noted: "Another source of uncertainty is acquisitions ... analysts are still reserving judgement about Inchcape's acquisition skills, given the problems arising from its 1986 foray into the insurance trade", a reference to the £40 million spent on Clarkson Puckle. The Inchcape team, however, felt that its post-acquisition efforts to improve the management of the company, and recently improved results, confirmed its judgment.

Dale Butcher saw the debate from the inside. "There was an understanding of the need for organic growth, but organic growth was always penalized because it would usually show a loss for a couple of years while you build up your business. It was much easier for George to stomach an acquisition, even with goodwill, and get profits from day one. So the accounting treatment drove George and his team primarily to acquisitions. We always say that it was the subsequent team that messed things up with acquisitions, but there were some fairly poor ones made in George's time as well, in the belief that you need to build scale."

Philippe Lasserre conducted sessions on "Managing Mergers and Acquisitions" during the Euro-Asia Centre programs taking place at this time. His research for these classes threw up the fact that between January 1987 and December 1990, Inchcape had approved eighty-two acquisition projects at a cost of £290 million. Of these, fifty-two projects had fallen below their target. All group members had been involved in one or more acquisitions during this period and he believed that there was a significant opportunity to learn from collective experience. One of his slides bore the simple message, "On average, mergers and acquisitions are bad news." As events would show, it fell on deaf ears.

A CHANGE IN DIRECTION

Turnbull had come into the group envisaging a reduction in the group's dependence on cars. He had reversed this policy to take advantage of the car sales boom, but by 1989 was again, under prodding from Stacey Ellis, thinking about a further strategy reversal. Both he and George were becoming more and more worried about the very long-term future of the Motors business, though Ellis had some revolutionary dreams.

In the future, Ellis could "see Inspection and Testing maybe going through to £100 million and insurance becoming a world league business and in my mind, I thought that we could probably come down to three legs with an international flavor. So I thought, we should build up these two big service businesses."

Did George share this vision? The two worked closely together, and Stacey saw George as "very independent. He loved Motors, but equally, he was a realist. He was no macho 'I'm right,' or 'You're wrong' type of thing. He would just sit through, I don't know how many meetings, and eventually he would say, 'I think ...' and he would sum it up and about nine times out of ten, he was about right."

While this agenda remained under wraps, Inchcape's results continued healthy. In 1991 the group recorded a record profit of £185.2 million before tax. This result (which included the sale of Inchcape's tea business) represented a 6.4% growth in pre-tax profits on 1990, and brought gearing down to about 20%.

Growth in the non-Motors businesses was vigorous, with profits up by more than a half in Services and nearly a tenth in Marketing. Of the two major regions in which it operated, while the Far East businesses largely continued strong throughout 1991, in Southeast Asia the Singapore-based Inchcape Berhad suffered a fall in operating profits due to declining demand in most of its businesses. Other factors affecting Inchcape's results were lower demand in the aftermath of the Gulf War, and the recession in the U.S. and Europe. The U.K.'s contribution to profits had declined from over a third of operating profits in 1987 to a fifth.

The results, according to comments made by Sir David Orr at the time, demonstrated once again "the inherent strengths of the Inchcape group. With a range of businesses and geographical spread, the group has been able to capitalize on those industries and regions that have continued to grow even as others have suffered from the recession."

Outside commentators also praised the group's performance, but the final accolade, as far as George Turnbull and his team were concerned, came on June 19, 1991, when Inchcape finally made it into the FTSE-100. As *The Times'* "City Diary" reported, it represented the culmination of a twofold ambition: "The first, Alpha stock status, was achieved within two years (in 1988). The second, to be rid of its outdated stock market classification as an overseas trader, happened last December." Quoted in the article, John Duncan said simply, "We're all delighted."

BARON AT THE GATE

By this time, the big question hanging in the air was the succession. Who would Sir George Turnbull anoint as his heir? There were three internal candidates: Charles Mackay, sector director of Inchcape Pacific Ltd. (IPL); David John, director of the Southeast Asian operations; and Stacey Ellis, the planning supremo. As Derek Whittaker observed, Turnbull was an expert at manipulating, and in particular playing off his ambitious senior executives against each other. But though each of them had good qualities, it was Mackay who had delivered outstanding results at IPL and he it was whom George finally favored. In an interview with *The Times*, Turnbull was reported as saying, "Mr Mackay had been earmarked as his successor from the day he joined Inchcape from Chloride in July 1986." The baron in the field, who had so often battled with those at the center, was about to change sides.

Since 1986, Sir George Turnbull had combined the roles of chairman and chief executive. In March 1991 it was announced that from January 1, 1992, the roles would be split. Charles Mackay, chairman of Inchcape Pacific, would first become group managing director, and later in the year take over as chief executive. Sir George would continue as chairman until 1997 to oversee the restructuring process.

In part, this phased move was meant to allay the doubts of those who felt that an unrestrained Charles Mackay might just be too great a change for Inchcape. Despite the excellent results he had achieved at IPL, some detractors noted that they had been achieved in very favorable circumstances. The reorganization he had executed there had been effective, but would the hard, aggressive performance culture implemented at IPL be suited to Inchcape plc? He had also, as several managers pointed out, left behind a difficult legacy: a lack of a clear successor.

Further doubts concerned his well-advertised commitment to global business streams. Under Turnbull, there had been a slow evolution in this direction, culminating in the announcement after the Torquay conference. O'Donoghue recalled that "George always had the intention that once we had the businesses under geographic control, he would turn it into a business-driven organization." But in the meantime, he had always allowed exceptions to allow for the vagaries of Inchcape local needs, and accepted their importance.

While Turnbull had let things proceed at their natural pace, Mackay was a hearty exponent of total global business streaming; it was his route to "focus." His faith in it came out clearly in an interview he gave at the time of the IPL business streaming. "We will be a lot more focused than we have been, and we'll get a lot more specialism in reporting …This is not a cost-cutting, but a top management focusing operation." His commitment to the geographical concept and the role of the country managers was, on the other hand, less evident. But although he had successfully implemented business streaming in the Far East, there it had operated on a regional basis. Could the same model be applied successfully to the whole group? It was the start of another long-running debate.

While Mackay had many supporters, and no-one doubted his intelligence and huge ability, most were relieved to know that George would be around to act as a moderating influence. Mackay's confidence had grown hugely, boosted by his high profile in Hong Kong, as *taipan* of one of the old *hongs*. Those who had seen him enjoy the limelight wondered how he would adjust to the relative calm and lack of notoriety of being head of a group that some analysts still failed to spell correctly.

John Duncan recalled talking to Turnbull about this and being told, "Don't worry, I will be there to guide him." Whittaker had similar conversations, and concluded: "I think George recognized that he had the potential to be brilliant, given the fact that he would have been watching over him. He saw him, realistically, as one of the major chief executives in the U.K. Several years' more experience, and George's coaching could have unlocked all that potential ... He was a good team player during his time at IPL. Charles helped us get Peugeot into Japan, Australia, and New Zealand. I suppose it was George's influence over him that made him into a team player.

In fact, Turnbull was well aware of all these concerns, and had tried to prepare the handover as thoroughly as possible. In doing so, he had enlisted the help of INSEAD's Philippe Haspeslagh, whose presentation to the executive board seminar had included coverage on various conceptions of corporate groups, the role of the center in a group, and the evolution of the life of groups.

Such a menu had great appeal for the Inchcape executives, and Turnbull, in particular, had been taken by Haspeslagh's comments about how the U.S. conglomerate General Electric (GE) had handled its last handover of power. As Haspeslagh recalled, "I was talking about the evolution of companies, using the example of GE and describing how each phase is usually associated with a new CEO. I stressed how one of the crucial things in this situation — because whilst you need to preserve and build on the old, you also need to break down some things in order to build the new — is that there should be a clear agreement and understanding between the outgoing and incoming persons about what needs to be accomplished in the next phase so that it does not cause bad blood. It is also a way of transmitting legacy. I told them the story of the handover between Jack Welch and Reg Jones at GE, and how they did it in the presence of an outsider, who happened to be Peter Drucker."

As a result, Haspeslagh was invited to play the same role for the handover from Turnbull to Mackay. This he was to prepare via a series of interviews with those two and various others. However, Haspeslagh had barely begun the process when he was contacted by Bob Goodall with the news that because of George Turnbull's ill health, the process would be speeded up.

The news of George Turnbull's illness was a tremendous shock to everyone. John Duncan recalled that he was in Malaysia when he got the message to phone Turnbull at 10 p.m., local time. "Then he gave me the news of his illness." Duncan played a key role in disseminating the news. "The first phase was to get the message over that this was not going to be a problem for the group ... We got that message across all right."

The design to ensure an orderly succession was completely nullified as Sir George was forced to retire prematurely in November 1991. Charles

Mackay became group chief executive immediately, and in June 1992 the great caretaker, Sir David Orr, once more stepped into the breach to act as chairman until the board appointed a permanent successor.

Sir David recalled, "When George became ill, we sat down and talked about what we were going to do. It was rather awful. There was no doubt that George knew he was going to die and approximately when, and that is what happened. George discussed it absolutely openly ... he was marvelous." To Sir David and all who had worked with him, Sir George's premature retirement in November 1991 was a moment of great sadness.

THE BARON ENTERS THE CASTLE

As Haspeslagh described, in taking over from Sir George, "Charles saw himself as the more entrepreneurial person, who was business-oriented. He had been sitting out on the periphery, but now the baron had to come into the castle." He pinpointed several concerns that Mackay might have had about his new role of poacher turned gamekeeper: "Having sat on the periphery, there was a certain amount of frustration with the bureaucracy and the role of the center. So he was concerned about how he would review and create the role of the center that would be small, and lean, and encourage entrepreneurialism."

It was clear there would be changes, not least among the top personnel who would not stay to serve under the new chief. Inevitably, the appointment of Mackay meant that Turnbull's team would eventually begin to break up. Also, unlike Turnbull, Mackay was not a Motors man, steeped in the culture of Inchcape's healthy but dominating business. What changes would he make there? Would he accept the new vision that Stacey Ellis had been forming in his mind? No-one would have put money on this. Derek Whittaker spoke for them all when he observed, "That was the great pity of George dying prematurely, when George's intention in appointing Charles was that he should be there guiding and providing his particular brand by common sense. To do the same to him as he used to do to Stacey — 'that is crackers, or that is brilliant'."

THE END OF AN ERA

In retrospect, the Turnbull era became bathed in a rosy glow. During this time, the story ran, the top team had worked together in harmony, there were no politics, the results were terrific, and Inchcape was the City's darling. Rod O'Donoghue summed up George's skills as a leader:

"George had a unique skill to put chemical combinations of people together that worked extremely positively in the corporate interest." Peter McElwaine, later deputy chief executive of Inchcape Middle East, agreed with this. "He had a rare ability to make people within the organization think they were of value to the organization, and that gave him a lot of credibility ... Leadership was the key to George's success." One member of the executive team had a colorful analogy: "If George had said, 'You frightened lot jump out,' we would have all jumped out with him. Anyone else, we would have said, 'You jump first, mate.'"

But perhaps in defense of those who took up the torch after him, there were some dangerous flaws in the edifice Turnbull bequeathed to Charles Mackay. John Whiteman observed that, "There is a great tendency to build up the myth of the Turnbull era. But it didn't all go wrong when Charles arrived ..."

The period 1986–89, he recalled, was a good period for the main businesses, with "Toyota knocking everything flat in front of it ... That was the base of the group when Motors' potential was truly realized. At the same time, we were knocking off the obvious problems and, starting with a broad mesh, it was quite easy to identify which ones to tackle. In a sense, the job was easier at that stage." But as another contemporary remarked, "Once the period of clearing out the basic rubbish, which was a great driver of growth, was over, if anyone had checked analytically what was going on, where the organic growth was going to come from — obviously there was not much." Rod O'Donoghue felt that, "We had reached the point when George died, where we were going into a different phase. There was going to be investment because the housekeeping had been done. We were in very good shape in the market conditions that existed, but more was needed."

As the results showed, when it came to bringing growth, the acquisitions record was not good, many of the core businesses remained "a mess," and Motors was still too dominant, despite Turnbull's stated desire to make it less so. Dale Butcher admitted, "Perhaps George invested too heavily in Motor Retail. Motors was his heartland — he understood where the market was." He divided George's term of office into two parts: "George had done a wonderful job sorting out the mess, sorting out the management team, and giving head office a proper role to play in the business ... However, the situation changed at the end of 1989, when the loss-makers evaporated. I think that's when the drive for growth became difficult for George and his team.

"That was when things started to unravel. George was not very well, and Stacey was questioning some of the businesses Charles wanted to invest in ... You could feel the tension in head office at this time."

Stacey Ellis thought that "George delegated very well. He didn't get involved in the detail, unless there was a problem. He just listened and said, 'OK, get on with it.' So people thought that they were getting on with their own business, and were happy. And it helped that we were successful." This attitude, Stacey felt, meant that George got the balance between the center and the barons in the field about right. "We didn't do everything they wanted, and vice versa. But the balance was good." David John agreed. "Once you had George's trust, you ran the business. He would get off your back."

Another question about the Turnbull era is the extent to which George dazzled his own managers, the City, and the business journalists about the real nature of Inchcape's turnaround. Was it sleight of hand by an accomplished magician to sell them a story that was not true? With one bound, Inchcape's share price was free and soaring high.

Colin Armstrong felt that Turnbull was "masterful at choosing the right people to help him in his "massaging" of the institutional investors, the fund managers, and the market perception of the company. He had this history, and he either got it or had it and enhanced it, a reputation that he was in charge of something that was going to be successful ... he seemed to give the right messages. I used to sit there looking at this from the inside, and then seeing what was happening on the outside because the share price movement bore no relation to our actual performance or immediate future."

Whiteman agreed, "We were underrated until 1990, and one of the things we consistently talked about was why the market gave us such a low rating. So we worked on communicating and the market assessment of us took off, because we were carrying on when the rest of the world was having a downturn ... And it is very hard when people keep writing positive things about you to say, 'No, that's not right; we're actually a bunch of small businesses operating in slightly out-of-the-way places.'"

Robert Morton, City analyst, felt that "George Turnbull came in with a great reputation. There was a huge hype internally about how strong he was, and how he was doing great things." However, he conceded, "Personally, I thought he did an OK job to sort out the root and branch problems within the business — and really got to grips with them."

Dale Butcher recalled: "At that time we were struggling because Inchcape was being reclassified from an overseas trader. There was a huge debate about being reclassified as a motors company, because motors companies had low P/Es ... John [Duncan] did a good job convincing the City that we were a marketing and distribution group, with some services as well."

But in the end, the epitaph for the Turnbull era came down to the undeniable fact that, under him, Inchcape had been effectively restructured and gone on to thrive, amidst relative harmony and cooperation among the top team members.

More importantly, Turnbull had delivered what he had promised, had concentrated on "doing what we do now, but better." As he himself had acknowledged in an interview, "That may not be as exciting as seeking the grand solutions and acquisitions ... but as Honda said, 'It is fit and finish rather than the redesign of a car' that produces success ... Always remember that success is mastery of the little things that have to be done well and in the right order — only rarely is it the grand design that brings total success."

Cutting Loose, 1992–94

Going Global

*"Organizational decisions depend on information,
estimates, and expectations that ordinarily
differ appreciably from reality."*

A good year for global, was 1992. A good word for business in the last decade of the twentieth century: short, punchy yet not aggressive, ambitious, complete, and non-partisan. "Global" conjured up positive images and rolled easily off the tongue. Turn it from an adjective into a noun and you had a grandiloquent term that might have come out of any self-respecting business school or strategic consultancy. Globalization was impressively "technical" and commanded instant respect. Of course, it wasn't new, but in the United States it was smart to talk of global brands and global markets, whether they were for consumer products or financial instruments.

The term was used with growing frequency from the mid-1980s onward. In 1983, Theodore Levitt wrote an article for the *Harvard Business Review*, proposing that companies would need, in future, to treat the world as if it were one large market. This influential article confirmed what many major U.S. consumer product companies were already doing, but gave academic respectability to that which other nations might see as ethnocentricity, or just plain laziness on the part of the Americans. Levitt argued that technology was driving the world toward commonality. Improvements in communications and travel were giving many more people access to information about new products and stimulating demand from across the world. According to Levitt, the standardization of products would enable huge economies and, more idealistically, that would translate into reduced prices. And the next consequence would be the demise of multinational organizations and their replacement by global ones. What Levitt was saying, corporations like Coca-Cola were doing, and had exploited from the Second World War onward. Coca-Cola also had a supreme understanding of the value of its global brand.

In the late 1980s the debate had moved on from marketing to the overall strategy and structure of the organization. Christopher Bartlett and Sumantra Ghoshal, respectively of Harvard and INSEAD, researched nine multinational companies and talked to over 250 of their managers. These companies were struggling to meet what were termed "multidimensional" strategic aims. Not only were they trying to compete through global efficiency, but they were also having to be responsive at a national level, while transferring learning across the organization and across the world. Bartlett and Ghoshal pointed out that few purely global, or straightforwardly multinational or international companies, now existed. The new organization format and the new terminology was "transnational."

In their research, Bartlett and Ghoshal were struck by how clearly the companies saw what to do, but how they were being held back by their organization structures and their capacity to change. They identified what they called an "administrative heritage." On the one hand, this could be the source of its key competencies. On the other, it could represent its most significant liabilities: the resistance of the organization to change and realign or expand its strategic capabilities.

They found that managers in highly complex organizations were, almost universally, making assumptions that simplified situations, rather than grappling with the complexity. Typically, they suppressed complexity by assuming that choices were a simple dichotomy: global integration versus national responsiveness; centralization or decentralization. Alistair Mant picked this up earlier in the 1980s in his book *Leaders We Deserve*. He traced polar or binary thinking back to educational experiences, and to cultural norms.

Bartlett and Ghoshal argued that product, function, or geography must not have the same level of influence on each key decision. Instead, the organization would need to ensure different roles for different activities, and become accustomed to the fact that nothing in the nature of a role would remain fixed. Responsibilities, relationships, and balances of power were to be in a state of flux. They saw this as the route to developing multidimensional perspectives and capabilities. They also observed that the more successful companies used training, conferences, and other forms of socialization to achieve a mindset in their managers that was attuned to handling complexity: "creating a matrix in the mind."

In 1992, one writer created a huge intellectual stir with his proposal that we were all heading toward a world where risking one's life for abstract goals or ideological struggles would cease to have relevance. Courage, imagination, and idealism would be shunted into the siding of economic calculation, technical problem-solving, environmental concern, and the satisfaction of sophisticated consumer demands. Taking a very long-term view, Francis Fukuyama noted that nationalism was a relatively new feature of social history. He foresaw the same economic forces that had fostered nationalism — those that had replaced class with national barriers and created centralized and linguistically homogeneous units — now encouraging the dismantling of national barriers and the formation of a single, integrated world market. Whether or not the political neutralization of nationalism would be complete within the present generation was not of concern to Fukuyama: ultimately, it would take place.

Kenichi Ohmae took the idea of nation states ceasing to be meaningful aggregates in another direction. His credentials were good: in 1990 he had predicted the collapse of the Soviet Union. Ohmae noted the flow of four "I"s across the old boundaries: industry, investment, individuals, and information. Investment would be less constrained by geography and increasingly made up of private money. Market forces were driving the global orientation of companies: knowledge and technology was being transferred to where it could be best exploited. Information technology made cross-border working far easier to realize and encouraged the setting up of strategic alliances. Because of better information flows, consumer taste would become more global, and consumers would look for value wherever they could find it. In effect, global solutions would flow to wherever there was a need, without the intervention of nation states. The middleman role of nation states would become obsolete; they would eventually be seen as unnatural or dysfunctional units of organization. In a borderless world, nations would become a nostalgic fiction.

In *The Competitive Advantage of Nations* Michael Porter argued for the importance of geographical clusters of related endowments. Ohmae endorsed this idea, but saw no reason why these clusters should be located exclusively within one nation's boundary. In fact, Ohmae suggested that these groupings might work even better when spread across boundaries. He saw "region states" as being the new natural economic zones, either as a specific part of a nation or straddling nations. In Europe, the Rhone-Alps region and its strong linkages with Northern Italy was a clear example. In the United States, the Bay Area and Silicon Valley of California was another; in Asia, Greater Shanghai or the Hong Kong/Guangzhou/Shenzhen/Macau area were other demonstrations of the region state.

The emerging economic world was neither a politically bounded patchwork of nations, nor was it Fukuyama's long-term vision of convergence and homogeneity. Rather, it was what Ohmae called a zebra: stripes of darker color separated by "white space." Convergence of buying power and demand would occur within the darker stripes, but the pace of convergence might be quite different in the white spaces. Managers of businesses would work along and in the stripes, unconfined by national boundaries. Conventional organization structures required rethinking. The old country management system might need to be supported by information management that picked up the regional flows of activity. Or, it might be better to retain the country management to handle politically biased matters of central government policy, and then weave a regional matrix of functions or business sectors across the nation states. Critically, Ohmae's proposed solution to the globalization issue was a market-driven, regional one.

In the first half of the nineties the Internet was moving rapidly from the academic to the business arena, but was still seen primarily in terms of its communication power. In the second half of the decade its enormous potential for commerce has become much more obvious. While there is no immediate sign that the ability of individual nations to raise taxes has declined, the Internet must pose a significant threat to the taxation of many sorts of transactions. Globalization itself is leading companies to relocate production wherever and whenever low tax opportunities present themselves. Globalization makes it harder to check the accuracy of reported profits, and easier for many more individuals to earn income outside their home base and hide some of it from the tax authorities. Unless nations can find other politically acceptable ways of raising tax revenue to provide the trappings of statehood, both the Internet and globalization may contribute to the eventual decline of the nation state.

In the early 1990s the academics were running well ahead of most of the field practitioners on the subject of globalization. Many corporations held on to the vestiges of local or political–regional structures long after the apparent globalization of their products and services. Often it was blurred by the use of terms like "matrix," but local operating knowledge and political influence were not things to be cast aside in the rush to globalize. Inchcape was about to embark on a major organizational change that would challenge its managers to handle complexity, and to use other than binary thinking. Like many other companies, the personality profiles of the successful operating managers had several things in common: the preferences for order and "tidiness" and for closing down the range of options, rather than opening them up. Binary thought dominated their decision-making processes. And, as in other organizations, it was the successful operating managers who were usually promoted to positions of greater strategic influence.

GLOBAL AMBITION

In the United Kingdom in 1992, "global" had a very specific relevance. The economy was in deep recession, with new car sales forecast to decline to about £1.5 billion compared with previous levels of £2.3 to £2.4 billion. The housing market was in hibernation. Consumer spending had stalled, and company after company came in with profit warnings. The "R" words — recession and redundancy — were peppering the media. Europe was going into deeper recession, but the United States was just starting to climb back into growth after a long period of depressed activity. Going global was a very attractive way to be heading if your domestic market was going nowhere.

"Global" was one of those words, like "international" and "multinational", that one could happily introduce into a conversation or an Annual Report without fear of some pedant asking for a definition. In a stock market hungry for good news, one could throw out a few "globals" and be sure that an eager audience would snap them up. Sometimes, though, the audience failed to distinguish between the real thing and the reverberation.

One man with global ambition was now firmly in charge at Inchcape. With a caretaker chairman in Sir David Orr, who himself was not in good health, Charles Mackay had few restraining forces around him as he set out to conquer the world. The team George Turnbull had so carefully put together was still intact, though it contained more than one individual who might have had his ambition thwarted. It came with a style of operating that was robust but collegiate: everyone could have his say; everyone would be listened to; everyone could expect to influence the decision at hand and then move on.

January 1992 was the start of a business-streamed Inchcape.

Interviewing Charles Mackay, *The Financial Times* said, "The former colonial trading house is trying to shed its traditional British image. It is setting out on the text-book route of corporate change, and is on its way to becoming a thoroughly 'global' organization ... The new 'global' approach mirrors the changes that have already taken place among Inchcape's customers in the motor and shipping industries. According to Mackay, who pioneered the change when he was head of the group's Far East operation, 'it offers focus and specialization'." Focus was another concept the investment community regarded as virtuous, and the word "core" was closely associated with it.

Through their contact with INSEAD, Inchcape's senior managers had already started to wrestle with the concept of core competencies. Searching for them in the geographically organized group led to repeated frustration, and was to become a recurring theme as the very shape and existence of the group was challenged. At least in the new business-streamed structure there was a greater likelihood of isolating a core competence or two. The theory was clear enough: what is it that you do so well that it adds value and is difficult for your competitors to replicate? The notion of collective learning residing in the organization was readily understood. So was the idea that a core competence could signpost the way for new business development. The theory was fine, but even in the relatively constrained diversity of a business stream it was still rather like looking for a needle in a haystack.

In January 1989, BZW's analysts were recommending Inchcape's shares for its "wide spread of service and marketing interests." By February 1992 they were highlighting the "reorganization along global lines" and "further moves to strengthen core activities." No longer were investors content to let the company spread their risk: according to the new dogma, the investor now had rapid access to so much information that he could manage his risks more efficiently than any company. What the investor wanted from the company was focus, because focus implied greater efficiency within that enterprise — and growth, in profits and dividends.

Structurally, Inchcape was doing two other significant things. The first was to appoint directors to head the business streams, but to base them in London. David John had moved from Singapore to London to run the Marketing stream, which then represented 25% of the group's profits. Alan Marsh and Derek Whittaker joined the board to head up the Toyota and "non-Toyota" parts of the Motors business. With the exception of Buying Services, the heads of Shipping, Testing, and Insurance were all London-based. To a man, they were all British.

The second action was to appoint country managers to preserve some of the benefits of the former geographical organization. Though he backed the idea of streaming, one of Sir George Turnbull's firm conditions was that the balance between business specialization and geography must be maintained. He did not want to see the original strength of the group — its local knowledge and status — being thrown out with the bathwater. Nor did he want to see any growth in overheads through duplicating roles or adding bureaucracy.

The country managers were more mixed in their backgrounds and included a Hong Kong Chinese, an American, a Chilean, a Greek, and an Australian, plus eight more British managers. They were all heads of existing businesses such as Marketing or Motors or Business Machines, and being appointed country manager was essentially an honorary extra responsibility. *The Financial Times* made an observation which came to haunt Inchcape: "The culture of a group with its roots deep in Britain's colonial past cannot be changed overnight. Change must also reach to the top — and Inchcape's board has only one member who is not British, a French non-executive Director." However, the cultural mix was not the main problem.

The Financial Times noted that, "Mackay is in no doubt about the relative importance of these changes. 'Globalization is 80 per cent of it and the country manager role is 20 per cent. Global is the watchword.'" *The Financial Times* went on to quote David John: "If a country manager and an executive have a falling out, it will be my job to fly in and bang their heads together." Whatever subtlety of organization Sir George may have wanted in the last days before he retired was already lost, but the potential for confusion was not.

Back in St. James's House in the West End of London and close to the gentlemen's clubs, the streams were busy setting up shop. Shipping and Testing were already organized along the lines of business streams, as were the two parts of Motors. Insurance stayed in the financial district of London, maintaining its independence and separation from Inchcape group. Each stream began to set up its own functional staff: typically someone on strategy or business development, plus a finance director and a human resources specialist, several of whom were recruited from the previous corporate team. What all of them were looking forward to was increased autonomy from the center, and most already had strategies or coherent plans in place.

MARKETING DOES NOT QUITE FIT THE MODEL

Marketing was different. David John was still traveling intensively and continued to attend board meetings of Inchcape Berhad in Singapore, so his leadership was sometimes remote. Worse, the stream had no strategy and even lacked knowledge of the businesses it contained. The reason was quite simple: Marketing was essentially everything that did not fit into the other streams, and sometimes things which should have belonged to other streams but were not assigned, for geographic or historical reasons. In many cases, Marketing represented the history of Inchcape and was the primary legal and visible entity in each country where Inchcape was operating. This was an added and costly burden for the stream to bear.

Its products ranged from liquor and tractors, to refinery catalysts, to beer kegs, to medical equipment, to chocolates and biscuits and dog food. It even included contract manufacturing of pharmaceuticals in Southeast Asia and the bottling of Coca-Cola in Chile. In short, it was a mess of monumental proportions. What was superficially simple to structure and project to the financial community was, in reality, a jumble of mainly small and mainly local businesses. A new group strategy director was soon to be appointed by Charles Mackay: his name was Andrew Cummins. Asked subsequently whether he thought Marketing could have worked as a global stream, Cummins said, "In reality, 'global' was a false word: it had no real relevance. We were trying to build coherent businesses with a sustainable competitive advantage. It didn't matter if they were global or not — the businesses were still local — for example, the Marketing Stream in the Middle East."

The first task of the Marketing team was to try to understand which businesses had scale and were making significant profits, and then to try to find coherence across them. An early attempt to extract gold from the silt of decades of entrepreneurial accretion was a nice confirmation of the well-known Pareto principle. Of several hundred businesses that had been identified, about 20% were making a positive contribution and of that fifth, only ten businesses were of real scale. The "tail" was extremely long, with minuscule profits tapering into losses. Moving from that analysis to real action was going to prove the real challenge: which businesses were "tired," and which were merely in the early stages of growth? Another problem was more emotive: would the act of discontinuing products or dismissing principals cause a lack of confidence in the remaining principals? Would Inchcape be seen to be in retreat from its traditional role?

Another challenge lay on the "people" front, as one of the authors was soon to discover. Marketing had a dense thicket of relatively senior and well-rewarded managers, some managing businesses that had shrunk underneath them and left their reward packages apparently bloated. Others also had responsibilities hanging over from the old geographical organization, such as the public companies in Singapore and Malaysia and the quasi-corporate structures in Hong Kong and Japan.

Generally being the older companies of Inchcape, the Marketing business units had mature cultures, which reflected more the Asian values of loyalty than the dominant Western value of reward for performance. Bonuses were seen as a right, rather than a variable component of pay, and in Japan the salary structure was still based on age and service seniority rather than job content or performance. In 1992, obtaining basic information about the businesses or the people who managed them was like pulling teeth. Not only was information localized and unstandardized in its format, but also the information systems were ineffective and unreliable. Under the old geographical structure, information systems had been centralized, but purely to gather financial data, and at a high level of aggregation.

Early on, David John had decided to recruit a marketing professional to join his central team and help rethink the overall strategy. He chose Ian Ross, who had made rapid progress in British American Tobacco (BAT) and had had a high-level career ahead of him in that organization. Ross brought in very structured ideas of what marketing and business planning should be about, but also wide experience of setting up in developing markets, including Chile and Vietnam. More unusual still, was his early background as a journalist in the world of pop music. As Ross observed, "I joined at the high of the company in terms of performance and reputation — it was growing strongly. The strategy looked sensible and very plausible: a transformation from a trading house to a sector-driven international distributor — on the face of it, all looked fine." But first impressions of the real task were less positive: "I didn't see anything I recognized as a business or market plan: I saw a series of budgets, and I didn't see a clear statement of what these businesses were trying to do — just numbers. Frankly, there seemed to be lots of managers of very small businesses, and not any kind of guiding light behind it. I was a bit shocked ... I got a gut feel that more than 80% of this was junk. Whether or not it was junk, there was no way that a head office could add any value to these businesses. They were not of critical mass; they didn't have the right management or a clearly defined market position. All you could do really was act as banker."

The view from the field was bound to be different, since it involved an inevitable loss of local autonomy and changes in the decision-making process. A longserving senior manager in the Middle East, Peter McElwaine, supported the need for specialization, but he was concerned about concentrating expensive expertise at a remote center rather than strengthening resources at the "sharp end" of the business. For him, the costs of employing just one expensive senior manager in London would have been better spent on engaging a number of salesmen locally. In Singapore, Stephen Looi had his doubts, too. "In the old style, there was no need to refer to London. Decision-making was quick, local knowledge was there ... Streaming adds bureaucracy and makes the geographic spread so great."

If there were doubts in the field, what was even more fundamental was the view of the man charged with making the Marketing stream work: David John. He recalled a discussion with Sir George Turnbull:

"I had absolutely no objection to the streaming of Toyota, because that was a stream with one principal. You needed to manage your communications with that principal superbly — and manage it at all levels. Also, you had to convince that principal you had a decent management development policy. Those were the two big deficiencies, in my view, of the former geographic structure of Inchcape. But I had severe reservations about the Marketing stream, because the units were not big enough to stream: there was a multiplicity of relatively small operations in forty countries or so. Each had its own culture and nothing was uniform.

"I had a discussion with George, saying, 'I reluctantly go along with it, but if you aren't careful your overhead is going to grow; secondly, you are going to lose focus on the bottom line; thirdly, you have got the cultural aspects to think through.' He said, 'Well, we are going to do it,' and I said, 'I will work it to the best of my ability, but I still have quite a number of reservations.' But it was not an atmosphere conducive to informed debate." Despite his concerns, David John decided to take on the challenge of setting up the Marketing stream. "You made your point, but once the decision was made you got on with it, without complaining." It was probably typical of other senior Inchcape managers who, despite what their intellect might be telling them, would respond positively to George Turnbull's forceful leadership style. For Stacey Ellis, this was "one of the attributes of a good manager." He cited the experience of Jim Thomas, who "did not like the decision to sell Tea and it caused him a lot of distress with his staff, [but] he carried out his duties as well as we could have wished and we all respected him."

Who Would be a Country Manager?

If the Marketing stream was struggling to work up enthusiasm about its new responsibilities, then so were the country managers, who were mostly responsible for a region, and some for single countries. In *Inchcape World*, Charles Mackay spelt out the theory of being a good country manager in each of their territories: be "Mr Inchcape"; provide central services; be the link between the business streams; and act as a source of knowledge on new business opportunities and local knowledge. In Singapore and in Malaysia, they had the extra responsibility of communicating with shareholders of their respective local public companies. In addition, they were responsible for running one major business stream within their territory, and it was this that directly affected their bonus and career prospects. Eight out of the twelve were responsible for the Marketing stream.

As ever, there was a gap between theory and the reality of life on the ground. Paul Cheng, who was country manager for Greater China, found that, "Global streaming created a lot of confusion in the minds of principals, because all of a sudden they now had to talk to London. Inadvertently, you cut out the authority from the field. If everything has to be decided in London, then why talk to Hong Kong? It makes the Hong Kong management totally ineffective." Philip Cushing, who took over from David John in Southeast Asia, saw this clearly from the moment business streaming was first publicly articulated at the Torquay management conference in November 1990. "I knew from that day that the idea of being left as country manager in Southeast Asia wasn't something that I wanted to do. It was quite clear that I would be pretty powerless and anachronistic. To the point that if a career opportunity didn't open up for me with a clear line of responsibility for a business, I would have left."

The country management debate was at the heart of the tensions generated by a shift from regional to global structures. It was an issue with which many other companies have wrestled, and obfuscated with matrix organizations. No red-blooded line manager is likely to be comfortable with shared accountability and compromised power. The country managers would be the losers, and local knowledge would be thrown out with the global bathwater. The oscillations between product and geographical organizations continue in other companies: as recently as September 1998, Procter & Gamble announced that it was going to split itself into seven "global business units." Sometimes the act of changing is more important than the change itself.

A TALE OF TWO ACQUISITIONS

While these structural changes were being digested, two major acquisitions were occupying the attention of the corporate team. The first to be completed, in January 1992, was Spinneys, a company that had grown from small beginnings in Palestine to become a substantial business throughout the Arabian Gulf and beyond. Stacey Ellis had stalked this quarry for several years, and watched as it was bought by a Swedish group for a price he deemed too high. This acquisition was a clear demonstration of the cautious but long-sighted approach Ellis adopted, and the way in which he influenced Turnbull. Ellis, at that time, handled all acquisitions and disposals.

On the subject of acquisitions and disposals, he recalls saying to George Turnbull: "We should never pay too much." What he meant by this obvious statement was that if the company went into the marketplace, buying only once every five years, nobody would remember whether or not the company had paid a generous price. However, running an active program of buying and disposing of so many businesses would attract attention. This implied more rigor about pricing. "So, on the sales side, I hope we were fair but if we said 'no' then we meant it, and the same on the purchase side. That was part of our culture and approach."

This culture and approach was essentially one of straightforwardness, and a rare willingness to lose a deal rather than pay over the odds, as Ellis was to demonstrate in his pursuit of Spinneys. "During the first discussions with Spinneys, someone came in and offered 30% more than us. But I said 'no' and walked away. Then it came up again and we got quite involved. A Swedish group came in and offered a silly sum of money and again I said 'no.'" As Ellis reflected, whatever conclusions one might draw from financial analyses, "you have to stand back a second time and say that it is a good acquisition, because you know you will wake up in five years' time and it will either stink or be brilliant." But, in this case, despite all the apparent synergies, Ellis still could not convince himself the price was right. His conservative approach paid off: "Later there was a recession in Sweden — 1991 — and hey presto, it came up again. The guy who had beaten me to the punch had been put in charge of selling it. We spent three months going through it and we got it for a steal!"

The "steal" was £32.1 million and a P/E ratio of 5.5. Not only was it remarkably cheap, but an almost ideal fit, strategically, operationally, and culturally with Inchcape's existing Gray Mackenzie business. There was some overlap of markets, but Spinneys added new countries like Jordan and Cyprus and operations such as supermarkets and important principals like Nestlé. The management team had similar skills and backgrounds to their counterparts in Gray Mackenzie, and, in many cases, already knew them socially. Within the first month, most of the senior managers in Spinneys had met one or more of the senior Inchcape team, and had been reassured about future intentions for the business and the integration process. Several noted how different this was from their experience of the previous acquisition: few, apparently, met any senior people, and their only encounters were with unfriendly accountants. At a stroke, Inchcape's presence in the Middle East had doubled. The Marketing team had something to be happy about.

Entirely overshadowing this acquisition was that of TKM. At more than ten times the price of Spinneys, and involving Motors, it was bound to attract all the attention. Negotiations had started the previous year, based on initial contacts between Charles Mackay and Sir Ron Brierley's New Zealand group. Despite being based in Hong Kong at the time, Mackay apparently persuaded Sir George that he should lead the negotiations. Those close to the TKM acquisition still wonder if the transaction would have proceeded if Turnbull had not been seriously ill. If it had gone ahead, they felt the price and terms might have been very different. As it was, the deal was struck at £382 million, and £376 million of that was raised by a one for three rights issue in January.

By March 2, the deal was consummated and Reg Heath, chief executive of TKM, joined the board of Inchcape. Inchcape had completed its first ever rights issue and made by far its biggest acquisition. TKM brought well-known franchises like Ferrari, Chrysler, Daihatsu, Mazda, and Subaru; it also added some lesser-known names like Lada, Proton, and Kia. Six thousand more people, mostly in the U.K., became part of Inchcape — though many of them were scarcely aware of this fact. The management team of TKM was left intact to run its business, without any senior appointments from the acquiring company, and largely without interference from Inchcape's corporate team. TKM brought an utterly different management culture into the Inchcape group, one that would soon affect that of its new parent.

Press comment was favorable. In the previous December, *The Sunday Telegraph* faithfully echoed the global buzzword: "The £376 million purchase ... will boost Inchcape's global car sales by a half next year. The City has greeted the deal as a triumph of timing. Mackay boasts he is buying TKM for £100 million less than the asking price 18 months ago. Most have assumed the groundwork was Turnbull's, but one non-executive says 'It owes a great deal to Charles's persistent negotiating skills.'" Writing in *Inchcape World* in April 1992, Mackay boasted, "It increases substantially our global spread in import and distribution, taking us into France and Ireland for the first time and considerably expanding our activities in the U.K. and Australia."

GLOBAL REVERBERATIONS

More good news followed as the company declared its results for 1991. Describing it as the world's largest independent car distributor, *The Asian Wall Street Journal* hailed a 6.4% rise in pre-tax profits. It quoted Mackay: "We're not looking for market-led recovery. We push our profits up with or without, and when the upturn comes, they'll go up that much faster." The bullish tone was echoed by the analysts' "buy" recommendations. BZW commented on the global reorganization, acquisitions, and strong exposure to the high-growth economies of the Pacific Basin. UBS Phillips & Drew also liked its exposure to the Far East, and noted that it was "a relatively complex company with ... a wide geographical spread of profits." Nomura Research Institute noted that few industrial companies had gone through the U.K. recession with their growth records intact, and praised the diversity of risk across the group. Inchcape was in danger of becoming fashionable.

TEAM TACTICS

With less than half the year gone, two more important management changes were to be made. Mackay recalled Philip Cushing from Singapore, putting him in charge of the Services businesses: Shipping, Testing, and Buying — but not Insurance Services, which maintained its relative autonomy. Cushing joined the Main Board on May 1, within just two years of joining the group. His view of the task ahead of him was succinct: "What I inherited was three interesting businesses in their different ways, all in various states of disrepair, and, to some extent, disrepute in the group. I don't think George was very interested at all. Charles had tried hard to do something with Buying Services but failed. Shipping meandered along, and Testing was in — disarray isn't the right word — because of what happened in Venezuela and Foreign Trade Supervision, profits had plunged. The one thing that you didn't do with George was come in with unexpectedly poor results." As he explained in *Inchcape World*, "Once I have familiarized myself with all three activities, I see my task as being to assist the growth of those businesses fast and profitably. They all have tremendous potential."

Mackay had made one change that would have long-term significance: he had another more pressing one to make. During the previous six years, the working relationship between Mackay and Stacey Ellis had at times been tense, but George Turnbull was seen to be content to let one act as a foil to the other. Stacey was the thoughtful, prudent, and cautious operator for whom ambition needed to be tempered with careful planning and exhaustive negotiating. This approach had served the group well in its "housekeeping" phase, and helped contribute to a run of surprise-free results that pleased the stock market. Eventually, the differences in style led to a parting of the ways.

The search was on for a replacement strategic development director, and headhunters Spencer Stuart managed to break convention by finding an Australian. Andrew Cummins joined the board on June 5, 1992, the date Ellis stood down. Cummins was a breath of fresh air, with a breezy, no-nonsense style. There was no mistaking he was Australian, and no mistaking that he was in a hurry. His speech was often machine gun-like, always struggling to keep up with his thought processes. The stereotypical "Aussie" bluntness was coupled with a passionate approach to business and barely concealed emotions. No-one could accuse him of being "Mr Cool." He had spent nine years with McKinsey and six-and-a-half years with Elders, the last two of which were spent sorting out the mess resulting from an unsuccessful management buy-out. He left Elders looking for a management buy-in, but failed to find the right opportunity.

He was clear cut about why he wanted to join Inchcape: "From my point of view, the job offered me the prospect of becoming a CEO once Charles stepped down. Inchcape was a big global company — or a big international one. It had operations all over the world that, to the City, made it international. I didn't want to work for a standard British plc. I didn't join for the money, but for the board position and the challenge … Inchcape to me had a lot of attractions — diversity, challenge. I wasn't disappointed in what I found, though the share market hyped it up because of the 'Asian bubble.' From £3.50, the share price went to £5. There was talk of Inchcape being 'a class act.' It was all exciting. And I like motor cars — I enjoy Ferrari days at Goodwood. So I was interested by the Motors and the international businesses, particularly those in Asia. I saw it as an opportunity."

Cummins was equally clear about his task: "We were looking to see where we could create a 'scale' business. At that time, the share price was way ahead of the value of the component parts of the business, so we were creating value for the shareholders by doing what we were doing. You could never make a case for breaking the company up in those first few years."

ANOTHER KNIGHT ROLLS IN

Also joining the board on the same date as Andrew Cummins was Sir David Plastow, who was nominated to succeed Sir David Orr as chairman on September 15. He had just retired as chairman and chief executive of Vickers plc, whose famous subsidiary was Rolls-Royce Motors. It was Rolls-Royce that had given Plastow his route to the top, and forty-two years' experience of the motor industry — albeit a rarefied niche of that industry. He was also joint deputy chairman of Guinness plc, and deputy chairman of TSB group, a banking organization. His was an archetypal British chairman's image: pinstriped suit, striped shirt, and a formal posture to go with a crisp, if courteous, manner. A self-made man, with a dedication to business, he was characteristically pithy about the reasons for taking on the job: "George was very ill; David Orr was very persuasive." Also, he felt that he had something left in him to contribute, drawing on his experience of serving on the boards of nine public companies, on both sides of the Atlantic. "So, perhaps I could do something. That is the reason I took it on."

He planned to spend two days a week at the St. James's office, "overseeing the board and communicating with shareholders." This latter activity was to become a center of interest for Plastow, who had taken to heart the pronouncements of the Cadbury committee on corporate governance. The narrow definition and broader responsibilities would be tested in the months and years to come. In less than twelve months, Inchcape had had three chairmen, all of them knights.

Charles Mackay now had his team in place, and with far less bloodletting than had been the case when he took over Hong Kong in 1986. And he was to have a chairman who would know little of the detail and complexity of Inchcape. The way was clear for his ambition to take off. It was now time to motivate the troops.

ACE and Other Slogans

◆

Sir David Orr sat down. He had just delivered a witty, and, at times, irreverent after-dinner speech. His audience was in good humor and applauded warmly. More than ninety of his board colleagues and senior managers were packed into L'Agath restaurant in Luxembourg Town. It was a balmy evening in early June, and the late evening sun suffused the room with a gold-and-pink glow. Though he was not leaving the board until September, this was effectively Sir David Orr's last public occasion inside Inchcape and a chance to say goodbye to people with whom he had enjoyed an excellent working relationship. Having returned as chairman for a second time, he was now in the process of handing over to his successor, and seeing a new chief executive set the company on a very different course. He had reminded everyone that one person was absent, and sorely missed: Sir George, who by this stage was seriously ill. This was the last evening of the group management conference, and there was no doubt in anyone's mind that one era was closing, and another had already opened.

Luxembourg was not an obvious place to hold a conference, but it was chosen with an eye on the "new Europe" and the fact that Inchcape, through its acquisition of TKM, had increased its presence in its home continent. Some long-distance travelers grumbled about having to change planes to reach this destination, but there were few complaints about the Inter-Continental hotel, and even fewer about the cuisine. For most of the delegates, the company conference — whether Inchcape's or a previous company's — was a familiar ritual.

They knew the drill: a welcome pack in the hotel room complete with a plastic name badge; a hastily converted ballroom; the usual parade of directors delivering set-piece presentations justifying their business or their function; over-sized syndicate groups dominated by one or two noisy individuals; stage-managed debates and a final exhortation to "up your profits." Oh yes, and the silly little chairs which were excruciating after a couple of hours, and the group photograph one would look at in years to come to see who was still around. But it was a time to meet old faces and catch up on the gossip in the bar and at coffee breaks, and with any luck, grab a game of golf or tennis. Expectations of this conference were correspondingly modest, albeit there was a new chief executive to tune into.

This time, however, there were also some new personalities to meet. Michael Hemery, chief executive of Spinneys, and Reg Heath of TKM were prominent, and with Reg were two of his closest associates: Maurice Rourke, who handled business development and Peter Caney, his finance director. Philippe Haspeslagh, the Belgian Professor of Strategy from INSEAD, was another new name to most of the delegates. The INSEAD link was strong. Haspeslagh had been a star speaker at Mackay's last Inchcape Pacific conference in Macau the previous year, and Mackay had gained his MBA at Fontainebleau. Inchcape was a founder member of Euro-Asia Centre at INSEAD and a regular user of its senior management training.

BEHIND THE SCENES

Preparation had been going on for some time. As Charles Mackay recalled, "We had a number of intensive sessions using Philippe Haspeslagh as a moderator to think through what we really wanted out of Inchcape. I suppose you could say that the work that went on before the conference, which was pulling the executive committee together to think it through, was fairly trendy in two ways. First of all, to get all the top people to go away on several occasions within six months, and use outside help from a business school. The second was that it was a fairly democratic process: it really was a group of people trying to come together to think it through. I didn't try and impose a solution on them — which was certainly not the way it had been in the past. I think it worked, at the time."

Two workshops were held off-site at a country retreat called Danesfield House, following a series of structured interviews and visits during 1991. "There were three constituencies: Charles, the corporate staff, and the heads of the businesses. That was the triangle that had to be put in place," recalled Haspeslagh. "So, basically, I was trying to get a commitment from them that returns could be improved. Some of them felt at that point, too few of them, that organic growth would be the principal way. They saw it as possible, but initially, if you take note of the results of the questionnaire we did, then they were probably looking more for acquisitions."

Out of these discussions, reflected Haspelagh, emerged "an ambition for Inchcape — to be by the year 2000 one of the top twenty companies, that would be first or second in each of its business streams. Basically, the idea was that there was a natural growth of about 4% in the streams, and that internal development and small acquisitions or acquisitions of principals could bring that up to 10%. Most of the conference was to be geared to 'how do we get that 10%?' — by bringing new solutions to customers and principals, investing in IT, solving agency issues, and generally working the organization faster and harder. Besides this, Charles said that he and his corporate development would take care of acquisitions in order to add another 10%. So while I was working with the organization to try and get them to commit deeper and make certain investments to get more growth, Charles would be making corporate acquisitions."

ON A TREADMILL

Bob Cowell, an investor relations consultant, started proceedings on the Sunday evening with an entertaining presentation. He gave an outsider's view of the company, referring to its transformation in corporate stature and elevation to forty-sixth position in the FTSE-100 from nowhere. His tone turned serious as he concluded with a set of stern warnings: "Your new premium rating demands premium performance; yesterday is history, it's tomorrow that matters; and greater market status means closer scrutiny. You are on a treadmill."

VAULTING AMBITION

Back in the ballroom of the Inter-Continental on Monday morning, the conference strap line came up on the screen: "The Next Leap Forward: 1992–2000" and the music pulsed for half a minute before dying away. It was something of an anticlimax when Mackay introduced Philippe Haspeslagh and he launched into a dry exposition of factors for enduring success. A shared ambition, focused businesses, leveraged core competencies, and a lean, empowered organization. Typical business-school speak. Various members of the audience were beginning to look bored or in need of strong coffee to overcome the effects of the previous evening's sessions in the bar. One could almost read the minds of those tired faces: "What the hell has this to do with selling more cars, chocolates, or photocopiers?" He then reinforced the importance of ambition, citing it as the biggest single predictor of accomplishment, and strategic intent as a key ingredient of Japanese success. Haspeslagh also reminded them that 40% of the 1980 Fortune 500 had disappeared one decade later: staying successful was the hard part. After David John had recalled the successes of the past six years, Charles Mackay took the stage, and set out his ambition for the next eight years. The message was carefully couched, but two things stood out and jolted his audience like twin bolts of lightning: 20% year-on-year real growth in EPS and £1 billion of operating profit by the year 2000.

Was this the message of a new Messiah? It was critical to one's career not to take a position on this too early, so it was with some relief when Andrew Cummins and Rod O'Donoghue took over the podium to explain in detail how this might be achieved. Both emphasized the need for a mixture of organic growth and growth by acquisition. O'Donoghue, in particular, left no doubts about the criteria for investment and the controls that would be required, but this was not really what the audience was interested in. Minds were already racing ahead on the twin tracks of personal and business agendas.

Mackay then rounded off the morning with remarks on the group's values. In the early 1990s every self-respecting large corporation needed a set of values, variously "to act as the glue that binds" or to articulate "the way we do things around here." This was Inchcape's first attempt at a set of values and they came out as a curious assembly of integrity, professionalism, teamwork, and "Yes, We Care." This latter slogan was Mackay's own culture change program from Hong Kong, which was now to become a group-wide venture.

The entire afternoon was devoted to syndicate groups who were given the task of working out how their business stream could achieve the "ambition." Groups of fifteen or more individuals gathered around a table rarely achieve constructive debates, and this was no exception. As the afternoon wore on, weariness with debating and the need to produce presentations led to the desired conclusion: "Yes, we can do it, but we will need to make some significant acquisitions." Each stream presented its findings, but one protested vehemently that it could not be done. Dale Butcher remembered, "The only stream that said, 'We cannot grow to the scale you want' was Testing, but we were told we were very unadventurous. We said, 'We are quite happy to grow organically, but not to spend silly money.' It was a rather naive strategy." Butcher thought that the drive for acquisition had come from outside the organization. Haspelagh's recollections were quite the opposite: at no time had he advocated an acquisition-led strategy. The drive was coming from within, and was more to do with ambition than strategy. But a consultant had unwittingly become the scapegoat.

Eventually, everyone was whipped into line and the figures were added up: £290 million from Motors A; £250 million from Motors B; £150 million from Services; £100 million from Insurance Broking, plus an extraordinary £320 million from Marketing. The total was £1.1 billion. Adjusted for overheads and other sundry losses, the final figure was deemed to be £1.06 billion. As one cynic was heard to mutter in the bar afterwards, "It's absolutely, bloody amazing where a bit of ambition can take you."

After Luxembourg, further work was done to refine the operating plans of the business streams. Haspeslagh realized subsequently that "there was also a very clear financial profile put forward, which I hadn't discussed but which was put together by 'corporate.' If you look at that profile, the total of the operating plans of the existing businesses, their forecast of profitability by 2000 was £849 million. This still left a gap of £225 million to be filled by 'major corporate acquisitions.'"

CORE COMPETENCIES — CONUNDRUMS OR CHIMERAS?

The next day was devoted to a search for core competencies, again led by Haspelagh. He was picking up on a new mantra that had emerged a couple of years earlier. "Top management must add value by enunciating the strategic architecture that guides the competence acquisition process. We believe an obsession with competence building will characterize the global winners of the 1990s. With the decade underway, the time for rethinking the concept of the organization is already overdue." Thus concluded an article in the *Harvard Business Review* by C. K. Prahalad and Gary Hamel. Prahalad and Hamel were soon to become the latest gurus of management thinking. Identify your competencies, reorganize around them, and you were on the way to competing more successfully, or so the message seemed to be.

As Yves Doz had pointed out, the origins of this latest mantra could be traced back to the late 1950s, with a considerable expansion of interest in the 1980s. Doz acknowledged that the theory had intuitive appeal to managers. He also noted a bias in much of the strategy literature of the 1970s toward analyzing the external environment; core competencies redressed the balance in terms of making a strong case for the firm's own resources and capabilities as a factor in corporate renewal. Yet he was concerned that the emerging theory had neither a solid empirical base nor a micro-theoretical foundation. He went on to expand on some of the difficulties it presented: "Competencies are not easy to manage. Competencies are not very tangible, nor measurable, and the more valuable competencies may well be the least manageable. Competencies are fragile. Unpracticed, they wither away; stretched too thinly they lose their cut; explicited too fully, they no longer improve; aggregated too widely, they lose substance and reality; cultivated too long and too tightly, they turn into rigidities, and breed incompetence in responding to new circumstances." Doz made another obvious yet critical point: that competencies could reside in the whole organization or with one individual — or at any other point on that spectrum. He concluded his paper with a reminder that allowing competencies to emerge was one side of the task. Managing them through development, diffusion, integration, leverage, and renewal processes was also necessary, and it was the job of top management to achieve the balance and turn these efforts into operational objectives.

One other problem with core competencies was the lack of rigor with which the term was used. As John Kay lamented, it degenerated into a pretentious phrase that described all the things a business normally does. For Kay, however, it was the one or two truly distinctive capabilities that a business possessed. It might have skills like bottling beverages which other people could acquire readily, but it might have a brand like Coca-Cola which was unique: its distinctive capability. Deploy the skills and leverage the distinctive capability in the right market sectors and one would have competitive advantage. Used rigorously, the concept could make a major contribution to a business. Clearly, if the business had a long list of competencies, they were neither core nor distinctive; if it had none at all, then it was likely that it had no competitive advantage.

As one of the most important influences on competitive strategy during this decade, it is sad to see recent writers concluding that its usefulness in business was so limited. Ian Turner captured this feeling: "After spending many hours in relentless pursuit of their company's core competencies, managers often concluded that the concept, while enormously appealing in the abstract, in practice merely gives rise to frustration and bewilderment." Core competencies were a pungent illustration of a yawning gap between the academics and the managers. The one side develops a powerful concept and sells it vigorously. The other side absorbs it intuitively but without enough rigor. The lack of rigor leads to early disappointment, often well before the issue of applying the idea has even been reached.

Meanwhile, back in Luxembourg on that summer day in 1992, there was a job to be done in getting the concept across to an uninitiated group of managers. Haspeslagh started off by contrasting competencies with technology. Technology was stand-alone, but competencies were embodied in systems. Knowledge about them was tacit rather than explicit. They were deeply embedded in the organization. They were difficult to unbundle and therefore hard to copy or acquire. They were built through a process of aggregation and integration rather than through discrete activities. The promise they held for Inchcape was a way of differentiating the company from its competitors, and making it the preferred partner for customers and principals. And, it would ultimately allow the company to earn extraordinary returns from ordinary business situations. It began to sound like magic dust.

He then took the delegates through "six essential tests for a core competence." The first was "definitional": does the potential core competence make a disproportionate contribution to the customer's perceived value? The second was "access": does it provide access to a wide variety of markets? The next was "defensibility": is the competence difficult for competitors to handle? Then "reality": is it better than those of our competitors with a similar competence? "Current criticality" followed: how critical is this competence in terms of the current position of the company in its industry? "Future criticality" rounded off the list.

Armed with the theory, the delegates set off in their syndicate groups. In some ways this was harder than working out what was required to meet the ambition. Everyone knew what the final figure had to be for ambition, but this was more elusive and qualitative. Furthermore, they were looking for something group-wide rather than in each business stream. Eventually, the answers emerged: marketing to principals, and systems-led marketing advantage. Marketing to principals was enlarged to include marketing to customers, since this was of greater significance to the services businesses.

As the debate continued, it was suggested that the group did not have an abundance of marketing skills. This was left largely unchallenged, which was strange given the level of sophistication and expertise that existed in Toyota (GB) or J.D. Hutchinson in Hong Kong, as just two examples. However, there was a growing perception that the company did not have the structured, classical approach of a fast-moving consumer goods manufacturer. But it seemed to have an inferiority complex about its "street smart" ability to market in "difficult" countries. By contrast, no comment was made on its systems capability, which was in a far inferior state, even at the level of gathering basic financial data. The concept of systems driving a marketing advantage was so far from reality as to be a hollow joke. Nevertheless, these were potential competencies and therefore aspirational, to use the jargon of the day.

As if to illustrate just how fast academic fashions were changing, in 1994 Prahalad and Hamel launched a bestselling book, *Competing for the Future*. They catapulted themselves into the ranks of guru strategists such as Michael Porter. But their critics were quick to point out that core competencies was only part of the formula for success: it was unwise and unsound to rely on this model alone. Michael Tracey and Fred Wiersma had begun to unpick examples of companies such as Briggs & Stratton that shared the same core competence of making small engines as Honda, and yet had not been so successful. Similarly, they thought it was going too far to imply that Intel's success arose solely from its competence in designing microprocessors.

Within a year, Tracey and Wiersma published *The Discipline of Market Leaders*. It, also, became a bestseller. One reason was its disarmingly simple proposition that there were three "value disciplines": operational excellence, product leadership, and customer intimacy. All a company had to do was to choose one of these disciplines in order to dominate its market. As fast as they displaced Prahalad and Hamel, another mantra moved in. This was the notion that cooperation might, after all, be better than competition. While the intellectual fashion wars rattled across new ground, Inchcape continued to wrestle with core competencies for the next five years. It was compelled to do so: it was the kernel of the logic of its continued existence as a complex group.

WITHIN AN ACE

Organization was the theme for the final day. Once again, Haspelagh led off with a theoretical input on the possible different organizational approaches for Inchcape plc: "Value creation in diversified companies is a matter of capturing value, and creating value. There are many types of diversified companies, ranging from investment holding companies through to integrated firms. If you are going to create value, you need to have a consistent organizational approach."

Then, after a few more charts of theoretical organizations, the punchline was delivered: Inchcape needed the best of both the diversified multinational and the conglomerate approach. Inchcape should have empowered and accountable business units, lean business streams, lean country management, and a small headquarters. As if by magic the acronym ACE was adopted for the conference and the last element had fallen into place: Inchcape's Next Leap Forward would be based on ambition, core competencies, *and* empowerment.

Though no-one recalled it, Haspelagh's papers for this conference repeatedly drew attention to the importance of the "people issue" in any attempt to change the structure or style of an organization. He went to pains to stress the need for thorough and constant communication. The very last item on the conference agenda, by which time the delegates' minds were on the journey ahead, was human resource management. No-one recalled this item, either.

SELECTIVE LISTENING

As they flew out the next day, what messages would Inchcape's senior managers take away? Which elements would they seize on, and what would they communicate back to their colleagues in the field? Memories of the Luxembourg conference are many and varied, which illustrates the old saw that people hear what they want to hear, but there was also some consistency in what they took away.

To Bob Goodall it was, "over-egged ambition … You can look at the Luxembourg speech. We are going to be a Hanson — 20% compound growth a year. But if you are going to do that in a business with no organic growth potential, what do you do? You go out and acquire."

Peter Whicheloe, a corporate planner from Singapore, thought that "Luxembourg was a high point. Charles Mackay was wonderful. There was a mood of euphoria — marketing was going to go up to £300 million profit alone. The humor of John Duncan — everything about it was an occasion, but it did more harm than good. It was out of touch with reality."

Having just joined the Marketing stream in London, Ian Ross also found the Luxembourg conference a "high." "I had only been in the group about three weeks. What I thought was so good about it was that it was very quick compared with BAT. And lots of great, ambitious statements were being made, and I was no longer constrained by the ponderous, bureaucratic nature of the BAT organization. What I didn't realize — the low is coming out the far side — was that the group didn't have the resources beyond money, in terms of people, way of doing business, systems — to actually effect this change. Worse … it didn't really seem to think it mattered. There was an assumption that an acquisition would work — by definition. Because we are just so jolly good!"

What Ross did not yet know, the board should have known. Two accountants in the group financial control department had updated a previous study of the performance of acquired businesses. They produced a paper in February 1991, a full year before Luxembourg. In it, they concluded that thirty projects worth £133.9 million were above target, and fifty-two projects totaling £160.6 million were below target. They also noted that, "If we achieved an average PBT of 25 per cent ROI for all our acquisitions, then we could have expected a contribution of £64 million in the 1991 Budget, as opposed to the PBT of £30.3 million that is actually incorporated." This was hardly a ringing endorsement for a strategy of growth by acquisition. By any corporate standards, the very existence of such a study was commendable. It was just sad that the warnings from such thorough and rigorous analysis appeared not to be heeded. All the external researching into the success rate for acquisitions, then and since, has said roughly the same. Inchcape's "batting average" was no better and not much worse than that of many other companies. Which is not to say a lot.

The worthy accountants went on to identify factors that had detracted from success: new business areas with limited experience; new countries with no previous experience; underestimating overhead savings or overestimating synergy benefits on rationalization; management problems in the company being acquired, particularly with entrepreneurial-type chief executives; and additional capital expenditure demanded by principals. It was all there, if anyone had cared to notice.

Views on the conference acronym were less complimentary. Ross dismissed it thus, "Take ACE: that is a typical example of a fad. Sloganeering. You know what I think about most management textbooks; I reckon you can get much more out of reading a good novel. To me, 90% of the time they are an aspirin." Another delegate was equally blunt: "Ambition, competencies, and empowerment: I thought it was naïve."

Philip Cushing saw the ambition as bordering on arrogance: "There is no doubt we had a corporate arrogance — not a personal arrogance — but, you know, the share price at £6, record profits year on year. Life was a series of extrapolations into the sky, Luxembourg being the absolute apex. Lots of companies have fallen into that trap, and they usually fall very hard, because the foundations are not strong enough. And we thought we were counter-cyclical: we were a very attractive stock — this is nothing to do with hype — when the U.K. was in recession in the early nineties. We were providing a safe geographical outlet for money that wanted to leave the U.K. We didn't argue with it, but our feet were certainly well off the ground in '90–'92."

For Andrew Cummins, it was his first real contact with Inchcape's senior management. His interpretation of what took place was, "What we said to people was 'we want growth.' The mistake was made at the Luxembourg conference. Basically, we said we have got to keep growing at 20% per annum, so please go out and find acquisitions. I arrived on the doorstep as this happened. 'Think big' was the catch cry. To some extent this was fine, because the problem Charles Mackay had was that people had always thought small. So, the company was full of little businesses in every country — worth £100,000 but nothing that would make a difference. But where we lost control was letting everyone across the company loose — it is hard enough to do a good acquisition. But the purse strings were loosened and they were all encouraged to grow their businesses. On top of that, regional executives like Paul Cheng wanted to grow big in China, which seemed like a great opportunity."

One person was absent from Luxembourg: the incoming chairman. Sir David Plastow recalled that, "The outcome of that conference, as I understood it, was to go on the acquisition trail and develop the group that way. I think that the emphasis on acquisitions really was over-sold. Everybody was 'gung ho' and there was a tendency to forget that the first priority is make your current assets sweat."

It should be added here that Inchcape was now a company with an enviably strong balance sheet and virtually no capital constraints. This was a vivid memory for Charles Mackay: "I remember David Plastow saying, 'What do you mean, there is no system of capital rationing?' And I said, 'Well, it's hard to believe, but we have enough cash flow to handle all the investments we want to make and without our gearing going too high.' Largely, this was because we were bringing our working capital down sharply. So, it isn't a question of saying, 'we've got three projects all above our hurdle rate of return, but we can't finance all of them.' We could say, 'As long as it makes "x" it goes ahead.' This was extraordinary. I don't think I have ever met that in any other company." An Indian summer, maybe, but who would not take advantage of such an opportunity?

What Charles Mackay was trying to do was no less than signal a fundamental shift in the culture of a complex and disparate group: a business that had won friends in the stock market with its caution and prudence in the preceding six years under George Turnbull. Mackay knew that change was needed to stimulate the level of growth he was seeking. He also knew that to cut through complacency and comfort, one has to shock one's audience and use a little hyperbole.

As he saw it, "I wanted to get away from the incremental approach of, 'How much can we commit to, but not go for too much in case we regret it?' Quite a lot of people in the company felt that if you committed to something and you didn't make it, then something must be wrong. And that was a major obstacle to growing the group. I wanted to turn this approach on its head and go for highly ambitious targets. Obviously, you won't make all of them — you can't. I have always said to people, 'I would rather go for 120% and make 115%, than go for 105% and make 110%.' My personal preference is to stretch people, but not to hammer them into the ground if they don't make it. But all parts of the organization have to understand the rules of the game, and this was sometimes difficult for the people at the center."

POWER PLAYS

The rules of the game mattered to Rod O'Donoghue. He supported fully the notion of lifting ambition levels, but he was concerned about how empowerment might be applied and interpreted. O'Donoghue contrasted the previous approach and the version that Mackay was expounding: "George had a view about accountability, which was not the fullest expression of empowerment. He would empower if he had total confidence in the individual: only then would he let that individual run. It was a conditional form of empowerment under George. Under Charles it became a theme that was all-encompassing rather than conditional. He was worried, I think, that I was going to destroy the concept of empowerment by my approach to something like control. I said, 'Charles, I don't want personal control, but I must ensure control exists and that we have it as a corporation. It doesn't have to be the same as in the past, but it must exist.' It was his feeling that I might block the concept of devolution; I wouldn't have done that. I believed in the positive concept of empowerment. But I fought very hard to ensure that the elements I perceived as control were maintained."

The reality of redistributing power was to be even more complicated than the theory suggested, as Charles Mackay recalled, "It was particularly difficult, I felt, to get the center really to back off — which was perhaps less surprising. But what was disappointing was the business streams, who were arguing strongly to be left to get on with it, with the minimum of interference from the center. The top management of the streams also interfered too much in the individual operations, probably because they knew more about the business and were focused on just one sector. Where the center had got away with asking for a few bits of information — largely financial — the stream would ask for a lot more detailed operational and financial data. So, when you talked to the field you found they tended to say, 'This empowerment thing is a myth — the financial controller of my stream is asking for ten pages, where before we sent in two!' It was empowerment from the center to business streams, but not down to the business units, where it was really needed."

So what did the ninety or so delegates take away and transmit as the genetic code of the new culture? According to Mackay, "I would have thought that the people in the field probably came away saying, 'Ambition — we really can up our game quite considerably; we can do much more than we have. It won't be easy, but let's go for it. Competencies — yes, we do have to put some serious effort into identifying and developing our core competencies. Empowerment — it will be great if it happens, and they seem to have taken the brakes off and let us go. But I'll believe it when I see it.' That was probably the view in the field. The people in the center were probably saying, 'That all sounds good in theory, but we have got to keep a close eye on things: otherwise the field will probably make a mess of it.' So, old habits die hard; and they did."

Looking back on Luxembourg, Haspeslagh could see a process that started with good intentions about creating focus, deepening and leveraging competencies, strengthening the organization, and becoming more entrepreneurial. "And that is done honestly and with great enthusiasm. Then, as it goes through successive stages, it starts to revolve around EPS growth and 'how do I get the acquisitions that fill that gap?' And it doesn't happen in one day: it's like a sideways shift over nine months. They took away with them the ambition, and to some extent this wasn't bad, as the purpose was to make them ambitious. But the ambition should not have been reflected by buying companies, but investing in businesses." The analysts had a different view. Barclays de Zoete Wedd had expectations: "The group protected a relatively strong balance sheet by financing the TKM acquisition by a rights issue. The group therefore still has significant scope to make acquisitions …"

In the new corporate culture, what would a typical "line" manager regard as important? In terms of where the power would lie in the future, they would be making sure that they were well aligned to the business streams and their senior managers. These would be the people to impress, and if it meant talking less than positively about the center and its staff, then that was just another instance of "all's fair in love and war." Their view of the chief executive was a paradox: though he was, by definition, from the center, his words and actions seemed to align him more closely with the business streams. Tactically, the typical "line" manager probably felt it would be unwise or even career limiting to disagree with the chief executive. If they had a vision about the future of the center, it would be of an emasculated group headquarters. They would shrink the center and its staff to a size and role more appropriate to that of a holding company format. One thing seemed to stand out: growth was everything, and acquisitions were needed — the more the merrier.

Was this a closer approximation to the new group values? Ambition was clear, but was empowerment supported by competencies and underpinned by accountability? Was ACE just a playing card with one spot, after all? Whatever it was, there was no turning back now. Luxembourg had let the genie out of the bottle.

"The Class Act of the Recession"

◆

A VIRTUOUS SPIRAL

T he notion of a positive feedback loop is a familiar enough concept. Seeing this in terms of how a company interacts with the stock market is a useful way to begin to understand what influences what. Add in another physical concept called "noise," and one is on the way to building a picture of the behavior of people in a company and the people who affect the valuation placed on its stock, day to day, and month by month.

The company produces some positive information, which it transmits to the people who influence the market valuation. They react positively, and re-transmit the information in a positive way, which causes the valuation to increase. Their comments and the new value reach the company as positive feedback. This makes it feel even more confident about itself, to the extent that it transmits more positive information. And so on, with increasing amplitude. Busy markets are "noisy" markets, and the attention span of the receivers can be only fragmented and limited. But the people receiving the information discriminate between positive and negative signals. If you are getting a lot of negative signals, the positive ones will stand out and claim your attention. Simple, but potentially dangerous. Thus it was with Inchcape and the London stock market in 1992.

By now, John Duncan had built up a sizable department to handle Inchcape's "corporate affairs." It was busy gathering information from inside the organization, and projecting this in a steady stream to the financial press and the analysts employed by the leading stockbrokers.

Delivering news of improved performance over several years had enhanced Duncan's credibility. Investors were impressed, not just by the increased profits, but also by the aggressive dividend policy, which ensured they were able to take increased gains in the short term. This had a positive effect on the value of the shares, which increased the market capitalization. On top of this, Inchcape was standing out like a lighthouse in the dark sea of recession in Britain. All the factors were in place for a virtuous spiral.

When Inchcape declared pre-tax profits for 1991 of £185.2 million — up 6% on the previous year — the market was impressed. It was especially impressed because this figure was about £5 million ahead of the forecast made three months earlier with the rights issue. The best performance came from the Services businesses, up 51% to £42.1 million. Even Marketing managed to come in with £57.2 million, which was an increase of 8.5% on the previous year. The way the group had been projected as having three "legs" also looked more credible now, with Services constituting 23% and Marketing 31% of the total profit. This was a further simplification of the ten businesses, and was designed entirely for external audiences. Underneath, the complexity continued. In an interview with *The Financial Times*, Charles Mackay was able to talk confidently of further progress in the year ahead. He made it clear that he did not see economic recovery in the U.K. until 1993, and went on to point out that domestic sales accounted for only 30% of the total. By implication, Inchcape's global spread was the reason behind its current and likely future success. Year-end debt was less than £100 million, giving a gearing ratio of 18% and plenty of scope for further acquisitions.

The Asian Wall Street Journal attributed success to "the company's wide range of businesses," which "allowed it to withstand recession in many of its markets." Lack of focus certainly did not seem to be an issue at this time. The newspaper also quoted a conglomerates analyst, Geoff Allum at County Natwest, who said, "It's quite an encouraging statement — one of the quality companies around." The effect of good results on the share price was an extra 13p, or 3% on the day. It was difficult to reconcile the drive for focus, which had become so fashionable, with this enthusiasm for corporate diversity. Or, perhaps, the analysts were simply better at handling apparent dichotomies than the managers of the organizations they assessed. And if challenged, they would probably have retorted that a well-managed conglomerate was better than a less well-managed, focused company.

"As Sir David Plastow slips behind the Inchcape wheel for the first time this morning, he will find a company that appears to be running as smoothly as any Silver Cloud that purred off the production line during his years in the driving seat at Rolls-Royce Motors." *The Times* also had a picture of three confident men: Sir David Orr, the outgoing chairman, flanked by his successor and by Charles Mackay. It went on: "The beauty of Inchcape is that whatever the number of swings, there are invariably as many roundabouts," echoing the virtues of a diverse portfolio. This seemed to hark back to the earlier strategic approach of Lord Inchcape. It was indeed bizarre that, as fast as the company was trying to present itself as more simplified and focused, it could win praise for its previous strategic positioning of spreading risk through diversity.

Sir David took over on the day Inchcape was reporting a 28% increase in interim profits generated from sales up 33%, thanks in part to the TKM acquisition. Even without TKM, sales growth would have been 20%. The 'Lex' column in *The Financial Times* cast doubts on the quality of these earnings. There was concern that distributing cars outside the U.K. would prove tough, and concern about the trend for manufacturers to repossess their distribution businesses — especially when they had watched a distributor like Inchcape make a success of it. Lex also picked up the fact that the boom in Hong Kong had masked difficulties in other markets. Despite these caveats, Lex conceded that "the strong management team appears to be absorbing TKM well, and savings should flow as TKM and existing distributors are rationalized." *The Financial Times* noted that gearing had crept up to 40%.

The analysts were less equivocal: most responded with "Buy" recommendations. BZW liked the dividend increase and suggested that "Inchcape represents a good each-way bet, with progress expected from its exposure to high growth areas (it is a major beneficiary of recovery in dollar-related currencies) and from the TKM acquisition; plus it has the kicker of exposure to U.K. economic recovery on the Motor side." A month later, Flemings were positive and saw Inchcape as a hedge against sterling weakness, singling out the prospects for the East Asian operations, which accounted for 44% of profits. In November, with the share price now at 515p, S.G. Warburg thought that, "The interim progress compared very favorably with U.K. plc and reflects the wide business and geographic base of the group." They went on to suggest that, "With a strong management team and balance sheet the shares should retain their premium rating."

ONE MAN'S LEGACY

Just before Christmas, the flow of good news was punctuated by the death of Sir George Turnbull. There was deep and genuine sadness among many of the staff in St. James's and further afield. The sense of loss was real, and once again thoughts turned to what might have been if he had survived to act as chairman to the new chief executive. *The Financial Times* was fulsome in its praise. "In one of the most dramatic and rapid of corporate rehabilitations, he gave Inchcape a clear focus, reduced to 10 the number of businesses in which it was involved, and expanded the Group's European operations. He drove profits to a record level and, two years after he had joined, the Stock Exchange value of Inchcape had doubled."

Judged solely on results, it seemed that Sir George had bequeathed the new management team a superb inheritance to take into 1993. When the previous year's results were declared at the end of March, the company reported 28% growth in pre-tax profits to a quarter of a billion pounds. Revenue was up by 36%, but this was to be the turning point for the operating margin, which from this point went into an inexorable decline. But for now it was a time to preen in front of the media and set the "global" reverberations going again. The chairman's statement drew attention to the fact that the group was well placed in growing economies, and implied that its geographic spread was a major factor behind its success. "Inchcape proves watertight," was the headline in *The Daily Telegraph*. "It will be a desperate world economy that catches out Inchcape. Trading in more than 80 countries and with nary a penny invested in manufacturing assets, it may not have immunity to recession but few come closer." Ahead of the results, on March 8, 1993, the share price had risen to 632p.

Mackay was the subject of an expansive profile in *The Observer* and a detailed interview in *The Financial Times*. The publicity machine was in overdrive. In the interview, Mackay referred to the handover from Sir George: "It worked very well because the TKM deal galvanized the whole company, pulling everyone together — it was very exciting. The rights issue was well received in the City and it gave us a sense of pride. The more fundamental thing was George's legacy — it didn't all collapse when George himself suddenly disappeared. Inchcape under George was remarkably free of company politics. That team spirit he fostered just rode on; the momentum was unstoppable." Most people in the company at this time would agree that politics were minimal, and teamwork at its best, under Sir George. Privately, fewer would agree with Mackay that the same team spirit had continued. The political machinations and maneuvering had probably started already.

Mackay went on to express his satisfaction with global business streaming, though he was amazed at the resistance to the spread of best practice. Best practice was another buzzword of the early 1990s, which sounded seductively straightforward. It was something that would always spread like butter, and was bound to be good for you. In a relatively homogeneous business, this might well happen and produce benefits for the whole organization. But in large parts of Inchcape, especially in the Marketing stream, the businesses were so localized and specialized that the logic was stretched to breaking point. On top of the logic sat the weight of the old cultures and the financial control systems, where sharing was not necessarily valued or rewarded.

Mackay's interview ended with some interesting observations on growth: "Acquisitions hit the headlines — and there's a danger there, both internally and externally, that everyone starts thinking that's what it's all about." He went on to state that he believed that 75% of growth in the Motors business should come from organic growth, which included "bolt-on" acquisitions, and only 25% from larger acquisitions. This was an interesting twist on the idea of organic growth, and too subtle for most of his audience inside the company, who really did think that acquisitions were "what it's all about."

The only part of the company where acquisitions were not a potential way of growing was the Toyota stream. For Trevor Taylor, head of TGB at the time, life was tough in the U.K. car market, but he kept his team focused on building market share and strengthening the dealer network. But he went further. "One of the decisions we took to help us support earnings during this period of reduced margins was to re-examine and then focus on how we could improve profitability around the vehicle. We concentrated on selling ancillary products such as finance, insurance, and extended warranties to increase the penetration of such products in our vehicle sales." One part of the organization was growing organically, in the real sense of the word. The approach was spread to the other countries in which Inchcape distributed Toyotas and the Toyota division performed strongly throughout the 1990s. Being a "cash cow," it was left to its own devices and stayed aloof from the politics. Some would say that this was a blessing in disguise for shareholders and employees.

The analysts were happy, too. Barclays de Zoete Wedd was positive and came out with a clear "buy" recommendation. They thought, "The integration of TKM has gone very well, particularly the consolidation of

Mann Egerton and Wadham Kenning which is expected to bring substantial benefits in 1993." On March 29, 1993, when the share price stood at 596p, Nikko Europe plc also said, "buy." "It is difficult to criticize a company at this point in the cycle that manages to report pre-tax profits up 36% ... and the dividend ahead 17%. We still rate the shares as a BUY because of the enormous growth potential in the Far Eastern economies, but also because of the progress being made elsewhere, in particular in Motors (8 smaller acquisitions since TKM)." Referring to the translation of profits, UBS commented on the company benefiting from the weakness of sterling, but noted that the strong yen was putting pressure on its import operations. UBS thought that "strong management should deliver outperformance" and gave another "buy" signal. The share price stood at 600p, capitalizing the group at £3 billion. It then started its long descent.

UNFINISHED BUSINESS: SPINNEYS

Away from the hyperventilating atmosphere of the media and the analysts, there remained serious unfinished business. Two major organizations were still to be assimilated into the Inchcape culture. In the case of Spinneys in the Middle East, work was going well. Senior management in Gray Mackenzie, and in the Marketing stream, had spent plenty of time talking to, and listening to, the Spinneys people. From the outset, the message was positive. Growth and investment were emphasized, and the career possibilities within a wider grouping were promoted. The previous Swedish management had starved the businesses of investment in a stark attempt to increase one ratio: return on assets. Spinneys' senior managers had a bonus scheme, which paid out on this singular ratio. Gray Mackenzie's bonus scheme was based on a broader range of business measures and personal objectives. This was quickly introduced, in place of the old scheme.

Alan Davies, Gray Mackenzie's chief executive, made it clear that promotions would be on merit and that Spinneys' people would be on an equal footing. When this began to happen, he was taken seriously. He was taken even more seriously when acquisitions in new markets were made, and when much-needed capital flowed into the operations. Fleets of worn-out vehicles were replaced; supermarkets and offices were refurbished. Many meetings took place at a local and regional level to get the two companies talking to each other about business issues; the social side was not neglected, either. Davies transformed the old colonial atmosphere by ensuring that Indian expatriates and Arab nationals were brought into the mainstream of the company and promoted as rapidly as possible. Davies was a natural verbal communicator and could generate enormous enthusiasm, especially with more junior staff. He was also a visionary who left the detail to others; and he was intensively protective of his team and his "turf." Davies' next plan was to bring about economies of scale by combining so-called 'back office' operations. Also, his previous experience with Rothmans had taught him the importance of clear brand identity and having everyone marching under the same banner. Integration was not just a buzzword — it was a pressing reality.

Davies was throwing his formidable energy and enthusiasm into this side of things, but his team was in danger of underestimating another front. Local legislation in most of the Arabian Gulf states had enforced localization through minority shareholdings for the foreigners. As in Gray Mackenzie, Spinneys were usually "49 per centers." The local partners, in reality, left management control in the foreigners' hands. Provided the local partners were kept informed and provided with a steady flow of dividends, they had provided little interference.

In only one or two generations, they had emerged from some of the poorest backgrounds in the world. Some had survived by pearl fishing, camel herding, or the most basic of trading, and several had a passion for falconry. Now they were among the richest people on earth, and had invested in their children's education. Some of the brightest and best were getting their MBAs at Harvard or Stanford and returning to Dubai or Bahrain with some sharp questions about the way business was working, and what it was the foreigners were actually doing to earn their 49%.

As his successor John Bartley, explained: "Our partners viewed these companies very much as their businesses — we just happened to work in them". In the Dubai community, as Bartley pointed out, "These were two competitive and separate companies — each with their own heritage — big names, locally". Spinneys' corporate colours were a striking combination of green and yellow and a Spinneys supermarket was instantly recognizable. Gray Mackenzie's were an equally definite red and white, and work had been going on to strengthen the brand image of their outlets. The next step was to merge Spinneys' identity. Losing their identity to Gray Mackenzie was one step too far for the Spinneys' partner. It was not only a matter of justifiable pride: he quickly articulated the business issues behind his reaction. This was a turning point in relations with the local partners. The pace and scope of integration would have to be throttled back, and the days of passive acceptance of the foreign managers were finished.

The management challenge of working in the Middle East is formidable: not only had one to satisfy the needs of retail and trade customers, but also major principals such as Nestlé or Heineken. Add in the dimension of majority-owning local partners who were becoming as sophisticated as the foreign managers they employed, and any executive team would have a complex balancing act to perform.

The process of engineering one organization out of two is often reduced to a set of financial and structural actions. That is the world of the corporate planner, the analyst, and the accountant: their skills are undeniably necessary to work out whether or not financial benefits are likely to emerge. In Inchcape at this time, the negotiation of large acquisitions was driven by numbers and run at a corporate level. The new concept of empowerment meant that the subsequent integration was the job of the business stream, and corporate staff could not get involved. In many organizations, the human relations issues are usually left as an afterthought, perhaps because they are so difficult and elusive. This applied in the case of Spinneys, and because of the doctrine of empowerment it was difficult for corporate management to make any constructive contributions. The streams were in charge of their own destiny.

Gray Mackenzie had one more human relations tripwire to deal with. Michael Hemery had been retained as chief executive of Spinneys, reporting to Alan Davies. Hemery was a respected local figure and had at least as big a personality as Davies. At a corporate level, Inchcape had agreed that Hemery should be part of the acquisition, and rationalized that retaining him would present a better "face" on the transition to one organization. The reality was obvious. Neither would find it easy to accommodate the other, nor would their styles ever blend. Hemery did his best to put a professional gloss on the relationship, externally. However, one of them had to go, and it was not going to be Davies. After time and energy had been used up pointlessly, and confusing signals had been sent to the rest of the organization, the inevitable decision was reached and Hemery retired within the year. This was another example of a decision that was delayed, and a delay that achieved nothing.

Apart from these hiccups and some lessons learned the hard way, the acquisition and integration of Spinneys was to prove a considerable success. The other acquisition was in a different league altogether.

UNFINISHED BUSINESS: TKM

"TKM was definitely a low. You could see what was happening, and this machine was coming towards you — despite the fact that it didn't make sense." John Whiteman was then the most senior corporate planner, reporting to Stacey Ellis and then Andrew Cummins. He recalled working on TKM from 1989 onwards: "It was the only obvious thing to go for. It was the right thing to do, but, in retrospect, we bought it at the wrong time and had the wrong perception of their strengths relative to ours. We could have afforded to be wrong on one aspect, but not both. In an analytical sense we didn't overestimate the value of TKM. We were aware of the problems with asset valuation. We were aware of the role of exchange rates. The vulnerability of Mazda, France; the quirkiness of Australia — which were two major profit centers. We were even aware of the operating style of Retail U.K. It wasn't that we didn't know what was going on. It seemed to me that there was no-one to hold things back because of George's illness."

According to Stacey Ellis, George Turnbull was not in favor of the acquisition, but he was fond of Mackay, whom he had brought into the group and had seen perform so well in Hong Kong. "If George had stayed on for another six months, I think Charles would have convinced him to do TKM, but in a different way — maybe broken it up in a different way."

Dale Butcher was also a corporate planner at the time. "You could see the warning signs, but I'm not sure we gave them proper attention. In terms of transforming the group, which was Charles' motive, in lots of ways a big acquisition like TKM was necessary to kick-start Inchcape into the next millennium."

In Bob Goodall's view, it was a deal that should not have happened at all. To him, it was simply a case of not following one's own carefully thought-out corporate strategy, which had identified two major concerns: an overdependence on Motors; and an overdependence on Japanese products, with the currency risk this implied. According to Goodall, "It should have been turned down before it even arrived on the table, as it didn't meet our strategic objectives … and, indeed, there was a strong body of opinion inside the group that we should not proceed with TKM."

Whether or not it was a sensible strategic move, and whether or not the negotiation achieved a sensible price, the deed was done. Inchcape would certainly not be the first or the last company to experience a "rush

of blood" when making an acquisition. What really counted was how
such a major acquisition would be managed and integrated into the
parent organization. On the contrary, it was left with considerable
autonomy for more than a year.

In Andrew Cummins' view, the main mistake was that "We retained
their finance director and let them run with systems we didn't
understand. We allowed their culture to erode the Inchcape culture."

For Bob Goodall, this was a fundamental issue: "It almost became a
reverse takeover, and TKM took over our Motors business. Charles
put walls around TKM on the basis that he was the only person who
could deal with Reg Heath." Perhaps the biggest mistake in the total
period was actually saying that I didn't accept it. 'Either I go in and
have equal status to gather some intelligence — that is as much my
patch as anywhere else in the group — or you find yourself a new HR
director.' I should have done that." Like Cummins, he found the new
culture unacceptable: "It had a totally short-term focus." Goodall felt
that it paid its top people excessively and everyone else badly and did
not care about staff turnover. "It had values that were nothing to do
with Inchcape values. We allowed that culture to become the
predominant culture for a couple of years. Of course, it didn't stop at
Motors, because everyone else saw it and thought that if it was good
enough for TKM, it was good enough for them. TKM was held up as
the example of how you could run a lean, mean business. How? They
didn't invest. In retail, TKM was very poorly regarded by the
manufacturers, because they hadn't invested in the dealerships. So if
you aren't investing in dealerships or people, you could run a lean and
mean business, but for how long? It was running on empty." In
Goodall's view it was very well run, in the sense that it was dressed up
for sale. But the long term was another matter. "Yet it was held up as
an example of how to run a business."

This counter-culture aspect of TKM went to the heart of things for
someone who had helped establish a distinct "Inchcape" culture. As
Goodall said, "George Turnbull had changed the culture in terms of his
beliefs. You cannot be a baron: you operate our way or you don't operate
at all. You accept central controls, central strategy, and you work as part
of the broader Inchcape. Your targets are subsidiary to the broader
targets. Overnight, that went with TKM." Organizational learning
should have prevented this capitulation: Anglo-Thai had turned into a
reverse takeover situation, and the memory of that disaster should have
been recent enough to set alarm bells ringing.

"I think I am apolitical." This was Rod O'Donoghue's comment on the period following the acquisition. "There will always be politics in some form, but to me corporate politics is where personal interest overrides corporate interest. People began talking about each other rather than the business. When that happens, in my view, you have begun to lose it, and the post-TKM period had a lot of that. For me, that was very difficult as a person, because it is anathema to me. I cannot abide it."

One general manager thought that the new regime was good at cutting costs and taking brutal action with poorly performing dealerships. He also observed that it damaged relationships with the motor manufacturers, who were looking for investment in facilities and training and a collaborative approach. Instead, they found penny-pinching and a combative relationship. The new regime managed to please its owners because, as this manager recalled, "The way the financial systems operated allowed 'buckets' to be built up." Money could be diverted into these "buckets" and later recovered at the most auspicious moment. This all too familiar practice could obscure the underlying trends of the business for some time.

Cummins thought that Reg Heath was not sufficiently committed to the business, at least not to Inchcape. "He seemed to just do his own thing, and I felt he should just have said, 'Pay me and I'll go,' which he did in the end. He walked away saying he never liked the place anyway. There was a huge culture clash between Reg and Charles — and everyone else, too."

"Reg Heath used to report the results separately, yet we were trying to integrate the two. It went on for eighteen months. Morale in the old Inchcape businesses went to rock bottom," concluded Goodall.

Despite the favorable comments of the analysts and the press, integration and assimilation of TKM was far from complete. It would take one major outside recruitment and the loss of another year to begin to sort out the mess and put the combined businesses back into an efficient state. Out of two major acquisitions, the record was mixed. One was a brilliant deal in "fit" and price, followed by a well-planned integration whose only faults lay in its undue haste and gaps in communication with local partners. The other was a questionable deal with all manner of human relationships problems getting in the way, and damaging morale in the parent company. It would be tempting to think that Inchcape would draw a deep breath before plunging into more acquisitions. In fact, the opposite was happening.

FURTHER DISTRACTIONS FROM ORGANIC GROWTH

Capital expenditure receives close scrutiny in many large, Western organizations. Often, it is reviewed with great rigor and the process takes on the mantle of a corporate ritual. What goes on under the heading of revenue, and what is happening in the marketplace, are often of much less detailed concern to a complex multinational. Capital expenditure is one area where the corporate team can exert some power, or, at least, create an illusion of power.

The group capital committee of Inchcape was no exception. Its routine business would include applications for refurbishing of a showroom, extending a lease, upgrading a computer system, or relocating an office. Sometimes the capital involved was as little as £100,000. The more interesting aspect of its work was the review of disposals and acquisitions of businesses and the setting up of joint ventures. Every meeting was faithfully recorded. Senior executives attended every meeting, often the chief executive, the finance director and his deputies, the strategy team and, sometimes, the chairman. In previous years, it had met about once a month. During 1992 it met increasingly often: in the eighteen months from mid-1992 it met no less than fifty-eight times. The minutes record the "ins and outs" of applications, resubmissions, and requests for more detail or revised figures. Disentangling these from the records is not a straightforward task, but it is possible to build up a reasonably accurate picture of what was going on. It appears that fifty-three acquisitions and joint ventures were reviewed, and the total value was over a third of a billion pounds. By any standards, this was a feverish work rate. One message from the Luxembourg conference had been received loud and clear.

The job of the committee was to filter out any inappropriate applications, and then pass the viable ones on to the Main Board for approval. The Annual Report and Accounts for 1993 show that a total of twelve principal acquisitions were completed at a cost of £88.3 million; underneath the headline were a further forty or so minor acquisitions. Every meeting consumed a significant amount of time, and even more time went into the staff work to prepare and revise submissions. Many ideas for acquisitions would start at a relatively low level, and then move up through the hierarchy of financial controllers in business units and streams, absorbing work as they went. It is impossible to calculate just how many hours, days, or weeks were consumed in this activity, but it was quite clear that less time and energy was left for matters of organic growth — or assimilation of these acquisitions.

Rigor is one of the characteristics one might expect of such a committee. Rigor was evident in the close attention paid to discounted cash flows and net present value calculations. Hurdle rates of return were set, based on the real cost of capital. Hurdle rates were adjusted for risk, within a country or a particular sector of business. The accountants and strategic planners were doing a sophisticated job. However, meetings have their own dynamics, and these were no exception. On more than one occasion, the team submitting an application was told that its projections for volumes or margins were too pessimistic. The Marketing stream was even criticized for having failed to bring sufficient acquisitions to a conclusion, and was urged to accelerate them. One person who regularly had attended meetings of the group capital committee was Bob Goodall. For him, enough was enough. "I stopped going. It never turned anything down. It turned Finland down once, but Reg brought it back later and they accepted it. These acquisitions had nothing to do with any strategic plan the group had ..."

The 1993 reported figures for goodwill were £52.1 million. Adding in 1992's extraordinary level of acquisitions made a total of nearly £400 million of goodwill in two years. There was a lot of recovery work to be done, and the drop in operating margin from 4.2% to 3.7% did not make the task look any easier. But there was still time to make two more significant acquisitions.

Cracks in the Edifice

A CASTLE IN THE AIR

"**H**ad we bought Danka and not TKM — who knows what?" reflected Stacey Ellis. Danka had approached Ellis in 1991 to buy them out for about £40 million. "We all had lunch or dinner together — they wanted capital to grow and satisfy their ambitions. And I thought they had put together quite a clever way of looking after the Business Machines business. I thought, had we got Danka — that was another area, sort of Consumer Products, sort of Industrial, where we dealt with the end customer — it could have been done on an international scale and could have been another business stream. We could have got in on the ground floor: today that business is probably capitalized at more than Inchcape." In fact, by late 1998, Danka's market value had collapsed, though it had been riding high two years previously.

While Ellis was pondering over Danka, and his future after Inchcape, Mackay had been talking to Ricoh in Hong Kong and to Gestetner about their office equipment businesses. Inchcape already enjoyed a close relationship with Ricoh, the Japanese manufacturer, built on a track record of success with their photocopiers in Hong Kong, mainland China, and Thailand; Australia was one market where success had proved more elusive. Mackay had managed the relationship with Ricoh out of Inchcape Pacific. He saw an opportunity now to expand with Ricoh on a global scale. Gestetner had a tired image in Europe and a number of pressing business problems, but its real significance was the fact that underneath the Gestetner badge, typically there was a Ricoh machine. Ricoh already held a 25% stake in Gestetner.

According to Butcher, the underlying logic of buying into Gestetner was that it would, in some way, bring Ricoh to say, "You have bought that share now; we had better give you our distribution rights for Europe." But Ricoh already had their own subsidiaries in Europe and neither Butcher nor others could understand that line of argument. The house journal, *Inchcape World*, proposed a different reason: it waxed lyrical about the forthcoming office revolution and the convergence of technologies around electronic processing. This was a market the company could not afford to neglect. However, to Mackay's new strategy director, Andrew Cummins, the business had more fundamental attractions for the future configuration of Inchcape. "Overall, I felt we should be trying to build the business and become what I call a high value-added distributor — that is, retain our diversity, but build the business around a portfolio of distribution-related businesses focused on the supply/distribution channel from factory gate to consumer — where there is the opportunity to add a lot of value-added services. So you would not just be moving product. In Motors, all the value added is in spare parts, PDI (pre-delivery inspection), marketing, etc. It's the same for Business Machines. I was heavily involved in this area when we took a stake in Gestetner in the hope of doing something with Ricoh."

London's *Evening Standard* praised Inchcape's 15.3% stake in Gestetner as "a neat and prudent means of preparing the ground for what has the potential to be a rewarding and more substantial long-term strategic investment." The initial stake had cost £36.8 million, and was being acquired from Chiltern, an Australian holding company. It left open the potential to acquire the whole of Chiltern's holding of Gestetner loan stock by July 1, 1994. That would increase Inchcape's holding to 24.6%. Cummins and O'Donoghue would become non-executive directors of Gestetner, along with three Ricoh directors.

What Inchcape was buying into looked grim: previous year's profits of just £27.2 million on £900 million revenue and a forecast of profits halving in the current year. The main problem was the downturn in European markets, which accounted for over half of the sales. Gestetner was in the process of writing off £45 million for redundancies and asset write-downs. The theory was that Inchcape and Ricoh would bring "both focus and vision to the Gestetner board" and that the way the deal was structured would allow Inchcape a long, hard look inside before committing more funds. Part of that long, hard look was Steve King, who was then number two to Rod O'Donoghue and his logical successor as group finance director. He was subsequently "shoe horned" into Gestetner, taking his career off in a new and unexpected direction.

The market reacted by marking Inchcape's shares down by 3p to 588p. The analysts were not impressed. BZW was clearly puzzled by the Gestetner deal and saw it as "mildly dilutive" but liked the two-stage approach, and noted that no formal due diligence had taken place. UBS expressed concern over the strategy, as did S.G. Warburg. However, Warburg went on to speculate about considerable benefits and thought that the market's reaction might have been overdone. They concluded, "The strong management and financial skills of the group should not be underrated." That halo was still shining brightly.

TYPHOON WARNING

In the meantime, one Japanese opportunity was being countered by a Japanese threat: the strength of the yen. Nineteen ninety-three had started with sterling weak, which was excellent news for the translation of profits back from other currencies. The yen began strengthening against all major currencies, and as early as April, UBS picked up the fact that the Mazda, Subaru, and Ricoh agencies would be hit by the yen, and estimated the damage to profits to be about £12 million. They did not mention Toyota, which represented a far bigger profit stream. By the time the interim results came through, the damage was clear. Pre-tax profits were still rising, more slowly — up 11.2% — but a currency gain of £16 million from sterling's devaluation was being more than outweighed by the strength of the yen. Under the heading "Inchcape's slow puncture," *The Financial Times* put its finger on the problem: "The market grew so excited about Inchcape's overseas earnings after sterling's devaluation it blinded itself to the countervailing margin squeeze that stemmed from the rising yen. By virtue of its big Toyota distributorship, Inchcape resembles a proxy Japanese company." *The Financial Times* went on to raise other concerns, but took heart from the long term: that Inchcape was "a well-managed way of riding the Chinese economic wave." Another halo was still intact.

Reaction to the strength of the yen inside the company was muted and stoic. It was another of those external events that one has no control over, but given time it would correct itself and the upward trajectory would resume. Indeed, all the outside experts at the time were basically saying the same thing: "Sit tight and it will blow over soon enough." Of more immediate concern was the steep downturn in the economies of continental Europe. Mazda France was being squeezed from two directions: by a dramatic drop in demand, and by the effect of the yen on its margins. Bridget Walker was then working for TKM as business development manager. She remembered how the bad news was received: "I sat in a board meeting when they talked to the guy from France, who said, 'I have undershot my budget again this month, which means cumulatively I have undershot it by a huge amount. But, it's all right: I will still beat it by the end of the year.' And, nobody really questioned him seriously about this. Eventually, about November, he had to come clean and say he really wasn't going to do it." It was ironic that just as Inchcape had significantly increased its exposure to Europe, the markets nose-dived.

ANOTHER CASTLE IN THE AIR

Insurance broking in the early 1990s was a business going through rapid change. And yet, to meet the people who ran it was to take a step backward in time. It was a special world, which the new, professional breed of managers in Inchcape had some difficulty relating to. If your formative years had been spent in companies like Ford, Merck, Unilever, or Beecham, you would have a straightforward view of business. Products were tangible and could be packaged and distributed. Controls, structures, and processes would be second nature. The organization was built on assumptions of meritocracy. Work hard, play hard, handle the politics adroitly, and anyone with the necessary drive and stamina could succeed.

While much of the financial services sector in London had changed radically following "Big Bang" in the mid-1980s, the insurance sector still retained elements of an older culture. In some ways it was a microcosm of the British class system. At the top were the expensively, privately educated men, some with double-barreled family names and more than the normal number of initials. Their speech was accented and clipped in such a way that they could identify each other instantly. Having a degree or professional qualification was neither an advantage nor a disadvantage, but having the "right" background most certainly was. A significant number had family wealth behind them; they all conveyed an air of confidence and "savoir faire." Their education had turned out confident communicators and outstanding networkers. Like other members of the financial sector, they favored stripes — dark, striped suits and loudly striped shirts and spotted ties. Expensive tasseled loafers or black brogues were the standard form of footwear.

This was a world where business was done face-to-face and often with a minimum of formality. Entertaining occupied a central role, whether it was in the paneled private dining room of a company or the hustle and bustle of a wine bar or pub. Titles were inflated to managing director or chairman for jobs which, in other industries, might just have been called sales manager. They paid themselves handsomely and organized an impressive array of benefits. Bonuses were an important feature of their rewards, but, to misquote J. K. Galbraith, often looked more like a gesture of considerable gratitude to themselves than an objective outcome of performance. This was not a place to apply techniques of modern human resource management, like HAY evaluations.

Below, was an army of supporting players: they processed the paperwork and generally tidied up the loose ends left by the people at the top. Some of them would be young men of similar backgrounds to the top men, and they would serve their apprenticeship in the bowels of the organization. The army was not paid well, and working conditions were often Dickensian: computerization was still very limited. But newcomers were already breaking into this stratified world. From within Britain came the bright "grammar school" boys, a state education providing them with everything except, perhaps, the social ease of their privately educated colleagues. From the outside came the Americans and the Europeans, and the threat of consolidation.

Bain Clarkson was Inchcape's insurance broking business. In a good year it would generate profits of about £20 million, but it was always subject to the cyclical nature of the insurance sector. If premiums were squeezed, so were Bain Clarkson's fees. In this respect, it had some of the characteristics of the commodity-type businesses like tea and timber. It was essentially a British business, though the operations in the Far East and Australia were quite successful and Europe was starting to be developed. Simon Arnold was its chairman and chief executive, and he sat on the Main Board of Inchcape but retained his office in the financial district of London. An outstanding salesman, Arnold cut an impressive figure in any gathering. With a large and erect frame and silver hair, he was always immaculately dressed and never at a loss for words. He had joined Inchcape in 1984 from Minet Holdings plc, and was seen as a considerable coup at the time. The cut and thrust of deals was what he enjoyed; the pedestrian stuff of processes and long-term strategies was for others to play with.

The theory was "scale": you had to have scale or you would not enjoy an independent existence for long. The theory was as valid for insurance brokers as it was for the big accountancy firms. The practical outcome was consolidation, and the only way to get there was by acquisition or merger. At the time, Bain Clarkson was tenth or eleventh in the world ranking of insurance brokers, but the dominance of the top three or four players was massive. Whether the theory of scale was built on the elegant ideas of economy of scale or the rougher notion of "dog eat dog" was not clear, but being middle-ranked was regarded as being bad news. If one were neither a dominant force nor a niche player, then one would be squeezed.

Insurance broking was a major preoccupation for the corporate planners. "We spent a fortune on consultancy advice," said John Whiteman. "We must have spent more on that business than any other, including Motors: McKinsey; SPA; Booz Allen. It was a hard industry to call. We knew that the role of broker was in decline. We knew that there could be consolidation." Andrew Cummins recalled that, "we felt that with insurance broking, we could do something on a real scale. There were sizable acquisition opportunities in this sector. We looked at Sedgwicks and some other big brokers but decided not to take on the big global players but to consolidate Bain Clarkson as a strong local player. In many cases this was Inchcape's strength — a strong local business ... There was a board debate about whether to get out or to get bigger within insurance broking. Bain Clarkson had been a successful investment."

For a while, the sentiment went in favor of floating off Bain Clarkson. Much work was done to prepare for this eventuality. In September 1992, merger negotiations started with C.E. Heath, another medium-scale British broker, but these eventually came to nothing because of a failure to agree the price. Meanwhile, several smaller acquisitions were made to improve the presence in Europe. In 1992, £21.9 million secured a 25% shareholding in CECAR, the third broker in France; then an increase in Revasa in Italy from 10% to 49% cost £1.7 million. In 1993 a 65% stake in Boels and Begault, a Belgian broker, was acquired for £9.2 million. A potential new chief executive was also recruited to replace Simon Arnold. Ron Forrest joined from the position of chairman and chief executive of Alexander and Alexander, New York, in 1994. Forrest was one of the bright self-made men without the private school polish. Short in stature, and sharp-witted, his Lancashire accent brought in a bluff, no-nonsense approach and a lot of ambition.

As time went by, the flotation looked less and less likely to succeed, and there was a return to the idea of buying size and scale. The target was to be the Hogg group, but before this was consummated, the results for 1993 had to be explained. Two weeks before the results, the Third Earl of Inchcape, and life president of the Inchcape group, died aged seventy-six. In the space of two years, the group had lost two of its previous leaders.

The strength of the yen and weakening demand in Europe, Japan, and China had done the expected damage to the growth in profit. Results for 1993 showed 8.3% growth, which was £271.4 million. Motors rose 7% and Marketing fell 7%; Services came to the rescue with a 27% rise. The chairman's remarks about 1994 also being a difficult year had the analysts revising profit forecasts downward. Sir David Plastow had taken to heart the principles of corporate governance, and believed in giving the shareholders as much advance warning as possible. It was late in the day for this approach and it took the investment community by surprise. The share price lost 37p, or nearly 7% at a stroke.

The Financial Times was kind enough to say, "It is a tribute to Inchcape's management skills that a consistent string of good results has masked the unforgiving nature of its basic business." Then it hit harder: "With operating margins of about 4 per cent, Inchcape remains highly vulnerable to disappointment. The inherent volatility suggests Inchcape should trade at a discount to the market rather than the premium it has recently enjoyed." Inside the company, the strong yen became the new mantra. It was the main excuse, the principal cause, the "Aunt Sally" for all ills. One story that went the rounds was that someone had greeted the chief executive with a cheery "How are you today?" to which he had replied, "Fine, apart from the yen, thanks." No doubt, it would soon fall back to normal values and then all would be well. Or so some people kept saying. In December 1993, Robert Fleming Securities Ltd. speculated about a sharp reversal in the value of the yen in the year ahead.

Despite profits warning earlier in the year, three suitors were pursuing the Hogg group: Hongkong and Shanghai Bank, Jardine Matheson, and Inchcape. Inchcape won the bidding with an offer of £176.6 million in cash. Buying a public company was something new for Inchcape. If it went ahead, the deal would lift Inchcape's insurance broking from tenth to seventh place in the world league. Not bad, but still significantly smaller in scale than the top three, and not a comfortable position to occupy for too long. At the top, the doors revolved smoothly: Hogg's chairman, Anthony Howland Jackson, would chair the new group, and Ron Forrest would become chief executive. Simon Arnold took the consolation of a deputy chairmanship on his way to retirement. Geographically, the match was good: Hogg would bring in coverage of North America, Australasia, Africa, and Latin America. A good fit, but the market took the news badly and marked down the shares by 2%. Lex, in *The Financial Times*, picked up the fact that acquisition would be unlikely to contribute to Inchcape's earnings in the current year, and the worries about the extent of Hogg's own trading difficulties. "At 40 times earnings, Inchcape is paying a full price. Writing off goodwill will knock more than £150 million off Inchcape's shareholders' funds, lifting gearing to 50 per cent." Gearing was one issue to become increasingly critical. Another was yet to emerge: the state of Bain Clarkson's own trading situation. Lex went on to speculate that the partial flotation of the combined business in the following two years could enable it to jump up to the top tier of brokers. "… Inchcape had to get bigger or get out of insurance broking. The merger and flotation may enable it to do both."

Inside the company, views about Hogg were mixed. Andrew Cummins saw it as an opportunity to prove himself as a negotiator and to prove a point about how to integrate an acquisition — in contrast to what was not happening with TKM. For his number two, John Whiteman, it was another example of the "numbers game." "We spent a lot of time doing projections, not just on Hogg, but in general in planning. I don't know how many man-months we spent coordinating figures, which I think were all absolutely worthless. Worse than worthless, because people took action on the basis of them … Bain's were projecting growth and Hogg's were projecting growth, so we said if we pay 'x' times for this, and if we exit at 'y' times on this, we'll still make money. I can remember being in a session where Charles was doing his back of the envelope stuff and I said, 'What if it doesn't perform?' and he said, 'It will.'"

Motivation was the issue on which another senior manager focused. "It was an outrageous price. Why did we do that? Basically, it was a mixture of consultant speak and to keep the new CEO of insurance happy. We should have asked, 'Today, Bain Clarkson is generating £18–20 million, so what is that business worth to someone else? Who is trying to consolidate the industry?'" For Bob Goodall, one of the grammar school meritocrats, there was another issue: "In terms of culture, was it a suitable business for Inchcape? Never. Absolutely not. We went for growth in a business where we didn't have potential, and in a business where we should have been out."

By June the share price had fallen to 480p. Kleinwort Benson still held a positive view and thought that the share price discounted current risks. They suggested Inchcape was a well-managed group and that it should grow in 1995. On Bain-Hogg, they replayed the company view about synergies and resulting improvements in profitability. However, they noted that the acquisition would have little effect on the group's profits in 1994 or 1995. Shareholders' funds had been pouring out in a torrent of ambition: how long would it take to see a return?

CORPORATE GOVERNANCE

Tiny Rowlands of the trading group Lonrho, and Robert Maxwell's publishing group had been important triggers in the United Kingdom. Some situations were outright scandals and abuses of power. They caused investors, public and private, to be concerned about the distribution of power at the top of large companies. More than this, they felt an increasing need for more translucency, if not transparency, in the workings of public companies. The phrase "corporate governance" had crossed the Atlantic and landed with a faint thud some years earlier. It was one of those portentous phrases that sounded obvious on the surface, but was hard to define with precision. It was a pity, because it was starting to throw light on some of the most fascinating aspects of the way boards of public companies actually work. It soon acquired the status of a buzzword, but it was in the United Kingdom, rather than the United States, where greater practical progress was being made.

In Britain, the Cadbury committee formulated a set of guidelines. Some of the larger enterprises had already been operating in a way that would fit the guidelines well. Cadbury was codifying "best practice." It was a voluntary code and it was assumed that peer group and investor pressure would be sufficient to make sure that it was followed. Inchcape's chairman was a man of integrity and he had a strong belief in straightforward communication. Sir David Plastow embraced the new concept wholeheartedly, and made it a feature of his chairmanship; some would say it was almost an obsession. In the early 1990s, most chairmen's statements in the Annual Report and Accounts would include a suitable paragraph on the subject. In the Annual Review of 1992, Plastow took two pages to explain the structure of the various board committees. There were four of them.

The chairman's committee consisted of all the non-executive directors and the chairman, and it met immediately before each board meeting. This committee reviewed the performance of the executive directors and senior management. It also reviewed succession planning. The audit committee was also composed of all the non-executive directors and was the forum for reporting by the group's external and internal auditors. The group chairman, chief executive, and finance director attended by invitation. The group's own audit director reported separately to the chairman of the committee. The remuneration committee was another committee of non-executive directors and was led by the group chairman. It reviewed the terms and conditions of each executive director, and no director attended discussions about his remuneration. The nomination committee was the fourth and the smallest. It was led by the chairman and consisted of the most senior non-executive, at that time Peter Baring, and the chief executive. Its job was to make recommendations on appointments to the board. If the reader has had the patience to reach this point, he or she might be justified in thinking that little had been left to chance.

As far as corporate governance was concerned, Inchcape was doing it by the book. Later, in the house journal, *Inchcape World*, Sir David gave employees an explanation under the heading "Playing by the rules."

Empowerment was the theme of an article by Jay W. Lorsch. He noted that the 1980s had been the decade of employee empowerment. It was part of the drive to seek improvements in productivity and quality to allow U.S. companies to compete globally. Without doubt, this was a response to Japanese competitiveness and a reflection of the fashion of emulating Japanese management methods. Lorsch went on to propose that the 1990s would be the decade of boardroom empowerment. Empowerment would result in outside directors having the independence and ability to monitor the performance of the top management team and the organization. Those outside directors would also be able to influence the strategy of the company if its performance failed to meet the expectations of the board. And, in a crisis, they could change the corporate leadership. When Lorsch was writing, over 80% of U.S. chief executives also chaired their companies and enjoyed a relatively high degree of autonomy; some would say it was a dangerous degree of autonomy. An empowered board would be a direct threat to the freedom of these company heads. Splitting the roles of chairman and chief executive was one of the most contentious and visible aspects of the corporate governance movement. The other was the perception that many CEOs were excessively rewarded for the relatively modest performance of their companies.

In the U.S. and the U.K., institutional investors typically did not want to sit on boards. They did not seek the role that the banks occupied in Japan or Germany. But they were ready to put pressure on boards to challenge their management, and were becoming skilled in influencing the financial media to augment that pressure.

Meanwhile, the corporate governance machinery rolled on in the U.K., and *The Economist* criticized it for continuing "to focus on narrow rules and regulations, to the point where producing rulebooks for boardrooms has become something of a cottage industry." The British love of committees was demonstrated by the interim report of the Hampel committee in August 1997. Sir Ronald Hampel of ICI chaired a committee that was reviewing the work of the previous two committees, those of Cadbury and Greenbury. Greenbury reported in 1995 and, ironically, retained his control over the chair and chief executive roles of Marks and Spencer until late 1998, after a very well-publicized battle for the succession. The Hampel report concluded that the previous recommendations had gone far enough toward making managers more accountable. The voluntary approach was working and the whole thing needed more time to bed down. Principles were more appropriate than rules. This drew heavy criticism from those who wished to see tough disciplines being placed on directors, and there was a suggestion that the government might need to impose a set of rules.

When Hampel finally reported in January 1998, he stuck to the same line: a voluntary approach was best. Essentially, he was saying that the shareholders should be the arbiters of what constitutes good corporate governance, armed with the best information with which they can be provided. He noted the interests of customers and employees, but such stakeholders would not have a formal role in this process. His committee put more emphasis on the notion that boards of directors should be aiming to make shareholders rich, and not just make managers accountable. As yet, it is too early to tell whether governing a company by these principles of the 1990s has any influence on the creation of shareholder value.

A NEW-LOOK BOARD

During the first flush of enthusiasm for corporate governance, the board of Inchcape was being transformed. At the start of 1992 it had sixteen members, and each head of business was represented. Derek Whittaker, George Turnbull's old comrade, retired in 1993. In 1994, three more executive directors retired: Simon Arnold; Alan Marsh, who had headed the Toyota division; and Reg Heath, from Motors International. David John added Toyota to his existing responsibilities for Marketing, and Maurice Rourke, an old TKM hand, was promoted to take over from Reg Heath but not to join the board. Inchcape's only director whose native tongue was not English also stood down: J.-P. Parayre. Three non-executives retired and three more joined.

The net result of all these comings and goings was a "new-look" board of symmetry: five executive and five non-executive directors plus the chairman. The executive directors were Messrs. Cummins, Cushing, John, Mackay, and O'Donoghue. The stalwart Peter Baring led the non-executives, plus Lord Armstrong, Jurgen Hintz, Tony Alexander, and Liam Strong. The latter two directors had pressing duties as chief operating officer and chief executive, respectively, of Hanson and Sears, major companies going through turbulence of their own.

The business streams now had their own management boards with their own chief executives. This structure was intended to give each stream greater control over the implementation of its strategy. The Main Board had redefined its responsibilities: the strategic direction of the overall group and the allocation of human and financial resources. In between the streams and the Main Board sat another body, the group management board. The GMB, as it was usually known, included all the business stream heads plus functional heads and was chaired by the group chief executive. The practical effect of this restructuring was to push some power down into the businesses, but to concentrate power at the top into fewer hands.

Following the Cadbury principles, the roles of chief executive and chairman had been split, and the most senior non-executive director, Peter Baring of Barings Bank, had the power to remove and replace the chairman if the need arose.

Before looking at the gap between structural intent and operating reality, it is worth recalling Sir David Plastow's words from *Inchcape World*: "In 1973 when I was running Rolls-Royce Motors, my chairman asked me, 'David, what do you think my job is?' I gave the usual answer: to ensure we had the right board, to oversee the balance sheet and strategy, to present the public face of the company. He said, 'Yes, but what is my *real* job?' Before I could answer, he went on, 'It's to fire you if you don't produce the right results.'"

These were to be prophetic words.

FORM AND SUBSTANCE

As Bob Goodall would point out, there was bound to be a difference between form and substance, and that was often more to do with style and personalities than structure. He did not see "a strong, effective relationship between the chairman and the chief executive, or between the executive and non-executive directors. There was a chasm between the board and the GMB — the GMB really had no access to the board — they didn't work in harness. In George Turnbull's day this didn't matter from our perspective, because the board rubber-stamped what the executive committee decided. We had non-executives — long-term retainer types — they all went in a bunch.

"There was a distance between the board and everyone else. For example, there was a chairman's committee, which met initially before every board meeting. The non-executives met the chairman. They then joined the rest of the executive directors, which created suspicion between execs and non-execs. No attempt was made to build up the relationship between the board and the GMB. John Duncan and I were the two GMB members not on the board who were invited to the strategy review. We sat at a table on one side and weren't allowed to talk unless spoken to."

The current chief executive, Philip Cushing, found relations between the center and the businesses quite difficult when he was heading Southeast Asia and Sir George Turnbull was in charge of the group. "At one level I enjoyed the company of George, Stacey, Rod, and people like that. At another level it was a very combative relationship … In other respects, I felt that the social structure of the group was good. There was a lot of good interaction on a personal level. I think people felt a good spirit. Looking back on the last eight years, even in times of substantial disarray, I feel the social interaction of the group has been one of its strong points: a lot of companies would do well to engender the same sort of spirit. The contrary view is that it was at the expense of being hard and sharp. I'm not sure I really know which is more true."

The coming storm would test working relationships and trust between key individuals. The balance of power had already shifted in a way that affected trust. Having the right structure was important, but the coming stresses and strains would seek out any weaknesses in relationships first.

ONE CASTLE COLLAPSES

On July 1, 1994, Mackay was explaining why it had been decided not to increase the holding in Gestetner. The official reason was that Ricoh, Gestetner, and Inchcape would work together to develop business, while maintaining separate distribution channels for the Ricoh and Gestetner brands — and this strategy did not require more investment. The share price went up by 5p as a result. But Lex in *The Financial Times* suggested, "The more negative interpretation, though, would be to question what Inchcape was up to in the first place … Inchcape has been left with a fair chunk of capital tied up in a different business … Still, Inchcape has more pressing issues to worry about. The inexorable rise of the yen against the dollar will be causing greater headaches given Inchcape's reliance on selling Japanese goods abroad."

RUSSIA AND THE REAL THING

By the end of July, the company had a more interesting announcement to make. It was investing more than £25 million in Coca-Cola bottling franchises in Russia. Coke was already there in Moscow and St. Petersburg, and offered Inchcape the opportunity to set up in some of the remaining large cities in the Russian Federation. The cities were Niznhy Novgorod, Samara, Volgograd, and Ekaterinburg. Undoubtedly, the success of the bottling operations in Chile had helped win the franchises from Coca-Cola. Since the rehabilitation of Latin America in Inchcape's eyes, much investment in facilities had taken place, and the return on that investment was outstandingly good. In Coke's eyes, the market share was also excellent.

A key figure with credibility in Atlanta was Sergio Mardones, who had put Chile on the Inchcape map. At the London end, Philip Cushing and Ian Ross were the drivers of the project. The Coca-Cola business had been spun out of the Marketing stream so that Cushing could give it closer attention. Cushing recalled that, "Charles and David John before me — we were all convinced we had to do something difficult in order to 'earn our spurs.' Chile was clearly regarded by Coke as too small and too easy. We were then encouraged by Coke to think aggressively; we made a big pitch and were successful in getting five franchises in Russia." Cushing knew that however difficult Russia might be, it was the route to gaining greater status within the Coca-Cola system. Gaining this would potentially unlock access to easier and more lucrative markets around the world. Cushing, and others around him, could see that Coca-Cola bottling offered the opportunity to build a major business that would reduce the dependency on fragile principal relationships. For now, the immediate task was to set up an organization "from scratch" in Russia. Once again, ambition was to run ahead of ability.

Reality Time

A Short, Sharp Dose of Leadership

◆

"One in three of your top three hundred managers say that their contribution is not welcome. Nearly a half said that they received only a small amount of feedback on their performance."

"When we asked them what it takes to succeed as a manager in Inchcape they said: 'Get results; keep to budget; meet commitments; work hard; don't surprise the boss.'"

STARTING AT THE TOP

T hese were just two extracts from a thorough survey of the opinions of that vital group of managers who sat just below board level. The survey had been conducted worldwide by a consultancy, taking in the 300 most senior managers. Typically, they were the management teams of the main business units, the boards of the streams and functional specialists in the corporate headquarters. These were the people who directly influenced the behavior of the group's 48,000 employees. This was a flavor of the culture of the organization at the start of 1995 when the survey was conducted. It was not the first time that the company's culture had been on the agenda.

The results echoed the work previously done by Andre Laurent during his sessions with the Inchcape managers attending the Euro-Asia Centre sessions at INSEAD. As successive groups of senior Inchcape managers attended courses in Fontainebleau, he was able to sample their views on the corporate culture. Over the years from 1987 he built up a solid database. Laurent had used a blue-and-green "color code" to describe the old Inchcape family culture, the new Turnbull culture, and the culture which Mackay had inherited and was in the process of modifying.

Students of organization culture will recognize the analogy of the time needed to change the course of a supertanker. After ten years, old green had been defeated and new blue was dominant, but the ambitious, empowered organization expounded by Mackay at Luxembourg probably existed only in the minds of the top thirty or so managers. The tanker had not started to turn in this new direction.

The paucity of the organization culture was not the only unwelcome feedback the group management board was receiving. They were getting their introduction to 360-degree feedback, on their individual leadership styles. The fact that they were in a comfortable country house hotel in the Sussex Downs was of little consolation. Nor was the share price: it was falling fast as they sat in their "workshop."

The GMB had been instructed by Charles Mackay to attend this pilot session for a leadership program, setting an example to the rest of the organization by kicking off a process that would be rolled out to all Inchcape's top managers around the world. It was certainly a high-profile way to launch the program: for the consultants who had designed it only days before, it was a time of ultra-high tension. Everyone had arrived at Horsted Place on a bright but chilly Sunday afternoon on April 2, 1995. All had followed the usual instructions to dress in the standard Inchcape way for such occasions: "smart casual." Despite the sweaters and sports jackets and open-necked shirts, they looked anything but casual. The body language said very clearly, "I do *not* want to be here."

The program director of the consultants, EDC Ltd., rose to introduce herself and her colleagues and to outline the contents and purpose of the next three days together. Rosemary Harper had held a high-profile position in British Aerospace and was no stranger to such gatherings. Despite this, her normal self-confidence seemed to have ebbed away and she strained to overcome the frigid atmosphere in the lounge of the hotel. Cocktails and an early dinner helped thaw out the chill. Soon the laughter started, but it sounded too hearty and forced. There seemed to be a set of different agendas being worked through; several individuals retired to bed with a sense of foreboding about the next day.

The events leading up to this board workshop had started with an advanced management program at the Euro-Asia Centre in May 1994. Andre Laurent had asked each of the twenty-one senior managers to answer a simple question and write their answers down confidentially on a slip of paper. The question was straightforward enough: "What does it take to succeed in Inchcape now?" The replies were equally straightforward: "Get results." What was remarkable was the unanimity of response and the total lack of any other factors being mentioned. When Charles Mackay came to Fontainebleau for the winding-up session, he picked up this bleak message and was appalled. He debated the issue at length with Bob Goodall on his return and came up with a proposal. He decided that a course providing "a short, sharp input of leadership skills" should be set up and administered to 300 of Inchcape's top managers. Bob Goodall and his team were left with the task of making it happen.

Goodall's assumption about the senior managers was that they would not stomach a behavioral change course, and that he would have to find a way of packaging the whole thing so that it would have a "hard" exterior and a "soft" center. In July, he presented a new group training plan to the board. Its centerpiece was something called "Leadership for Shareholder Value." As he had hoped, the shareholder value component grabbed their attention and the board endorsed the overall plan with the leadership program. Armed with this mandate, a detailed specification was put together and fourteen business schools and consultants were invited to tender. The word spread to other consultants, so that eventually nineteen organizations expressed interest. It was striking that the business schools took a relaxed approach, ranging from "we could have a look at your problem if you advance us £50,000" to completely failing to produce a proposal.

In December, Philip Cushing, Maurice Rourke, and Alan Davies met with Bob Goodall to act as a subcommittee of the GMB and make a choice between the finalists. The result was a split vote, between EDC and Forum Corporation. EDC were late entrants and by anyone's reckoning outsiders. By contrast, Forum Corporation had the resources, the reputation, and the presentation skills one had come to expect of an American consultancy. They had one other advantage: General Electric's Jack Welch was one of Philip Cushing's heroes and they had done major work for GE over a sustained period. A final showdown was arranged for a Friday afternoon just before Christmas in the boardroom at St. James's Square. EDC produced a sparkling presentation, which challenged their audience to "identify value-destroying symptoms" within the group. In complete contrast, Forum failed to generate energy and gave a strangely lackluster performance. Against the odds and against internal predictions, the business was awarded to EDC, at the same time cutting the overall budget. This was to be one of several sleepless nights for the EDC team who wondered what they had really won. Despite misgivings over costings and time-scales, they were elated that they had achieved a "David and Goliath" result.

Working over the Christmas holidays of 1994, EDC designed a comprehensive opinion survey, which went out early in January to all of the top 300 managers. Charles Mackay's accompanying letter urged them to reply promptly and told them that their turn would come to attend a program. Meanwhile, the members of the GMB received questionnaires for the Myers-Briggs Type Indicator® and a bulky instrument called the Leadership Effectiveness Analysis™.

The LEA™ was a 220-item survey of their leadership behavior: to be completed by themselves, at least three peers, and three subordinates. It was also to be filled in by their boss, which in every case was Charles Mackay. Paper flew backward and forward across the world. By March, EDC had processed the opinion surveys and discovered to their astonishment a return rate of over 80%, and lengthy written comments on a significant number of them. EDC had also carried out focus group discussions in Hong Kong and London, within each of the main business streams. The design for the board workshop was finalized just two days before the event. All was set for a productive three days …

WHO IS IN CONTROL?

At this point it is relevant to recall some of the events in the preceding eight months. The Interim Results in September were effectively a profits warning, and the shares fell to 408p. Toward the close of 1994, the financial services arm of Bain Hogg in the U.K. and Hong Kong, and the Hogg group's U.S. interests were sold off to a U.S. broker, Accordia. The sales raised a total £42.9 million. The disposal of TKM's Kenning car rental business raised another £26 million, and attracted favorable comments from *The Independent* newspaper about "sharpening focus." The shares picked up 11p to 438p.

Nineteen ninety-five kicked of with news of a global alliance with

®Myers-Briggs Type Indicator (MBTI) is a registered trademark of Consulting Psychologists Press, Inc. Oxford Psychologists Press Ltd. is the exclusive licensee of the trademark in the U.K.

™The Leadership Effectiveness Analysis (LEA) is a trademark of Management Research Group, Inc.

Accordia designed to give Bain Hogg access to the U.S. market without the need to commit capital. The analysts' reaction was muted and the shares fell 4p. At the end of January, a ten-year exclusive distribution agreement for Asia-Pacific was signed with Timberland, the U.S. footwear and outdoor clothing group from the rural state of Maine. Inchcape was now investing heavily in the branded lifestyle business: the immediate bill was £15 million for the Australian and New Zealand businesses of Timberland. More was required for an ambitious upgrading in Japan, and working capital would soon be sucked into inventories. Another profits warning swamped this good news, and immediately took the shares down 20% to 311p. The company had warned that profits for 1994 could be 10% down on the previous year.

The factors being blamed were weak car markets in the U.K. and Hong Kong and, as ever, the strong yen. *The Financial Times* adopted its familiar kind-but-cruel approach, by saying that "Inchcape's second profits shock in less than a year says more about its business than its management." It picked up the point about "shrinking margins in a low margin business" and then went on to emphasize "Inchcape's exposure to trading risks that are outside its control. Its fall to a market discount rating seems deserved." The talk was now more about quality of earnings than quality of management. According to *The Daily Telegraph*, the analysts had reacted angrily to the sudden bad news. No-one likes unpleasant surprises — least of all a stock-market analyst. Confidence had been spiked, and the remarks made by Bob Cowell in Luxembourg just two-and-a-half years ago were coming home to roost.

On March 2, a new job was created — that of group managing director — and Philip Cushing filled it. Charles Mackay remained group chief executive and became deputy chairman. The reasons for splitting the roles were to give Mackay more time to communicate with the stock market, and to concentrate on longer-term issues and relationships with suppliers such as Toyota and Coca-Cola. Others saw it more starkly as giving someone tough a chance to tighten operational control. At forty-four, Cushing was relatively young and known to be someone who would quickly get to the root of an issue or problem. Nonetheless, there were others in the top team who would have felt equally capable of the task, and at least as well qualified.

There was just time before the Annual Results to announce another deal. Out of the confusion of the Gestetner adventure was to emerge a new company: Inchcape NRG, based in Hong Kong. This 50:50 joint venture was based on Gestetner and Inchcape each putting in £20 million of net operating assets. It would distribute office equipment sourced from Ricoh plus other manufacturers such as Hewlett Packard, Konica, Mita, and Murata. Charles Mackay was quoted in *The South China Morning Post* as saying, "The company would achieve critical mass in the region." No longer was "global" the catchword; the reality was regional.

Profits for 1994 were marginally above analysts' forecasts, but the predictions for the first half of 1995 were sufficiently pessimistic to cut estimates for the full year to £200 million or less. This third profit warning within twelve months took the shares down a further 7% to 278p. There was some speculation in the press about a takeover bid, and *The Financial Times* quoted Sir David Plastow as saying that press rumors of boardroom disagreements were "absolute rubbish." In *The Times*, Mackay explained, "We were never in any doubt that 1994 was going to be a challenging year. In the event, we were also confronted by a number of external factors that, quite frankly, were beyond our worst predictions and almost entirely out of our control." A less favorable backdrop for a board-level workshop would be hard to imagine.

HEARTS AND MINDS

Monday was one of those bright, early spring days when the light seems all the harsher because of the bareness of the trees, and when the sun lacks the strength to overcome the chill of the wind. Sylvia Handler had the first slot of the day. She was an American economist with senior management experience in the United States, and was a Sloan Fellow of London Business School. Then employed by Coopers and Lybrand, it had been her presentation on the creation and destruction of shareholder value that had helped EDC win the business in the "shootout" with the Forum Corporation back in December. She struggled hard to engage her audience in something that now seemed remotely academic, compared with the reality of the last few days on the stock market. Though there were important lessons to be learned from her presentation, the mood of the group was hostile and she found it difficult to retain her composure. This was one element that would be "designed out" of the program.

Next on was Claudia Heimer to talk about cross-cultural management. As a Brazilian-German working in France and with a Masters degree from Birkbeck College in London, she had some natural authority as well as academic credentials. Cross-culture was a component that Charles Mackay had insisted on including in the program. Apart from the fact that he wanted maximum "value for money" from the four days, he retained a strong impression that other senior managers would always seek out British expatriates rather than mix socially with the locals. This colored his view of the cross-cultural dimension. The reality was rather different: most of Mackay's board colleagues were experienced and capable in this area, by any external standards. Some had a facility and an attitude that would be the envy of many leading companies. So, Claudia's task was an uphill one, and though her audience treated her civilly, this was another element to be discarded.

Two down and one more to go, that day. The last session was to prove a great success: it was something known as the Myers-Briggs Type Indicator. The MBTI® had, by now, become very widely used in U.S. corporations, as well as in an increasing number in Europe. Several million people now had experience of it, mainly in business but also in a range of non-commercial organizations. As a personality indicator, it had several advantages: it was robust and based on a vast amount of data; it could be normed for different countries or occupational groups; it was non-threatening and no-one appeared to be a "loser." Most of all, in the right hands, it could be a lot of fun. Sally Plummer made it fun and lifted the mood of the whole team. Sally, along with Nick Allen, was from Castleton Partners and working on a collaborative basis with EDC. A confident and jolly person, she made light work of explaining the theory and then each director was given his own "type," which was expressed as four letters, either E or I, S or N, T or F, and J or P.

There was a total of sixteen possible combinations: these could be laid out on a four-by-four grid. After making sure that everyone was comfortable with their own four-letter combination, she invited them to share the results with the rest of the team. Plotting them on the grid was revealing. The majority landed in one box called the ESTJs; some were ISTJs. "E"s typically would get their energy from people and activity; they would think with their mouths wide open. "I"s needed to recharge their batteries by escaping from people and finding solitude; their fault was often to think of something brilliant to say after the moment had passed to say it.

Taken together, the STJs prefer an orderly world based on systems and procedures, facts and figures, and hierarchies and functional specialists. For them, the future would typically be an extension of the present and they would be at their happiest with detailed plans and budgets. If change were needed, they would most likely change the structure. In short, they were typical managers, but not necessarily leaders. STJs were the most common "type" in organizations because they thrive on administration and control. However, in any group of a dozen or more people, one might expect to find a spread of Myers-Briggs types. The Inchcape top team was clearly dominated by STJs.

Only one individual had an "F" in place of "T." "F" stood for Feeling and "T" for Thinking. According to the theory, this person with an "F" would prefer to take decisions based on his value system, rather than solely on the cold, detached logic that would be the preference of the "T"s. Within organizations, these people with the "F" preference would, typically, represent the corporate conscience. Because of their concern for the customer, they would often gravitate to sales roles. The top of Inchcape had one such, lonely person. The N–S dimension was slightly better balanced, with three "N"s in the team. These "intuitives" would prefer to see the whole picture, rather than break things down into the detail liked by the "S" or "Sensing" types. Future-oriented, the "N"s would be the ones to spot trends, and be more likely to move on to the next deal, leaving others to pick up the pieces. Their STJ colleagues would probably seem dull and plodding at times.

The whole point of the MBTI exercise was to throw some light on how they might work as a team. A balance of different types would usually be more effective, but one could definitely not recruit around Myers-Briggs types. All you could do was work with what you had inherited and make adjustments and intelligent use of the differences. Myers-Briggs made a great deal of sense to the Inchcape top team, but one fact was inescapable: ESTJs were the dominant type. A writer on the subject, William Bridges, had taken the Myers-Briggs Type Indicator one stage further and applied it to organizations. He postulated that organizations would differ in their personality in the same way as individuals. Therefore, it was possible to have sixteen different types of organization, each with its own distinctive character. It had clear implications for organization development and, in particular, culture change. As the leadership program was rolled out to the remaining 300 managers across the group, the same pattern would be repeated. Inchcape was an ESTJ organization.

You could predict that it would be good at sticking to plans and schedules and not spinning off into wild ventures. Status and "turf" would be important, and dissenting voices would not be tolerated easily. An ESTJ organization would be happiest in an environment that did not change too fast, and would tend to preserve and protect the established way of doing things. It might even deny that the world had changed around it, and that its way of doing things was becoming inappropriate. Under extreme pressure, its people could become disoriented and quickly turn the smoothly running machine into chaos.

THE THEORY OF CHAOS, SUITABLY ADAPTED

Chaos was the subject of the next day, and Professor Ralph Stacey was the man to take the GMB into this newly fashionable area. Another economist, Stacey had also worked as a corporate planner and with a City of London stockbroker. At first, his calm exposition of how random events might have unforeseen consequences impressed his audience. But as he moved into the working of organizations, discomfort levels began to build rapidly. Denial was setting in. How could this maverick individual suggest that the board might not be able to control or predict events? How dare he imply that capital investment appraisals were largely a waste of time and an elaborate charade for decisions that had already been lobbied for and taken in the corridor, rather than the boardroom?

This particular ball had started rolling in 1963 when a meteorologist, Edward Lorenz, noticed that cloud patterns sometimes seemed random and at other times highly organized. He wrote an equation to try to predict this behavior. At the heart of the theory was the notion that minute changes in the beginning of a chain of causation would lead to huge changes at the end. The beating of the wings of the butterfly leading to a hurricane became the familiar metaphor. The mathematics behind the theory was that of non-linear equations.

In the 1970s, computers were beginning to make an impact on the fund-management business. By identifying relationships in financial and market data, it was hoped to build mathematical models that would predict investment outcomes — or at least reduce some of the uncertainties of market behavior. Work continued in the next decade with more powerful computers and more complex models. However, a great deal of subjectivity still conditioned the inputs to the models and the search continued for better solutions. Meanwhile, exponents of chaos theory had noticed that when the results of chaos equations were plotted graphically, they looked quite like price movements in the financial markets. A number of fund-management companies invested in applying chaos theory to their businesses. For a variety of reasons, the outcomes were disappointing and chaos theory was displaced by newer approaches like neural networks and genetic algorithms. However, chaos theory helped to spread the wider idea of "non-linearity": that events did not occur in some predetermined way. Rather, that things would happen in fits and starts and would be subject to a vast number of influences.

Ralph Stacey's interest was in the world of organizational behavior. He saw organizations as a network of human relationships and as non-linear feedback systems. Organizations exist in an environment containing other organizations, and do not simply adapt to the environment — they evolve with each other and re-create the environment as they go along. A human network in a state of stable equilibrium would simply repeat its past behavior. The nearer the system moves toward the edge of disintegration, the greater the likelihood of new behaviors emerging from the mixture of order and disorder. And those new behaviors would be the source of creativity and innovation.

Stacey's argument was that, in the real world, organizations compete with each other for customers and resources so that they can never settle into stable equilibrium. But success will go to those that innovate and, therefore, operate closer to the edge of disintegration. Competitive selection would weed out those stuck in a state close to stable equilibrium. One implication for the managers of successful, innovative organizations is that they are unable to know the long-term outcome of their actions, and no-one is really "in control" of the future direction. Rather, the organization will emerge through a process of self-organization in which disorder, unpredictability, and "messiness" play a vital role.

Stacey's message for managers was twofold: first, the harder you try to control the outcomes of an organization, the more you push it toward stability and squeeze out innovation. The organization will ossify and either go out of business or be taken over by a more successful one. Second, managers need to learn to let go of the controls while vigilantly avoiding tipping the organization into total instability. As Stacey saw it, the leadership role was less about foreseeing the future and controlling the journey, and more about containing the anxiety of the members of the organization so that they can create and discover a future that no-one can truly foresee. In a turbulent world it is impossible to be in control; therefore, one should abandon the fantasy of control and set about harnessing the creative energy of complexity and disorder.

Nick Allen, one of the team of consultants, was sitting at the back of the room while Stacey put forward his controversial ideas: "He then took them through all the rational decision-making around the TKM deal. Then he asked them to describe what really went on. All the politics came out. That was part of Ralph's hypothesis about how organizations really work: the shadow organization. All that real decision-making took place in the shadow organization. This then came into the theme of hurdle rates. If you set it too high, people concoct a way of getting over the hurdle rate. They concoct reasons why they cannot deliver on the figures they put in to get to the hurdle rate."

Stacey continued his assault on the sacred cows of rational management. Who was he to criticize the validity of annual budgets and three-year plans? At a time when the share price was still falling and the yen was still rising relentlessly, against all predictions, this hurt deeply. The ESTJs had seen chaos and they did not like it. "There were people there who were positively angry about Ralph's approach," said Bob Goodall. "I can remember him challenging them: 'If you can't even predict your next quarter, how can you produce a ten-year cash flow for an investment, that has any meaning whatsoever?' I thought it was wonderful, but most people just hated it."

360-DEGREE FEEDBACK

It was now Rosemary Harper's turn to introduce the LEA, which had been winging its way across the world in the past two months gathering feedback from peers, subordinates, and bosses. For most of the individuals sitting around the table, the boss was Charles Mackay and this added to the tension. Equally true, was the fact that the people sitting around the table were his subordinates who had provided feedback to him. Again, the theory was carefully explained, and then applied straight into a template for leadership in the "new Inchcape," which the GMB designed, working as a group. Then it was time for each individual to discover his feedback, which came in great detail and would require careful interpretation. As Bob Goodall recalls, "This was our first experience of 360-degree feedback. It was really quite a courageous experiment to start at that level. One or two people were a bit taken aback by their feedback: it was a bit of a jolt and people had to come to terms with that. By and large, the reaction to 360 degrees was very positive, and coaching support was there immediately so you could go and talk about it." Not everyone around the table supported the ideal profile of a leader. One highly competitive individual had scores on teamwork that were almost off the scale — in the sense that consensus, cooperation, and empathy were almost non-existent — and he was proud of it.

That evening the group management board went out to dinner and had an uproarious time, compensating for what had been a demanding and difficult day. Without a doubt, one of Inchcape's unofficial core competencies was entertaining, whether it was for principals, customers, or themselves.

BOILING POINT

The next day was a renewed search for the official core competencies and key success factors, and an attempt to combine the implications of the LEA and MBTI information to find a more effective leadership style for the future. This was the heart of the program: defining and adopting the behaviors that would support the strategy of the business. The theory was good, but the tension simmered just below the surface. Soon the discussion got into the detail of how the business should be run and became very personal. The tension exploded.

One member of the board could no longer contain the pent-up feelings of the last few months: "I cried in sheer frustration." This moment was a profound shock and, to some extent, it was a turning point. What followed was a concerted effort to find common ground as a team, and try to reach a positive outcome for their few days together. In Goodall's view, this was only papering over the cracks. "In a sense, the leadership program, far from pulling us together as a team, probably finally said, 'This team cannot function together any longer.' There are points when teams become dysfunctional. I think all the members of the GMB knew it but didn't want to admit it. We had come together on the leadership program to become a team, and yet everyone went away knowing that it had to break up. It was the start of the process that led to Charles going and Philip stepping up. David would go and so would Andrew, so it was a big turning point in the company."

Other views of the leadership program were less charitable. One participant criticized not so much the program as the motivation for running it: "The terminal point as far as I was concerned was the leadership exercise down in Sussex … I think that and the ACE theme of the Luxembourg Conference was an example of fashion impinging on policy, and management fashion being a surrogate for grip and ideas to drive the group forward." Cummins thought it was a waste of time: "It was the wrong time to do it. You cannot do a culture change when strategy is unclear and the share price is going down, and everyone is in despair."

The EDC team were also close to despair, having invested a huge amount of effort to do all the research and preparation, worldwide, against tight deadlines — and having used up all their reserves of emotional energy trying to keep the group together over the previous few days. It looked now virtually certain that the whole program was "dead in the water." At the end of the workshop there was an intense debate, and several strongly dissenting voices. And yet, "to the credit of the GMB, despite quite a lot of negatives, I think they had the wisdom to recognize that there were some real strengths in the program. Instead of throwing the whole thing out because it hadn't worked in its entirety, and had been uncomfortable, they said, 'Let's sort out the good bits.'" In Goodall's view, these were understanding the use of a repertory of different personal styles to get business results; the balancing of teams; and the awareness and empathy for other people's styles and contributions. A decision was made. The leadership program would go ahead.

The Trojan horse of shareholder value was wheeled away: this was now to be unambiguous training in behavioral change. And because of the almost accidental discovery of team-working, another important decision was taken: instead of running it in geographically-based groups of mixed businesses, it would be run on a business stream basis, starting with each stream board. Rosemary Harper was too exhausted to be elated, but she was aware that "what had started just as a series of training programs (which was a shot of good old leadership), actually began to turn into a change process. There was a realization that there was a need to do more than just training."

Within a month there was a rare piece of good news: the buying services business had been sold for £40 million to the Li & Fung group of Hong Kong. The shares gained 10.5p. Another global ambition was abandoned and a thousand people in eighteen countries found themselves part of a new family. Richard Tam knew Li & Fung well. "They are quite successful and quite flexible. In fact, our buying operations have become more successful under their management."

CARNAGE ON KING STREET

"People were so gob-smacked that this could be happening to them ... I was given the rather thankless task of taking letters round to everybody and people said, 'Here comes Melanie — she knows what's happening — who is staying and who is going.' I had only been there six months, and I had only been taken into the loop the day before because I had to type everything up. Going through the building the atmosphere was terrible — people in tears — it was pretty bad. When I joined it was all 'Footsie 100,' gilt-edged, blue-chip, and suddenly this massive redundancy in head office. I thought then, and still do, it was a knee-jerk reaction."

If Melanie Price, Bob Goodall's secretary, was taken aback, her colleague Alison Davies was even more shaken by the events of May 1995 in the King Street, St. James's headquarters. Alison had joined as compensation and benefits director for the group, from the relative stability of Smith Kline Beecham. "I arrived in the group and within a fortnight we were cutting a third of head office. I refer to this as a 'slash and burn' exercise, because although I had had a lot of experience before of redundancy exercises, I had never seen anything done with so little planning. It will stay with me for a very long time, because what we essentially did was simply slash names out to save costs.

"Morale just plummeted to a degree that I have never seen before. We had people sobbing in the corridors, and the whole place practically ground to a halt and became totally dysfunctional. Some of this spilled over to other head offices around the world — Hong Kong and Singapore felt the cold wind. It marked people very badly, and it took them a long time to recover from that. The morale problem never really lifted for the rest of that year. The crazy thing was that shortly afterwards I was having to talk about replacing people who had gone, as they just couldn't cope with the workload that was left."

There was no doubt in the minds of a number of senior managers that costs could have been saved. There was equally no doubt that natural wastage could have achieved the same result without the damage to morale. Voluntary redundancy and early retirement would have been attractive to a number of individuals, but the effect would have been less dramatic. It was deemed necessary to send a signal to the investment community that tough and quick action was being taken: head office was the customary "soft target."

Communication was another issue. Though the heads of departments were consulted about whom they would choose to let go from their teams, the communication was through a letter on individuals' desks and a bulletin the same day. It was as if senior management had retreated behind the barricades.

"Our Most Valuable Asset"

May was also the month of the annual general meeting and a time to talk to the shareholders and the media. The chairman repeated his cautious view of profits for the first half of 1995 and avoided predicting the full-year outcome. In *The Financial Times*, he was quoted as stressing that the group was taking action. "We have, however, for some time been cutting back hard on costs and will continue to do this as a high priority. We have already reduced staff numbers significantly." The shares went up by 4.5p.

During the same month, head office staff received another bulletin. This one urged them to find ways of saving stationery and turning the lights off to save electricity. The American cartoonist, Dilbert was not yet well known in the U.K., but he would have relished the irony.

Falling from Grace

◆

No News is Bad News

W hen a company stops talking about itself, you can be sure something is wrong. When the torrent of news is reduced to a trickle, the press and analysts will smell a rat. It was obvious — and they would build it into their assessments.

"Corporate PR had too big a role," thought Robert Morton. He had been analyzing Inchcape since the early 1980s, first with Simon & Coates, then with De Zoete's, which subsequently became BZW, and since 1992 with Charterhouse Tilney. "In the early 1990s it just went completely over the top. And then it just shut down communications so that expectations went adrift, leading to shocks and surprises. The uncertainty associated with this shutdown of any meaningful information flow obviously increased the risk of holding Inchcape and damaged the share price ... One does expect a dialogue in general terms about trading, etc., so that outsiders and shareholders in particular — who, after all, are the owners of the business — know what is going on and don't have surprises sprung on them six months later."

The man on the other side of the fence was John Duncan, who headed up corporate affairs for the group. "We were always honest and realistic. But later on, we were more and more governed by what we could, or could not, say to the market: the regulators were watching closely. In the old days of PR, if you had a good story you would go to the Balls Brothers wine bar in Paternoster Square on a Friday night — it was called the Friday Night Drop — and let them have it. You couldn't do that later."

Referring to the phase of greatly increased acquisition activity following the Luxembourg conference, including the major acquisitions of Hogg and Gestetner, and the tensions within the management team,

Duncan concluded that "All this led to real problems with the analysts. There was a tougher and tougher regulatory climate and then we clammed up. The real reason was that the wheels were starting to come off, but we didn't want to say so, or why. So we alienated the analysts and we stopped being open. We had great communication problems.

I would say that from 1986 for five or six years there was trust between us and the analysts. Those were the good times. After that, the trust was eroded, and it all happened within a very short space of time. They saw the wheels coming off, though they were astonishingly excited about the TKM acquisition and the rights issue. But that was because of the trust. The market loves you if you bring in year-on-year steady growth: it doesn't like surprises. We gave them surprises and, by and large, the acquisitions didn't work. If we had gone on growing steadily, we would still be the market's darling — if we had weeded out the bad businesses and bought more wisely. And the big mistake was not talking to the press. You can't turn them off like a tap."

The analysts would simply call it the risk discount and the shares would be marked down accordingly. In April 1995, with the share price at 305p, James Capel could see logic in the shares as a "long-term buy." Their report noted that any more bad news would remove the stock from the FTSE-100, but thought a break-up bid for the group unlikely. "Mutiny mounts at Inchcape," shouted a headline in a Sunday newspaper. The article went on to refer to the "strange mix" of businesses.

The next month, Charles Mackay was in Singapore opening a Toyota service center. He told the local *Business Times*, "The rising yen has made the current generation of Japanese cars too expensive." The familiar yen excuse was rolled out again. He went on to paint a picture of a rapidly growing market for cars in China, and drew attention to the growing Inchcape presence there. China was a renewed source of fascination for companies and investors: all those billions of people and all that potential demand.

It had echoes of the apocryphal story of the two shoe salesmen sent to West Africa earlier this century to explore the market. One came back and said that hardly anyone was wearing shoes and doubted if the market was worth going for. The other came back and said they could sell 100 million pairs because only a few people had shoes. In the mid-1990s it was clear that China was still communist rather than capitalist, and that the vast majority of its citizens were still among the poorest in the world. It was equally clear that central and provincial governments gave the highest priority to investment in manufacturing facilities.

China needed to employ its own people producing goods for export first and domestic consumption second. China would welcome inward investment in factories and new technology. But why would China wish to import products such as cars in any quantities, especially when organizations like Volkswagen had invested long term in local manufacturing? It was difficult to see a secure role for a foreign trading company, despite Inchcape's long association with China. And yet James Capel in April had looked forward to the lifting of austerity measures in China, and SBC Warburg suggested that Inchcape's "exposure to the Pacific Rim remains a positive factor, particularly China."

The next piece of news was the announcement at the end of July that David John would take over as chairman of BOC, leaving Inchcape at the end of the year. One potential candidate for the top job had given up the struggle and found a new future for himself. The next day it became clear that Inchcape had two weeks previously sold its stake in Gestetner to Ricoh, allowing Ricoh to make a £179 million offer for Gestetner. On August 2, it was Japan that was making the news when its Ministry of Finance revealed a package of measures to encourage its investors to put their money abroad. The aim was to help depreciate the yen. The *Evening Standard* headline was: "Rush for Inchcape as Footsie shines." "There is now a rush to buy Inchcape stock, up 8 1/2p to 305p because it is cheap, yields 5.8% and gives a highly geared play into a depreciating yen." After a quickly arranged meeting with the analysts, the conclusion was that the year's profits would remain depressed but that profits would pick up fast in the following year. Up went the shares by 19.5p, or nearly 7%. *The Financial Times* was not impressed: "Given the nature of Inchcape's business, profits can pick up extraordinarily rapidly. Nonetheless, its recent difficulties demonstrate the poor quality of earnings."

And it wasn't just the yen that was affecting sentiment: on the same day, the company announced that 2000 jobs would be cut across the group on a worldwide basis. The estimated savings were £30 million. The reality was that the job-cutting had been going on for several months, following hard on from the one-third cut in head office staff, which was designed to send an unambiguous signal to the operations. The company just had not had an opportunity to mention it until recent events with the yen caused it to talk to outsiders.

STRAINS AND STRESSES AT THE TOP

One week later, Sir David Plastow announced his retirement at the end of the year. Within a month, two key figures on the board had decided to leave. Sir David explained to *The Financial Times*, "I feel that it is a good time for me to make way for a new Chairman who is in a position to commit his time to Inchcape for several years to come. I am also anxious to play more golf." The newspaper went on to record that Sir David and Mackay had again strenuously denied rumors that they had fallen out. Sir David said: "It is absolute rubbish. The only thing I hate about Charles is his insistence on decaffeinated coffee." The banality of this line spoke volumes. The search was on for a new chairman; he was to emerge from an unlikely direction.

For those staff working in head office the tension that followed was only too obvious. "In the interregnum between Sir David Plastow stepping down and the new chairman coming on board, there was a real vacuum in the company and it became very difficult," as Alison Davies recalled, "It was appalling — quite difficult to handle."

With much less fanfare, Trevor Taylor stepped up from chief executive of Toyota (GB) to become head of Inchcape's Toyota businesses worldwide. This plugged the gap that was left by the forthcoming departure of David John, and helped calm the nerves of Toyota Motor Corporation. It also calmed the nerves of investors, since the Toyota business was clearly the solid backbone of the whole group and a major stream of profits. Taylor was well known and highly respected by TMC and had made a great success of the Toyota operation in the U.K.; he was a good example of the need to have solid "backbone" managers in the succession plan.

By late August the yen had fallen 25% in five months and Inchcape was one of the top-performing stocks in the FTSE-100. It was now capitalized at £1.8 billion, which lifted it just clear of the bottom of the league.

Meanwhile, Bain Hogg was busy announcing a new client retail service network. It was, of course, global. In an article in *Lloyds List*, reference was made to "a number of strategic disposals" and that, following these disposals, the revenue had dropped to £216.1 million. This gave Bain Hogg a world ranking of eleven. After one year and £176 million of acquisition, the insurance broking business had gone from eleventh to seventh and back to eleventh in the world. So much for the theory of buying "scale."

Just ahead of its interim figures came the opening of Inchcape's first Russian Coca-Cola plant in Volgograd, and the announcement that a further £25 million would go in over the succeeding two years to open another five factories. It was a bad half-year. Profits were down from £125 million to £18.6 million, but the charge to exceptional expenses was £64.7 million. There was even a decision to move out of the impressive St. James's headquarters. It was time to deliver the bad news, take the pain, and then move on to a fresh and more austere start.

In early November, Sir Colin Marshall (later Lord Marshall) joined the board of Inchcape in order to take over as non-executive chairman from the start of 1996. "It happened in part because I knew Charles Mackay and he was a member of the British Airways board of directors as a non-executive," recalled Lord Marshall. "He was therefore familiar from the inside with my plans to step down as chief executive from British Airways at the end of 1995, and to assume the part-time non-executive chairmanship of the company from the beginning of 1996." In fact, he was also a non-executive director of British Telecom and the Hongkong and Shanghai Bank, and was lined up for the presidency of the Confederation of British Industry. He was involved in a wide range of other corporate and public activities.

"Charles told me of the plan to seek a new chairman for Inchcape —in fact, I think I had already read it in a newspaper anyway — and he asked me if I would have any interest in it. I said, 'Well, let me reflect on that.' In reflecting, I felt that because of Inchcape's presence on a global basis, and being to some considerable extent a service organization — service, retail, etc., it was something with which I had lots of familiarity. And because of my own past experience of being in business on a global basis for almost all of my working life, I said, 'Yes, I could be interested.' So, we then went through the usual procedure by talking to the search firm that was appointed to seek a successor to Sir David Plastow. Then, of course, meeting with other members of the board — the executive directors as well — and we came to the conclusion from that process."

Press reaction was universally favourable and the investment community saw it as a considerable coup to secure the services of such a business leader. The staff of Inchcape could not help but be impressed by the chairman's style: here was a courteous man who greeted everyone and had an extraordinary ability to remember names and faces. Here was a man who was clearly brilliant at time-management, and who seemed able to open gaps in his diary, despite such a workload. One of his passions was "customer care" and it was clearly more than just a slogan. But behind the bland and amiable exterior lay a cutting edge that would be put to quick effect.

REVOLT

A motel on the edge of an industrial estate and a ring road in the English Midlands in early November was an unlikely setting for a corporate drama. Several of the stream boards had now had leadership programs of their own. Motors' and Shipping's were held in the U.K., and Inspection and Testing had theirs in Ithaca, close to Cornell University and near the site of a large acquisition, the Edison Testing Laboratories. It had been decided that it was important not to leave out the corporate team of senior managers. The late decision resulted in a scramble to find a suitable location. Staverton, near Rugby, was the compromise choice. These managers were the senior finance team: specialists in consolidation, tax, treasury, and audit; the human resources team; corporate planning; and several senior people from the Inchcape Pacific headquarters in Hong Kong who did not fit into a business stream structure. In terms of seniority in the group, they were in the organization level just below the group management board. Feelings about being there were generally negative, and the events of the recent months had left a pall as heavy and leaden as the grey November sky in Warwickshire.

Following Mackay's wish, the programs usually started on a Sunday night, as a signal of their earnestness. For people who already spent a large part of their lives traveling, losing even a fragment of a weekend while in England was a further irritant. In the bar that night, there was already a sense of anger and frustration. The next day, the program started with details of the internal survey that had been conducted earlier in the year. By now, the feelings expressed in the survey about communication and the value placed on individual contributions had intensified. And yet, the survey of Inchcape's top 300 managers was saying that the problem lay with "corporate." These were the people sitting around the conference table in Staverton. Were they the cause of the problem, or were they suffering the problem? How could they exert leadership if the GMB did not recognize their abilities or listen to their advice? Were they impotent or just ineffective? How could they demonstrate responsible behavior? These uncomfortable questions came to the surface as the debate swirled. "They were basically in denial or confusion," according to Rosemary Harper who was the consultant directing the program.

Anyone who had thought that this was going to be a comfortable, anodyne training program knew that this was not to be. There was still an expectation that external help was at hand. The consultants would surely have answers to some of their problems, at least. But the mood was to turn ugly by the middle of the first morning. In a departure from previous events, including the now famous pilot program with the GMB at Horsted Place, Ralph Stacey's session on chaos theory had been brought forward to accommodate his university teaching schedule.

Stacey talked about the way we all make sense of the world by constructing our own simplified models of it, based on our experiences and on our interaction with other people. As a result, we would each have our own version of what constitutes reality. And that version of reality would be truncated by whatever mental models we had built up. Culture — national or organizational — was an example of a mental model that was very resistant to change. We would tend to see what we expected to see: we would ignore anomalies. This process was as automatic as riding a bicycle and worked below our level of awareness. As he introduced his propositions, the reaction was either mild curiosity or rejection. How was this relevant to the professionalism of an auditor, for instance? The mood of rejection was taking over.

Then he went a step further: he suggested that the corporate team members were in danger of becoming "skilled incompetents." Their skills of analysis and presentation had been burnished to a high degree, but had become increasingly irrelevant to what was actually going on in the outside world, and to how organizations really worked. The reality of the outside world had changed, but their mental models had not kept in step. They needed to learn how to construct more complex models of the world by bringing in greater awareness of their thinking processes; otherwise, they would not survive.

This lit the fuse. Anger boiled over and Stacey was taken to task by several managers. How dare he suggest that they were becoming irrelevant? The truth was that, by design or default, he had lanced the boil. The delegates were no longer prepared to listen. Stacey articulated his anger at not being given a fair hearing and suggested that they had become "hopeless." The session broke up completely and a majority of delegates left the room. Those who remained attempted to apologize to Stacey who was by now red in the face with emotion; he decided that he wanted no further insults and prepared to leave. Eventually, emotions cooled enough to persuade Stacey to stay and finish his session.

When he resumed, Stacey explained how complex learning involves creative destruction and is bound to create anxiety and tension. "If you are working on an issue where you are far from agreement, and far from certainty, then you will be uncomfortable: you will be close to chaos." "Turbulent times will generate huge emotions." "A new strategy will emerge from the confusion and discomfort, but only if you stay in that area long enough. Don't retreat to agreement and certainty about less important issues." "Strategic direction is not just the vision of a powerful person; it is the result of spontaneous self-organization." "You are in danger of creating a myth around George Turnbull as a leader." In essence, Stacey was trying to get the delegates to face up to their responsibility for influencing the organization. In their turn, the delegates rejected that as unrealistic, because they were simply not listened to anymore.

The discussion shifted to the mental models of the executive directors, and how they needed to change. One of the consultants noted that the executive directors were identified as the scapegoats for all that had happened, and that some of the delegates had a sense of "failed dependency." The people in whom they had put their trust had failed them. Stacey worked hard to broaden out the discussion to all the other factors that were bearing on Inchcape and its key decision-makers, but the black cloud of anger stayed attached to the executive directors. "What can be done about it? Why don't you invite them to come and discuss these issues here with you?" His questions caused anxiety in the group, but eventually they decided to put this suggestion into practice.

For the three Chinese managers from Hong Kong, this had been a deeply disturbing episode and something quite beyond their previous experience. For Alison Davies, who had joined just six months before and had her baptism of fire in the head office headcount cuts, this was "an extraordinary and unpleasant experience. It was very clear that the functioning of management had broken down — or that is what it felt like. I felt strange because I was detached and didn't have the emotional reaction to what was going on."

After Professor Stacey had completed his sessions and left, the debate and anger rolled on. It found coherence around the way to invite the chief executive and his colleagues to Staverton to listen to the concerns and ideas of the delegates. Just to listen. Several phone calls later, it had been arranged. The next day, Charles Mackay, Philip Cushing, Rod O'Donoghue, and Bob Goodall drove together up the M1 motorway and joined the meeting. It was a brave move. To their credit, they listened carefully for a couple of hours to the anger and frustration of a group of people who felt increasingly alienated and impotent. Keith Lawler and Nelson Chan acted as spokesmen for the corporate managers. "There was enormous anger in that program," recalled Bob Goodall. "The whole thing brought about a great awareness to everybody that we were really in a very, very serious situation. The preoccupation we had with 'results' was not only *not* getting us results, but it was also causing us huge morale and motivation problems. People were looking for a different type of leadership from the GMB than they were getting." By the end of the debate, a lot of heat had gone out of the situation and it allowed a neat side step to take place. It was agreed that the "Staverton" team should present their views and recommendations for action to the last meeting of the GMB of the year — just before Christmas. "We did actually see at that point a significant step forward from the corporate team," according to Rosemary Harper. A change process had started. As before, in the last years of Kenneth Inchcape, it took a crisis to provoke change.

In the weeks that followed, the e-mail system became the network to design a presentation for the GMB. E-mail also turned into a support mechanism to keep up spirits and provide some sense of purpose. The so-called Staverton Team had widened its circle to include other head office managers who were left out of the original workshop because they were considered not senior enough to attend. Several of the team dropped out of e-mail contact at an early stage: their minds were already set on defecting from the organization.

The presentation to the GMB was going to be made by four representatives: Keith Lawler, Alison Davies, Dale Butcher, and Peter Stubbs. It was clear to most of the team that what was needed was a radical shift in corporate culture. It was equally clear to them that the ESTJ-dominated GMB was not ready for the term "culture." Operating style was decided upon because it sounded more practical and down-to-earth. Its essentials were honesty, respect, teamwork, and consistency: honest, straightforward communication; respect for individuals and their views; cooperation rather than competition between streams and corporate; consistent messages and behavior that matched the messages. It would require absolute and long-term commitment from the whole senior management team.

Charles Mackay chaired the presentation on December 21. He asked that the presentation be heard out without any interruptions. It was — in complete silence. Without seeking an overall reaction, Mackay asked for a repeat, slide-by-slide. This turned into a dissection, which began to lose itself in detail. The four presenters found themselves frustrated by the way that the GMB functioned. One director thought this was the most important presentation he had ever listened to in his time with

Inchcape: the voice of middle management was at last coming through. Eventually, the presentation team was invited to comment, and they told the GMB that they were encouraged that some of the issues had been debated, but felt that others still had not been recognized. Mackay proposed that each member of the board should go away and review his leadership style in the light of their 360-degree feedback and test it out against the new operating style. It was another side step, but the team knew they had made a lasting impression.

ENDING A YEAR TO FORGET

At the start of December, there was another hammer blow to morale: Inchcape was pushed out of the FTSE-100 index and relegated to the second division of FTSE-250 companies. Philip Cushing was quoted in *The Financial Times*: "There is a long history of companies dropping out of the top 100 only to come steaming back." Sir Colin Marshall was quoted as saying that he believed Inchcape had "taken most, if not all, of the action required."

One man's career was in the ascendancy. In fact, its trajectory was more like that of a rocket. Peter Johnson, the man who had been brought in to run and sell the U.K. Motors Retail business, stepped up to head Inchcape Motors International, which embraced all the motors franchises outside of Toyota. He displaced Maurice Rourke who had come in with the TKM acquisition and later replaced Reg Heath at the top. Rourke's forte was business development: building relationships with manufacturers and bringing in new franchises. The steady grind of consolidation and performance improvement in existing businesses was not for him. Johnson's route to the top was not a smooth one, however. In the summer of 1995, he had spent his first four months with the group preparing U.K. Retail for flotation. He was at an IMI board dinner when "Charles Mackay arrived and announced to everyone that he had changed his mind, and he wasn't going to float Retail. He didn't bother to tell me beforehand. I found it disconcerting."

Japanese humor is well known for its slapstick, knockabout style. It has another, more whimsical side, as Osamu Narita, chairman of Inchcape Marketing Services in Tokyo, showed. "We had a visit from the Royal Ballet in Japan and invited many guests from major principals and customers to the performance. We were so proud that Inchcape contributed to the new version of stage production of 'Sleeping Beauty.' We thought we were working in a great company."

DECISION TIME

It did not take the new chairman long to make up his mind. As he put it, "… all that tended to be overwhelmed by the cost to the company of what had happened with the rising value of the Japanese currency. And we needed to act to restore the strength of our balance sheet. Therefore, we were going to have to exit some of our businesses. We embarked on a rapid exercise to determine which businesses we should move out of, and which we should stay in. It was really a review of the strategic direction of the company going forward and in the end happened quite quickly. We did it — I recollect — within sixty days or so of my assuming the chair.

"The financial imperatives were very considerable indeed, and yes, they were clearly a driving factor. Plus, of course, the way in which the investment market was looking at Inchcape. Although Inchcape had already moved out of a whole succession of businesses over quite a long period of time, there was still confusion as to what really was the strategic direction of the company. There was a need to try to address the concerns of the investment market, while at the same time recognizing a need to strengthen the balance sheet of the company."

It was time to declare the Annual Results for 1995. On March 25, 1996, Sir Colin Marshall revealed the outcome of the strategic review the company had been carrying out since January. Inchcape would focus on distribution. Testing would be sold, and Insurance Broking would be floated off or demerged. The analysts estimated that this could bring in £550 million, taking care of the balance sheet problems and leaving the group some cash to play with. The Marketing stream would relocate to Asia, basing itself in Singapore, and consider introducing new partners or local shareholders. The dividend would be cut. And Philip Cushing would take over as chief executive, with Charles Mackay remaining as deputy chairman until June. He would then leave. It was a classic "clean-up" job, but impressive for its scope and clarity. The new leaders were firmly in charge and the shares responded by picking up 10p.

At his farewell party in the staff dining room in the St. James's headquarters, Cushing and Mackay swapped anecdotes about Russia and China and appeared well disposed to each other. Whether the jocularity was forced was difficult to tell. The staff gathered there, standing stiffly with a drink in hand, were startled by Charles Mackay's last request for them to look after the group because he wanted his share options to perform over the next six months.

Press reaction was accommodating. Most newspapers saw the dividend as unsustainable and therefore a cut was inevitable. The strategic overhaul pleased: it released shareholder value, increased focus, and would strengthen the balance sheet. Dropping the chief executive was seen as part of the process of "wiping the slate clean" ready for a fresh start. The blame for all the troubles was not entirely management's, because external events had clearly been extraordinarily adverse. Anticipating the announcement, *The Sunday Times* commented: "Those who know the company well say Marshall has acted on the advice of non-executives and operational executives who laid the blame for the company's problems at Mackay's door. He and Marshall have a close business relationship. In 1993 Marshall invited Mackay on to the British Airways board, a post he is leaving, and they both serve as non-executive directors of the HBSC banking group." Marshall had no time for sentiment.

SUCCESSION UNSTITCHED

Anyone who has monitored succession plans for any large company will know that much of what passes for a plan is part political game and part "wish list." The acid test of checking plans against outcomes will reveal just how solid or realistic was the thinking that went into those plans. In many cases, even on a time scale as short as one year, the gap between plan and reality is dramatic.

This is not necessarily the fault of the people drawing up the plans. They are usually unaware or have out-of-date impressions of the ambitions of the individuals whose future they are planning. They have to make judgments about how someone may perform at the next level in the organization, and that next position may demand very different abilities and attitudes. Often they are making their judgments without the help of any independent psychological or behavioral profiling; such intrusions are often seen as unnecessary or offensive at a very senior level. Then, add in the fact that the organization itself is changing shape continuously as people come and go and jobs are re-jigged to cope with emergencies. Extra change comes from reaction to organizational fashions and shifts in the marketplace. Perhaps the biggest "spanner in the works" for any succession planning is the effect of mergers and acquisitions.

Despite all these uncertainties, succession plans are often constructed around the current structure of the organization. Filling in boxes and preparing neat charts is a comfortable displacement activity for more open-ended thinking about matching potential resources with potential organizational needs. In Myers-Briggs terms, traditional succession planning is made for STJs, but its very neatness can be a mental straightjacket. The NFPs and those comfortable with the implications of chaos theory would be much happier making a broad match between the talents of the top team and the range of scenarios for a future organization — and leaving it at that as far as a formal plan is concerned. They might expend more of their energy on developing those talents and increasing the diversity of the top team, in order to cope with unanticipated change.

Planning one's own successor is often regarded as one of the most important tasks facing any chief executive. George Turnbull had a long-term plan for his succession based on one individual.

There was no doubt that the style of Mackay was an abrupt change from that of Turnbull. Certainly the senior management found it difficult to adjust to. George Turnbull had been noted for his ability to delegate fully once he had confidence — and not get involved in the detail. In the Middle East, Peter McElwaine recalled that "We often felt that Charles was operating at a higher intellectual level, but that is not always how to bring people along with you." One senior board member reflected on "his strong intellectual appreciation of the numbers."

Paul Cheng, one of Mackay's recruits, had clear views on the change in leadership style: "Charles is highly intelligent, highly analytical, and highly numerate, but his intelligence and enthusiasm for a project sometimes leave little room for other people." The love of detail and numbers struck Ian Ross forcibly: "I remember sitting with Charles and David in Bangkok, going through those interminable quarterly reviews. I have never found anything so boring in my life. Just number, after number, after number. 'Your working capital ratio in this business (which turned over just £1 million a year) has gone from 10.2 to 10.4.' It was as if by getting deeper and deeper into the numbers then you would suddenly find gold about how the business works."

However, the ambition of Mackay transmitted itself into the corporate culture. For many, this was an attraction and one of the reasons they joined the company. Osamu Narita joined in 1991 and found, "We were enjoying ourselves being called an 'expansionist' group and actually excited to read about new acquisitions in every newsletter from St. James's House. At the same time, we were very proud of 'glocal' management style with heavy autonomy by local management." Back in Hong Kong, Richard Tam thought differently. "If we had been more conservative between 1991 and 1992, we could have sustained our success. We were too ambitious and overconfident." Ambition expressed itself in another way for John Bartley: "The changeover of styles when Charles came in with his McKinsey background — he was a highly cerebral, high-flying, contemporary manager, but perhaps trying to do too much too quickly."

The other high point of Mackay's career with Inchcape was to come back to London and, as he said, "to put in place a global structure for the business. This had the blessing of George Turnbull and the non-executives but, initially, there was a fair amount of resistance from some of the executive team who had grown up under Inchcape's local company structures. We applied the same basic ideas of putting ambitious strategies in place, and putting managers in a position where they could achieve them. For two years it worked pretty well and we began to believe that we could really become a major company in Britain. Turnover grew from £3 billion to £6 billion, so it was a time of exceptional growth. Then things started to go off the boil."

The dynamics of any top team are fascinating and crucial to the success of any organization. A platitudinous statement, maybe, and one that is generally and intuitively true but elusive in close-up. Commonly, the so-called top team is not really working as a team for much of its existence; nor does it necessarily need to, except in times of crisis. When it meets formally, each player will follow his or her agenda and avoid criticizing fellow members of the team, for fear of reprisal. Decisions are made sometimes by default, through disinterest, or out of collusion. Typically, decisions emerge from "conversations in the corridor," from particular one-to-one relationships, or "kitchen cabinets," exactly as Professor Ralph Stacey had identified in the leadership programs. Observations on how just two individuals worked together can sometimes illuminate the inner workings of the overall team. For example, John Whiteman found his department was making little impression on strategic thinking in the early 1990s because, "Andrew and Charles had a bit of a love–hate relationship. Charles was not always a good listener and Andrew was not always a good arguer. Both could be emotional." One can imagine the effect this might have had on any attempt at a team-based decision. Mackay's own view was that he would have done one thing differently. "When I came back to London, George had built his own team that had been increasingly successful. I kept going with the same team at the center. Although we put a lot of new people into the streams, the center stayed much the same. I don't

244   Managers and Mantras: One Company's Struggle for Simplicity

think that was a very smart thing for me to have done. It is nothing to do with the individuals, who were very good. After you have had a strong leader who has built his own team, it often doesn't work to run the same team with a different leader and style."

The succession of Mackay was built on one premise which became self-serving: that George Turnbull would be chairman and act as Mackay's mentor, as well as check any excesses of ambition. No-one challenged the basic flaw in this plan: the possibility that George Turnbull might not be capable of acting as chairman when the time came for the handover of power. As Derek Whittaker put it, "Charles Mackay without George did not prove to be the man ..." "Without George," said Rod O'Donoghue, "there were going to be bruised egos whatever happened, but George would have managed those. I think Charles, who is a fine executive, was in a very difficult condition when he found himself *the* paramount authority in a business he was hoping to learn more about before he was faced with the immense tasks ahead. David Orr was in transition. David Plastow was new to the business. It was very difficult." Bob Goodall was also working to the same premise: "Charles Mackay was bright. He had clearly done a great job in IPL. And I think to this day that if he had come in under the original terms, George would have sat on the ambition and controlled it. Not stifled it, but managed it. I think it would have helped Charles contain his ambition in a more strategic framework."

Mackay found himself not only without his mentor but with rivals. "The other thing that I would not do is to allow myself to be in a situation where there were at least three people who thought they should be chief executive — if not now, fairly soon. You need to have succession in place, but it is unhealthy for the organization to have people competing the whole time for the top job. That said, I don't like people who surround themselves with 'yes men,' though it would have been easier when the going got rough." And the going did get rough. Mackay's own view of the conditions was, "If we had realized how bad the yen was going to get, and how long it would last, we would have started battening down the hatches in 1994. All the experts kept saying the yen would fall back, but the reverse happened; it went on for several years. We were therefore too slow to take our foot off the growth accelerator. We probably lost a year."

The last word on this subject should come from the man who succeeded Charles Mackay, Philip Cushing, who was asked if he was surprised to become chief executive. "I was, perhaps, more surprised by the speed with which Colin Marshall dealt with the subject. As to the circumstances, Charles on a personal basis was extremely good to me, right from when he decided he wanted me to come back to London, rather than anybody else — and he had several choices — to run the Services businesses. So, on a personal basis, I owe him a lot."

A New Mantra: One Company, One Team

OUR FOCUS FOR THE FUTURE

A Portuguese colony on the edge of China was an unlikely place to launch a new leadership, a new strategy, and a new operating style. Macau had little of the gloss of its larger neighbor, Hong Kong. Indeed, some aspects of Macau were distinctly tacky. Yet, it had the advantage of being half the price of Hong Kong, and having a spacious hotel looking out to sea. Inchcape's senior managers had met last for a conference four years before, in Luxembourg. The only echo of that conference was the convoluted journey. After the flight into Hong Kong, it needed a taxi to the ferry terminal and then a jetfoil trip through the islands and across the Pearl River delta, followed by a minibus to reach the hotel. Everything else was changed. The mood was somber; the main ambition was survival. There were no outside speakers, no gurus; the only highlight was the presence of the new non-executive chairman, Sir Colin Marshall. Most of the delegates were keen to see how Philip Cushing would grapple with the task of putting the group on the road to recovery. Many also had expectations about a new vision for the business, and hope for the future after the battering of the past two years.

Cushing's approach was down-to-earth and sincere. He was also in acute pain, having strained his back playing squash the previous evening. There was no doubting his conviction, and much of his exposition of the new, focused strategy was familiar to his audience. Describing the group as specialists in international distribution made a number of people uncomfortable, who felt that it failed to do justice to the whole business and played down the high-profile aspects of Marketing. But Cushing was deliberately trying to shift the emphasis back onto operating efficiency: "Doing what you do now, even better." No longer would it be possible for growth to come solely from acquisitions. Organic growth would be the driver from here onwards. Disposing of businesses that did not fit would raise the cash to invest in those businesses that had a future.

Following convention, it was time for the heads of each stream to justify their business. Joe Newcombe talked positively about the joint venture with Ricoh and about the convergence of technologies and products in Office Machinery, with the occasional flash of dry Australian wit. Michael Cooper gave a typically detailed account of greater efficiencies in Bottling in Chile, and progress with the new acquisition in Peru and the delayed start in Russia. Everything in the Toyota division was absolutely under control, according to Trevor Taylor, whereas Peter Johnson saw Motors International having "everything to play for." Richard Nelson proudly declared that Testing was doing better than ever, and Simon Morse gave the most entertaining and creative presentation about one of the smallest businesses, Shipping. It was the turn of Marketing, which was now represented by Andrew Cummins, who had taken over responsibility following the departure of Alan Davies. Cummins was typically plain-speaking and had difficulty in disguising his doubts about the overall viability of the Marketing stream and the need for drastic pruning. Those managers in the audience from the Marketing stream found little to cheer about.

It was the turn of the functional heads. Rod O'Donoghue spoke convincingly about ways of strengthening the balance sheet and speeding up financial reporting. However, this was not the man who had spoken so firmly and positively at Luxembourg: the past four years had visibly aged him. He lacked the old enthusiasm and conveyed a sense of weariness. Bob Goodall launched a new human resources strategy, which had been endorsed by the group management board and amounted to a thorough manifesto for a change program. It was a direct response to all the messages that had come out of the leadership program in the previous year, culminating with the "Staverton Team" and their revolt.

The impact of all this missed the audience completely. Question after question was about bonuses and share options. Many of the delegates had missed the financial targets for their bonus, and had been awarded lower bonuses solely on the strength of their "personal goals." Typically, bonuses for the previous year were paid in March or April, so they had felt the pain in their pockets only a month or two before. Share options had held the promise — at some point in the future — of a bit of capital to pay off the mortgage or plan for their retirement. As luck would have it, many share options were issued at or near the peak of the share price. With the share price at less than half its peak, the prospect of the options paying out looked increasingly remote. Most agreed with the idea of tying a proportion of rewards to performance, until performance faltered. Human nature being what it is, everyone really expected a one-way bet. Goodall was angry about being dragged down into the bear pit, after all the work that had gone into his new strategy, but that was the reality of human resource management. "Never mind the big ideas, what about my pay and rations?" Reflecting later on this, Goodall made the point: "It's remarkable that it must be at least five years since anyone made a penny out of their share options. We have no long-term incentives in this group, but people continue to work, and work hard, and are motivated. What I have learned, if anything, is that financial reward isn't the key motivator."

There was, however, a more fundamental reason why the senior management was failing to engage with the new human resources strategy. That reason was about to emerge.

ALL CHANGE

It was time for Cushing to make his keynote presentation and bring the conference to a formal conclusion. He began to speak with conviction and some passion about creating "One Company, One Team." Behind the slogan was the idea that internal competition was destructive and that Inchcape needed to present a united front to the outside world of customers and principals. By supporting each other and sharing knowledge, the individual businesses could exploit the benefits of belonging to a powerful group. This could range from the sharing of best practice to the cross-referral of business leads. New life was being breathed into synergy.

He then declared that the group would live by five values: service; teamwork; innovation; respect; and results. The values had come directly from the survey conducted for the leadership program eighteen months previously. Three hundred managers had answered a range of questions about the group and its culture. Two were critical: "What does it take to succeed in Inchcape now?" and, "What should it take to succeed in Inchcape in the future?" It was the top five responses to the second question which generated the values. This was not something generated by a copywriter or a public relations department. It was the senior managers' aspiration for their company and it would form the basis of a new operating style. The term "culture change" still was not in the Inchcape lexicon, but that is what Cushing was asking for.

For some weeks before the Macau conference, Cushing had been looking for something else dramatic to announce. He wanted something for people to get excited about and he needed a vehicle that he could put his stamp on. He wanted a symbol that would demonstrate that the group could add value to its constituents. Cushing had a conviction that the general level of management skills was inadequate, particularly in the area of marketing and logistics. It was time for more "hard-edged" training than the behavioral program introduced by his predecessor. His was an intuitive approach, and no formal analysis had been done. There was much discussion about the target audience. Eventually, all agreed that the program must reach 600 managers in the first year to have the greatest impact. This was more than double the rate of progress of the leadership program, which had proven to be a tough logistical exercise in itself. The new program was nothing if not ambitious. At Macau, Cushing unveiled it and admitted that the design of the content had not started: he would consult with line management to arrive at an appropriate configuration, but that would not be allowed to delay its introduction. It would be called the "Accelerator."

The conference wound up with a question-and-answer session. A number of questions were about the future for the group: after the hard slog of improving performance and tidying up the portfolio, what lay ahead? What was the big picture? Cushing's reply was honest if uninspiring. He admitted that he did not have the answers and that it was necessary to rebuild the fundamentals of the business first. Then it would be appropriate to start thinking about grand strategy again. The conference ended on a flat note. The group was now in the hands of a hardheaded pragmatist. But where was the vision and inspiration to sustain motivation? Was that all there was? The reason the human resources strategy failed to inspire was now obvious: it stood orphaned, without the framework of an inspiring corporate strategy.

The closing dinner took place in the grounds of the hotel in the open air: the warm, humid air of a South China summer evening. The old "work hard, play hard" culture of Inchcape lived on in the form of a number of noisy high jinks that took over the proceedings. This was definitely the Anglo-Saxon way of releasing tension and bonding together with one's colleagues. Before long, several of the Chinese executives had disappeared discreetly, probably in search of more sophisticated entertainment in the town. The South Americans stayed on but found it difficult to come to terms with the vulgarity and light-hearted style of the evening. They thought it was entirely inappropriate for a company still facing serious problems. Building a common culture went much deeper than slogans: national cultures and corporate cultures were rubbing together uncomfortably.

HUMBLE PIE

The move from the luxury of St. James's in London's West End to a couple of floors in a nondescript office block in Cavendish Square, just off the crowded shopping area of Oxford Street, was both practical and symbolic. The rent was halved. The image of the company was now down-to-earth, but for some of the corporate staff it was a sign of decline rather than frugality.

In the spirit of the new Inchcape, the design of the new Accelerator program would be subject to consultation. An ideal opportunity presented itself with the annual international management program at Ashridge Management College, which lies in lush countryside to the northwest of London. The delegates were asked to recommend the content to their chief executive. Cushing had already made up his mind about what was required and expected the thirty line managers from around the world to come up with a similar prescription for a set of "hard," quantitative topics.

They did not. They asked for a program that would make the five new values come alive. At first, Cushing said nothing, but his body language said it all. Summoning up restraint and patience, he asked for justification. One delegate from Malaysia summed up their feelings: "If you can't get the foundations right, then we will just waste time and money: the values are the foundations and we need to get them in place first." Cushing agreed, and so the basic design for the Accelerator was set. It was a defining moment: a chief executive had not only listened but changed his mind, radically. It was also clear that the middle managers were serious about changing the culture.

From this point onward, the senior human resources team, essentially four people, worked hard on the detail of the design for the Accelerator and the processes that would be needed to support it. One of these was an in-house 360-degree feedback system. This was based on internal research, coordinated across several continents and business streams. Not only did this greatly increase the face validity of the system that quickly emerged, but it also saved considerable amounts of expenditure on consultancy. Consultants were used to bring in technical solutions such as e-mail feedback and self-processing of that feedback by the managers on their computers. The overall aim was to reduce dependency on consultants and the human resource function, and give managers more control and involvement in their own development. Much effort also went into communicating: making sure the messages were clearly understood by both the local human resources managers and their operating contemporaries. Both groups would be required to carry on the communication and leadership process locally. Consultants were still making valuable inputs, but a much healthier balance between internal and external resourcing had been struck. Not surprisingly, it started to generate enthusiasm and motivation.

FOCUSING DOWN

By late summer, the press was talking about a reinvigorated Inchcape and making mildly optimistic comments. *The South China Morning Post* was typical: "The market has slowly begun to give the company the benefit of the doubt, and credence to its strategic overhaul." On October 9, the sale of Testing Services to Charterhouse Development Capital was announced. The price was £380 million, almost £100 million more than some analysts had previously estimated. According to one newspaper, "The price tag is a personal triumph for Cushing." It certainly seemed an excellent deal and would go a long way to plugging the hole in the balance sheet. It was ironic that Stuart Simpson of Charterhouse was quoted in the same article as saying, "We believe we could float it now but it has such high growth potential, we are likely to hold on to it for about two or three years." The only other component of Inchcape's portfolio with high growth potential was the Coca-Cola business. To several members of the board, it seemed as if selling Testing was selling the family silver.

A few days later came the surprise sale of Bain Hogg to the American insurance group Aon for £160 million. The planned demerger had been overtaken by events. Several months earlier, Bain Hogg was being valued at £250 million, but pressure on margins and unmoved insurance rates washed away £90 million. There would be a £195 million write-off of goodwill on disposal. The grand strategy for insurance was in ruins, and shareholder value had been destroyed on a breathtaking scale. In *The Evening Standard*, Cushing distanced himself from his predecessor's problem child: "Inchcape would now be looking at increased investment

levels in its existing businesses as well as bolt-on acquisitions. No
diversifications are planned." "The group has been straightened out from
a portfolio point of view. Now we have to get on with it," he said.

With the share price at 272p, HSBC James Capel downgraded its
recommendation to "hold" and showed its impatience: "We recognize
that the company is improving, but have a concern that this is now a
two year story." Within their report was a more sophisticated approach
to valuation than the customary sum-of-the-parts calculation. Concepts
such as economic profit and the weighted average cost of capital were
being applied. The analysis was becoming more penetrating: there were
fewer places to hide.

MANAGING CHANGE

As a follow-on from Macau, Cushing starred in a lengthy video of
questions and answers, staged in Hong Kong with a large group of
managers. The video was sent around the Inchcape world and received
with positive and sometimes bemused reactions. Occasionally, it was
simply not shown or was actively suppressed by line managers who
decided that it was irrelevant or distracting for their staff. The next step
was to identify a senior line manager to lead what was already being
called the change program. His or her immediate task was to drive the
Accelerator program; the more difficult one was to ensure that the GMB
and the next level of senior management were supporting the change
process and demonstrating the new values. Parallel with this, the
leadership program was now revisiting the top fifty managers. A
significant number of them had been identified by their middle
managers as "blockers." Peter McElwaine was selected as project director,
reporting to the GMB. He was senior and he was from line management
rather than human resources; therefore, he would be more credible.

Philip Cushing set up a change committee under his chairmanship.
Gradually, he disengaged himself from the committee. He was
increasingly delegating the process of culture change to others. The
others were the members of the GMB, the project director, and, of
course, the human resource professionals in head office. Out in the
operations, some line managers saw this as a centrally funded
opportunity. They took hold of it with enthusiasm and genuine
commitment, often adapting it to fit in with parallel programs inspired
by their principals. Cushing's detachment gradually became more
obvious and eventually threatened to undermine the whole process.
Because he had started off so strongly and with such personal

conviction, his detachment was all the more of a contrast. Now he seemed to be more preoccupied with the future strategy of the group. In any case, he had always preferred the operational and numerate aspects of business, and there were plenty of reasons to pull him in this direction, too.

Another video emerged and it was from an unlikely source. Saatchi and Saatchi had been called in to advise on the corporate image, and while discussing the culture change program, they mentioned a short film about geese, which they had used internally. The images of geese flying in formation were spliced with simple messages about teamwork and respect. Not only were the images strikingly beautiful, but the music had a powerful, modern beat. It was "tailor made" to support "One Company, One Team." Soon copies were being produced in all the main languages within Inchcape, and sent out with a multilingual booklet. Perhaps the most memorable message the video contained was, "The geese flying in formation *honk* to encourage those up front to keep up with their speed." *Honking* entered the company's vocabulary as a way of speaking up and being empowered. The close alliteration with a more vulgar English expression caused much amusement. Because of its imagery and the trouble that had been taken to translate it, it had an extraordinary impact. Some of the older, more straight-laced staff found this new way of communicating quite extraordinary; some wondered what on earth the group was doing by wasting its money on such frivolity. Most simply enjoyed it and felt that the company really was changing and losing its stiff, colonial attitudes. Bizarre but brilliant, it sent a powerful message right round the Inchcape world.

The Coverdale Organisation had won the business to produce the Accelerator program, mainly because they had a large enough team of consultants to train 600 managers worldwide within one year. They also had the unusual ability to train in several foreign languages. As a consultancy, they had a long history but a slightly dated and unsophisticated image. What they offered was simple, engaging, and fun. It would strike a chord. After all the difficulties and depression of the previous two years, it gave people something to rally round and a reason for fresh hope. It was essentially a very basic management program with"add-ons" to reinforce the new culture. It avoided the big issues of strategy and structure and leadership: to some observers, it was a sugarcoated distraction from reality.

Coverdale started off with focus groups in the Far East, Southeast Asia, and the U.K. to sample opinions. They picked up most of the issues and concerns which the previous research for the leadership program had done. One thing was clear: the values would work at all levels and across cultures, with one exception. That exception was "respect." In the Anglo-American sphere of influence it had an egalitarian meaning, overlaid with the more contemporary valuing of an individual's diversity of background. In the East and some parts of South America the same word meant deference, and sometimes subservience, to those older or more senior in the organization.

While Coverdale were assembling their resources to train the top 600 managers in the New Year, the GMB met for a second leadership workshop, this time in central London. Peter McElwaine had formulated seven questions for them to tackle:

1. What are we trying to achieve? (Mission)
2. How are we going to get there? (Strategy)
3. Are we different enough to succeed? (Competitive advantage)
4. What operating style do we need to achieve our personal and corporate aims?
5. What behavior do we need to demonstrate when going about our business? (Values)
6. How will we know we are succeeding? (Feedback)
7. What are the reward and recognition drivers?

This went to the heart of the culture change and the GMB's leadership of it. Answering these questions in the two days would have been a sufficient task, but Cushing insisted that they also tackle the "Vision and Mission" for the group. Peter Grey of EDC led the consultants' team. He recalls that "it was a huge struggle," and that, "It required a team that was coherent and ready for open working — they were not — yet they were dealing with issues where the group was far from agreement and far from certainty." It was again a time of high tension. "A huge amount of impatience with the process surfaced. It was a difficult process, with difficult questions: sheer frustration surfaced. People got very impatient with the whole area of operating style, and chose not to deal with it on that occasion. However, they struggled manfully with some absolutely fundamental questions like the mission statement." Reflecting on the role of facilitator, Grey felt that, "From the consultants' side we set ourselves up a bit. We strongly recommended that they didn't try and do it all in two days. But they were very strong-willed people, very determined, and the net result of that was that instead of coming out on a high, and saying 'Great, we've done three-quarters of a difficult agenda,' there was a low feeling about unfinished work."

Inchcape's "Vision and Mission" were to take a good deal more work before they saw the light of day, and needed the intervention of external wordsmiths to produce short sentences of clarity. Clarity had to be achieved in a way that would embrace all the different businesses Inchcape was engaged in. When it finally emerged, the Vision was admirably succinct: "Together we deliver the brands the world demands." The only problem was that the Vision was no more inspiring than the corporate strategy was imaginative. To the connoisseurs of such prose, the Vision was much closer to a mission statement. All this effort and frustration around what should have been a natural and relatively straightforward task led right back to the perennial question no-one wanted to tackle: "Why does the group exist at all; what is the logic?"

Throughout 1997, the Accelerator program drew consistently high ratings, and individual after individual found it so inspiring or satisfying that they wrote personal notes to the consultants; some e-mailed their chief executive directly. This group-funded program had a simple structure: three days working through 360-degree feedback, Myers-Briggs, and the Five Values. Three-hundred-and-sixty-degree feedback was now an internally designed system. Because it was seeking subordinates' views, several thousand Inchcape people had direct contact with the process and helped open up communications — upward and laterally.

The Accelerator was fun, tightly structured, and highly predictable. It filled a hunger for certainty and uncomplicated learning of some basic management techniques, and undoubtedly gave hundreds of people fresh hope about the future. As one manager put it, "It was something to rally to: a sense of belonging." It was difficult to find anyone with negative comments about it. Ian Ross was fascinated: "Everyone loved the Accelerator. To go on the Accelerator, to see the enormous enthusiasm of the people — it took me back — it was like the first level of nursery school. I couldn't believe that people had been through that. In BAT, even before you started managing, you go through that. It indicates something about the lack of business process and the lack of sophistication."

"What this actually did was to intensify the feelings towards Inchcape and make people feel proud to belong to this group," said Kalpana Prathap about the view from the Middle Eastern team on culture change. As an Indian and a woman, Prathap was concrete evidence of the changes taking place in what had been one of the most "colonial" parts of the group. All her predecessors in the role of human resources directors had been British males. "This was the first time that London has really offered a whole host of support and leadership. Philip Cushing sponsored it. The reason that this is more successful — contrary to 'Yes, We Care,' which looked at everything from a distance — is that this has gone to the crux of the matter by getting to the individual and telling him why this matters. The individual says, 'I can see what Inchcape are trying to do for me and I want to progress and be a better person; I will learn and I will give it back to the employer.' There is more buy-in because there are very tangible benefits to the individual. 'Yes, We Care' was negative in effect because it created extreme cynicism in people. That did more damage, because no-one was listening, and top management didn't support it."

Top management support was also a concern of David Newbury, who headed Inchcape Motors, retail business. "I don't think the various programs have been as successful as we would like them to be, because there has not been sufficient buy-in at senior management level. Charles Mackay had 'Yes, We Care' in Hong Kong and attempted to spread it wider in the group. One of the previous general managers in Motors allegedly stopped that information being spread — he didn't want anything to do with it. Unless you get buy-in at that very senior level, and real ownership for cultural change, it won't happen." Newbury's approach was to adapt what the Inchcape group offered and fit it around his organizational needs, and those of the manufacturers they represented. "We have a program called 'Operational Excellence' which is definitely bearing fruit for us. That is very much culture-oriented: it integrated the Inchcape values. But I think that companies sometimes have these sorts of programs, like business process re-engineering, which are really about downsizing and taking cost out — instead of being a cultural generator of what we do, or a generator of efficiencies."

Peter McElwaine's background as a line manager had imbued in him a respect for budgets and controls and managing through numbers. His experience of the change project changed him. "One of the great successes of the Accelerator program and the change process has been that for the first time we have concentrated on our people and not bottom line figures. The message that has sent around the group is incredible. It's just a great shame that while the bottom line has improved, it hasn't reflected itself in the share price."

In Goodall's view, "In the first year, the change program was an enormous success, though it has lost some momentum. It was a very good initiative that we needed: it was commercially relevant and had a significant impact on morale."

For Cummins, the deal-maker, it was not just irrelevant but a distraction. At that time, his plans for merging the Marketing stream into a foreign group were blocked by Cushing, leading to his decision to resign. As Cummins put it: "… and money was being spent on crap like culture change."

"Marshall aid turns Inchcape's fortunes." This was the headline in the *Investor's Chronicle*. "Inchcape has been a classic destroyer of shareholder value. Now run by ex-British Airways boss Sir Colin Marshall and helped by currency movements, some of the balance may soon be redressed." It concluded, "Sir Colin and his team still have a lot to prove. But if they succeed, the upside on the shares will be huge. Buy them."

IN WITH THE NEW

In March the company announced that Paul Cheng, its only Asian director, would stand down at the AGM in May, and would leave his position as chairman of Inchcape Pacific. It also announced that a new finance director had been found, and not from within. Les Cullen would join in April and take over from Rod O'Donoghue from July 1. O'Donoghue would remain as an executive director until his retirement the following year. Cullen was coming from Goodman Fielder, where he had been chief financial officer for this large Australian food company. A Scots accountant with an MBA, Cullen had packed plenty of experience into his forty-five years, having worked for seven companies and seen plenty of restructuring. His route to England was via Southeast Asia and several of Inchcape's businesses.

THE EXTRA DIMENSION

"There isn't a model that I have seen at business school or in textbooks, which deals with the issue of principals. Business models are very good at dealing with customers and suppliers and adding value, dealing with finance and so on. The idea that you are absolutely dependent on the principal is something that most models don't incorporate — which is the complexity, and the weakness and strength, of Inchcape." Many Inchcape managers would recognize the truth of this comment made by one of their colleagues. The familiar territory of stakeholders —

shareholders, employees, customers, and suppliers — had an extra, special component that went way beyond the normal sense of supplier. This component shaped the thinking and the strategy of the whole group, and ultimately arrested the speed of its transition into a simple focused business.

In practice, relationships with principals take a variety of different forms, but the idea is simple: a manufacturer has a product to sell and the agent or distributor has some special access to a market that makes it attractive for the producer to channel that product through the distributor. From the last century until the present day, manufacturers, or principals, needed help to sell their products in unfamiliar, difficult, and developing markets. Sometimes, this was because they did not want to invest time and money in finding out about the new market, and then setting up salesforces or logistical operations to deliver their product to the end customers. Sometimes, local laws forced them to pass their products through the hands of a local agent. This latter practice was very common in the Middle East, for example. Companies like Gray Mackenzie, which were the foundation of modern Inchcape, would collect agencies almost like postage stamps. The local markets were unsophisticated and the "good chaps" from Scotland or England could turn their hand to selling anything from biscuits to beer, and manhole covers to fire extinguishers, with a little help from their Indian colleagues.

The more products their salesforces handled, the better the overhead would be spread. More products might call for a bigger "godown," or warehouse, and a few more trucks, but little else. Contracts with principals were often sketchy or non-existent and notice periods perilously short. However, agency law would protect them by granting exclusive rights within a particular territory. And inertia, on the part of the principals, would ensure that agencies would survive long after a relationship was producing any significant gain for either party. It was a cozy world, which could not last.

First, the markets would grow more sophisticated in their demands and call for greater specialization. Agency law would be tilted in favor of businesses that had a majority of local ownership. Principals started to wake up to the fact that more specialized partners could be found to move their products — or at least ones who were hungrier for the business and more nimble in their approach. Then the principals would covet the juicy margins being made by the distributor or agent, and want to take over the territory for themselves. The world of the intermediary was becoming ever more turbulent and insecure. The answer, in the

1970s and 1980s, was to ensure that the bucket was always being filled at the top, as fast as principals leaked out of the bottom.

Inchcape's Marketing stream inherited this domain. It was not all bad, by any means: under the old geographical organization, Inchcape's local subsidiaries had a sound reputation for understanding the intricacies of a market. They also stood out as ethically upright, which was an important consideration for principals who did not want their reputation or their brand sullied by corruption or sharp business practices. And, when it suited them, the local subsidiaries would play their trump card: they belonged to a major British multinational organization with powerful resources. This was a feature which a member of the finance team was quick to spot: "The group did not understand that one of the dangers of being in the third party distribution business is that principals want to deal with somebody who they know will have to deliver, and is capable of financing that delivery. Therefore, strong balance sheets, strong financial resources, and an international reputation to protect, made us an attractive target for people to enter into contracts with."

One of the anomalies of financial control in many organizations is that capital expenditure is closely monitored, but other avenues for spending money are not. In the Turnbull era, the limits on capital expenditure were tightly set at each level of the hierarchy. The general manager of a business unit might find himself having to work hard to justify spending a thousand or so dollars on a photocopier. To get round the problem, he or she might decide to rent it so that it was "lost" in the accounts as a revenue item. Sometimes this made sense, sometimes not, depending on the local tax regime. However, taking on a new principal was uncontrolled. It was normal for a business unit to enter into an agreement with a manufacturer without any clearance from the group. The first thing a new principal would suggest was a commitment to stocks. Being new to the product, the Inchcape manager would typically rely on the manufacturer's advice about appropriate levels. They were rarely conservative in their advice. This was a source of a ballooning growth in working capital, and the Marketing stream was the worst culprit in the group. It was also symptomatic of another source of tension in the relationship between the principal and the distributor. The principal's overriding aim, especially if they were Japanese, was to maximize market share. Maximizing the return on funds employed was the paramount aim of the distributor. Profit margins, stock levels, and promotional costs would be the ground over which these conflicting aims would be fought for, day in and day out.

In the Marketing stream, much thinking and talking was done around weeding out the small volume, time-consuming principals and concentrating on the ones with high sales and major brands. Nestlé, Heineken, Procter & Gamble, and Timberland were the sorts of companies the stream management wanted to be associated with. Down at the operating level, there was guerrilla resistance to losing any principal. There was always the excuse that a particular product or brand was yet to come good: sales forecasts were always "J" curves, starting two years out. There was also the concern that deliberately sacking a principal would cause other principals to lose confidence and "jump ship."

The planners and strategists had difficulty with one cluster of products. These were the so-called industrial lines: abrasives, tools, workshop equipment, and so on. For someone brought up in consumer marketing, they were an anathema. Products that lacked brand visibility, that were not backed by advertising campaigns, and which sold by word of mouth or through public tenders, were a grubby nuisance that did not fit the models. Products that had very local selling patterns and lacked any global or regional potential were of little interest. They brushed aside the fact that their margins were often far higher than the fast-moving consumer goods; they turned a blind eye to the durability of the relationship with these principals.

These were some of the problems at a micro level. At a macro level, the word went out that building relationships with fewer, bigger brands was the way forward. Inchcape would be a global player with global brand-holders. It was an ambition that encompassed scale, specialization, focus, and simplicity. All the mantras would commingle into one chant. The paradox was obvious: fewer, bigger relationships meant higher risks for the whole group when, and if, one relationship stumbled or fell. It was another twist on the familiar portfolio theory. There never was an easy answer.

"Inchcape's business was very much as an 'intermediary' and this is a fragile and precarious business with low-quality earnings," said David John. "You are having to carefully manage your partners, principals, and your people with the in-built, inherent clash of interests. You have, effectively, to earn a profit while holding the ring. Therefore, it calls for great skill in leading, motivating, training, and, indeed, retaining your management. Otherwise, they walk off with the principal! You have to demonstrate that you have a better understanding of your local market, local culture, and customer base than your principal, and you have to provide him with excellent distribution. I don't think this was recognized in the latter years, where the atmosphere was one of over-penalizing failure and under-recognizing success."

In the United Kingdom, the Toyota franchise was so successful that it became a critical component of the group's overall profits. In 1990, it had become clear that something had to be done to secure this distribution agreement for as long as possible. Toyota had announced its intention to build a European plant in England, which would start production in 1992. The agreement then hammered out by Turnbull and his colleagues was extraordinary by Inchcape standards, and certainly unusual by any other standards. The agreement was for eighteen years. Toyota Motor Corporation took a 4.9% stake in Inchcape itself and put up the cash for a half-stake in Toyota (GB). The cash injection was a very welcome £110 million. The catch was that Inchcape's controlling interest in TGB would progressively decline. By 1997 it would become a minority partner. It was a way of securing a diminishing share in what was projected to become an increasing stream of profits, as the U.K. production offered the prospect of greater volumes. The only negative factor was that greater volumes would mean moving from being a niche player to competing in the mainstream of the market, where margins would be significantly slimmer. But it had proved to be one way of addressing the problem of fragility, and provided Turnbull's successors with a very solid base from which to operate.

In the case of Marketing, many of the principals lacked the size of Inchcape and depended heavily on it. A few were much larger and more powerful, such as Nestlé and Heineken. Rarely was the relationship symmetrical. In the case of Motors, it was skewed heavily in favor of manufacturers like Toyota or Ford who had infinitely more resources and leverage. This set two more constraints. The first was that having more operations in more countries or with more retail outlets did not allow Inchcape to exert leverage as a major buyer. Reflecting on this, Stacey Ellis compared the situation to that enjoyed by the major British supermarket chains: "What competitive advantage did a corporation like ours bring to a retail outlet? We couldn't find one because the motor makers would not allow us to buy at a more competitivete rate because of our size. They didn't want us to become a Sainsburys or a Tesco." The second constraint was geographical: motor manufacturers like Toyota were reluctant to hand over too many of their markets to one distributor organization. They did not want all their eggs in one basket, and Inchcape already represented a significant part of their third party distribution.

If these were buffers holding back major growth, then the attitude at operating level was essentially pragmatic. There was a job to be done in extracting the maximum long-term value from the relationships the group already enjoyed, and this is what obsessed Trevor Taylor and his colleagues in the Toyota division. "There must be an excellent relationship and a reputation with one's principals that goes far beyond any legal agreements between the two companies. Thus any problems can be talked through to a sensible solution. Obviously, one must understand as far as possible what the principal is thinking. I take the view that once one has to resort to agreements, then relationships begin to deteriorate and that cannot be good.

"Nonetheless, having established a good relationship one should then plan always to exceed the principal's expectations in every aspect of the franchise business. Consequently, if you have a good reputation with your principal and you can outperform their expectations, then it is less likely that, other than maybe for strategic reasons, they would seek alternative representation."

Sir David Plastow was equally clear about this relationship: "It is a two-way thing: you build a partnership by superlative performance on your part, and in that context then you can begin to negotiate the sort of terms, the sort of cost base that makes sense to you." Talking about Trevor Taylor's consistent approach, he said: "He was a genuine model as to how to handle franchises. He worked like hell on relationships with the Japanese in a consummate manner. There was no hot and cold: he just constantly went along, made his point, never shouted and screamed."

There is a sense that the arguments about the fragility and sustainability of a distributor are overdone, especially when set in the broader context of commerce. All business is inherently risky, and the argument that the holder of the brands is somehow in greater control of their destiny needs challenging. For a manufacturer, the risk of a new product failing in the marketplace is high, and especially so with fast-moving products. The statistics are frightening, and only the stronger companies can sustain development under such conditions of attrition. They too have to fill a leaking bucket, and their investment in research and development, and in new product development, can be staggering. Pharmaceutical companies face risk over particularly long time scales, and in markets that are far less comfortable than they were under unrestrained public health spending. Markets can collapse overnight, and changes in technology can render products obsolete in short order. Nonetheless, Inchcape was bound to see a future where it was increasingly boxed in and unable to grow its traditional businesses rapidly.

16

Storm Clouds Gather

◆

AN ASIAN FOG

A butterfly flaps its wings in an Amazon rainforest. It sets off a chain of events that culminates in the destructive energy of a typhoon in the South China Sea. This was typical of the allegories used to convey one of the messages of chaos theory. In the middle of 1997, Southeast Asia suffered from a long spell of unusually dry and hot weather. Indonesia and Malaysia suffered huge forest fires that burned out of control for months. Ignorant or greedy farmers were blamed, but sometimes nature itself was the fire-raiser, in the shape of electrical storms. Whatever the cause, the effect was dramatic and widespread. Cities like Singapore and Kuala Lumpur were wrapped in an acrid haze that sometimes thickened to a fog. Ash fell on gardens and shiny new cars. People choked and their eyes watered. Ships collided and aircraft had to make diversions. In Kuching, schools and offices were closed. In September the World Health Organization warned of respiratory and heart ailments unless the smog cleared in the near future. There was even talk of seeding rain clouds with dry ice. Most people were simply waiting for the monsoon rains of November to arrive.

The effect on tourism was devastating, and this had a knock-on effect for other businesses. As business confidence sagged, cracks in the edifice of the financial structures of various countries began to appear. First Thailand, then the Philippines, Indonesia, Malaysia, and Korea began to reveal the extent of imprudent bank lending, and each saw a run on its currency. Singapore tried to stay aloof, but even its rock-solid economy was being dragged down by the woes of its neighbors. On July 2, Thailand had unpegged the baht from the US dollar, and the baht promptly fell 15%. This was the trigger for instability in all the currencies of the region. During August the currency turmoil spread to the stock markets. In early September, Hong Kong's market fell 15%, and they were not even directly affected by Southeast Asia. The common view from New York or London was that this was a little local difficulty and it would sort itself out in time. Those who looked narrowly at the patterns of world trade judged the impact on the world economy to be negligible.

Inchcape had delivered annual results for 1996 that showed a 12% increase in profits; most of the profit increase came from the Motors business, and especially from the Toyota franchises. *The Financial Times* quoted Cushing as hailing the profit improvement as "the beginning of a brighter future." He added, "The things we have done this year are creditable but it is our ambition to push this Group much further." The shares moved up against the market trend to finish 13p higher, at 268p. *The Times* was attracted by the effect that Coca-Cola Bottling would have on the margins, and noted that £80 million was being spent in Russia that year alone. Morale inside the company began to pick up, and people felt they were turning a corner even if they had doubts about the way ahead. The shares continued their recovery through the spring and summer.

BOARD CHANGES

Andrew Cummins lost the fight to take the Marketing stream off into a merger. Cushing had insisted on the internal restructuring route, despite the inherent difficulties, delays, and costs. This had been much more than a business issue for Cummins: it was a point of principle and he was not prepared to compromise. With the chairman and the chief executive in charge of strategy, and without a business to run in a way that he believed in, Cummins was a man without a role. At the AGM, it was announced that he would leave at the end of the year. The board would no longer have a strategy director.

Paul Cheng Ming-fun stepped down from the Main Board and his role as chairman of Inchcape Pacific. Cheng left with a sense of frustration: "For me, aside from the first part of my career in Inchcape, my strengths were not fully utilized. Obviously, as a British company your senior management is British, by and large. Deep down, local management in the field is not totally trusted by head office. Deep down we can tell, or at least feel the mistrust." He was replaced by Raymond Ch'ien Kuo-fung, who took over both roles as a non-executive. He had left his position of managing director of the Hong Kong-based Lam Soon consumer products group. On the surface, this looked like a straightforward and adroit replacement. However, *The South China Morning Post* pointed out that, "While Mr. Cheng was noted for his good contacts with Beijing and was a member of the Preparatory Committee, the Provisional Legislature and the Legislative Council, Mr. Ch'ien will be part of Mr. Tung's inner cabinet, running this territory after the handover." It was more of an indication that Inchcape was putting a greater emphasis on protecting its position in Hong Kong, rather than exploiting its position on the mainland. In the same article, Cushing defended the amount of time Raymond Ch'ien would spend on Inchcape: "The time he does spend with us will be important in assisting development of our business in China." Since Hong Kong would soon be part of China, this statement could not be faulted.

The fact was that Inchcape had 6000 people in Hong Kong and 1500 in the mainland, spread through twenty cities. The business streams had never been happy with Mackay's centralist approach to China, and did their best to avoid working through or with the regional head office run by Paul Cheng. They saw this as an unnecessary overhead and interference. They also questioned just how much business they could really build when they occupied the role of intermediary rather than manufacturer. One business that had been set up in the late 1980s was a logistics company in Shanghai, and that had prospered. Clearly, this was one form of business that could flourish. Reflecting on several years of building a corporate image and an infrastructure in China, Richard Tam said, "Our name was quite well known in the labor market, commercial, and government circles. All these point to the fact that we had done the right thing in setting up the infrastructure. We didn't have a very good business strategy for China, which should be long-term, not short-term. We tended to close down some of the businesses too soon. We closed down many of our offices in 1996/97 and that was a waste of funds and resources. We built it up in a period of three to four years and were pulling out too soon." Tam was exaggerating to make a point, because the Inchcape presence in China continued, albeit with a much lower profile. However, as for many other companies, the promise of China and its 1.2 billion consumers had turned into a chimera.

Two new executive appointments to the Main Board were announced. They would take effect from the start of 1998. Peter Johnson would represent Inchcape Motors International and Trevor Taylor Inchcape Toyota division. Motors mattered; none of the other business streams was represented directly on the board. The future direction of the group was crystallizing out.

Panic in the Markets

By May 9, 1997 Inchcape's share price had recovered to 307p. This was the peak, and despite a gradual softening there was a sense of confidence that recovery was now firmly established. Just when it seemed that a long run of bad luck and jinxes was coming to end, bad news struck again. The turmoil in the Asian markets hit those groups heavily exposed to Asia, like Cable & Wireless and Standard Chartered. Inchcape was no exception and fell 13.5p to 271.5p at the end of August. Two weeks later the interim results showed the underlying earnings of the group had increased by 15%. However, *The Independent* thought that "the results raise as many concerns as they answer." It worried about the spread of currency problems from Thailand and Malaysia to Inchcape's big markets in Hong Kong and Singapore. It drew attention to the £55 million costs of restructuring the Marketing stream and the fact that this was projected to increase earnings by only £9 million per annum.

The main concern of *The Independent*, though, was clear: "just why the group is investing huge sums of money into Russian Coca-Cola bottling plants." It noted that the total investment would soon be nearly £100 million, and yet the business was still in loss, to the extent of £7 million in the first half of 1997. *The Times* referred to the group's big ambitions for its Coca-Cola businesses, and suggested that "the group is otherwise making a good start to its recovery." In the press, Philip Cushing was at pains to point out that "only 5 per cent of Inchcape's assets are in Far East markets." Within the narrow definition of capital assets, this was true.

Russian Roulette

The decision to invest in Russia was a bold one. Roger Pudney of Ashridge Management College had observed the group for a number of years. He thought that, "Increasingly you were very entrepreneurial, and that is what makes the Coca-Cola business work. Very happy to take on tough markets, tough parts of the world, and build things from nothing. That is Inchcape at its best: get out and change the world!" The original decision to invest in Russia was one of the more difficult ones the group had faced. For David John, the Coca-Cola relationship was crucial to the future of the organization. In the longer term, he thought that the nature of the group's business as an old-fashioned intermediary was likely to be unsustainable. He had already demonstrated the way that contract manufacturing of items like shampoo and toothpaste offered a way of building a position behind tariff barriers, and of securing long-term relationships with consumer product brand holders. For him, this was also a practical route to tackle the market in China. Relatively "low-tech" manufacturing, in partnership with a powerful brand holder, offered a sustainable way forward. And, it would play to Inchcape's strength in handling developing markets. The particular attraction of Coca-Cola was the extraordinary strength of its global brand and a principal whose policy encouraged the building of a long-term relationship. The model had already worked well for Inchcape in Latin America and relations with Atlanta were excellent. "That was why I was very keen on the Bottling business. We had the financial clout so that we could exploit that business." The task was to convince Coca-Cola to make new territories available. After several other forays, eventually Russia came on the table, but David John thought that, "In Russia, we allowed ourselves to be pushed too far, too fast by the principal. We should have said, 'Let's get one operation right first.'"

Paul Cheng's memory of the Coca-Cola decision was that "I was a lone voice on the board. I kept asking the question why, and they said: 'Paul, you don't understand — you have to make a commitment to Atlanta.' They were mesmerized by the mystique of Coca-Cola, the power — you know, when you go to Atlanta and visit Coca-Cola's headquarters. My view is that we had a very good operation in Chile, where it is a manageable unit, and part of the reason for success. Because we wanted to create Coca-Cola into a stream, we started cultivating relationships with Atlanta. One must always put oneself in the other person's shoes to reflect on how they are thinking. The way I saw it was, 'Here is this group trying hard to cultivate our relationship: we might as well use them in some of the difficult situations.' They made us feel we had to prove ourselves.

"I kept asking, I said, 'Fine, I understand all that, but where is the main course? After you have proven yourself, where is the big market we are going to get to give us the type of returns we are looking for and recoup some of our investment — where is it?' China is gone, the United States is basically very well established, and it goes from generation to generation, so we got Russia. I said, 'Gee, Russia. Pepsi-Cola is not a bad company, but they have been struggling in Russia for ten years. What makes us think that we can do better?' So I said, 'Be very careful.' Again, they said, 'Paul, you don't understand. We are going to make sure they really understand we are committed to this business.' I said that I understood that, but when you make this scale of investment, there has to be at least an understanding that if you do well, say in two years, we will certainly give you serious consideration and give you some lucrative markets. Otherwise, it's all one way. I would never go into a commercial relationship when I can see very clearly that it is one-sided." Colin Armstrong was the man who had brought the Coca-Cola business into the group, and fought for its retention and subsequent reinvestment. Reacting to the suggestion that Inchcape had to "earn its spurs" in Russia, he said, "Well, they certainly fell for that one. Maybe there was some truth in it, but there is a question of whether they should have gone to the extent of building four plants."

The man given the task of setting up in Russia was Ian Ross. It was just the sort of challenge that suited this most international of managers, who had cut his teeth on markets like Vietnam. He was no expert in the arcane world of beverage bottling, but saw the main challenge as being a marketing one — and something that would respond to well-proven principles of marketing consumer products. Gradually, the Coca-Cola business was separated out from the Marketing stream and constructed as a stream in its own right.

At the top of the new Bottling stream would be the quiet and introverted Michael Cooper, who headed the Chilean business, and whose patron was Sergio Mardones. Despite his name and English family connections, he was thoroughly Chilean in education and culture. He was also the ultimate bottling technocrat and knew all the minutiae of the business. Tight running of operations was his specialty and Atlanta respected his expertise. Around him in Chile were his functional team, all bar one of whom was Chilean. Their working language was Spanish and, by good fortune, Ross was fluent in the language. In their head office in Santiago they were eight hours behind Russia in time and a long way physically; typically it would take thirty-six hours to fly from Santiago to one of the plants outside Moscow such as Ekaterinburg. Ross remained in London and reported initially to the group chief executive and then to Cooper. Cooper subsequently joined the group management board; Ross did not, though he saw himself as potential head of the stream.

One of the selling points to Coca-Cola had been the "strength in depth" of the management and the ability, through the business stream, to deploy resources into new operations. This was based on the solid track record and well-resourced teams in Chile. As ever, there was a gap between the promise and the reality. It was true that there were managers and technicians in Chile who could be released to help set up the Russian operations without damaging the Chilean business. But, in Russia, ideally one would need to acquire some knowledge of the language to be able to survive and operate effectively. It was also true that the next best language was English, because many of the younger Russians had learned English and had a huge motivation to polish it further. Even the most senior Chilean managers lacked total fluency in English; at the next level, the knowledge of English was distinctly poor. So there was an immediate practical barrier for a Chilean working in Russia, even if only for a short project.

The thought of moving to Russia, with its instability and harsh climate, was not an attractive prospect for someone who enjoyed a stable country, a delightful climate, and magnificent scenery. Little wonder, then, that few, if any, Chileans put their hands up for a transfer to the distant east. "We never delivered the systems out of Chile or the senior management to run it," said Ross. "We had to recruit the whole lot from outside; we had to get the systems from outside. That is just acting as a bank. Not surprisingly, the operational management — myself included — got way behind schedule because we were spending all of our time trying to recruit people. And once we had recruited people, we had to decide how to control these businesses — rather than actually building the business in the first place."

To some extent, the people who were recruited were self-selecting. They needed to know about bottling operations and they needed money or an adventure, or both; otherwise, why would they subject themselves to the vicissitudes of newly capitalist Russia? In came some "larger than life" characters with checkered histories, some leaving behind complicated domestic situations. Most had experience of developing countries, and some were old hands of Nigeria or the Philippines; they had a tolerance for chaos and ambiguity that would stand them in good stead. Most were British, leavened by an Americanized Russian, an Indian, an Irishman, and sundry other nationalities. Several were refugees from the great rival, Pepsi-Cola. One of their common characteristics was sturdy self-dependence, which did not bode well for teamwork.

These were the leaders; under them came the young Russian managers and technicians. Not only were they very young, but they were also highly educated and highly ambitious. The idea of the long grind up the promotion and experience ladder was outside their concept of management. If you were clever, studied hard, and worked hard, then why should you not rise from plant manager to regional director in three years — or less? That was the right of the new young capitalist Russian. And, if Inchcape was not prepared to promote them, then they would find another employer who would. This was no idle threat in a labor market hungry for English-speaking locals with a minimum of business experience. All the foreign companies operating in Russia found labor costs rising far faster than they ever expected or had budgeted for. In turn, construction costs rose dramatically. Delays in obtaining materials and plant were legion. Projects fell behind plan and extra money had to be spent to keep the wheels moving. Personal security called for special precautions that were not just inconvenient but also increasingly expensive. At the individual level, the sacrifices made by Russians and foreigners in the Bottling team were extraordinary. Working seven days a week for long periods and traveling within Russia put huge strains on their personal and family life. Ross knew this only too well, as he put up with a peripatetic existence between London and Moscow and the operations.

The head office was in Moscow and it had soon grown its own culture, which became despised by the plant managers. While there was some substance to the criticisms coming from operating management, it was very typical of the "head office versus operating unit" antipathy in any other organization. What exacerbated the issue was the rugged individuality of the members of the so-called top team in Russia. Valiant attempts were made to address this through team-building workshops; ultimately, resolution lay in the departure of a number of the original recruits and a more measured approach to finding or promoting their replacements.

As time went by, pressure increased to get plants open and to control costs. To Cooper, it was a nightmare: not only did it seem out of control, but the managers he relied upon were hard to handle. In Chile, there was respect for seniority and commands were followed. In Russia, the potpourri of nationalities had no instant respect for anyone. Cooper and his team would fly in from Chile, genuinely trying to help. By the time they had recovered from the journey and adjusted to the climate, they had to adjust to a world of chaos which irritatingly failed to fit within their own mental frameworks. Denial of this dissonance would lead them to assume negatives about their colleagues in Russia: they were unprofessional, inefficient, lazy, or badly led. The answer was to scrutinize the plans and the budgets in ever-greater detail in a ruthless search for the truth. There is no doubt that both sides had the best of intentions for the business, and each was working incredibly hard to get things right.

The reality of cross-cultural management was that a significant gap had opened up between them. One of the obvious remedies was to transfer some senior Chileans into Russia on a long-term basis, or at least move the head of the Bottling stream close to the country that needed help. With Chile running smoothly, Cooper could have moved to Moscow or London to devote more of his time to the "problem child." That he did not, was probably due to his personal preferences on lifestyle and the fact that another Coca-Cola operation was also claiming his attention. It was in Peru.

The original stake in the loss-making Embotelladora Latinoamerica in 1996 was 25%. Within a year, the Chileans had imposed order and control, and secured greater operating efficiencies in the plants and in distribution. Two senior Chilean managers were based in Lima on a full-time basis. The Peruvians spoke the same language and operated in the same time zone as the Chileans. Though there were considerable differences between the two national cultures, managing the Peruvian situation contained far more positive factors than did Russia. The interim results of 1997 confirmed the swift turnaround: Peru was in profit.

Not only was this a cause for celebration: there was a brand-new, state-of-the-art plant to open in Vina del Mar, a smart coastal resort and a major city. The new plant replaced an old and cramped one closer to the city, and offered greater output and more local employment. Before the celebrations, thirty of the senior managers of the Bottling stream came together for a conference. They were from Chile, Peru, and Russia. A significant number had never met before. One of the aims of the meeting was to break down barriers between Latin America and Russia, so that each could learn from the other. No outside speakers or consultants were involved. At the end of two days, serious business issues had been aired within the context of theories about national cultural differences.

Everyone knew there were differences between Russia and Latin America, but the real surprise was the gap between Peru and Chile. Feelings ran high when it was suggested that the Chileans were perpetrators of the "seagull syndrome": flying in from a great height and then flying out again, leaving the mess behind. Emotions cooled but the point went home, and the Chileans admitted that they could have been arrogant or insensitive in their approach. At the social level, and intellectually, barriers were just starting to break down. Another day would have cemented their progress, probably in terms of cross-cultural project teams to tackle some of the more pressing issues. Unfortunately, that third day was not available and the Bottling stream was destined never to meet again.

The day was given over to a grand opening of the plant by the President of Chile and a swathe of the Chilean establishment, including notables from the military and the church. Senior executives from Coca-Cola spoke in resonant terms about the Latin American market and the favorable business climate that existed in Chile. In a surreal tableau, a giant Coke bottle, some ten meters high, rumbled along a track onto the stage. Its giant cap blew off and water poured out in a brown torrent and in an unexpected direction, nearly dousing the distinguished guests. Apart from this incident, everything ran like clockwork. Over 400 guests were entertained in a giant marquee to a banquet and lively, modern entertainment. Among the guests was a party of analysts who had been taken on a tour of the group's Latin American businesses; they were making up their own minds about the "new Inchcape." The day was brilliantly organized: Cushing, Cooper, and Mardones could be justly proud of the achievement. Shortly after, came the announcement that the company had invested a further £41 million in Peru, giving it a majority interest in a business that controlled 90% of the country's sales of Coca-Cola.

"We did take the Russian opportunity, and history will probably say it was a mistake." Cushing reflected on the mistake: "In itself, it is clearly because of the financial results, but we would not have got Peru without having Russia first. Peru is, on its own, worth significantly more than Russia. I think Michael Cooper would agree with me that the Peruvian opportunity only opened up once we had shown the size of our ambition and taken on Russia. I think we undermanaged it, under-resourced it, underestimated what it would take to get it right — and we didn't have much luck either. We certainly didn't have much support from Coca-Cola during that period.

"On the other hand, spinning off Coca-Cola generally has been a tremendous success. To think that Chile plus Peru will leave this group with a value not far short of Motors. When I started my involvement it generated £5 or £6 million, so things change and move on ... I think the Coke thing from 1983 to 1998, as an overall view, would be regarded as a tremendous success. Sergio's doggedness in the 1980s in the face of, at best apathy in London, and at worst 'when can we get rid of it?' is a lot to do with that. I am pleased that I have been part of it, but there was nearly nothing to be part of. I think we all make mistakes and in the eighties the business wasn't viewed through bottlers' eyes — it was seen as a factory that makes soft drinks. The real opportunity wasn't seen, which was unfortunate. I am very pleased to have been involved with Coca-Cola, who, despite their frustrating bureaucratic ways, are a fantastically professional company."

The problems in Russia had not gone away, but external events were set to override any local operating issues. "Big names calm in the face of HK's storm." This was the headline in London's *Evening Standard*. The Southeast Asian storm had finally arrived in Hong Kong and the stock market was plunging downward at an alarming rate. Companies exposed to the region were taking a pounding in the London stock market: Standard Chartered Bank's shares had lost a third of their value in three months. Inchcape lost 32p that day, closing at 250p. Five days later the shares stood at 204p and the newspapers started talking about a global market crash.

SINGAPORE FLING

Months before, when the share price was recovering and prospects looked so positive, plans were made for another conference for the group's senior managers. It was to be in mid-November. The idea was to reinforce the culture change and make sure that the leaders of the business really were acting in the spirit of "One Company, One Team" and "walking the talk." The design was innovative and in complete contrast to any previous meeting. The idea was to demonstrate the new Inchcape and use shock to make a point. When the delegates arrived in the Singapore hotel, there was no agenda: just a sports shirt and instructions to arrive the next morning in the conference room wearing the shirt.

Next morning, the conference room was in semi-darkness and delegates were shown to their seats in what was effectively a "theatre in the round." They found they were in four blocks according to the color of their shirt; there was no hierarchy and no top table. The room lights went out and on the stage was a beautiful Asian gymnast going through her warm-up routine. This was the Olympic Games. For the next half-hour a team of professional actors brought to life the politics of the International Olympic Committee, as they sought to balance the demands of the various nations competing in the Games. The allegory was clear: the Inchcape group was the IOC. At the end of the scene, a TV-style interviewer invited the delegates to act as consultants to the actors about how they should play the next scene and how they should handle the issues that had emerged. This was not just theatre, but interactive theatre. The delegates found that they had another way of interacting: each had a TV-like controller that would register their vote about any issue, anonymously, and the votes would be displayed graphically on the screen.

The impact of the first morning was undoubtedly powerful and there was an air of excitement and energy among the delegates. In the afternoon, the debate began to center on the vision for the group. What really is the strategy? What is the long-term view? What is the added value of belonging to the group? More of the questions were directed at Philip Cushing. His responses were pragmatic but flat. He described the need to work hard to strengthen all the existing businesses, before moving on to any new opportunities. If suitable new opportunities emerged, then they would get serious consideration. The true picture was coming through: there was no vision and without a vision what was the purpose? All the energy of the morning was draining away. The adrenalin rush was replaced by weariness.

The following day, there were earnest attempts to raise spirits and work through new debates, but the energy and commitment had gone and were replaced by cynicism, and by nervousness about the markets. There was also a sense among the delegates that the board had made their minds up about the future of the company, but were not willing or able to reveal what it was. The closing dinner was held in the grounds of Singapore's Night Zoo. Whatever concerns people might have had, they put them aside. After a buffet and a few drinks, a live band appeared and got the dancing underway. Then the band found they had three new members: Rod O'Donoghue, who had just given a retirement speech, took up the bass guitar; Simon Morse, the head of Shipping, took over the drums; and John Stevens from Guam took over the lead guitar. They rocked and rolled for half an hour, to the amazement of the band and quite a few delegates. Inchcape may not have had a vision, but it knew how to party.

CHAOS THEORY BECOMES REALITY

The share price continued to fall. When the board met just before Christmas it was down below 160p. By the end of January it was at 138p and, by most reckoning, significantly less than the break-up value of the group. The Asian economic crisis had come home to roost.

CHAPTER

17

From Fizz to Focus

◆

---

*"They caught us at Christmas when were flat on our backs,
partly because of the share price." John Whiteman was
referring to the advice the board had been receiving from
Barings, the merchant bankers. "Also, I perceive the Singapore
conference in November being quite an ingredient. I think
Philip went away from that conference really frustrated that he
couldn't express a strategy that he and the audience could
believe in. The strategy of focusing the group on Motors and
Bottling and finding a way out of Marketing: he couldn't say
that. There was such a sense of knowing you had a strategy
but couldn't openly state it. This and other ingredients get you
to a point where people say, 'To hell with this, let's just bust
the group up.' I had a feeling that one day we would split."*

THE ANCHOR BOTTLER DREAM

f the Singapore conference had been a source of extreme
frustration for Cushing, then the future of the Coca-Cola
business was a source of fundamental concern. It would become
the trigger for a final re-think of the shape of the group. Establishing five
businesses in the Russian Federation had proved much harder than
anyone expected, and the news from Russia was rarely good. Keeping
overheads under control was one major preoccupation. Another
preoccupation was marketing. Not only was the Russian distribution
system relatively primitive, but it had aggravating "leakages." Product
arrived from other franchises and cannibalized Inchcape's sales. And
Coca-Cola's drive for market share cut across Inchcape's desire to raise
prices to cover costs.

Despite the problems in Russia, the relative security and high returns of Coca-Cola Bottling had come to look increasingly attractive, especially when compared with the far greater challenges posed by the Marketing stream. The experiences in Chile, and subsequently in Peru, had been so positive that Russia was regarded simply as a tough stepping-stone to more lucrative Coca-Cola markets. It had the potential to reshape the whole group. Getting Russia right was just a matter of time and hard work.

As Colin Armstrong had said back in the 1970s, "There are two big businesses that always survive whatever happens in the country; one is the brewery, and the other is the soft drinks bottler." Armstrong omitted to mention the brewery owned by Inchcape in Tehran, and sequestered by the Iranian government, following the Islamic revolution; but he was undoubtedly right about the soft drinks business. Apart from its survival characteristics, the other attractions of Coca-Cola bottling are typically high returns on assets, the probability of a quick payback, and healthy net present value calculations for capital expenditures.

The Coca-Cola business in Chile had demonstrated the potential, and the return on investment was more than satisfactory. Adding more countries was a reasonable objective, but much of the Coca-Cola world was already spoken for, and one had to wait patiently for opportunities to arise. Changes of ownership, or failure to perform, were reasons for franchises to become available, but there was always competition to secure these franchises. Philip Cushing and others could see beyond the addition of the odd country to a large and sustainable business that could be run as a major business stream. They first had to convince Coca-Cola that they were serious players, and Russia was part of the apprenticeship; Peru did not count. There was another aspect to this global ambition: it went under the name of "anchor bottler status."

"There was the very strong belief that becoming an 'anchor bottler' was actually the thing that could help transform the quality of the group's earnings." A relative newcomer to the board had soon noted the latest mantra. "Hence the desire to get Russia sorted and to have unified management for the Bottling stream."

The concept of "anchor bottler" first emerged in 1981. Roberto Goizueta, the relatively new chairman of Coca-Cola, authorized a 30% stake in the San Miguel brewery in the Philippines. The idea was to perform a turnaround on a bottler, using the minority stake as a way of influencing the management of that bottler. In early 1981, Pepsi was outselling Coca-Cola by a two-to-one margin: by mid-1983, Coke had reversed the sales statistics. This proved the concept. It set Goizueta on track to build Coke's whole international operation around taking minority positions in bottlers that were, typically, underperforming in markets of high potential. Coke would work with local management to improve production and marketing, while constraining its own investment to the absolute minimum. This was economic value added theory working out as a reality. As the approach was refined, Goizueta would only sanction investments in anchor bottlers if they beat a 20% return on Coca-Cola's capital.

By 1989, Goizueta was ready for a big investment: $500 million in Amatil of Australia. This was followed quickly by another big one: Coca-Cola Swire Beverages Ltd. was a joint venture set up to cover the Hong Kong, China, and Taiwan markets. By placing Coke executives on their boards, he was able to drive through change and lift the companies to the level of Coca-Cola's global standards. Goizueta adapted and refined the anchor bottler approach in the light of experience, and kept it from the glare of publicity. In the early 1990s, he began to articulate the anchor bottler strategy more openly. He went even further and suggested that the days of the conglomerate were over and that major companies should follow the Coke example. He was arguing that companies should operate from a core business, making financial investments in companies in related businesses that would allow them to exert management influence.

In 1996 the concept was fully mature. By having a stake in the bottlers, it could ensure that the marketing programs generated in Atlanta were followed closely. The integrity of one of the world's most powerful consumer brands could be preserved and enhanced. In each market, Coca-Cola would benefit from the market and political "savvy" of its local partners. It would also benefit by selling more of its syrup and by the return on its equity investments. And because the local partners would multiply Coke's own investment, this meant their businesses were better capitalized than Pepsi's in the rush to grab market share in the developing countries. Coke was winning the cola war and the anchor bottlers were prospering mightily. This was the exclusive club Inchcape had wanted so much to join.

ALL CHANGE IN ATLANTA

Cushing and Marshall went to Atlanta at the end of January 1998, against a backdrop of continuing problems in Russia. They were on their annual round of pressing for more territories and, more importantly, promoting the idea of Inchcape as an anchor bottler. The originator of the anchor bottler concept, Roberto Goizueta, had died at the end of October 1997, and a new leader had already assessed his priorities. That leader was Doug Ivester, the very man who had set up the first anchor bottler in the Philippines in 1981.

It became clear that the new leadership did not welcome the idea of trans-continental anchor bottlers, which ruled out Inchcape's attempt to span South America and Russia within one business stream. Furthermore, the new view was that the South American continent already had sufficient anchor bottlers. When Cushing returned to London, it was clear that the dream was over.

CIRCUMSTANCES DRIVE STRATEGY

As Cushing reflected, the journey that had started thirteen years before was now reaching a major turning point: "When did all this start? In some ways, it started in 1984; in other ways, it started with the 'blue bag.' In another sense, we really started looking at it seriously only in 1997, a year after I took over as chief executive. The first year was absolutely flat out on recapturing the momentum of the group and pointing it in the right direction to set off again. There was no time for any strategic work; it was all about making people believe again, that we had a future.

"Then, about January–February 1997, we started doing serious strategic work. I think the issue there very much revolved around Coke. The Marketing business was continuing to go up and down; Shipping up and down; Inchcape NRG had started well; the Motors business was powering away. What could we make out of Bottling? Could we get to this treasured anchor bottler status or not? A lot of the analysis and strategic planning at that time was geared around this issue. Eventually, at the beginning of 1998, we had been working on these plans, we had the Asia collapse, which had shown the continued vulnerability of the group to whatever wind was blowing. To my view, what has happened in Asia is not a fundamental change; it is one of those things that happen. I remember two years ago, shareholders were saying, 'Why don't you get out of Motors in Europe, because it is losing money, and has for the past few years?' I said, 'You don't make decisions that way — we're here for the long term.' I regard the Asian collapse as temporarily exaggerating a condition that already existed.

"Then the Coca-Cola future became clearer, although, to this day, Coca-Cola would be happy for us to carry on as a bottler. But, we needed to have enough comfort to build a twin-legged substantial group, and we needed our business with Coke to be five times the size that it was, and we weren't going to get there. That was probably the final element in it that said, 'OK, if that's true, then we need to look at a different version of the future, which immediately sets up Motors as the solo business of the group. And the optimum solution is to sell the parts.'"

As Lord Marshall put it, "The decision was, in effect, to break up the company, but it was a tough decision to take. We looked at all sorts of alternatives, and we had many iterations of this issue before coming to a final conclusion, and making the announcement. Obviously, we had a substantial amount of external advice from the banking sector, from our brokers, and from our lawyers as to how to go about the restructuring of the company yet again."

THE RUMOR MILL GETS IT WRONG

During February 1998 the staff in the head office at Cavendish Square noticed a number of small and highly confidential meetings, and remarked on the fact that the company secretary and human resources director had frequent discussions. The rumor mill ground on, and most were betting that the head office staff was about to face another ritual culling. The announcement of March 2 stunned employees around the world.

Preliminary results for 1997 showed headline profits before tax of £184.1 million: a 12% increase, following a similar increase in the previous year. The press release was straightforward:

"Inchcape plc has announced that it intends to focus entirely on its international Motors operations, which include import and distribution, retail and related financial services activities. Inchcape is the world's largest independent importer and distributor of motor vehicles. This is the next phase of the Group's strategy, set out in 1996, to enhance shareholder value by focusing on fewer, larger, businesses, and which has been reflected in the improved financial performance announced today."

The press release continued:

- "Significant value is expected to be created for shareholders by the demerger and listing of the very successful South American Bottling business, with ADRs in New York.

- Additional shareholder value is expected to be released by the demerger and listing of Marketing Services Asia Pacific and the Middle East as a single entity on an Asian Stock Exchange.

- Bottling in Russia and Shipping Services will be divested.

- The total process is expected to be completed by mid-1999."

The chairman, chief executive, and group finance director would lead the restructuring process, and when it was completed Philip Cushing and Les Cullen would leave Inchcape. They and some of their corporate colleagues would fall on their swords. Shareholder value was the stark new mantra.

The new, purely Motors, Inchcape plc would be run by Peter Johnson as chief executive, with Sir Colin Marshall as chairman, and Trevor Taylor as his deputy. The goal of simplicity and focus was finally in sight. All those photographs of chief executives and chairmen posed in front of cars had proved prescient, after all. Having once reputedly said, "I hope they don't turn my business into a garage," Kenneth Inchcape was probably turning in his grave.

Conclusion

◆

*"I like buying companies that can be run by monkeys —
because one day they will be."* (U.S. fund manager)

I Managers ...

In a book of this nature, one is obliged to pick out the peaks, and
then apparently ignore the richness of life spread out in the fertile
valleys below. Major events and big issues claim our attention, and
time and opportunity have restricted our interviews to a relatively tiny
cross-section of the players. Over the past decade, the authors have had
conversations with hundreds of employees, and many "outsiders" who
have transacted in some way with Inchcape and, as a result, we are acutely
aware that the existence of a group such as Inchcape meant much more
than simply maximizing shareholder value. Based on our observations of
Inchcape, the answer to the question, "Why do companies exist?" can
never be reduced to an economic equation.

Seductive indeed is the idea of the company as a "black box"
mechanism for processing inputs and producing outputs in an orderly
and predictable way. The more technologically inclined would probably
feel at home with the analogy of computer programs with lines of code
being worked methodically and minutely through a central processing
unit. The reality that an organization might be a shifting and swirling
coalition of interests, subject to a variety of external influences, and
endless permutations of choice, is less comfortable. Less comfortable still,
is the sneaking suspicion that the whole thing is only partly under any
form of control or guidance: how it will react to an influence or an event
is often unpredictable. What goes under the name of strategy is
sometimes little more than the post-event rationalization or "patterning"
emerging out of the chaos. Is a large organization more of a Catherine
wheel than a cruise missile?

The further one travels down this route, the more one questions the
real effect of those people who are supposed to know how complex

businesses operate. How much can we trust the advice of the consultant? How useful is the latest, immaculately argued proposition from the business school? How much does the investment analyst really understand? How effective or influential is the board of directors of the company? How far does the leader of the organization actually shape its destiny? What do managers really manage, and whom should they believe in? Why do people become passionate about belonging to an organization, when logic might tell them "to jump ship"?

We invite the reader to take the plunge with us as we review each of the main constituents in this forty-year history. We ask you to prepare for paradox, and to practice the old skill of juggling with several ideas simultaneously. Above all, we ask you to use your judgment: one thing that helps to distinguish us from machines and monkeys.

THE LEADERS

The Third Earl, Kenneth Inchcape was an early example of what would subsequently be termed the "entrepreneurial" approach to business. Having transformed the diverse collection of companies he inherited into the Inchcape group, he then expanded it through acquisition into a successful conglomerate that spanned most of the world.

The stock market applauded his creation, since they liked the idea of a company that didn't have all its eggs in one basket. To manage this far-flung empire he built face-to-face relationships with his people, and trusting them was his way of running what had become a complex business. As he told a then young manager in the Middle East in the 1950s, "Never forget, Macaskill, you cannot have profits without people." His fame spread, and he gradually became involved in other business interests and the affairs of his country. Then, occasional spectacular business failures began to undermine the stock market's confidence. Eventually, he came to realize that he needed help and could no longer run the company single-handedly. Very reluctantly, but with great dignity, he handed over the controls to the new breed of professionals. In nearly a quarter of a century as leader, he had seen profits grow eighty-fold and the market capitalization rise to more than £250 million.

Sir David Orr had experience of running businesses around the world until his retirement. Skilled with words and an expert committee man, he was also good at spotting opportunities and had a strong competitive streak. He saw the need to bring in more specialization or focus. As he set about looking for a new, younger head of the business, he also realized that the rest of the center's team were approaching retirement age and needed "fresh blood." With any vision of a part-time job fast disappearing, he subtly upped the pace of work at head office by setting an example of parsimonious and speedy meals. Not for him the two-hour formal lunch served by butlers and accompanied by fine wines. Times had changed.

Then came news of huge losses in Thailand, owing to dubious financing arrangements. The stock market was not amused, and marked the shares right down. This made it all the harder to attract a new leader, but, eventually, he found George Turnbull: older than he had originally envisaged but a man with top-level experience around the world, and a reputation for cutting a swathe through problems.

David Orr stayed on to allow his successor to visit all the operations before deciding on a course of action. Noted for his urbane and witty approach, he will be remembered as the "bridge" between the old and the new.

George Turnbull's reputation preceded him. Contemporaries knew him as a tough, competitive operator and the stock market had high expectations of him. Turnbull knew that he had to make friends with the shareholders if he was to get the support he would need to lay the foundations for growth. His other goal was to build a good team around him: professionals who believed in the "work hard, play hard" ethic. Together, they could introduce a new style that would drive out the old culture. He sent out a clear message to all managers: they could no longer operate their companies as fiefdoms. They were either part of the team or they were out. They would perform, and there would be strict financial controls. Their job out in the field was to produce regular profits, year on year. Entrepreneurialism was a dirty word.

He and his team traveled exhaustively round the group, ensuring the message was understood. There was a sell-off of loss-making or ill-fitting operations. As a leader he was visible and won respect from all levels of the staff, in every country. He understood the operational side and always appeared ready to roll his sleeves up and get stuck in. As each year went by, the results improved steadily and no opportunity was lost in telling the stock market or the media.

However, the media and the market still had difficulty understanding the businesses, so it was decided to group the business into categories to reduce the apparent complexity. The external audiences were satisfied for the time being, though the complexity — some would say muddle — remained. The real problem was that nobody really knew which businesses to pick as winners, and that included the highly paid consultants. Eventually, five "stars" and five "cash cows" were picked and justified; history tells us that the cows became stars and vice versa. For the loyal head office team, all the hard work was beginning to pay off. They realized (though few would admit it) that running a business like this was immense fun and intellectually stimulating.

By now, the steady improvement in performance and a lack of surprises had restored Inchcape's once tarnished reputation. The stock market was ready to accept the company into its top ranks and into the glare of the spotlights. Inchcape was a rising star, and George Turnbull was rewarded with a knighthood.

Sir George will be remembered for the transformation of the group's financial fortunes, as a man who generated great respect and whom a wide cross-section of people were ready to follow — perhaps the only definition of a "true" leader. At least as important was his ability to build a strong team around him and to neutralize politics. In six years, he achieved a great deal.

His protégé was also a rising star. He had passed out top of a leading business school, and worked with a top-flight consultancy. He then applied his sharp brain and high energy to the hothouse atmosphere of Hong Kong and the Pacific region where, acting decisively, he had succeeded in dramatically improving results. Sir George's premature retirement brought Mackay to the leadership role a year earlier than he expected, and without the wisdom and counsel of his patron. Inchcape was now a well-heeled, high-profile organization that stood out in an otherwise depressed marketplace. Turnbull had prepared the ground: now the market wanted growth. The pressure was on.

Under Mackay, acquisition became the order of the day. Financial controls were relaxed to encourage a climate of faster growth. The managers happily bought up companies in all parts of the globe, and as the group once more expanded, there was scarcely time to graft the new onto the old rootstock. Unfortunately, this worked against the idea of focus, which had led to the setting up of business streams. As new regional offices were set up under their noses, the central team saw their power dwindle and costs climbed yet again. Teamwork at the top began to crumble and politics filled the vacuum. Then came a problem with the Japanese currency, which went on far longer and became far worse than anyone had predicted. Moreover, the European markets were suffering too. Profits were sliding and the financial health of the business was under threat.

Hoping that it would all turn around quickly, Mackay became less expansive in what he told the stock market, and they became concerned about the leadership of the group. It was probably an intensely lonely and pressured position to be in. If, as was said, he became more analytical and less decisive as the stresses and strains built up, then it would be little wonder.

Mackay became the scapegoat for the group's ills and eventually a new operating head was appointed under him; subsequently, he resigned and left the business. In less than five years he had presided over a record high share price, capitalizing the business at £3 billion, and seen one of its most precipitous falls. He will be remembered for his enormous ambition for the group and a powerful intellect, as well as his achievements in Hong Kong. As a leader, he seemed to find it harder to generate the warmth of relationships that would attract a broad range of followers, or surround him with a supportive team.

His successor, Philip Cushing, was also noted for his intellectual prowess. He had had an excellent education and clear confidence in his own ability. In character, he was more in the George Turnbull mold of "work hard, play hard" and came across as an individual with his feet securely planted on the ground. Still in his mid-forties, he was strikingly younger than his predecessors.

One of his important mental models was simplicity and focus. It was curious, then, that his first actions were to try to restore a sense of pride and belonging to the group. That is not to deny the need: morale was shattered and there was a great urgency about putting the whole management team back on its feet. The expectations out in the field were of a period of slash and burn, of rationalization and sell-offs. Yet, getting everyone to rally behind a new slogan like "One Company, One Team" seemed like heart ruling head. To talk of building a new corporate culture across the disparate business streams was fascinating, but totally unexpected. The intellectual justification for holding the group together was still an unresolved issue; the fashion in the marketplace had long since abandoned conglomerates as anachronistic. The market was not interested in the idea of managers spreading their risk. The group should specialize and take any risks on the nose. If it succeeded, then it could expect more funds; if it failed, who cared?

Cushing rushed around the group with great energy, used video-recorded mass meetings to help spread the message, reinforcing it with training provided by consultants. His enthusiasm was infectious and spirits rose. The old, complex business lived on and the center began to feel relevant and even loved again. Performance picked up and for two consecutive years profits recovered by more than 12%. Only one thing was missing: a vision of where everything was heading. Cushing did not appear to have one, or was not ready to talk about it; nor did the rest of the senior team. Was it just a question of waiting for an opportunity to turn up?

What actually turned up was a severe economic crisis in Asia and the investors fled, leaving the share price down at a level not seen since the early days of Turnbull's leadership. Then another blow struck: a Russian economic crisis. Leadership became increasingly remote and then an announcement followed. Complexity was dead. The other businesses would be sold off, leaving a one-product business, and the current leader would resign when the auctions were completed. Assuming completion by mid-1999, his time in charge would be just three years.

THE EXPERIENCE OF LEADERSHIP

The five leaders of Inchcape the public company were very different in their personalities, skills, and backgrounds, the only common thread perhaps that of self-confidence. Their effectiveness was clearly conditioned by circumstances and timing. For more than three decades, leadership was vested in a sole individual. The split role of chair and chief executive of the last seven years coincided with far closer public scrutiny of the group's affairs, whereas the earlier leaders were largely masters of their own destiny and could operate more easily. As Sir David Orr said of Kenneth Inchcape: "He was a very effective chap. He did not consult or delegate but was a very good operator. He had very high ethical standards, wanted people to behave properly and have a conscience. It was very much a one-man company, as he didn't delegate. He did it all himself. If he said he would do a thing, he would do it. He was ruthless in a lot of ways but very straight. A very good man." Another senior director put it more pithily: "He was a decision-maker: he made decisions and followed them through ... He was the boss." Later leaders have had both greater expectations placed on them and more constraints on their freedom to act.

Business literature abounds with homilies about leadership and anodyne biographies of former chief executives. The two most recent chief executives of Inchcape give us a glimpse of what it actually feels like to be in a leadership position. Charles Mackay faced a looming problem in 1992 when he took over: what to do with Marketing? Did it make sense as a business stream? What should he do with all the under-performing companies? He described some of the dilemmas: "With the benefit of hindsight, we should have put the knife in but earlier, in many cases we were not sure how much the under-performance was due to poor management, and how much was more fundamental. I suppose we were nervous about cutting sizeable pieces of Inchcape out, and demoralizing our principals and partners. Also, in places like Japan, there was a huge cost of getting out. It seemed cheaper to continue with relatively under-performing businesses than take massive write-offs and have all sorts of social problems. And, of course, Inchcape as a whole was doing relatively well. So, there were rational reasons for soldiering on and trying to make something of the under-performing businesses, and in some cases succeeded in doing so. However, looking back five years later, you can say we would have been better off taking the pain much sooner."

His successor, Philip Cushing, had also concluded that swift action was desirable in difficult situations. "In no circumstances that I can think of, did any sort of delay help. Whether it was over people and their adequacy for the job at hand; whether it was to wait for a business to prove itself; whether it was to accept or approve an offer. I am not aware of any circumstances where it was better for waiting." He was frank about his experience at the top: "I do not have a problem with the generality of being chief executive of a public company. But the first six to nine months were the toughest time I have ever had in my career."

Asked about the most crucial attributes for the job, he replied: "I think of it in two — the personal characteristic stuff, and then the specific skill set. The personal characteristic stuff: it is enormous emotional reserves to try to inspire people, not just by an academic approach, but by leadership. I found that more than ever in my life, I never stopped thinking about things. In any other job, to a greater or lesser extent, apart from very specific periods or projects, I could shut the door and go home. When you are number one, you don't shut the door and go home: it is there all the time.

"There is the need for emotional reserves, so that you can help people whenever they need it, and remember that when you see them you can impact them either positively or negatively by what you say. That is not easy sometimes. You have to have the personal capacity to say constantly to yourself, 'What is the worst that can happen here? Will life come to an end as a result?', as a way of protecting yourself from being dragged into the morass and driving yourself mad — which you can do. I think you have to be physically strong. Those are personal attributes: leadership rather than management.

"Multi-tasking: I find that more than in any other job I have ever done, you need the ability to have your brain running on twenty things, more or less at the same time, so that you can keep them all moving. And, not to be too focused on any one problem: because you are coach, jockey, and all those things, at once. There are more obvious things, like straightforward brainpower: to absorb a large amount of information and draw on it when you need. But it is not magic; a lot of it is just hard work."

Lord Marshall, who has seen his share of chief executive performances, summed up the problem: "Lots of people can be successful or appear to be successful when something is really growing and they are in an expanding marketplace. The real, tough issues and when managers are proven is when they have to face the alternative and go in the other direction: that is really hard going. And it is tough on the morale of the organization."

COLLECTIVE LEADERSHIP

Discussion of company leaders necessarily involves reference to their boards. For the first thirty-three years of Inchcape's history as a public company, the distribution of power between the leader of the group and the board was unequal. Put more aggressively: it was simply "no contest"; the destiny of the company was literally in the hands of one person. The board seemed to have little or no collective influence over crucial succession decisions.

So, although Lord Inchcape was the head of a public company, by all accounts, he treated it as his fiefdom. By virtue of his personality, history, and the less demanding shareholder environment, he was able to run the group as if it were still a private company. What we have been able to capture of the flavor of board meetings suggests a field marshal being briefed by his able staffers. The non-executives added the benefit of their wisdom or connections. The dialogue was crisp and cryptic. Instructions would flow from Lord Inchcape with a minimum of debate. As Lord Tanlaw described, "He knew precisely what he wanted, and where the group was to go. He would go through an agenda, he had read all the papers and done all the preparation and was able to run a board of directors with extreme efficiency ... Decisions were made and implemented with speed."

When Sir David Orr took over as the interim head, he brought with him a consultative style and contemporary notions of strategy and control. Sir George Turnbull strongly reinforced the controls and paid great attention to satisfying the shareholders' needs for steady results and adequate information. There is no doubt that he delegated responsibility fully and clearly, but there is ample evidence that, as chairman and chief executive, he was fully in control of the board. He consulted and then made the decisions. Sometimes he made the decisions and then presented the board with a *fait accompli*. As one director recalled: "George Turnbull called me in one day and said, 'We have decided to sell that business.' I was the director in charge and I said, 'Excuse me, I don't recall this being discussed at the board: this is a major decision.' I had to force the proper exercise and discussion at the board." Because the majority of decisions were eminently sound and sensible, there was little or no criticism of his methods. People still talk with nostalgia about the sheer speed of decision-making and the sense of drive and momentum. He had a good team, but there was no doubt about who was captain. In this, pointed out Lord Tanlaw, he resembled Kenneth Inchcape: "George was also a decision-maker ... Under him, the board was basically a collective decision-making body but again, you had great difficulty disagreeing with George."

Toward the end of his term, Turnbull bowed to outside pressures and recognized the call for the roles of chair and chief executive to be split. He constructed his succession plan on just one individual — and the premise that he would control that individual from his position as chairman. It is conceivable that he really saw himself continuing to control the group for several years, while his "apprentice" learned his master's trade. All this happened just before the corporate governance movement swung into effect. In theory, no board would now allow such a succession plan to be enacted.

In practice, even the mightiest companies are still having problems with succession. The problems are not with understanding the principles of good succession planning, nor with the strictures of corporate governance. The fault line appears to lie with the lack of collective will of the non-executive directors, if one assumes that the executive directors are often more concerned with self-preservation. At the time of writing, the non-executives of another company eventually reacted to intense shareholder pressure, rather than appearing to work from their own sense of what was good for the organization and taking responsible action.

The next leader came to power in 1992 in the new circumstances of corporate governance, with a non-executive chairman over him. By then, felt Lord Tanlaw, the board was far more bureaucratic and so less transparent. "When I left in 1992 we used to read through over a hundred pages of board papers (as opposed to about twenty under George), which was absurd. This was typical of the centralized bureaucracy that Inchcape had become in the 1990s." Whatever the "rules" indicated, the effectiveness of their relationship would depend upon a sharing of the burden and the development of trust. It was obvious to many "insiders" that the trust had never blossomed. Within the senior executive team, the teamwork and camaraderie that had been such a strong feature was replaced by politics.

But unlike the time of Lord Inchcape, this was a far more demanding public arena, where every action was subject to close scrutiny. All through the turbulence of 1995, the board struggled to act collectively to put things right. By a huge stroke of misfortune, three of the non-executive directors had overwhelming problems in their own companies to deal with. The chairman himself probably found the support of his non-executive directors wanting, at the very time he would have needed it most. For more than a year, a large organization appeared distracted by this period of indecision.

This outcome could be blamed on an extraordinary and never-to-be-repeated set of circumstances. Rather like insurance, one needs a board most when one is in adversity. It is clearly out of order for the authors to draw conclusions or advance recommendations based on one situation. Yet, we feel sufficiently concerned to question whether the current constitution of public company boards in Britain enables them to be as effective as they might be. Whether non-executive directors and chairmen should be able to hold a clutch of other positions, full or part-time, and whether the non-executives' rewards are commensurate with their responsibilities, are two issues that might justify further investigation.

THE INCHCAPE MANAGER

From Inchcape's top management, we turn to an often-overlooked part of the organizational hierarchy, the operating manager. One of our goals, at the outset of this book, was to consider the role of middle-ranking Inchcape managers during the last forty years. What were their relative strengths and weaknesses? How did they change over time, and what effect, if any, did the mantras and training they received, or the organizational changes they went through, have on their and Inchcape's performance?

Under the Third Earl, the Inchcape managers were generalists to a man, working their way up the ranks out in their own geographical areas and becoming, as Macaskill put it, "Jack of all trades and hopefully, master of some." The quality of these managers was, as John Bartley and other contemporary observers described, variable. Some grew lazy under the loose rein of control exercised at this time, but the majority repaid their leader's trust by dedication to the company, using their immense local knowledge and contacts to seize any profitable opportunities that came along.

During their time, the group grew and flourished, though with occasional black spots. It was extravagantly praised by the City and business press and then, under pressure of economic hard times and a falling share price, suffered heavy criticism and was forced to restructure.

This generation was largely swept away by the new leadership and replaced by a different breed of professional, specialist managers. They were disciplined and controlled, though again the quality was variable. This finding seems to confirm Colin Armstrong's remark that attracting high-quality managers is one of the perennial problems of small companies, which many of the Inchcape businesses were. In addition, as Alan Reed observed when speaking of the difficulties in finding and training a successor in Motors Retail, "Traditionally, the car business just hadn't attracted the right people. It is difficult, most people drift into it anyway ... and it is easy to climb if you are good, because there are so few that are good. Inchcape says it wants graduates but you have to start at the bottom — you can't come in half way up in our business. Plus we are open seven days a week and work long hours. Do bright graduates want that?"

However, this later set of managers benefited from attending carefully planned training courses, and met up at group conferences and other internal courses designed to give an opportunity to forge links and hear about future plans. Afterwards, they were urged to return to the office and cascade the message down among the ranks. In contrast to their predecessors, the activities of this set of professional managers were much more strictly controlled by the center; business plans set out their objectives, and their performances were regularly appraised.

Despite all this, during their time too, the group grew and flourished, though with occasional black spots. It was extravagantly praised by the City and business press and then, under pressure of economic hard times and a falling share price, suffered heavy criticism and was forced to restructure.

To paraphrase a well-known tag, '*autre temps, autre managers*' — but similar outcomes. What conclusions can we draw from this?

In fact, our research has shown that notwithstanding the differences in training and skills, the views expressed by managers from both generations were remarkably similar. Despite efforts to promote the Inchcape name, for example, many of them still felt quite remote from the group. Just as managers from Gilman or Dodwell had felt quite separate from Inchcape in the 1970s, so twenty years later one longserving manager could claim, "My only relationship with Inchcape is when I look at the share price and see it has gone down again." Even in 1997, many still identified more with their business unit, and often had no awareness of other managers in the same business stream, let alone in a different one. Clive Hall, a general manager who first joined the group in 1981, recalled that he only met someone from Inchcape in 1996 when he attended an Accelerator program. "This was an eye-opener, listening to the views of people from many different parts of the world, many saying the same as us in the U.K."

But perhaps most striking was the way that the complaints of managers from Lord Inchcape's era bemoaning the way that Turnbull's controls were crushing entrepreneurialism and cutting across the group's core strength of local know-how, were echoed by a later generation who worked under Charles Mackay and Philip Cushing. They shared the feeling that they had a relevant contribution to make, but were not being heard by those at the top. Was this opinion justified?

The 80% return rate received by EDC in response to their opinion survey of Inchape's top 300 managers conducted in January 1995, and the lengthy written comments accompanying those replies, demonstrated the eagerness of the Inchcape managers to contribute and be consulted. Similarly, the representations of the Staverton team, and the influence of middle management on the design of the Accelerator program, showed that they could have a positive and valuable input into strategic and cultural decisions. Faculty who ran the group's training programs at the Ashridge Centre found that "Inchcape people were known around Ashridge as having lots of energy, lots of enthusiasm, open to new ideas. They were really keen to learn and get a lot out of the experience." The Euro-Asia Centre professors noticed the same positive, enthusiastic attitude and eagerness to contribute. Representatives from the corporate office who attended sessions were bombarded with questions and suggestions — not all of them polite.

Unfortunately, as one director observed of the group in the 1990s, "The style at the center was far too self-centered. There were not the skills to do with bringing people through and having confidence in them." David Newbury from Motors felt that "There was not a mechanism for spreading best practice round the group, was there?" This, despite the fact that "There is an awful lot of skill, knowledge, and ability in the company, at all levels, and there is a lot of skill and knowledge in the marketplaces where we operate, whether at local or national level."

The operating managers agreed. Necessarily, as they frequently pointed out, their outlook was colored by direct experience, which could give them potentially valuable insights into the way their businesses worked today, and how this might change in the future. But it seemed that their opinions were rarely taken into consideration by company strategists whose thinking, they felt, tended to take place within the confines of corporate head office and was based on input from business heads and reports commissioned from outside experts. For the final sessions in the Euro-Asia programs, the operating managers would produce a sheaf of well-argued presentations giving an analysis of their business within a local context, and their thoughts about future strategy, threats, and opportunities that might arise. These slides would be carefully collected and handed to the corporate representative to take back to London. But few of the managers who put so much work into their presentations felt that their contribution would be looked at again, or fed into the planning mill.

Several of Inchcape's leaders thought the managers were right to feel that their local know-how gave them a valuable edge. David John admitted that, "I find it very hard to understand how somebody sitting in London can second guess the guys who are in the market every day, 2000 miles away." He also agreed that the central imposition of certain controls and strategies had crushed vital managerial strengths. As a result of Marketing global business streaming, for example, "Inchcape's skill — managing joint venture partnerships in alien cultures — was latterly greatly underestimated." Lord Tanlaw spoke trenchantly of the effects of specialization: "These new business people may have got the company finances organized, but nowadays nobody seems to know who or what 'Inchcape men' are doing in, for example, East Asia. They may be beavering away like mad overseas, but as *foreigners* not *insiders*. As a result, they will often be the last rather than the first people to hear of good local business opportunities which are often offered to friends at social events in the area — like the weddings or funerals of the ruling business families. These offers are rarely extended to outsiders or 'men in suits from the West,' which could describe 'Inchcape men' of today. It never used to be like that." But as Stacey Ellis argued in defense of central discipline, "At the end we need more ideas than money, and our job at the center is to pick those that are winners. It's intellectually perfect, but emotionally disastrous."

Derek Whittaker, too, appreciated the importance of the men on the ground. "It was something I learned from Weinstock, as he always said, 'If I pick the right man for the corner office, he will make sure he has the right people supporting him — that is the long and short of it.'" In a group such as Inchcape, the importance of the man in the corner office working in some far-flung place and able to spot lucrative business opportunities was particularly true.

The frustrations of a Sergio Mardones were a good example of this. Operating out in Chile with contacts and a knowledge of the market for tractors and bottling built up over many years, central ignorance was highly frustrating. Under George Turnbull, the central strategy of getting rid of non-core businesses almost meant the sale of Coca-Cola Bottling, despite strong opposition from himself and Colin Armstrong. In this case, the strategy would not let him do what he knew was the right thing, invest and expand the business. At one stage, he and his fellow managers even formed a company to prepare for a management buy-out for US$30 million. Luckily, their visit to Santiago led O'Donoghue and Turnbull to change their minds.

From the Inchcape experience, it seems that this knowledge is frequently not tapped by those at the top. The managers were asked for financial figures and projections, but were not asked for their input, or involved in setting the *"grandes lignes"* of a strategy they would then be asked to implement, one that they may know instinctively is flawed.

A company's managers, while often lacking the jargon of the business schools, automatically carry out many of the analytical tasks taught there. Working daily in the marketplace as they do, to know the key factors for making money in their business, who the biggest customers are, what the competition is doing, the history of their particular industry, future regulatory or technological changes that will affect it, and so on, is as natural as breathing, and has been built up over years of experience. They automatically cultivate their core competencies, and to them, focus is not a mantra, but the central tenet of their working lives for without it, there will be no profits. The demands from corporate are often a distraction that gets in the way of this focus. "As managers," one field executive remarked, "we have a lot of demands coming from above — doubtless for good reasons. But my prime function is to sell motor cars. I find it very frustrating."

In their preoccupation with external pressures, senior managers sometimes seem to forget to engage their own people. In doing so, they risk overlooking an important source of expertise — and one of their most valuable assets, for as Peter Johnson observed, "Find a good manager and beneath him you find good people and beneath that is a good business." Perhaps it is time to tilt the pendulum back toward "the poor bloody infantry." The best way to start is by talking to the managers and, above all, listening to them. But this may be too revolutionary an idea for many companies to take seriously.

II … and Mantras

In the introduction to this book, we suggested that consultants, business schools, and the stock market formed a potent mixture, each putting forward their own mantras for success. We described this combination as a Bermuda Triangle, in which a company might lose sight of its own capabilities and best interests. Did this theory hold up in the light of what we found at Inchcape? What impact did these three powerful institutions have on the group's strategies and performance over the forty years covered by our research? How did Inchcape use the mantras it tried to adopt, and how influential were they — for good or bad? We begin with a round-up of the three groups making up our triangle.

THE MANTRA MARKETEERS
This Model Should Run and Run

Management consultants or advisors, whether they are academics topping up their income, or accountants extending their original line of business, or former managers, or newly-minted MBAs, all work under pressure. The expectations of them are that they will bring some expertise to a company. They will come bearing the label of "corporate strategy" or "total quality" or "human resource management" to distinguish themselves in their highly fragmented marketplace. Their label is often a constraint on their usefulness. How often does a company commission a rethinking of its overall strategy, which results in a change of structure, but which stops short of many of the human resource issues? Conversely, how often do companies engage consultants to introduce fashionable new human resource techniques when the culture or the strategy runs in a contrary direction? And how many mergers are constructed entirely on the basis of financial engineering and market shares?

Why do managers engage consultants? In part, their success is connected with companies falling victim to the fashionable mantra exhorting them to become "lean and mean." Too often, this has left them with a lack of in-house expertise, or what used to be known as experienced management. Thus, when later faced by problems, they find themselves having to outsource expertise that used to exist free of charge. Additionally, some organizations have become so "lean and mean" that they genuinely lack the time and resources and engage consultants as a temporary or virtual workforce. And what begins as a real need can turn into a pernicious habit: why not get someone else to do one's thinking for you, then blame them if it goes wrong?

All the familiar reasons for bringing in consultants were present in Inchcape: to get an independent view; to bring in outside perspectives of a market sector; to give credibility and articulation to an existing line of thought; to show action where indecision exists; to do some of the "dirty" work the managers would prefer to avoid. Stephen Looi, working out in Singapore, concluded from his own experience that, "Consultants were used to do something that you had already decided to do — as a justification. Often, they would only look at specific things in their brief. This was made worse when you employed different consultants in different places, destroying any chance of a cohesive view ... In the end, consultants depend on you as a client, and not many will really argue with you. They will tell you what you want to hear." Alison Davies at the center felt that, "Maybe we have done far too much analysis. Perhaps we have had far too many gurus crawling over the issues and you end up in paralysis. Whose advice do you take?"

Despite these apparent hazards, it is difficult to identify any instance of where consultancy might have led Inchcape seriously astray. Advice on ambition and empowerment was sound enough, if one studies the detail of what was proposed. The way that managers chose to interpret and apply it led to unintended outcomes. Even the advice on the need for 'scale' in the Insurance business was relevant. John Whiteman reflected that the future configuration of the Insurance sector was difficult to predict, and that the company had spent a considerable amount of money on consultancy advice. What was the advice? "I think they were probably ambivalent. We had to make up our own minds." In fact, timing and luck turned a sound approach into a significant loss of shareholder value. On the other hand, much of the advice about strategy and structure pointed in the same direction — that of radical simplification — but was just not acted upon.

As if to illustrate that, in this area, there is bound to be ambivalence, Bob Goodall noted: "We've always used consultants. I would question whether that has contributed to where we are now. But I very much doubt we got value for money and it has sometimes led us down routes we should never have gone."

In fact, consultants hired by Inchcape to tackle very specific issues remember being acutely aware that their particular approach, or offering, begged questions about the overall strategy and the group's culture. However, because of their specialty they were unable or unwilling to make their voices heard. Sometimes, it was just a case of getting on with the job in hand and being grateful to pick up the fees, and hope that one's efforts might have a beneficial effect on the whole organism. Was that collusion or pragmatism?

Have We Got a New Model?

"Just as there are only about six basic plots in the whole of fiction, covering everything from Cinderella to Catch-22, so there are only a handful of truly original ideas in the world of management."

Business schools have to sell themselves in a market where the competition is increasingly fragmented and less differentiated. The processing of MBA students and selling of lucrative executive training courses helps to fill the coffers and fund research activity. Research should help to produce new insights, and make sense of the evolution of all aspects of business. The ability to stand back and really think through the fundamentals is a luxury given to the academic, but largely denied to the manager.

Unfortunately, the selling of courses demands new concepts and new messages. Academic careers depend on writing papers and books. In this overcrowded arena, each writer is looking for a new niche to explore and new message to cut through the "noise." New models sell courses and new models sell books. If the model is sufficiently different but simple enough for a busy manager to grasp quickly, then that academic might even achieve the temporary status of guru. But, as any MBA could tell you, the effect of too many theorists chasing after too many excellent companies, in which they hope to mine the latest management idea, inevitably leads to an inflationary situation and possibly a dilution in the quality of the output.

The result of all these pressures is subtle but pervasive: the models have to be simplified versions of reality and they will typically tackle one aspect of a problem, rather than work on the total system of the organization in question. Sometimes the effect is insufficient to overcome the inertia of the whole organization; sometimes it will create an unwelcome distortion of the effectiveness of the whole. Perhaps most often, they are never sufficiently worked through to have any discernible effect, other than as an entertainment or diversion from reality.

In this imperfect market, the company can end up being the ultimate victim. Pressures from books and the media give the impression that companies which do not try out the latest management idea risk falling behind their competitors. So, confidence undermined, the company turns to outside consultants for support, and recruits the products of the business schools. The existing management is made to feel, at the very least, irritated and in the worst case, inadequate by the brash young newcomers arriving on the scene, complete with incomprehensible jargon and the latest theories. Some have begun to voice their doubts about "the Emperor's new clothes," but only in a whisper.

Often, the speed with which MBAs gallop through their intensive courses allows little time for them to examine the complexities of these theories, while the rapid expansion of the business school sector has itself generated a huge demand for faculty. This has led to the recruitment of people fresh from a doctoral program who are again strong on theory, but weaker on business experience. Since the younger faculty are often directed to teaching core MBA courses while their more experienced colleagues get on with their research and consulting activities, there is a risk of perpetuating a vicious circle of inexperience.

A recent interview given by George Bain, ex-principal of London Business School, seemed to confirm these weaknesses. "Having an MBA," he was reported as saying, "will never make a good manager out of unpromising material, but it will teach a few tricks of the trade ... At business school you learn half of what you need to know, and it is the less important half." Management education, he conceded, is "... a new area, so there is lots of room for charlatans ... I think there is also a lot of good stuff. The trick is to be able to separate the wheat from the chaff."

In companies, the ability of young MBAs to damage a business through overconfidence in their management skills may, hopefully, be limited in scope by their immediate bosses. Potentially more damaging, it might be argued from the Inchcape experience, is when these young graduates become City analysts. If, lacking any practical business experience, breadth of knowledge about the industry sector or real supervision, they dogmatically apply the ratios and models they have learned to judge a firm's performance, it could have serious consequences for the survival of that company and its workforce.

Business school programs offer a unique opportunity for managers to meet up with colleagues from different companies, industries, and countries, away from the stresses of everyday office life. They provide state of the art training in specific fields, and provoke new insights into old practices. At their best, business schools can challenge the way managers look at their business and help them to think more strategically. A business school introduced the ideas of core competencies and corporate culture to Inchcape's managers a decade ago. Many of them suspected that the struggle to identify both these features across their group raised a question about the existence of the group in its complex form. Despite this, it has taken ten years and a crisis to recognize what this insight might have been telling the board and its corporate staff.

At their worst, business schools will collude with the managers to apply specific models to deep-seated issues and help to upset the balance of the whole organization. Empowerment is one such example: a powerful idea, but lethal if the systems and processes and corporate culture are inadequate.

A Market Model

As we researched this book, we frequently heard the phrase, "The stock market does not like surprises." We were told repeatedly that the stock market is becoming more sophisticated. We were reminded that the stock market is a highly efficient mechanism and that, ultimately, the market will provide the answers. We took these notions on face value. Our context was, of course, the London stock market.

In order to deal quickly with large amounts of information, investors filter the data through their mental models. Whether they are private investors, fund managers, or stockbrokers' analysts, they will tend to "pigeon-hole" companies so that they can make comparisons between them. For example, within a certain category one might expect to find a particular range of price/earning ratios. When "overseas trader" was still reasonably respectable as a business format, Inchcape's bedfellows in this category were the likes of Harrison and Crosfields, and Lonhro. In the early 1990s, Inchcape was reclassified as "business services" along with BET, Rentokil, Hays, and Salvesen. This was a more highly rated sector, and it coincided with the elevation of the shares into the FTSE-100.

By 1994, Inchcape found itself reclassified yet again: this time in the distributors sector. Among its supposed analogues were Premier Farnell, whose products were electronic components. At the other end of the spectrum were Lex Services and the Cowie group, primarily domestic and dedicated to automotive distribution. When the British car market dipped just 1%, Inchcape's shares would be marked down in sympathy. Yet Inchcape's total profit before tax in 1994 was £230.6 million, of which 62% came from Motors worldwide and 41% of this from the U.K.: just a quarter of its profits.

Inchcape was at odds with the investors' models and seemed destined to be a misunderstood misfit. This was surely a factor in the drive for simplicity and focus: if only the company was simple enough for the market to understand, its shares would be valued fairly, or so the thinking seemed to go. Lord Marshall saw another reason: "I would not say the market was that confused about the businesses that Inchcape was in, but we were still seen as a bit of a conglomerate and conglomerates were completely out of fashion. Therefore, the market just refused to accept the intrinsic value of the company."

Worse difficulties were to follow. Whilst some of the analysts made genuine efforts to understand the group and unravel the fundamentals of the business, even they were handicapped by the way that they related to the company. Their first line of contact was through the chief executive and the finance director. What they understood of the company, beyond the figures made available to them, came to them through the filter of these two officers of the company. They would form an impression of these individuals and use it to frame their assessment of the company. If it were favorable they would maintain a positive view until their trust was betrayed. If it were unfavorable, they would remain suspicious and doubting. Rarely did they have contact with any other senior managers, and only occasionally did they visit operating units to understand better the business they were analyzing. As Inchcape dropped out of the top 100 companies and languished between 190 and 200 in the rankings, it attracted even less attention.

"The fund managers are effectively administrators: they often have a very rigid house policy about which stocks they can and cannot invest in, and they may have very limited room for maneuver." Bridget Walker,

Inchcape's investor relations manager, went on to describe how, "they look at so many stocks and have very limited time to look at each stock. Even if the analysts did do fundamental research and had a story to tell, they often don't read the research. They just read the summary, and then overlay that with their own view of 'we don't like that market' or whatever." Additionally, the London stock market had developed to a point where a small number of very large companies, such as Glaxo or BT, dominated the performance of the index. "If they bought 5% or 10% of Inchcape or another mid-cap company, it would be only a tiny part of their portfolio. Even if we did phenomenally well and our share price doubled in six months, it would make very little difference to their overall performance — so why bother?"

The movement of the FTSE indexes through 1998 illustrated this bias to larger companies: the 100 index gained 14.5%; the 250 index rose a meager 1.4%, and the SmallCap fell 10.4%. What is unclear is whether the large companies were seriously overvalued, and the remainder valued more sensibly, or whether a whole clutch of middle-ranking companies were undervalued and might have been better off in private hands.

Private ownership was a point that one senior executive picked up: "The reason the directors get put into that position is that the City analysts are not good enough at, in real time, identifying what is driving a business, and why a business might be heading into trouble. Which is why, for businesses that are complicated, traditional investment routes through the stock market may not be the right method. If you are not a utility or a pharmaceutical company, or something that is very easily analyzable and you know your competitors, then it is probably not worth the City's while to invest in good research and get good access to management. If you are a combination of being a complex business and with a market capitalization of less than a billion, then it may be that private equity is a better means of owning it. Because you can have a dialogue with the private equity owner without having to worry about the next six months' results or insider dealing rules."

By late 1998, directly and indirectly, U.S. investors held around 40% of Inchcape's shares. This was in a market where about 10–12% of the top 100 and just 4% of the FTSE-250 companies were held by the Americans. "The difference in the U.S. is that the so-called value investors start bottom up, where they look at the fundamentals and the cash-flow characteristics of each particular business ... The U.S. investors do so much more research. They are incredibly thorough," said

Walker, "and they talk to our bankers and brokers and people in Coke and South America. They have a much more business school-oriented approach, using evaluation techniques instead of P/E ratios, and look at economic value added and that kind of thing." So much for the sophistication of the London stock market.

So in the end, what can we say of the stock market? Did it serve Inchcape well, or not? Clearly, it enabled the group to raise capital and grow over a long period. The blame for the "overvaluation" of the shares in the early 1990s must be shared between company and market. The shareholders did very well and no-one was heard complaining then that the shares were too high. The fall from grace, and subsequent difficulties with "undervaluation," have been brutal: they reflect the simple models that the market uses to get its job done. Those are the rules of the game if one chooses to remain a public company in the London market. The cost of capital, the apparent superficialities and the imbalances of the London market might suggest that it is becoming an anachronism when compared with its competitors. Whether it will transform itself or be overtaken by other ways of financing business in other locations is a matter for speculation.

Charles Mackay noted that the City was a fair weather friend: "The same people in the City who said what a brilliant deal TKM was, a year later were castigating us for over-exposure to the Japanese motor industry and hence the yen. But, that's life." Rod O'Donoghue was equally realistic: "If your results are good, your theories are acceptable; if your results are bad, your theories are unacceptable ... but we were always complex and there was a lot to look at."

A last word from a London-based fund manager, commenting on the apparent unfairness of the London market: "If you look at Inchcape's charts — their profitability, their EPS — then we have had one or two disappointments to live with as well. I am trying to be fair. We did not understand the animal: that was certainly a factor, but against that, we could see certain weaknesses."

USING THE MANTRAS

Take Focus and Simplicity ...

Two intertwined questions have dominated Inchcape's top management thinking for nearly two decades: what businesses should we be in, and how should we organize ourselves to support them? Underlying this relatively practical pair of issues was a darker train of thought: why do we exist at all? Much time, energy, and outside advice was expended on this nexus rather than, say, improving IT systems or building logistics expertise. The mantras of focus and simplicity have found expression through various individuals, as a thread running through this book. Yet, the reality of simplicity is only now being delivered, and under pressure from external events. If the externalities had been kinder, it is possible that Inchcape could have continued into the next millennium in its complex, multi-business format. Which raises a question: what is it that prevented a much earlier move to a simpler, focused form of organization?

... and Add Synergy

Whether or not it was articulated as such, much of Inchcape's strategic thinking has been influenced by the idea of synergy. Variously, the synergy mantra was used as an intellectual justification for the parenting role of the Inchcape group, the existence of a group headquarters, business streams, the fostering of a common culture, a company-wide human resource policy, a change program, the value of the shares and, most notably, growth by acquisition. Applied in this way, synergy was the counterweight to simplicity and focus. However, conveniently, the two ideas were not mutually exclusive. For example, the creation of a business stream could meet the criteria of focus and simplicity whilst generating potential synergy within the stream. One could actually have one's cake and eat it. Yet, as Goold and Campbell point out, creating vertical linkages is the easy bit: horizontal synergies are much more elusive. Finding linkages between streams had always proved elusive. Because they were elusive, it was difficult to prove one way or the other whether, for example, "the group" added value or destroyed it. Hence the tortuous debates and the agonized navel-gazing.

The concept of parenting was used as a framework for portfolio analysis and as a justification for holding the group together. "We struggled with parenting: it is a terribly obvious idea but difficult to do anything practical with it," reflected John Whiteman. "What can you 'parent,' other than what you have got at the moment? Oddly, we sold Testing and did the parenting analysis for a replacement business. The analysis came up with a business about the same size as Testing and the same cost. So what was it about Testing that led us to not to continue parenting it? We never managed to make the parenting idea work as a criterion." Even if it was ultimately discarded by the strategic planners, the notion of parenting had a long life, and helped delay decision-making about the structure.

Right outside the normal realm of corporate planning lay one other looming excuse for not taking radical action, and that was the perennial fear of what the principals might think. Yet in Sir David Plastow's view, "The way to handle that is back to my word 'partnership.' You can discuss it with the principals, saying, 'This is our idea: you will benefit and we will benefit.'" Lord Marshall agreed with the notion that the fragility of the role of intermediary was over-played: "There is no doubt that principals can be in a very difficult position themselves. As a principal, you have to continue to come forward with new concepts, new ideas, new products — whether you are in the services business, or whether you are in manufacturing or engineering. Without that you are destined to die or get absorbed by others."

If radical action on the strategy was delayed until the "eleventh hour," that was not the case with the structure. Under Lord Inchcape, extreme decentralization was the model, but Sir George Turnbull swung it firmly back into centralization. Then the business stream approach, which Sir David Orr had started, and Sir George advanced pragmatically, was applied globally, in one bound, by Charles Mackay.

With global business streaming, the balancing factor of the country managers disappeared, all but wiping out the core competence of coordinated local knowledge. Business streaming also shifted power and control away from the center, and added another layer of bureaucracy and overhead. Centralization of the group translated into centralization in the business streams. With one eye on the stock market, all the exertions and disruptions of restructuring gave an impression of activity, but dissipated energy that might have been directed into more fundamental strategic actions. Structure had obscured or obstructed strategy.

The Inchcape experience illustrates the ongoing debate over the "appropriate" structure that large, diversified companies should adopt. It has been going on for a long time. "I remember my first general management course at Ashridge in the sixties," recalled Colin Armstrong. "The big, fashionable question then was whether you should be centralized or decentralized. A director came from Shell to talk about it. He said, 'I'm not going to tell you the answer. Neither one nor the other is the answer for any length of time. You have got to change and the judgment is about how often you change.' I never forgot that." Where the pendulum will swing next probably awaits the next round of research from the business schools.

What is not for speculation is the fact that the dominant mantra of the last decade has been "focus and simplicity." It took a long and wearying battle and a significant loss of shareholder value before the inevitable was recognized. Inchcape is not the only company to fight this particular battle, but the market has the overwhelming force. The outcome is invariably the same. The only difference is the route to simplicity and the time it takes to get there. Which leads us on to consider Inchcape's route to focus more closely.

WAS RADICAL CHANGE INEVITABLE?

If you run a public company and your shareholders run their mental models in a way that does not align with your configuration of organization, then you have a choice, albeit a limited one. You can persist with the unfashionable format and modify it gradually, whilst improving efficiency in every possible way. To some extent this is the route followed so spectacularly well by General Electric, and as long as the shareholders are well rewarded, no one will worry for long about the particular shape of the organization. Others have tried but have been obliged to take a different course: Michael H. Jordan took over the helm of Westinghouse Electric Corporation in the early 1990s with a dream of restoring the failing industrial conglomerate to new health. In the end, he sold off most of the traditional operations and transformed it into a major media concern that took over the name of another icon which it had acquired: CBS.

There was another reason why the fashion had changed and this was financial, as one director pointed out: "Inchcape is not alone in that U.K. accounting, and the way the City looks at companies — until the latest changes over the last two or three years — favored normal earnings. This meant two things: first, the cash and balance sheet allocation and risk were completely ignored; and, second, costs that you had incurred in acquisitions or in reorganization were ignored. The way the results were reported probably "fooled" us as to how the business was doing, both internally and externally. In the old days, you could basically take something over and lose all the costs of reorganization."

The approach taken by the former British conglomerate, Williams Holdings, was one of steady evolution. Over a period of years, it has sold operations that did not fit its core activity of fire protection and security systems, whilst acquiring businesses which fitted this strategy. It is now one of the largest specialists in this field in the world. If an incremental response to the fashion was unlikely to succeed, one could move quickly to a radical break-up, and there are plenty of recent examples of this approach, including ICI, Dalgety, and Courtaulds. Another option is take the private capital route, as in the case of Virgin, or through substantial private holdings, as in the instance of Rentokil. Then there are the venture capital firms, which are effectively the new conglomerates. They can operate out of the glare of the short-term pressures of the stock market. Time will tell if this offers a real alternative.

Inchcape could have followed the incremental route in the early 1990s. By then, its strength in the automotive sector was well established and it was financially robust. The fact that it did not is the result of a combination of factors. First, there was a change of leadership and a shift in the dynamics of the board. Then there was its increased status in the investment community coupled with the over-hyping of its Far Eastern exposure. "Inchcape was riding on the back of the Asian dream," said Lord Marshall, "which was an amazing factor within the market itself."

Finally, there was a tendency to start believing its own public relations' messages. "How often the communication has taken over the message, and we have ended up being more defined by our propaganda," reflected John Whiteman. In response to the stock market pressure for growth, the organization went off in a direction that weakened its finances and control systems, leaving it cruelly exposed to changes in currency and market problems outside its control. For a while after this, it appeared to be following the evolutionary route, and then another calamity pushed its weary management into radical break-up. On the other hand, with a nod to the fickle finger of fate, Stacey Ellis believed that, "It took just two decisions to be wrong. And every company is like that — it comes down to one or two decisions. If you get those right, then all the rest is peanuts."

We will never know if Inchcape could have found its way more gradually to another organizational format and whether the stock market would have been sufficiently patient. Nor will we ever know if it could have transformed itself into a super-efficient yet still complex group. It just could have been the highest form of intellectual challenge for managers to tackle. Back in 1984, Ansoff predicted that the principle of requisite variety would replace "minimal management" principles such as, "keep it simple," "decentralize," and "minimize the size of corporate management." Strategic management would ensure that the complexity of the firm's responses would be matched to the complexity of the challenges facing it. There is no evidence that his prediction is about to materialize. After forty years as a public company, and nearly one and a half centuries as a business, Inchcape is finally becoming a simple and focused business, in line with the fashion. It lives on.

EFFECTS OF THE MANTRAS

Did the mantras have a negative, positive, or merely negligible effect on the destiny of Inchcape and, by inference, other large companies? Having interviewed a wide cross-section of the players, and set their observations in the context of what actually happened, we came to an unexpected and paradoxical conclusion.

In our view, most of the mantras had rather less effect than their promoters might have intended or expected. Some, such as ambition and empowerment, had unintended and strongly negative effects. Others, such as core competencies, were researched with zeal and correctly identified, listed, and publicized throughout the group. Unfortunately, the implementation of other theories cut across and destroyed them. The real issue is not the idea in itself but its application. A mantra has the potential to be misinterpreted, or applied to a complex situation without taking into account some of the other important variables. Thus, Alastair Macaskill, David John, and several others blamed the business streaming theory for diminishing the importance of Inchcape's vital strength or core competence — the ability to exploit local know-how. "Please, take care of the country management," Macaskill had pleaded with Turnbull at the time of the Torquay conference in 1990. "You abandon it at your peril." But then "Charles applied business theory to a much greater extent, because that was his background. Essentially this disenfranchised country managers and local managers."

We described a large organization as a swirling coalition of interests. We have also suggested that complex organizations may be only partly under control as they interact with their environment. Chaos is always just around the corner, and management is often more about steering the organization back from the brink than running a logical machine. The real danger of the mantra is that it may lead to a single input that affects the balance of the delicately balanced whole. Clearly, the manager has just as much responsibility for avoiding this danger as does the advisor.

We believe that every manager worth his or her salt will welcome new insights into management. We also believe that every manager should beware of seductively packaged and simplistic approaches to singular issues. Business schools have moved a long way in the past decade to develop a more integrated approach to their study programs. Despite this, there is still a steady output of very specific and narrow advice on offer. This will only change when the buyers of such advice — the managers — insist on integrated, system-wide thinking. That said, in the spirit of solidarity with our business school and consultancy colleagues, we would like to offer one final mantra, based on the Inchcape experience, from which other companies might profit in the future.

"MIND THE GAPS"

To impose a pattern on the development of a complex group like Inchcape is almost impossible, but the concept of gaps proposed below does provide a framework to identify some important fault lines affecting the group over time. The theory behind it is simple.

Gaps appear in an organization where vital linkages are either missing or have broken down, and so affect a firm's overall functioning. They can be identified in areas of management, culture, business, communications, strategy, implementation — the list is a long one, and every manager will be able to add his or her own favorites. For this is a game everyone can play: an MBA is not obligatory, but managerial experience is.

All firms have some gaps in their organization; these reflect tensions and shifts as the whole system evolves and realigns itself continuously. As soon as one gap is covered, another may appear. Some may be easily identified and dealt with; others may remain invisible for some time, only emerging at times of crisis to compound a company's problems. It is not the existence of gaps themselves that is important, but the number and depth of them, and it is the firm that has too many gaps that must beware. Eventually, there may come a time when the gaps start to overlap or even join up, so that a company can find itself like a boat holed beneath the waterline. The top managers may frantically rush trying to plug the gaps, but in vain.

This simple concept can be applied to any organization. Using it, the Inchcape saga over the past forty years can be characterized as a search to plug a series of gaps that affected its operational efficiency and profitability during that period. Some were readily visible and recognized by the leadership and successfully bridged — for the moment, at least. Some were more subtle, lying half-hidden and working insidiously over time, until their full impact emerged. Others were recognized too late.

THE BUSINESS GAP

The Inchcape business gap had several arms. The first was characterized by the never-ending search, beginning under David Orr and continued by every subsequent leader, to find a major profitable business on which the group's future fortunes could be based. Various candidates were tried — Inspection and Testing, Insurance, Coca-Cola in Russia — but ultimately, none of them proved suitable. As a result, this gap remained unplugged. While times were good and the other businesses thrived, the existence of this gap was more of a nagging worry than a serious preoccupation, acknowledged but sidelined. But when the economy turned down, it emerged as a serious hole that then joined up with perhaps the most critical business gap of all, that between performance and the expectations of shareholders and the analysts. When this happened, the Inchcape leadership knew it was in trouble.

Another arm of the business gap concerns acquisition activity, and has two aspects. The first is the gap between the price paid and performance, between the hopes and projections at the time of buying — the actual performance — and, too often, the eventual disappointments when the time comes to sell. The second type of acquisition gap, the one between acquisition and integration, is potentially even more lethal.

Their existence was fully recognized by the top teams, from Lord Inchcape to Philip Cushing. Charles Mackay observed that, "Acquisitions hit the headlines, and there is a danger there, both internally and externally, that everyone starts thinking that is what it's all about." In fact, Inchcape's record on buying was not by any means all bad news: Spinneys in the Middle East, and ETL in the Testing Services business were both real successes.

The main damage was actually caused later by the gaps between promise and performance opening up among the many small, poor acquisitions that were the product of a buying frenzy rather than a measured strategy. John Whiteman recalled how "Everyone got on the acquisitions bandwagon, led by Charles, encouraged by the press and the City," whilst John Bartley described how, "I think we tried to do too much too quickly in the early nineties. If someone came along with an idea from any country that you were not in and wanted to plant the flag in it ... the Genghis Khan mentality ruled. We will do this ... that ... instead of having a well thought-out plan and a proven competence that would travel, that we could transplant somewhere else. We just did all sorts of things in all sorts of difficult, unknown markets, most of which had to be reversed in the ensuing years." Lord Inchcape sounds positively restrained by comparison.

Rod O'Donoghue agreed that, "At this stage in our development, there was nothing inherently wrong that our expansion strategy should be based on acquisition and organic growth. As long as we stuck to the criteria and as long as we were investing, ultimately, in where our focus should be." But unfortunately, focus and simplicity were overrun as expansion by acquisition rather than organic growth led the group once more into complexity, and opened up a perception gap. Andrew Cummins later saw this clearly: "The culture of the company was not to lose things. So we were continually trying to grow across too many fronts we could not manage. In retrospect, the business was a mess underneath. We were too complex. Our overhead costs were too high. Inchcape was fighting on too many fronts, and its past finally caught up with it."

The integration gap has been well documented by the business schools and in the media, yet it was another trap into which Inchcape fell. Sir David Plastow was well aware of how it affected the group. Looking at the aftermath of the TKM acquisition, he recalled that, "Rule one in an acquisition is that on the first day of completion a team go in and build the systems to fit the company, and really get into the skeletons. It never actually happened." Instead, it seemed like a reverse takeover by TKM."

MANAGEMENT GAPS

This category can embrace several subsets such as communications, control, leadership, and cultural gaps. Severally they can be borne but when, for example, communications and control gaps join up, then it is time to be on the alert.

Into this category fall the obvious gaps in communication and control between field and center that almost led the group to disaster under Lord Inchcape. George Turnbull devoted a lot of time and energy to bridging this gap, and for a time succeeded. But it re-emerged later as economic circumstances deteriorated, and the field managers felt that some corporate managers were once again behaving like practiced exponents of the seagull theory.

Then there was the quality of management gap, one that Inchcape tried to bridge by training but which remained a constant problem. This was not a fatal gap, but rather a cumulative one. More serious, perhaps, was the big gap left by the rooting out of the entrepreneurs with their local know-how. Paul Cheng was clear that, "Inchcape's strength is really its knowledge of Asia. What I saw, with all due respect to the stream directors who were good people, that most of them lacked experience of living and working in the Asian culture for many years. Therefore, how could you rely on feedback from the field?"

Also in this category comes the leadership gap. This proved very dangerous during the various times of crisis the group went through for, as Macaskill observed, "When the chief executive wavers, the analysts pounce." First there was Lord Inchcape, who was sidetracked by P&O, and then later, Charles Mackay was said to have "immersed himself in detail" at a time of great turbulence. The lack of coherence between the leadership and the board was an additional gap, recognized and rued by many, who then linked its effect to the company's performance.

Below this came the gaps in the top team, perhaps most serious following the disbanding of George Turnbull's team. For this gap was filled not by harmony and balance, but by politics. Dale Butcher felt that with the departure of Stacey Ellis, "The balance of the team at the top was wrong. Stacey put discipline into these wonderful strategic moves that nobody else seemed to ... We missed that balance, that rigor." Nick Allen noticed at the GMB workshop in April 1995 that, "There was so much politics at the top level, and there was a lot of jostling for power — and money. In no sense were they a team." The lack of balance and diversity in the personality types of the members of the top team possibly accounted for some of the problems. John Whiteman mused that, "Maybe it is back to your NFs versus STs. In theory, we are ST in our approach ... that has driven the course of events. We had tended to regard strategies as projections. We have not worried about the actions to achieve them."

THE CULTURE GAP

Cultural issues gave rise to another series of gaps; one of the most insidious being the one between the statements at the top about 'people being our greatest asset', and the actions of management, especially at the time of slash and burn. Bob Goodall recalled an example of this in connection with the TKM acquisition: "On the one hand the group was saying 'Yes, We Care,' and here on the other hand was the group demonstrating quite obviously we did not care because we were quite happy for a totally different style of management to be allowed if that fitted our purposes. So, it was totally inconsistent."

From his experience with Motors, Peter Johnson put another spin on this. He believed that Inchcape as a corporate entity had values "that are very important and that it genuinely believes them, but that it has not been particularly good at delivering them. I think there is a genuine recognition of the need to give service to customers and through to principals. I actually believe there is a great desire to offer respect to employees, but this has seldom been delivered. There has been a gap but this is not because Inchcape hasn't wanted to deliver it, but because respect comes at the end of a long process Inchcape has hardly started. You can't say, 'respect me'; it comes after years of doing what you say you will do."

Another culture gap, that between the different businesses, led to the lack of understanding and trust that underpinned the failure to make the whole greater than the sum of its parts — that is, the synergy gap. And even within a single stream, cross-cultural gaps could appear and be damaging, as the Chile–Russia bottling experience demonstrated.

COMMUNICATION GAPS

As Melanie Price noted, "This has not been the forte of the group. It has been through very structured channels, up but mostly down … it could go up a little, and then stop." When Alison Davies joined, one of the first things she noticed was "an almost total lack of communication about what was going on. There was this big gap in communication …" This, several people believed, had a particularly devastating effect on morale when the group was downsizing.

Peter Johnson agreed that, at Inchcape, "the most important communication of all, which is management communication, was poor." One field manager recalled how the senior executive in charge of his division "didn't like people getting together, so he wouldn't allow meetings where you could discuss things. You didn't know who your colleagues were. His divisional directors didn't have an opinion because once you did, you were on your way out." This was an extreme case, but often communications suffered just as much from neglect. Peter Johnson believed this could not be justified. "It is not good enough to say we are an internationally-based business, one in different time frames — you have to take the time." It was a gap he was determined would remain plugged in the future.

A very important gap which Inchcape recognized and made intensive efforts to bridge was the comprehension gulf that yawned between the City and the company about just what sort of an animal the group was. Charles Mackay recalled that, "People from the City said, 'I do not understand why Inchcape is Inchcape.' We came up with plausible rationales but, to be honest, they were to some extent, *post facto* rationalizations of where we had got to in Inchcape's historical evolution." Attempts to bridge this gap in fact only led to the opening of an ultimately worse perception gap, between the story sold by corporate affairs of a focused, healthy group, and the reality of the still mixed bag of mainly small businesses laying underneath. Ian Ross noted that the "class act was a sham — there was always this huge gap between the ambition and the reality."

With hindsight, Charles Mackay felt that, "Undoubtedly, we had far too much press exposure for a company of our size which contributed to City expectations running ahead of reality — and that was dangerous." As Stacey Ellis described, "The business was growing well and we were getting kudos from the City; it became an escalator, a treadmill that keeps on going."

This, again, was a very dangerous gap, especially when compounded by the addition of a communications gap as the company turned down the volume once the bad times began. For, as Paul Cheng pointed out, "Once you have sold it to the City, if you change they will say, 'You do not know what you are doing,' or 'It is not working; that is why you are changing' … If you are a limited company and in the hands of institutional investors, it is very brutal. If you do not perform, you are gone, because they have their own performance to worry about."

This was an example of a gap that stayed submerged for long periods, but was always there, waiting to re-emerge and deliver a strong blow. For in September 1996, after twelve years of re-engineering, what had been projected as a focused, globalized distribution group was described in the press as a "sprawling empire" — the same tag given the group in Lord Inchcape's day. It indicated that Inchcape's journey had in fact been a circular voyage, that the organization had indeed behaved more like a Catherine wheel than the cruise missile it aimed to be.

IMPLEMENTATION GAPS

Strategy ...

There is a series of implementation gaps, of which the first obviously concerns Inchcape's strategic planning. From 1981 onward, the group produced endless, beautifully crafted strategy documents — Group Reports for the 1980s, "The Way Ahead," Individual Business Stream Strategies, "Inchcape's Direction in the 1990s," "For the Year 2000" — each one immaculately argued. Yet, as Robert Morton remarked of the late 1980s, despite all this work, "I do not think there was a strategy except to let things carry on as they had been doing and then when it hit the buffers, the strategy seemed to be 'Let's concentrate on fewer things, so we have fewer problems to worry about.'" Ian Ross, who joined the Marketing stream at the high point of the group's fortunes in 1992, remembered he was shocked to find that "I did not see anything I recognized as a business or market plan: I saw a series of budgets, and I did not see a clear statement of what these businesses were trying to do — just numbers."

David Newbury also identified "this lack of strategic focus, coming right from the heart of the company … to make the broad [strategy] picture work, you have to put some detail into it. That has not always been the case." John Whiteman observed that, "The streams gave us plans which showed growth, but we did not focus on the actions that were underlying them." Reflecting on the annual strategy conference, he felt that, "Some of it is about whether or not it suits the people involved to be heroes and stand up and say 'This is a waste of time. You are not looking at the real world.' They wanted an entertaining conference. So we delivered one, so that they all went away feeling good." This optimism gap was one many recognized; the one between the hopes expressed in speeches, conferences, and company publications both to its own managers and the outside world, only to be dashed as the results failed to deliver and the headlines yet again turned from "Inchcape on track" to "Inchcape disappoints."

THE MANTRA GAP

No framework would be complete without this final implementation gap, that between the theory and advice picked up from the business schools and consultants' reports, and its practical implementation throughout the organization. One of the great mantras of the group, and of the business world since the mid-1980s, has been globalization. At Inchcape, this led to the imposition of global business streaming.

In Paul Cheng's view, "The streaming concept was not wrong — it was just applied incorrectly … We got caught up by the globalization theory, but without looking carefully to see what kind of business we are." Charles Mackay, too, felt that it was implementation that brought the problems, and, in particular, that "The country manager concept definitely did not work in practice."

John Bartley was one of many who believed that Inchcape had thrown out the baby with the bathwater in adopting global streaming. "One of the good things in the old days, having watched Inchcape in the 1970s in

Malaysia and the 1980s in Hong Kong, was that they had a lot of geographical knowledge and experience — people knew all the local ropes … I just feel that when Inchcape adopted streaming, they lost their way a bit … Frankly, you had competent, experienced managers down at the operating level who really were not allowed to do anything."

Both he and Paul Cheng agreed that business streaming had also opened up a serious gap between Inchcape and its partners, especially in the Middle East. "Those guys in the old days, they were close, they knew the partners. Mention the name 'Alastair Macaskill' or 'David John,' and out goes the red carpet. They integrated — became one of the family, one of the tribe, and then you can do what you like within reason. At the moment, unfortunately, you take a long time to get a reputation and a relationship with the Arabs, but you can lose it quickly, and it takes a hell of a time to get it back." It was almost a vindication of Lord Inchcape's old crew.

In fact, there is almost unanimous agreement that the implementation of global business streaming led to the destruction of Inchcape's greatest skill, its historic ability to operate as a local player. Rephrased in the 1990s, this had become the mantra of core competencies. The gap between speeches about building on this particular competence, while simultaneously eroding its effectiveness, was ultimately one of the most dangerous of all in the way it affected the group's performance.

Core competence was not the only mantra nullified by business streaming; it also put the final nail in the coffin of focus. For as Paul Cheng explained, "The concept of focus and specialization in principle is correct, but we should have applied it only on a regional basis, so that you can achieve the balance between geography and product specialization, and capture the best of both worlds …" And whereas regional streaming had eliminated extra overheads, "with global streaming, you are rebuilding them all over again, and doing it under a different label … You have gone the full circle, except it is a different name: you then have a Motors or Marketing stream, instead of Gibb Livingston or Dodwell."

Managers at all levels will, if they are honest, recognize the existence of some of these gaps in their own companies, although few will have to wrestle with the number that Inchcape encountered — some self-inflicted, others arising from the complex set of businesses it was in. Many were identified and bridged, but it proved to be only a temporary respite, and when they did re-emerge simultaneously, the group found itself almost back to square one. History, it is said, repeats itself because nobody listens the first time. How many companies are, like Inchcape, in danger of going round in circles because the same gaps in their systems reopen over time? Using the Inchcape gaps framework, and perhaps adding new ones particular to their circumstances, readers can examine the extent of linkage or disconnection that exists within their own organizations, and judge how many holes there are in its structures. Taking care to "Mind the gaps" might help them to avoid sinking.

Inchcape is by no means unique in the challenges it has faced, or in the solutions it has adopted. In the U.S., the break-up announced in June 1995 of that "quintessential conglomerate," ITT, "a collection of hundreds of businesses held together not by the logic of their activities but by the force of their management," provoked an article in *The Economist* that could have fitted Inchcape's case perfectly. In September 1998, Procter & Gamble announced a shake-up that would split it into seven global business units based on product lines, so ending its previous geographic focus. Ironically, Unilever had just reorganized in the opposite direction — going from global product units to regional divisions. In Europe, speeches by the heads of companies such as Siemens, Veba, Philips, and Cable & Wireless and Williams Holdings in the U.K., about the need to restructure — often in response to a dip in their share price — are a distinct echo of those made by Inchcape leaders over the last decades.

The debate about the benign or malign influence of the City is also prominent in the business press; in November 1998, auto components group Lucas Varity shareholders were asked to vote on whether or not to move its base to the U.S. because "the analysts in the City just don't understand the company." Meanwhile, as a result of the Asian economic crisis, conglomerates in South Korea, Indonesia, Thailand, Hong Kong, and Japan are facing the same need to adapt and restructure their businesses. For them, too, the most frequently delivered advice is to find focus and simplicity, whilst following a strict regime of financial control. There is no shortage of outside helpers waiting in the wings to tell them how to do it, but perhaps, finally, the message from this book is the need for managers to find the most effective way to live with paradox, rather than just feed on mantras.

However, as London Business School's ex-principal, George Bain, observed, "Managers are very insecure and always looking for new ideas. People are never convinced by reason, but by experience. There are certain lessons that each generation must learn for itself."

Epilogue

◆

A t the time of writing, Inchcape had declared its preliminary results for 1998. Pre-tax profits before exceptionals were £106.1 million. However, the exceptional charges turned that profit into a pre-tax loss of £297.6 million, due in most part to goodwill write-offs and lower asset valuations associated with the businesses sold during the year.

Four businesses were sold: Bottling in Russia and Latin America; Marketing in Asia; and Shipping Services. They were expected to raise a total of £550 million. It was expected that two more businesses would be sold by mid-1999: Marketing in the Middle East, and Office Automation. It was anticipated that they would raise a further £100 million.

On March 9, 1999, *The Financial Times* commented, "Inchcape is understood to be considering returning £570 million to shareholders through two special dividends as the former trading company completes its transformation into a focused motor distribution business. Inchcape has followed the modern mantra of focus. But while the restructuring may have been text book stuff, the business it is left with is not exactly at the glamour end of the market."

Damned if you do, and damned if you don't!

References

PART 1   THE END OF AN ERA
Chapter 1   From Merchant Prince to Colonial Dinosaur
Page

1   Barrie, Sir J. M. (1995), *What every woman knows*, Act II, Oxford Drama
            Library.

4–8   Jones, Stephanie (1989), *Trade and Shipping, Lord Inchcape 1852–1932*,
            Manchester University Press, pp. 19, 31, 52, 62, 78, 67, ix, 120,119, 127,
            173–4, 187, 140, 188–9, 197, 186.

6,16   Commander Wall, Michael, Public Relations Controller (1988), Interview,
            London.

10–11,   Jones, Stephanie (1986), *Two centuries of overseas trading, the origins and
13,15   growth of the Inchcape Group*, Macmillan in association with Business History
            Unit, University of London, pp. 244, 249, 251, 272, 269, 277.

12   Waters, Hugh, OBE, Board member, Inchcape plc, 1960–77, (1983),
            Interview in *The Times of Inchcape*, 25th Anniversary Edition, p. 1.

12–15   Tanlaw, The Lord, ex-Board member, Inchcape plc (1999), Interview,
            London, January 19.

12   Campbell, Colin, Director, Group Accounting and Treasury (1988),
            Interview, London.

13–14   Armstrong, Colin, ex-Board member, Inchcape plc (1998), Interview,
            October 1, London.

16   Lester, Tom (1974), "The Inchcape Caper," *Management Today*, July,
            pp. 74–79, 116–20.

17   Ellis, Stacey, ex-Board member, Inchcape plc (1998), Interview, August 13,
            London.

Chapter 2   Entrepreneurs, Fiefdoms, and Shocks
Page

18   Inchcape, Kenneth, Third Lord, Director and Honorary President, Inchcape
            plc (1988), Interview, London.

19–20   Parsons, Sir Michael, ex-Board member, Inchcape plc (1999), Letter,
            March 24.

20   Wood, Christopher (1984), "Moving the Inchcape Rock," *Far Eastern
            Economic Review*, August 9, p. 51.

21   Chandler, Alfred Dupont (1962), *Strategy and structure: Chapters in the history of industrial enterprise*, The MIT Press, Cambridge, Massachusetts.

21, 24,   Armstrong, Colin, ex-Board member, Inchcape plc (1998), Interview,
28, 31   October 1, London.

22   Chandler, Alfred Dupont (1977), *The visible hand: The managerial revolution in American business*, Harvard University Press, Boston, Massachusetts.

22   Burns, T. and Stalker, G.M., (1961), *The management of innovation*, Tavistock.

23   Emery, Fred and Trist, Eric (1965), "The causal texture of organizational environments, " *Human Relations*, Vol. 18, pp. 21–32.

23   Lawrence, Paul R. and Lorsch, Jay W. (1967, rev. edn 1986), *Organization and environment: Managing differentiation and integration*, Harvard Business School Press, Boston, Massachusetts.

24, 30, 33 Commander Wall, Michael, Public Relations Controller, (1988), Interview, London.

24, 25–28, Tanlaw, The Lord, ex-Board member, Inchcape plc (1999), Interview,
31, 35–6   London, January 19.

25, 27, 29 Owens, Richard, Managing Director, Oman United Agencies LLC (1989), Interview, November, Inchcape Advanced Management Program, Fontainebleau.

25   Leavers, Philip, IT Manager, Inchcape plc (1998), Interview, London.

25   Duncan, John, ex-Corporate Affairs Director, Inchcape plc (1998), Interview, September 30, London.

26–8, 30, Macaskill, Alastair, ex-Board member, Inchcape plc (1998), Interview,
31, 33   December 1, London.

27   Lester, Tom, (1974) "The Inchcape Caper," *Management Today*, July, pp. 74–79, 116–20.

31, 36   Simpson, Anthony, Managing Director, Inchcape International Trading (1988), Interview, London.

32   Hall, Clive, General Manager, Mann Egerton Toyota (1998), Interview, July 22, Nottingham.

32   Bartley, John, Chief Executive, Inchcape Middle East (1998), Interview, August 4, London.

33   Ashworth, Brian, Group Planning Director, Inchcape plc (1988–89), Interviews, London.

34   Carpenter, Robert, Analyst (1988), Interview, London.

34   Morton, Robert, Analyst, Charterhouse (1998), Interview, September 25, London.

36   Cowell, Robert, Analyst (1988), Interview, London.

Chapter 3 Enter the Consultants

Page

37 "The new shape of management consulting" (1979), *Business Week*, May 21, pp. 98–104.

37 Chandler, Alfred D. (1990), *Strategy and Structure*, The MIT Press, Cambridge, Massachusetts, Introduction.

40 Kiechel III, Walter, "Playing by the rules of the corporate strategy game," *Fortune*, September 24, pp. 110–12, 114, 118.

40 Peters, Thomas J. and Waterman, Jr., Robert H. (1982), *In search of excellence: Lessons from America's best-run companies*, Harper & Row, New York.

41, 46 Commander Wall, Michael, Public Relations Controller (1988), Interview, London.

41–3 Extracts from Summary of CCG Report and subsequent discussions, October 30, 1980.

45, 47 Ashworth, Brian, Group Planning Director, Inchcape plc (1988–99), Interviews, London.

45–6, 52 Simpson, Anthony, Inchcape International Trading (1988), Interview, London.

47–9, 54 Inchcape Group Corporate Strategic Review, 1982–87.

50–51 Inchcape Group Corporate Strategic Review, 1983–88, including Policy for Group Development, February 1983.

52 Armstrong, Colin, ex-Board member, Inchcape plc (1998), Interview, October 1, London.

53 Lasserre, Philippe, Professor of Strategy and Asian Business, INSEAD-EAC (1988), Inchcape plc case studies, Teaching Note.

53 Orr, Sir David, ex-Chairman, Inchcape plc (1998), Interview, October 1, London.

Chapter 4 The Great Caretaker Takes Great Care

Page

55–6, 61, 62, 65 Orr, Sir David, ex-Chairman, Inchcape plc (1998), Interview, October 1, London.

66 Haspeslagh, Philippe C., Professor of Corporate Strategy and Organization, INSEAD (1998), Interview, November 3, Fontainebleau.

68–9 Wood, Christopher, "Moving the Inchcape Rock," (1984), *Far Eastern Economic Review*, August 9, p. 50.

PART 2   TURNBULL TURNS IT ROUND, 1986–92
Chapter 5   *"You Will Achieve"*

Page

73   Turnbull, Sir George, Chief Executive and Chairman, Inchcape plc (1986), Chief Executive's Address, Inchcape Group Conference.

74   Orr, Sir David, ex-Chairman, Inchcape plc (1988), Interview, London.

74–5   "Profile: George Turnbull" (1984), *Inchcape Magazine*, no. 18, September, pp. 6–7.

74   Anslow, Maurice (1987), "Inchcape of Good Hope," *Financial Weekly*, July 9, pp. 38–41.

75, 82   Whittaker, Derek, ex-Board member, Inchcape plc (1998), Interview, September 8, London.

77   Butcher, Dale, Development Director, Inchcape Motors (1998), Interview, August 25, London.

77   Macaskill, Alastair, ex-Board member, Inchcape plc (1998), Interview, December 1, London.

80   Allen, Nicholas, Director, Castleton Partners Ltd. (1998), Interview, October 21, London.

81   Ellis, Stacey, ex-Board member, Inchcape plc (1988), Interview, London.

83   Goodall, Robert, Group HR Director, Inchcape plc (1988), Interview, London.

85   O'Donoghue, Rod, ex-Board member, Inchcape plc (1988), Interview, London.

87   Duncan, John, ex-Corporate Affairs Director, Inchcape plc (1998), Interview, September 30, London.

87   Ellis, Stacey, ex-Board member, Inchcape plc (1998), Interview, August 13, London.

Chapter 6   The Glory Days

Page

88   Inchcape Group Strategic Plan, 1984–86.

88   Anslow, Maurice (1987), "Inchcape of Good Hope," *Financial Weekly*, July 9, pp. 38–41.

88   Turnbull, Sir George, Chief Executive, Inchcape plc (1988), Interview, London.

89, 96   Turnbull, Sir George, Chief Executive and Chairman, Inchcape plc (1986), Chief Executive's Address, Inchcape Group Conference.

89   Butcher, Dale, Development Director, Inchcape Motors (1998), Interview, August 25, London.

90   Macaskill, Alastair, ex-Board member, Inchcape plc (1998), Interview, December 1, London.

90   Orr, Sir David, ex-Chairman, Inchcape plc (1998), Interview, October 1, London.

90, 94–6   Ellis, Stacey, ex-Board member, Inchcape plc (1998), Interview, August 13, London.

93   Ansoff, H. Igor, ed. (1969), *Business Strategy*, Penguin Books Ltd., p. 22.

93   Kay, John (1993), *Foundations of corporate success: How business strategies add value*, Oxford University Press, pp. 345–7.

94   Goold, Michael and Campbell, Andrew (1998), *Synergy: Why links between business units often fail, and how to make them work*, Capstone, Oxford, p. 224.

94   Goold, Michael and Campbell, Andrew (1998), "Desperately seeking synergy," *Harvard Business Review*, September–October, pp. 131–143.

94   "Synergy: The First Steps" (1991), *Inchcape World*, May, issue 11, p. 14.

97, 102, 103, 104–5   Duncan, John, ex-Corporate Affairs Director, Inchcape plc (1998), Interview, September 30, London.

98   Goodall, Robert, Group HR Director, Inchcape plc (1998), Interview, May 27, London.

100   O'Donoghue, Rod, ex-Board member, Inchcape plc (1988), Interview, London.

103   Beva, Judi (1987), "New tricks give bite to an old dog," *The Sunday Times*, February 8.

103   "Insight: Log'em and Leave'em" (1989), *The Sunday Times*, June 25.

103   "Inchcape: Turnbull turns it round" (1987), *Financial Weekly*, July 9–15.

105   Foster, Geoffrey (1988), "Inchcape's less perilous passage," *Management Today*, January.

105   Popiolek, Mark (1989), "Inchcape eastern promise," *Investors' Chronicle*, June 30.

105–6   Carpenter, Bob, Analyst at Kitcat & Aitken, Investment Research (1988), September 13.

106   Workman, Richard and Warner, Rufus, Analysts at Hoare Govett (1988), UK Company Comment, November 18.

106   Havard, Bob, Analyst at James Capel (1988), Morning Meeting, September 16.

106   Haille, Bob, Analyst at Morgan Stanley International (1988), Industrial Holding Companies Report, September 22.

106   UK Research Department, Cazenove & Co. (1988), October 27.

106   Mackay, Charles, ex-Chairman, Inchcape plc (1988), Interview, London.

111   Ed Krafft, Peter, "Inchcape wrestles on growth track," *Daily Telegraph*, April 22.

Chapter 7 "Like Speaking a Swiss Language"

Page

111, 129   The Inchcape Song, composed by Advanced Management Participants, INSEAD-EAC, Fontainebleau.

112   Laurent, André, Professor of Organizational Behavior, INSEAD, (1998), Interview, Fontainebleau.

113–4   Schein, Edgar (1992), *Organizational culture and leadership*, 2nd ed, Jossey-Bass Publishers, San Francisco.

114   Hofstede, Geert (1980), *Culture's consequences: International differences in work-related values*, Sage Publications, Beverly Hills, California.

114   Trompenaars, Fons and Hampden-Turner, Charles (1987), *Riding the waves of culture: Understanding cultural diversity in business*, 2nd ed, Nicholas Brealey, London.

115, 119   Laurent, André (1997), "Reinventer le management au carrefour des cultures," L'Art du management, *Les Echos*, April 4–5, pp. v–vi.

117   Mardones, Sergio, President, Williamson Balfour S.A. (1997), "Williamson Balfour S.A., Decline and Rebirth, 1981–97," Chile, June, p. 8.

117   Reed, Alan, General Manager, Mann Egerton Jaguar (1998), Interview, October 2, Nottingham.

120   Prathap, Kalpana, HR Director, Inchcape Middle East (1998), Interview, June 22, Dubai.

120   Cheng, Paul Ming Fun, ex-Board Member, Inchcape plc (1998), Interview, July 2, London.

121   John, David, ex-Board member, Inchcape plc (1998), Interview, July 16, London.

124   Cheng, Paul Ming Fun, ex-Board Member, Inchcape plc (1990), Interview, Hong Kong.

126   Looi, Stephen, ex-HR Director, Inchcape Berhad (1998), Interview, June 19, Singapore.

126   Looi, Stephen, ex-HR Director, Inchcape Berhad (1990), Interview, Fontainebleau.

128   Philips, Richard and Pudney, Roger, Ashridge Management College (1998), Interview, August 26, London.

Chapter 8 What's My Line?

Page

130   Cowe, Roger (1990), "Outlook", *The Guardian*, April 3, p. 21.

130   Carpenter, Bob, Analyst at Kitcat & Aikken, Investment Research (1989), April 13th.

131   Jones, Stephanie (1989), *Trade and Shipping, Lord Inchcape 1852–1932*, Manchester University Press, p. 197.

131   Foster, Geoffrey (1988), "Inchcape's less perilous passage," *Management Today*, January.

131–2   Morrison, J. Roger, McKinsey & Company, Inc. United Kingdom (1988), Interview, London.

132   "A Singular Englishman, (1990), *Singapore Business Times, Weekend Edition*, July 21–22.

132   Cushing, Philip, Chief Executive, Inchcape plc (1998), Interview, August 17, London.

133   Inchcape plc (1989), Press Release, July.

134, 140, 144, 150–151, 152   Butcher, Dale, Development Director, Inchcape Motors (1998), Interview, August 25, London.

134   Bolger, Andrew (1992), "Trading Places," *Financial Times*, January 27.

135   Anslow, Maurice (1987), "Inchcape of good hope," *Financial Weekly*, July 9, pp. 38–41.

135   Waller, David (1987), "Striving to shake off the colonial image," *Financial Times*, September 28.

135, 148, 149   Haspeslagh, Philippe C., Professor of Business Strategy and Organization, INSEAD (1998), Interview, November 3, Fontainebleau.

136–140, 142, 143   Ellis, Stacey, ex-Board member, Inchcape plc (1999), Letter 261G, May 17th.

136–7, 141–2, 151   Armstrong, Colin, ex-Board member, Inchcape plc (1998), Interview, October 1, London.

141   Mardones, Sergio, President, Williamson Balfour S.A. (1997), "Williamson Balfour S.A., Decline and Rebirth," 1981–97, Chile, June, pp. 10–11.

142, 147, 150   O'Donoghue, Rod, ex-Board member, Inchcape plc (1988), Interview, London.

143, 144   Houlder, Vanessa (1989), "Inchcape up 27%," *Financial Times*, April 11.

145   Lasserre, Philippe, Professor of Strategy and Asian Business, INSEAD-EAC 1992), Inchcape EAC Advanced Management Program.

145, 151   Ellis, Stacey, ex-Board member, Inchcape plc (1998), Interview, August 13, London.

146   Times City Diary (1991), June 20.

146   Tate, Michael (1991), "Turnbull to split Inchcape roles," *The Times*, March 6.

147   Marchand, Christopher (1987), "Inchcape sets up unified regional headquarters," *South China Morning Post*, January 16, p. 6.

147–8   Duncan, John, ex-Corporate Affairs Director, Inchcape plc (1998), Interview, September 30, London.

147–8,
149

Whittaker, Derek, ex-Board member, Inchcape plc (1998), Interview, September 8, London.

149

Orr, Sir David, ex-Chairman, Inchcape plc (1998), Interview, October 1, London.

150

McElwaine, Peter, Deputy Chief Executive, Inchcape Middle East (1998), Interview June 20, Dubai.

150, 151

Whiteman, John, Director of Strategy, Inchcape plc (1998), Interview, June 8, London.

151

John, David, ex-Board member, Inchcape plc (1998), Interview, July 16, London.

152

Morton, Robert, Analyst, Charterhouse (1998), Interview, September 25, London.

152

Turnbull, Sir George, Chief Executive and Chairman, Inchcape plc (1986), Chief Executive's Address, Inchcape Group Conference.

PART 3   CUTTING LOOSE, 1992–94
Chapter 9   Going Global
Page

155

Cyert, R.M. and March, J.G. (1963), *A behavioral theory of the firm*, Prentice-Hall.

155

Levitt, Theodore (1983), "The globalization of markets," *Harvard Business Review*, May–June, pp. 92–101.

156

Bartlett, Christopher and Ghoshal, Sumantra (1987), "Managing across borders: New strategic requirements," *Sloan Management Review*, Summer, pp. 7–17.

156

Mant, Alistair (1983), *Leaders we Deserve*, Robertson, Oxford.

157

Fukuyama, Francis (1992), *The End of History and the Last Man*, Hamish Hamilton, p. 275.

157–8

Ohmae, Kenichi (1996), *The end of the nation state: The rise of regional economies*, HarperCollins, pp. 2, 5, 12, 16, 64, 80, 108, 111.

157

Porter, Michael (1990), *The Competitive Advantage of Nations*, Free Press, New York.

160–1

Bolger, Andrew (1992), "Trading Places," *Financial Times*, January 27.

160

Morton, Robert (1989), "UK-Overseas Traders: Inchcape," *Barclays de Zoete Wedd Research Ltd.*, January 6.

160, 168

Morton, Robert (1992), "Inchcape: Motoring steadily on," *Barclays de Zoete Wedd Research Ltd.*, February 3.

162,
169–70

Cummins Andrew, ex-Board member, Inchcape plc (1998), Interview, July 17, London.

162

Inchcape Marketing Stream (1992), Internal memo. Inchcape plc, London.

163

Ross, Ian, Chief Executive Russia, Inchcape Bottling (1998), Interview, August 7, London.

| 164 | McElwaine, Peter, Deputy Chief Executive, Inchcape Middle East (1998), Interview June 20, Dubai. |

164   McElwaine, Peter, Deputy Chief Executive, Inchcape Middle East (1998), Interview June 20, Dubai.

164   Looi, Stephen, ex-HR Director, Inchcape Berhard (1998), Interview, June 19, Singapore.

164   John, David, ex-Board member, Inchcape plc (1998), Interview, July 16, London.

164–5   Ellis, Stacey, ex-Board member, Inchcape plc (1998), Interview, August 13,
166–7   London.

165   "The Inchcape Country Manager: Our Man on the Spot" (1992), *Inchcape World*, April, issue 13, pp. 14–15.

165   Cheng, Paul Ming Fun, ex-Board member, Inchcape plc (1998), Interview, July 2, London.

165, 168   Cushing, Philip, Chief Executive, Inchcape plc (1998), Interview, August 17, London.

166   Alexander, Garth (1998), "P & G gambles on shake-up to beat crisis," *The Sunday Times*, September 13, p. 10.

168   Levi, Jim (1991), "Globetrotter settles at Inchcape." *Sunday Telegraph*, December 15.

168   "Inchcape drives into TKM" (1992), *Inchcape World*, April, issue 13, pp. 10–11.

168   "Inchcape's Pretax Profit Rose 6.4% in '91" (1992), *Asian Wall Street Journal*, March 31. Interview with Charles Mackay.

168   "Inchcape: Analyst Report" (1992), *UBS Phillips & Drew*, February.

168   Harris, Tim and Pick, Charles (1992) "Inchcape: Preliminary Results," *NRI Nomura Research Institute Europe*, March 31.

169   "At your service: Profile of Philip Cushing, Director of Inchcape plc" (1992), *Inchcape World*, July, issue 14, p. 9.

170   "Inchcape's New Chairman — Sir David Plastow" (1992), *Inchcape World*, July, issue 14, p. 3.

170   Plastow, Sir David, ex-Chairman, Inchcape plc (1998), Interview, December 31, Kent.

Chapter 10   ACE and Other Slogans
Page

172,   Mackay, Charles, ex-Chief Executive, Inchcape plc (1998), Interview, July 8,
181–3   London. pp. 6, 7, and 9.

172–3,   Haspeslagh, Philippe, Professor of Corporate Strategy and Organization,
175, 178,   INSEAD (1998), Interview, November 3, Fontainebleau. pp. 3, 5, and 8.
183

173   Cowell, Robert (1992), "An Outsiders View," speech given at Inchcape's Senior Management Conference, Luxembourg, June 14.

174   Butcher, Dale, Development Director, Inchcape Motors (1998), Interview, August 25, London.

175   Prahalad, C.K. and Hamel, Gary (1990), "The core competence of the corporation," *Harvard Business Review*, May–June, pp. 79–91.

176–7   Doz, Yves (1993, revised 94), "Managing core competency for corporate renewal: Towards a managerial theory of core competencies," INSEAD (Working paper).

176   Kay, John (1996), "Happy combination: If identified and used properly, core competencies can drive a uniquely successful strategy for a Company," *Financial Times*, October 25.

176   Turner, Ian (1997), "The myth of the core competence," *Manager Update*, Summer, vol. 8, pp. 1–12.

178   Hamel, Gary and Prahalad, C.K. (1994), *Competing for the Future*. Harvard Business School Press, Boston, Massachusetts.

178   Treacy, Michael and Wiersema, Fred (1995), *The Discipline of market leaders*, Addison-Wesley, Reading, Massachusetts.

179   Inchcape Group Management Conference (1992), Luxembourg, Conference papers.

179   Goodall, Robert, Group HR Director, Inchcape plc (1998), Interview, August 13, London.

179   Whicheloe, Peter, Corporate Planner, Inchcape plc (1998), Interview, July 2, London.

179–80   Ross, Ian, Chief Executive Russia, Inchcape Bottling (1998), Interview, August 7, London.

180   Simpson, Andrew and Jordan, Anne (1991), Review of acquisition performance, Group Finance Control Department, Inchcape plc, February.

180   Cushing, Philip, Chief Executive, Inchcape plc (1998), Interview, August 17, London.

181   Cummins, Andrew, ex-Board member, Inchcape plc (1998), Interview, July 17, London.

181   Plastow, Sir David, ex-Chairman, Inchcape plc (1998), Interview, December 31, Kent.

182   O'Donoghue, Rod, ex-Board member, Inchcape plc (1998), Interview, July 9, London.

183   Morton, Robert (1992), "Motoring steadily on," *Barclays de Zoete Wedd Research Ltd*, February 3.

Chapter 11   "The Class Act of the Recession"
Page
186   "The class act of the recession" (1991), Lex column, *Financial Times*, December 11.

186   Inchcape plc Annual Report & Accounts 1991.

186   Fuller, Jane (1992), "Inchcape beats rights issue forecast with 6% improvement to £185.2m," *Financial Times*, March 31. Interview with Charles Mackay.

186   "Inchcape's pretax profit rose 6.4% in '91" (1992), *Asian Wall Street Journal*, March 31. Interview with Charles Mackay.

187   "New driver for smooth-running Inchcape" (1992), *The Times*, September 15.

187   "Inchcape" (1992), Lex column, *Financial Times*, September 15.

187   Scott-Malden, Nyren (1992), "Inchcape," *Barclays de Zoete Wedd Research Ltd*, September 15.

187   Smith, Mike and Gibson, Robert (1992), "Inchcape 'Ying zhi jie': A 'sterling hedge'," *Flemings Research*, October 28.

187   "Inchcape Recommendation" (1992), S.G. *Warburg Engineering & Motors Interim Results Review*, November, pp. 7, 43.

188   Turnbull, Sir George — obituary (1992), "Leading figure in turbulent car industry. *Financial Times*, December 24.

188   Inchcape plc Annual Report & Accounts 1992.

188   "Inchcape proves watertight" (1993), The Questor column, *Daily Telegraph*, March 30.

188–9   Vincent, Lindsay (1993), "Inchcape's True Brit: Charles Mackay," *The Observer*, April 4.

188   Bolger, Andrew (1993), "Inchcape Motoring to Strong Performance," *Financial Times*, March 29.

189   Taylor, Trevor, Deputy Chairman, Inchcape plc (1998), Interview, London.

189–90   "Inchcape: Positive Stance Confirmed" (1993), *Barclays de Zoete Wedd Research Ltd*, February 3.

190   Kirk, Stephen (1993),"Inchcape: Final Results," *European Equity Research, Nikko Europe plc*, March 29.

190   Shepperd, Mark (1993) "Inchcape: Exchange Rate Gain," *UBS Global Research*, April 19.

191   Bartley, John, Chief Executive, Inchcape Middle East (1998), Interview, August 4, London.

192–3   Whiteman, John, Director of Strategy, Inchcape plc (1998), Interview, June 8, London.

193   Ellis, Stacey, ex-Board member, Inchcape plc (1998), Interview, August 13, London.

193   Butcher, Dale, Development Director, Inchcape Motors (1998), Interview, August 25, London.

193–5,   Goodall, Robert, Group HR Director, Inchcape plc (1998), Interview,
197   August 25, London.

194–5   Cummins, Andrew, ex-Board member, Inchcape plc (1998), Interview, July 17, London.

195   O'Donoghue, Rod, ex-Board member, Inchcape plc (1998), Interview, July 9, London.

196   Inchcape Group Capital Committee minutes 1990–93.

196   Inchcape plc Annual Report & Accounts 1993.

Chapter 12   Cracks in the Edifice
Page

198   Ellis, Stacey, ex-Board member, Inchcape plc (1998), Interview, August 13, London.

198–9   Butcher, Dale, Development Director, Inchcape Motors (1998), Interview, August 25, London.

199   "Revolution in the office: Why Inchcape has taken a stake in Gestetner" (1993), *Inchcape World*, October, p. 9.

199, 203   Cummins, Andrew, ex-Board member, Inchcape plc (1998), Interview, July 17, London.

199   "Focus and vision key to Gestetner success" (1993), *Evening Standard*, May 11.

200   Scott-Malden, Nyren (1993), "Inchcape: Gestetner stake mildly dilutive," *Barclays de Zoete Wedd Research Ltd*, May 12, p. 2.

200   Sheppard, Mark (1993) "Inchcape: Interim Preview," *UBS Global Research*, August 27.

200   Murphy, Mike *et al.* (1993), "Inchcape: Stockbroker Report," *S.G. Warburg Research*, August 4.

200   Shepperd, Mark (1993), "Inchcape: Exchange Rate Gain," *UBS Global Research*, April 19.

200   Bolger, Andrew (1993), "Strong yen takes its toll on Inchcape," *Financial Times*, September 14.

200–1   Walker, Bridget, Investor Relations Manager, Inchcape plc (1998), Interview, October 1, London.

203, 205   Whiteman, John, Director of Strategy, Inchcape plc (1998), Interview, June 8, London.

204   Orry, Maggie (1994), "Inchcape ahead in 'tough year': Motor retailing improves on the back of a recovery in the UK," *Financial Times*, March 29.

204   Smith, Mike *et al.* (1993), "Inchcape: A warrant on East Asian recovery?" *Flemings Research*, December 8, p. 1.

204–5   Lapper, Richard (1994), "Inchcape makes agreed £176.6m bid for Hogg," *Financial Times*, April 23.

205, 209–10   Goodall, Robert, Group HR Director, Inchcape plc (1998), Interview, August 13, London.

205   Wright, Ed and Fell, Colin (1994), "Automotive Update, No 207," *Kleinwort Benson Research*, June 1, pp. 1–4.

206   Plastow, Sir David (1992), "Corporate Governance," *Inchcape Annual Review*, pp. 30–31.

207, 209   "Playing by the Rules: Chris Blackhurst interviews Sir David Plastow" (1994), *Inchcape World*, September, issue 22, pp. 3–5.

207   Lorsch, Jay W. (1995), "Empowering the Board: How do Boards draw the line between monitoring performance and managing the Company," *Harvard Business Review*, January–February, pp. 107–17.

207   "Reforming the firm" (1997), *The Economist*, August 9.

210–41   Cushing, Philip, Chief Executive, Inchcape plc (1998), Interview, August 17, London.

210   "Inchcape" (1994), Lex column, *Financial Times*, July 1, p. 20.

PART 4   REALITY TIME
Chapter 13   A Short, Sharp Dose of Leadership
Page

215   "The Inchcape Organisation Survey" (1995), Executive Consultants Development Ltd., London, March.

215–6   Laurent, André, Professor of Organizational Behavior, INSEAD (1998), Interview, Fontainebleau.

218   Hotten, Russell (1994), "Inchcape sharpens focus with £30m sale," *The Independent*, December 6.

219   "Inchcape's Motor stalls" (1995), Lex column, *Financial Times*, January 27, p. 18.

219   Pratley, Nils (1995), "Inchcape warning as yen hits costs," *Daily Telegraph*, January 27, p. 23.

220   Kohli, Sheel (1995), "Inchcape in £40m Asian deal," *South China Morning Post*, March 16.

220   Wighton, David (1995), "Inchcape issues warning as high yen takes its toll," *Financial Times*, March 28, p. 23.

220   Bagnall, Sarah (1995), "Profits and shares slide at Inchcape," *The Times*, March 28.

222   Bridges, William (1992), *The Character of Organizations: Using Jungian type in organizational development*, CPP Books, Palo Alto, California.

223–5   Stacey, Ralph, Professor of Management, University of Hertfordshire (1996) "The importance of mess, Part Two," *EDC Newsletter*, Autumn, pp. 2–3.

223   "Chaos under a cloud" (1996), *The Economist*, January 13.

224–5   Allen, Nicholas, Director, Castleton Partners Ltd. (1998), Interview, October 21, London.

225–7   Goodall, Robert, Group HR Director, Inchcape plc (1998), Interview, May 27, Paris.

226   Cummins, Andrew, ex-Board member, Inchcape plc (1998), Interview, July 17, London.

227   Harper, Rosemary, Director, Executive Consultants Development Ltd (1998), Interview, July 8, London.

227   Tam, Richard, ex-HR Director, Inchcape Pacific Ltd. (1998), Interview, June 17, Hong Kong.

227   Price, Melanie, Secretary to Group HR Director, Inchcape plc (1998), Interview, June 10, London.

228   Davies, Alison, Compensation Director, Inchcape plc (1998), Interview, July 1, London.

228   Wighton, David (1995), "Inchcape warns of further cuts," *Financial Times*, May 24, p. 24.

Chapter 14   Falling from Grace

Page

230   Morton, Robert, Analyst, Charterhouse Tilney (1998), Interview, September 25, London.

230–1   Duncan, John, ex-Corporate Affairs Director, Inchcape plc (1998), Interview, September 30, London, pp. 4, 9.

231–2   Wilkinson, Anthony and Beaufrere, Paul (1995), "Inchcape: Valuation after the Fall," *James Capel*, April.

231   Tyerman, Robert (1995), "Mutiny mounts at Inchcape," *Sunday Telegraph*, June 11.

231   Vasuti, S.N. (1995), "Inchcape plc expects soaring yen to dent car earnings," *Business Times (Singapore)*, July 18.

232   Inchcape (Reuters INCH. L) (1995) *SBC Warburg*, August 4, p. 3.

232   Neill, Michael (1995), "Rush for Inchcape as Footsie shines," *Evening Standard*, August 2.

232   "Inchcape" (1995), *Financial Times*, August 5.

233   "Plastow bows out at Inchcape," (1995), *Financial Times*, August 11, p. 9.

233, 237   Davies, Alison, Compensation Director, Inchcape plc (1998), Interview, July 1, London.

233   Gibson, Fiona (1995), "Bain Hogg unveils network: Initiative will focus on servicing clients with international insurance programmes," *Lloyds List*, September 6.

234, 240   Marshall, Lord Colin, Chairman, Inchcape plc (1999), Interview, January 7, London.

235, 238   Harper, Rosemary, Director, Executive Consultants Development Ltd. (1998), Interview, July 8, London.

236–7   Stacey, Ralph, Professor of Management, University of Hertfordshire (1996) "The importance of mess, Part Two," *EDC Newsletter*, Autumn, pp. 2–3.

237–8   Goodall, Robert, Group HR Director, Inchcape plc (1998), Interview, May 27, Paris.

239   Burt, Tim (1995), "Inchcape's yen to bounce back: Explains why the Company is intent on restructuring," *Financial Times*, December 6, p. 24.

239   Johnson, Peter, Chief Executive, Inchcape Motors International (1998), Interview, August 14, London.

239, 242   Narita, Osamu, Chairman, Inchcape Marketing Services, Japan (1998), Dialogue via e-mail, August 14, Tokyo/London.

241   Olins, Rufus and Waples, John (1996), "Mackay out in shake-up at Inchcape," *The Sunday Times*, March 24.

242   McElwaine, Peter, Deputy Chief Executive, Inchcape Middle East (1998), Interview, June 20, Dubai.

242   Cheng, Paul Ming Fun, ex-Board member, Inchcape plc (1998), Interview, July 2, London.

242   Ross, Ian, Chief Executive Russia, Inchcape Bottling (1998), Interview, August 7, London.

242–4   Tam, Richard, ex-HR Director, Inchcape Pacific Ltd (1998), Interview, June 17, Hong Kong.

243   Bartley, John, Chief Executive, Inchcape Middle East (1998), Interview, August 4, London.

242–4   Mackay, Charles, ex-Chief Executive, Inchcape plc (1998), Interview, July 8,
244   London. pp. 1–2 and 14–15.

243   Whiteman, John, Director of Strategy, Inchcape plc (1998), Interview, June 8, London. p. 5.

243   Whittaker, Derek, ex-Board member, Inchcape plc (1998), Interview, September 8, London. p. 4.

243–4   O'Donoghue, Rod, ex-Board member, Inchcape plc (1998), Interview, July 9, London. pp. 12–13, 15.

244   Goodall, Robert, Group HR Director, Inchcape plc (1998), Interview, August 13, London.

244–5   Cushing, Philip, Chief Executive, Inchcape plc (1998), Interview, August 17, London.

Chapter 15   A New Mantra: One Company, One Team
Page

248, 257   Goodall, Robert, Group HR Director, Inchcape plc (1998), Interview, August 13, London.

251   Kohli, Sheel (1996), "Market grows fonder of reinvigorated Inchcape," *South China Morning Post*, September 24.

251   Kahn, Stephen (1996), "Inchcape's £380m for sell-off," *Daily Express*, October 10.

251–2   Ford, Jonathan (1996), "Bain Hogg sale to US nets Inchcape £160m," *Evening Standard*, October 15.

252   Lloyd, Edwin (1996), "Inchcape: Changes take time. UK Company Report," *HSBC James Capel*, November 22.

253   "Inchcape: One Company One Team: 'Lessons from Geese'," — video (1997), Inchcape Group Corporate Affairs, London, March.

254   Grey, Dr Peter, Managing Director, Executive Consultants Development Ltd (1998), Interview, June 29, London.

255   "Inchcape: Our Vision and mission: What we aspire to and How we will achieve it" (1997), *Inchcape World*, February, issue 26, p. 1.

255   Ross, Ian, Chief Executive Russia, Inchcape Bottling (1998), Interview, August 7, London.

255–6   Prathap, Kalpana, HR Director, Inchcape Middle East (1998), Interview, June 22, Dubai.

256   Newbury, David, Chief Executive, Inchcape Motors Retail (1998), Interview, July 17, London.

256   McElwaine, Peter, Deputy Chief Executive, Inchcape Middle East (1998), Interview, June 20, Dubai.

257   Cummins, Andrew, ex-Board member, Inchcape plc (1998), Interview, July 17, London.

257   "Marshall aid turn Inchcape's fortunes" (1997), *Investor's Chronicle*, January 24, p. 42.

260–1   John, David, ex-Board member, Inchcape plc (1998), Private Correspondence, October 29, Surrey.

261   Ellis, Stacey, ex-Board member, Inchcape plc (1998), Interview, August 13, London.

262   Taylor, Trevor, Deputy Chairman, Inchcape plc (1998), Interview, July 14, London.

262   Plastow, Sir David, ex-Chairman, Inchcape plc (1998), Interview, December 31, Kent.

Chapter 16   Storm Clouds Gather

Page

263   "WHO pollution: An Asian pea souper" (1997), *The Economist*, September 27.

264   Tieman, Ross (1997), "Inchcape profits rise by 12%: Vehicle importing recovery and cost cuts help improve margins," *Financial Times*, March 25.

264   "Inchcape" (1997), Tempus, *The Times*, March 25.

264,   Cheng, Paul Ming Fun, ex-Board member, Inchcape plc (1998), Interview,
267–8   July 2, London.

265   Kohli, Sheel (1997), "Lam Soon Chief Ch'ien to join Inchcape Board," *South China Morning Post*, May 23.

265   Tam, Richard, ex-HR Director, Inchcape Pacific Ltd. (1998), Interview, June 17, Hong Kong.

266   "Inchcape on track for recovery" (1997), Investment column, *The Independent*, September 16, p. 24.

266   "Inchcape" (1997), Tempus, *The Times*, September 16, p. 28.

266   "Inchcape provides mixed blessings" (1997), *Daily Telegraph*, September 16, p. 23.

266   Phillips, Richard and Pudney, Roger, Directors of Studies, Ashridge Management College (1998), Interview, August 26, London.

266–7   John, David, ex-Board member, Inchcape plc (1998), Interview, July 16, London.

268   Armstrong, Colin, ex-Board member, Inchcape plc (1998), Interview, October 1, London.

269   Ross, Ian, Chief Executive Russia, Inchcape Bottling (1998), Interview, August 7, London.

272–3   Cushing, Philip, Chief Executive, Inchcape plc (1998), Interview, August 17, London.

273   Walsh, Fiona (1997), "Big names calm in face of HK's storm," *Evening Standard*, October 23.

Chapter 17   From Fizz to Focus

Page

275   Whiteman, John, Director of Strategy, Inchcape plc (1998), Interview, June 8, London.

276   Armstrong, Colin, ex-Board member, Inchcape plc (1998), Interview, October 1, London.

276–7   Greising, David (1997), *I'd like the world to buy a Coke: The life and leadership of Roberto Goizueta*, John Wiley, New York, pp. 92, 180, 279.

278–9   Cushing, Philip, Chief Executive, Inchcape plc (1998), Interview, August 17, London.

279   Marshall, Lord Colin, Chairman, Inchcape plc (1999), Interview, January 7, London.

279   Inchcape plc (1998), "Inchcape Announces Preliminary Results for 1997 and Plans to Focus on its Motor Activities," *News Release*, March 2.

CONCLUSION

Page

281   Lynch, Peter (1998), "US Fund Manager," *The Times*, December 23, p. 20.

282, 291, 307, 311   Macaskill, Alastair, ex-Board member, Inchcape plc (1998), Interview, December 1, London.

286   Orr, Sir David, ex-Chairman, Inchcape plc (1998), Interview, October 1, London.

287, 302,   Mackay, Charles, ex-Chief Executive, Inchcape plc (1998), Interview, July 8,
309, 313   London.
314–5

287–8   Cushing, Philip, Chief Executive, Inchcape plc (1998), Interview, August 17
London.

288, 300,   Marshall, Lord Colin, Chairman, Inchcape plc (1999), Interview, January 7,
304, 306   London.

288–90,   Tanlaw, Lord, ex-Board member, Inchcape plc (1999), Interview, January 19,
293–4   London.

291   Reed, Alan, General Manager, Mann Egerton – Jaguar (1998), Interview,
October 2, Nottingham.

292   Hall, Clive, General Manager, Mann Egerton – Toyota (1998), Interview,
July 22, Nottingham.

292   The Inchcape Organization Survey (1995), Executive Development
Consultants Ltd, London, March.

293, 314   Newbury, David, Chief Executive, Inchcape Motors Retail (1998), Interview,
July 17, London.

293   John, David, ex-Board member, Inchcape plc (1998), Interview, June 8,
London.

294, 306,   Ellis, Stacey, ex-Board member, Inchcape plc (1998), Interview, August 13,
313   London.

294   Whittaker, Derek, ex-Board member, Inchcape plc (1998), Interview,
September 8, London.

295, 312   Johnson, Peter, Chief Executive, Inchcape Motors International (1998),
Interview, August 14, London.

296   Looi, Stephen, ex-HR Director, Inchcape Berhad (1998), Interview, June 19,
Singapore.

296, 312   Davies, Alison, Compensation Director, Inchcape plc (1998), Interview,
July 1, London.

296–7,   Whiteman, John, Director of Strategy, Inchcape plc (1998), Interview,
303, 306   June 8, London.
309, 311,
314

297,   Goodall, Robert, Group HR Director, Inchcape plc (1998), *Interview*,
311–2   August 13, London.

297   Kennedy, Carole (1998), "Cinderella: Great minds think alike," *The Director*,
May.

298, 317   "Simple advocate of no nonsense: The Head of London Business School
separates the gurus from the charlatans," (1996), *Financial Times*,
December 12, p. 15.

300–2   Walker, Bridget, Investor Relations Manager, Inchcape plc (1998), Interview,
October 1, London.

302, 310   O'Donoghue, Rod, ex-Board member, Inchcape plc (1998), Interview, July 9, London.

303   Campbell, Andrew and Goold, Michael (1998), *Synergy: Why links between business units often fail and how to make them work*. Capstone, Oxford.

304, 310   Plastow, Sir David, ex-Chairman, Inchcape plc (1998), Interview, December 31, Kent.

304   Armstrong, Colin, ex-Board member, Inchcape plc (1998), Interview, October 1, London.

306   Ansoff, H. Igor (1984), *Implanting Strategic Management*. Prentice-Hall International, p. 471.

309–10, 315   Bartley, John, Chief Executive, Inchcape Middle East (1998), Interview, August 4, London.

310   Cummins, Andrew, ex-Board member, Inchcape plc (1998), Interview, July 17, London.

311, 313–5   Cheng, Paul Ming Fun, ex-Board member, Inchcape plc (1998), Interview, July 2.

311   Butcher, Dale, Development Director, Inchcape Motors (1998), Interview, August 25, London.

311   Allen, Nicholas, Director, Castleton Partners Ltd. (1998), Interview, October 21, London.

312   Price, Melanie, Secretary to Group HR Director, Inchcape plc (1998), Interview, June 10, London.

313   Ross, Ian, Chief Executive Russia, Inchcape Bottling (1998), Interview, August 7, London.

313   Bolger, Andrew, "Inchcape Motoring to strong performance" (1996), *Financial Times*, March 29.

314   Morton, Robert, Analyst, Charterhouse Tilney (1998), Interview, September 25, London.

316   "The Death of the Geneen Machine" (1995), *The Economist*, June 17. pp. 74–76.

EPILOGUE

Page

317   Voyle, Susanna (1999), "Inchcape ponders special dividend option," *Financial Times*, March 9.

Index